BEST LITTLE STORIES

from the

AMERICAN

REVOLUTION

BEST LITTLE STORIES

from the

AMERICAN

REVOLUTION

C. Brian Kelly

with Select Founding Mothers
by Ingrid Smyer-Kelly

Cumberland House
Nashville, Tennessee

Published by
CUMBERLAND HOUSE PUBLISHING, INC.
431 Harding Industrial Drive
Nashville, Tennessee 37211

Cover design by Bateman Design, Nashville, Tennessee.

Library of Congress Cataloging-in-Publication Data
Kelly, C. Brian.
    Best little stories from the American Revolution / C. Brian Kelly : with Select founding mothers by Ingrid Smyer-Kelly.
        p.   cm.
    Includes bibliographical references and index.
    ISBN 1-58182-006-2 (pbk. : alk. paper)
    1. United States—History—Revolution, 1775-1783—Anecdotes. 2. United States—History—Revolution, 1775-1783—Biography—Anecdotes. I. Smyer-Kelly, Ingrid.
    II. Title.
E209.K44   1999
973.3–dc21   99-18836
                                                                               CIP

Printed in Canada
  7 8 9 — 09 08 07

Dedicated to
Chandler, Larkin, and Clemme;
Kristin and Daniel;
Sophie and Will;
Ben and Will

Contents

VIII. Final Throes   343

IX. Last Glimpses   381

X. Select Founding Mothers   415

Introduction

MANY YEARS IN THE MAKING, eight long *and rough* years in the resolution, it was an incredible moment in the course of American history, a drama to rival the later Civil War and opening of the American West.

Not merely survival, but the very birth of a nation at stake, it was—in a sublime way, it still is—the American Revolution.

Just how incredible, how dramatic this Revolution was and is really lies in the details, as I've rediscovered in the course of writing this book. And I plead guilty to ignoring or forgetting many of those details until engaging in that recent exercise. I'm just wondering, though, could I be the proverbial Everyman (or -woman) in that regard? It's my sneaking suspicion, with all the historical attention devoted to the Civil War, World War II, the Civil Rights Movement, Vietnam, and various other historical events, that many of us tend to take the Revolutionary period for granted. Or is it just me?

Oops, recast that question, please. *Was* it just me?

In any case, I was well aware that there was the original settlement of the New World, the development of thriving colonies on the eastern shelf of a vast and still mysterious continent. Thirteen such colonies, of course. And then came . . . the Revolution!

No mystery there, naturally. Cataclysmic event of American history, even of world history. That moment in time when some pretty amazing and farsighted Founding Fathers got together and invented a new government . . . a new *form* of government. One dedicated to independence collectively and to liberty individually. That moment when an inspired colonial populus rose up in righteous anger, smote the wicked, and successfully fought the Mother Country . . . war over, end of story. Move on from there.

As I of course rediscovered, there was more, a great deal more, to the great drama than just that. And what a thrill in an author's post-academic life to discover, to begin apprehending, the true drama of it all! What excitement for an ex-journalist to find one story after another just begging for rediscovery. Hard, glittering gold!

As in the case, little known I warrant, of the mysterious American on a white horse who rode against the British the day of Lexington and Concord. And every time he lifted his rifle, said an early local history, "His aim was death." For that matter, the really major battle of that historic day in Massachusetts was neither Lexington nor Concord, but a place then called Menotomy and today known as Arlington, Massachusetts.

Details, details. The story is in the details. It's one thing to know, as any schoolchild surely does, that Thomas Jefferson wrote the Declaration of Independence, but how many of us are likely to recall that he did so as a member of a legislative committee just like the congressional committees of today (only smaller), that the committee included John Adams and Ben Franklin among its members, and that they made suggestions and even changes?

Picture the still young, publicly reticent Jefferson having to sit by as Adams, the head of the committee, managed the proposed document on the floor of the Continental Congress. Imagine the esteemed Jefferson groaning inwardly as the membership of the whole made one change or deletion after another in the great document we revere today.

Then, too, there was that stoic (some even suggest, *wooden*) figure, the Father of Our Country. Always resolute, correct? Overall, yes, but George Washington surely had his . . . more *human* moments. Picture the usually unflappable Virginian one day in 1776 at the future intersection of Forty-Second Street and Lexington Avenue on Manhattan Island, New York. Picture him shouting, yelling, hurling his hat on the ground in frustration as his militiamen turned tail and ran from the advancing British, as they threw their equipment to the ground and streamed past, paying little heed to their furious leader. It happened, as I've rediscovered in researching the book now before you.

Fortunately for his fellow Revolutionaries, his fortunes gradually improved, but we forget—at any rate, *I* forgot—the many perils he survived both before and during the war. Fortunately for the future nation, he skated past a bout with deadly smallpox; a plunge in an icy, rushing river; and the pre-Revolutionary massacre of British General Edward Braddock's column marching against the French and their Indian allies near the site of today's Pittsburgh, Pennsylvania. Then, during the Revolutionary War itself, never one to shirk the battlefield, he survived one perilous situation after another.

More than any other figure, I must confess, George Washington appeals to me as the very symbol of that war's successful outcome. Not merely as the widely respected commander in chief, but for the unexpected and very human detail one can discover watching this gentleman farmer from Virginia in action. Doing his wartime sleeping in more than one hundred different venues, seemingly always on the move, he left his beloved Mount Vernon plantation on the Potomac one day in 1775 . . . and didn't darken its door again for six long years.

Don't we *all* forget that history is only yesterday's headlines? That it wasn't all dry and dusty doings by wax-museum figures? Indeed not. These were real people doing the things—in great moments and small—that real people do. Thus, we can easily imagine the combined fury and embarrassment George Washington must have felt in dealing with Benedict Arnold's young, hysterical, and scantily clad wife the day that Arnold openly deserted the American cause.

But the story—both in today's headlines and in history—often is about the "little" people rather than the leaders . . . and I hope that fact comes through in the details related after these introductory words. For instance, the heroes and the rogues who briefly emerged in the bloody civil war fought in the Carolinas, only to be largely forgotten in the centuries since. One was the horribly disfigured Loyalist David Fanning, another was his murderous Patriot rival, Philip Alston, both ranging the North Carolina sandhills famous today as the Pinehurst and Southern Pines resort area.

Still another guerrilla fighter, an innocent at the start, was a mere teenager, a tailor's apprentice who amused himself one lonely day making a suit for a pet cat, but who shortly thereafter was gathering intelligence for his Whig friends, then taking part in internecine battles and watching people kill other people, then roll over the bodies to check the fallen's bullet wounds.

Another teenager who springs to view, incidentally, a resentful captive struck by a British officer's sword, barely a survivor of smallpox, was future President Andrew Jackson. Already fatherless, he would lose two brothers and his mother to the vicissitudes of the Revolution.

Speaking of mothers—women—my dear wife and collaborator in our *Best Little Stories* series of historical books, Ingrid Smyer, has added an illuminating section, more stories of great and "little" people for sure, about the often-forgotten women of the Revolution. "Select Founding Mothers," we call them.

But I had better stop right here and now: I'm getting fascinated all over again, ready to retell all those stories that make up the book that follows. No need for that, obviously ... but one real need: Please, for further reading, keep our sources in mind, since we owe so many of our facts to others who have gone before us, whether as historians probing the primary research materials, or as participants telling their own stories in print.

I owe thanks also to Garland Publishing's encyclopedia, *The American Revolution, 1775-1783*; *Country's Best Log Homes* magazine and *Military History* magazine for their respective permissions to reprint pieces contained in this book that first appeared in the pages of those publications. In addition, my stories on Thomas Paine and the adoption of the Declaration of Independence first appeared in the now defunct *Washington Star.*

Finally, the Garland compendium cited above has been a mainstay as both a factual source and fact-checking resource for many of the stories presented herein.

Meanwhile, please read ... enjoy. It's been a thrill to rediscover the many, many stories of the American Revolution. I just hope a little bit of my own excitement rubs off on you, the reader.

C. Brian Kelly
Charlottesville, Virginia

BEST LITTLE STORIES
from the

AMERICAN

REVOLUTION

I. Early Stirrings

The First American Revolution

Aside from local gossips, hardly anyone in colonial Virginia thought twice one spring day in 1674 when a young English gentleman stepped off a wooden sailing ship at Jamestown, bustling hub of the richest, most populous of the British Crown's new American provinces.

He had left England under a bit of a cloud, a tale of extortion, whether as a dupe or willing partner, trailing behind. Further, his wife's father had disinherited her for marrying the squire's son from Sussex.

In Virginia, however, the young couple could seek their fortune, enjoy a fresh start unsullied by bad memories or damaged reputation, since here, apparently, nobody knew.

More important, not even the principals of the pending historical drama had any idea what awaited them at the hands of Cambridge-educated Nathaniel Bacon Jr., then all of twenty-seven years. Instead, Bacon's wealthy cousin Nathaniel Senior, prominent steward of the colony, and even the aging royal governor, Sir William Berkeley, hastened to welcome the slender, dark-haired young man and his wife, Elizabeth.

If only they, if only *someone,* had been equipped with a crystal ball! Wouldn't they, wouldn't the entire colonial population of well over forty thousand, have been amazed—even the enigmatic Bacon himself?

For in just two years' time, it was the frontier homesteader Bacon—now self-proclaimed "General, by consent of the People"—who was the virtual ruler of the colony, with Governor Berkeley driven off to a narrow coastal strip, the Eastern Shore. It was young Bacon who burned Jamestown, America's first permanent village, first Virginia capital, first English settlement, to the ground; Bacon, who had become America's first real Revolutionary, who rallied "the people" and declared himself their leader and their spokesman against oppressive rule.

Risen, then fallen, like a comet across the colonial skies, Bacon instantly passed into U.S. history as one of its most bitterly debated—and now, today, most widely forgotten—hero-villains ever. On the latter point, take your pick. If you choose villain, you would be in estimable company. Future U.S. Chief Justice John Marshall, for instance, called him a "rabble-rouser." But Bacon did have his defenders as well.

It takes some searching, but in a Virginia courthouse, at Gloucester, there is a plaque on a wall proclaiming young Nathaniel "Soldier, Statesman Saint" (yes, someone forgot that second comma). He died not far away, of malaria apparently, and yet was not exactly buried nearby or in any other commonplace way. In fact, Bacon's final resting place is as unknown today as it was shortly after his death in the fall of 1676.

Oddly, it *was* the year 1676 when all this happened, exactly one hundred years before the "Second" American Revolution, and so much of the dispute, so many of the principles proclaimed, all sound so much the same. Unfair taxation by the Crown was one cry. Oppressive, aristocratic rule—in this case by the apparently senile Berkeley—was another.

Bacon was by all accounts a riveting, persuasive speaker, and the solutions that he offered were forward-thinking. Outright, public defiance of Berkeley was one Baconian development. Outright defiance of the Crown and its reinforcements due from England was another *Baconian* proposal. Still another, according to one contemporary source, was the possibility of an autonomous union of colony states, sort of a federation . . . sort of a *United Colonies!*

Then, too, there was legislation enacted by the Virginia Assembly at the time of Bacon's meteoric ascension in the summer of 1676—new laws, *Bacon's Laws,* giving the people more say-so in their own lives, chipping away at the privileges of the aristocratic leadership.

And in Bacon's various proclamations and manifestoes, one of them signed, "General, by consent of the People," later historians saw the first true pronouncements of democratic principles in America.

But as for the people who were Indians—Native Americans—Bacon unabashedly called for their extermination. And it was Indian troubles—raids, murders on frontier lands—that triggered Bacon's Rebellion in the first place. When Governor Berkeley hesitated to mount an expedition in pursuit of the marauding Indians, their exact identity arguable at best, Bacon and his fellow homesteaders at the outlying edges of the Virginia Colony went after Indians of their own choice anyway, without authority, in open defiance of the royal governor's orders.

Bacon's actions, his demeanor, and the things he said all apparently had their popular appeal. Despite being branded an outlaw by Berkeley, Bacon was elected to the House of Burgesses. This was an oddity in itself, for as Berkeley's young protégé just a year earlier, Bacon had been appointed to the strictly blue-ribbon Council of State. Now he was both an aristocrat and a populist!

At one point, on the theory that the "rogues shall harbor here no more," Bacon indeed did burn Jamestown. He raised chivalrous eyebrows, too, when he used a thin line of captured women, his "white aprons," as a screen forestalling enemy fire while his troops busied themselves behind the ladies in digging defensive earthworks outside of Jamestown.

In any case, the argument between Bacon and Berkeley—the colony-wide upheaval, the occasional civil war—swayed back and forth all summer in 1676, on into the fall, with Bacon virtually ruling the Virginia Colony. But in October, on the heels of another Indian expedition in a grim swampland, Bacon succumbed to fever and, quite suddenly, was gone.

In rash fury of his own, a resurgent Berkeley now tracked down and executed more than two dozen of Bacon's key followers as the late rebellion collapsed. Within a year, back home in England to give an accounting to King Charles II, Berkeley died as well.

Young Bacon's burial place was kept secret because of his followers' conviction that a vengeful Berkeley would exhume the body and hang it upon some gibbet in chains until it rotted away, an occasional custom of the day. It is said that a coffin filled with rocks was buried for Berkeley's later discovery, while the real burial was secret—it might even have been in the nearby York River.

Whatever the case, not only his burial place is unknown today, but his image, too. No known portrait exists of this firebrand who nearly toppled the royal governor of the Crown's vaunted Virginia Colony in the First American Revolution.

To Prevent Civil Insurrection

HERE'S A SHOCKER HEADLINE ITEM from both Boston and New York—in the 1680s, mind you. *Colonists in revolt. Royal Governors sacked and booted out. Colonists running their own governmental affairs.*

Unlikely report? Not at all. Not in context with Virginia's recent upheaval of the 1670s, known as Bacon's Rebellion. For here was a revolt, an insurrection, whatever you may wish to call it, that was so sweeping it drove a powerful royal governor onto a narrow slice of land called the Eastern Shore; destroyed Jamestown, the colony's capital; and produced all kinds of defiant, democratic-sounding, even "liberal" legislation known as "Bacon's Laws."

It's difficult to say now just how far into real revolution the incendiary events of 1676—thoughts, too—might have carried England's richest, most populous American colony, except for the rebellion's collapse with the death of Nathaniel Bacon from a fever at the very zenith of his revolutionary career.

Bacon today barely rates a footnote in the history of America. The leaders of the real American Revolution that came along a century later hardly ever mentioned him . . . but here's one irony. Patrick Henry in 1765 delivered a stinging speech in the Virginia House of Burgesses, by that time meeting in the eighteenth-century colonial capital of Williamsburg. Henry responded to listeners shocked to hear his defiance of the Crown with the epithet, "If this be treason, make the most of it!" Oddly enough, just ninety years before, in a field at Middle Plantation—later the site of Williamsburg itself—Nathaniel Bacon allegedly told his listeners much the same thing: *If this be treason, so be it!*

Interesting, too, that while Bacon's Rebellion only ended in collapse and was never foremost in the minds of America's Founding Fathers a century later, it did have one lasting, unsettling effect: It brought the king's troops to the American colonies and brought them to stay!

The first troops, perhaps as many as one thousand, plus an

artillery train, were sent across the Atlantic in response to Royal Governor William Berkeley's pleas for help in stamping out the upstart Nathaniel Bacon's rebellion. By the time the troops reached Virginia, however, Bacon was dead, and the rebellion was all over. But the troops were there. Thrust upon a population of only 40,000 they were the equivalent of "more than 150,000 soldiers poured into the state of Virginia in 1980 [population then more than three million] for the purpose of suppressing civil disorder," estimated Douglas Edward Leach in his 1986 book *Roots of Conflict: British Armed Forces and Colonial Americans, 1677–1763.*

The redcoats arrived in wintry January 1677 to a colony "ravaged and wrecked" by the recent civil war, its capital of Jamestown "in ruins," its residents spread out on "scattered farms" and struggling merely to provide for themselves. "So it was that many of the soldiers had to remain unhappily quartered on board their fetid ships for a further period of time [after an Atlantic crossing taking weeks], until the army could establish a base camp at Middle Plantation. Men sickened and many died."

Eventually, a good many surviving soldiers were sent back to England, but not all. Some stayed on voluntarily as settlers. What really irritated the colonists, though, was the retention of about two hundred troops as a standing garrison—"a constant reminder of royal authority," wrote Leach. To make matters worse, they had no barracks, no housing of their own—"many of these soldiers had to be quartered in civilian dwellings or outbuildings as unwelcome guests." The promised rental compensation often came late . . . and so did pay for the soldiers themselves. "The soldiers and officers are now farr in arreare and the soldiers cloathing of all sorts quite worne out, soe that if they be not provided for against winter they will inevitably perish," lamented their commander at one point.

In the end, in 1682, the garrison was disbanded, with most of its members apparently melting into the colonial populace . . . but with bad feelings on both sides still remaining. On the one hand, the Colonials were smarting at the insertion of regular troops in their midst; on the other, the military professionals from England resented the hostility they felt among the Colonials.

Move now to Boston, 1686: King James II had ordered a gigantic reshuffle and combination of the northern colonies. The once separate entities of New Hampshire, Massachusetts, Rhode Island, and Plymouth Colony were all thrown under one administrative roof, one royal governor, as the Dominion of New England. Soon after, New York, New Jersey, and Connecticut were tossed into the same pot. For a time, all of these colonies were ruled by newly appointed Royal Governor Sir Edmund Andros.

Andros came to Boston and its Puritans as a military professional with no intention of granting them new freedoms, as the suspect minion of a Roman Catholic king, as the commander of a newly placed garrison of troops backed up by a warship in the harbor. He soon set about emplacing cannon that could sweep the waterfront and various streets nearby. Perhaps worst of all, he drafted Massachusetts men to join an English-led, mid-winter expedition against Indians in the desolate Maine woods to the north. It was no time to attempt such a foray. The conditions were hard on the local men, but even tougher were the torturous abuses allegedly inflicted by their British officers.

That mission occurred in the winter of 1688–1689, and matters in Boston came to a head that spring. On April 18, some crewmembers from the frigate HMS *Rose* joined the townspeople in a bloodless coup that saw the ship's captain taken prisoner on a Boston street. Later in the day Andros and his chief lieutenants surrendered themselves to the insurgents as well.

Missing from that roundup was the former commander of the Boston garrison, Colonel Francis Nicholson. He, it turns out, had been dispatched earlier as a deputy governor for New York and New Jersey when they were conjoined to the Dominion of New England—with small redcoat garrisons stationed in Manhattan and Albany. The news of the uprising reaching New York from Boston in late April of 1689, of course, served to undermine his already none-too-popular regime. Although Nicholson, like Andros, was an Anglican, he was widely suspected of being a "closet Catholic" working against the best interests of local Protestants, especially the Dutch who actually founded New York and now were known to chafe under English rule.

It didn't help the cause of tranquillity when a few soldiers from the disbanded Boston garrison arrived to bolster Nicholson's Manhattan ranks—the fact that they were Irishmen made them suspect as Catholics as well. With trouble obviously brewing, one of the English regulars stopped a local militiaman from carrying out an order given by a militia officer. In a confrontation with the aggrieved officer afterward, Nicholson completely lost his temper and "flew into a rage," reported historian Leach, "brandished a pistol and threatened to have the whole troublesome town set ablaze."

Already waiting in the wings at that point was New York militia officer Jacob Leisler, "a prosperous and influential merchant of German background who shared the anti-English resentment felt by most of the Dutch." He also was "a staunch Calvinist" who "had become convinced that the integrity and perhaps the very life of the province [New York] were threatened by a secret Roman Catholic conspiracy involving Nicholson himself." Now, thanks to his imprudent outburst, the deputy governor had played into the hands of his critics. The very next day, May 31, the militia arose and quietly took over Fort James in Manhattan. The disarmed regulars melted away. So did Governor Nicholson . . . aboard a vessel setting sail for England. The volunteer who then took command of the fort, the local militia and, in effect, the affairs of government was Leisler.

With Protestant (and even Dutch-born) King William and Queen Mary now on the throne of England, Leisler apparently was happy to serve them as a loyal subject—and rump governor. So things drifted until January of 1691, when two companies of regulars, under Major Richard Ingoldesby, suddenly arrived in Manhattan. Colonel Henry Sloughter, a newly appointed royal governor, was said to be on his way as well.

Leisler now took a fateful step . . . or two. He refused to relinquish control of Fort James to Ingoldesby in the absence of Governor Sloughter himself. By difficult negotiation, it then was agreed that Ingoldesby and his troops could occupy the town hall as their headquarters. Soon, there were minor brushes between their overlapping patrols. The newly arrived Ingoldesby managed to attract several hundred local men to his side as reinforcement for his regulars. Leisler also was busy recruiting added numbers for his own force. Then on March 17, the date now celebrated in New York as St. Patrick's Day, Leisler issued a demand that Ingoldesby dissolve his local force. The English officer refused, and with new Governor Sloughter's approaching ship nearly on hand (it arrived March 19), shooting broke out between the two vying factions. It wasn't all-out war, but it did have serious repercussions—not only were two persons killed and a number wounded in the gunfire, but Leisler two months later was hanged. It also was a historical benchmark. As Leach wrote, "Here for the first time in North America an armed, organized force of provincials was in actual combat with the standing army of the Crown." (Nathaniel Bacon's rebellion in Virginia, by contrast, was more a civil war between insurgents and the royal governor's faction; the king's troops were still on their way to Virginia when the rebellion's bubble burst with the death of Bacon himself.)

With the advent of William and Mary in England and the troubles in Boston and New York, the experiment of an amalgamated New England colony soon came to an end in North America. Connecticut and Rhode Island were allowed to tend their own knitting as "largely self-governing colonies." New Hampshire, New York, and New Jersey would be royal colonies. Further, "By terms of a royal charter issued in 1691, Massachusetts Bay and Plymouth Colony, along with the line of coastal settlements in Maine, became a single colony with a royally appointed governor and elected legislature."

In the years ahead, until the very eve of the American Revolution, England and her satellites would be fighting four wars against the French and their various allies, both in the New World and the Old. As one result, the American Colonials often accompanied the British on expeditions to Quebec, Louisbourg, the Caribbean, and against the French in the Ohio territory. Rather than fully cooperating as steadfast allies in those situations, the Colonials and the British military often were at odds with one another. The professional British military considered the Colonials to be an unkempt, undisciplined, unreliable, even rowdy lot, while the Americans found the British to be arrogant, abusive, and unwilling to delegate authority to others.

In sum, the seeds of enmity planted at the time of Bacon's Rebellion simply multiplied thereafter. "There can be no doubt," wrote Leach, "that nearly a hundred years before the Declaration of Independence, redcoats in a colony were viewed by Americans as the arm of repressive authority." From then on, as Leach also noted, "Every colonist, whatever his political stance, understood that the king's forces were there to prevent civil insurrection."

Not for nothing would Thomas Jefferson's Declaration of Independence "indict" the king of England "For quartering large bodies of armed troops among us."

Rising Hope of Virginia

PICTURE THIS: AN ICE-FLOED RIVER in the wilderness of colonial America. White waters churning . . . bubbling, boiling along. And out on the seething surface, two men perched on a makeshift raft.

Their precarious platform, we are told by the younger of the pair, took hours to assemble with their "one poor Hatchet." The chopping, trimming, and shaping were "a whole Day's work" for himself and his companion. It was not until the early darkness of winter that they pushed out into the chilly Allegheny River for their eastward crossing.

And then, "before we were Half Way over," their raft became jammed—"jammed in the ice in such a Manner that we expected every Moment our Raft to sink, and ourselves to perish."

Who is speaking here? Who was it caught in this moment of peril? And worse, about to be hurled into the freezing water itself? To wit: "I put out my setting pole to try to stop the Raft, that the Ice might pass by, when the Rapidity of the Stream threw it with so much violence against the Pole, that it jerked me out into ten Feet water."

The man in the water was young, only twenty-one, not yet the Father of His Country, but rather an inexperienced militia officer at a moment of peril on the future nation's frontier.

Never mind that his location today would appear rather tame, an X-mark on a map of Pennsylvania. The reality surrounding the young Virginian and his companion was a primitive wilderness where bear and buffalo still roamed—Indians and the French, too.

Fortunately for George Washington (and for the future United States), he was able to react quickly after he was thrown into the water. With the raft still intact and close by, he found a handhold among the rough logs and managed to hang on. He and his companion, woodsman Christopher Gist, then found their craft too unwieldy for passage to either riverbank, so they left it for sanctuary on a nearby island, where they spent a cold December night—so cold, in fact, that the next morning they were able to *walk* across the now frozen river. The wilderness-wise Gist, acting as George Washington's guide, suffered frostbite of fingers and toes, but not the young man with him. Washington, still fairly new to frontier life, had come through his river dunking with no harmful effect.

As he now turned homeward for Virginia, he could count himself fortunate in more ways than one. It had been, overall, quite a risky mission to undertake alone and at such a tender age on behalf of his government, the British government of the middle eighteenth century. It had been an affair that would have intimidated many an older, experienced diplomat, soldier, or frontiersman. And the newly appointed militia major and adjutant for eastern Virginia was certainly not, by any definition of the word, *experienced.*

The young George Washington, though, was an impressive, powerful-looking figure of well over six feet. All his life he would be noted for his large hands—the largest, said the Marquis de Lafayette many years later, he had ever seen on any man! He was well-traveled within the prestigious Virginia Colony's highest social circles, from the entourage of the Crown's governor in the capital city of Williamsburg, Lord Robert Dinwiddie, to the ranking gentry of the Northern Neck region running between the Rappahannock and Potomac Rivers, up to the site of today's Washington, D.C.

His only foreign travel had been with his tuberculosis-stricken half brother, Lawrence Washington, to the Caribbean, during which journey young George had contracted, and survived, that dangerous disease of the day, smallpox. He still would have bouts with various fevers, malaria, pleurisy, perhaps even TB as well, but now he at least had overcome "the pox" for life.

He had learned surveying as a teenager, a trade that soon became the source of a moderate income for the young man. As a surveyor, he was indispensable to many an expansionist landowner of his day. As a result, he had spent some time "roughing it" in the Shenandoah Valley and other unimproved lands, and yet he was not a real frontiersman. On the contrary, he had spent his life in a colonial region that had been settled for generations. The frontier was pushing westward, to be sure, but so far, few Virginia Colonials or Englishmen had ventured past the Allegheny Mountains and into the Ohio River Valley beyond.

The widow Mary Ball Washington's son was a meticulous note-taker, but he still had much to learn in English grammar and composition, according to his latter-day biographer, Douglas Southall

Freeman. "Socially," added Freeman in his seven-volume work, "he was capable of entering the best of colonial society without embarrassment. He could not sing or play any instrument, and he probably felt a certain awkwardness in the presence of young women, but he could dance and he had a proficiency in cards and billiards."

He wasn't known as a great shot, but "he squared accounts by the superlative excellence of his horsemanship."

Thanks to his surveying tasks and his blue-ribbon contacts, George was a major landowner by 1753. He owned nearly 4,300 acres of "unencumbered" land, noted biographer Freeman, 2,000 of them in the Shenandoah Valley. "With the advantage of immunity from smallpox, he could travel freely," noted Freeman. He was accustomed to excursions that were short of the harsh frontier but offered few frills. According to Freeman, young George "was strong and was able, without complaint, or great discomfort, to sleep out of doors, in his clothing and on the ground."

It was early in 1753 that George Washington, on the eve of his twenty-first birthday (February 22, by today's calendar), was commissioned as a militia major and one of the Virginia Colony's four military adjutants. Since he could not claim one iota of experience as a soldier, the appointment was a testament to his recently deceased brother Lawrence's standing in the colony—and to George's own reputation as a bright young man on the rise.

His assigned area, or district, was, of the four in Virginia, "the most remote and the least interesting," wrote Freeman. The day was coming, though, when *Major* Washington's prospects for excitement and meaningful duty would take a startling turn.

First, however, he must instruct himself in the comportment of an officer, that he might then instruct his several lesser-ranking militia officers, many of them older than he, in the proper training of their own men at county level. He had at his disposal the months before the general musters of the militia in September, a useful respite, it seems. "Now, with the thoroughness that marked all of his acquisition of new knowledge and his every performance of his daily work, he—Major George Washington—was to learn the duties of District Adjutant of Virginia."

Now, too, only dimly perceived by the English and their colonists on the eastern seaboard of the future United States, the French were on the move—ominously so, and not quite as far away as French Canada, either.

In the spring of 1753, a small army of 1,500 Frenchmen appeared along the southern edge of Lake Erie, laying down some stretches of road and building Forts Presque Isle and Le Boeuf. As vague word of the incursion reached Virginia, Governor Dinwiddie had good reason to take alarm. Very obviously, the French were moving into the Ohio watershed, while the English were doing little to nothing in defense of the vast and rich territory that they claimed as their own.

In June of 1753 Dinwiddie sought authority from England to build his own forts in the Ohio territory to stop the French, and in late October he received King George II's instructions to first warn the French, then, if necessary, to "repel force by force."

In Dinwiddie's first effort to deal directly with the French, a pair of envoys sent to warn against encroaching upon "English" territory failed to reach the French frontier outposts.

As the end of October neared, Dinwiddie had passed along the king's instructions to his fellow colonial executives of British North America and issued a call for the Virginia General Assembly to meet in special session at Williamsburg on November 1. Excitement clearly was in the air when a young man arrived in town October 26 and soon paid a call upon the governor's handsome palace of red brick.

One of the colony's four adjutants, he was there to volunteer for the obvious. Someone must carry the English king's warning to the French to clear out. And young George Washington was determined to be that someone.

Dinwiddie's reaction? Permission promptly granted.

So it was that the untried militia major George Washington became Governor Dinwiddie's emissary to the French. So it was that young George undertook a mission that Chief Justice John Marshall later would describe as "toilsome and hazardous." As Marshall also wrote: "The Envoy would be under the necessity of passing through an extensive and almost unexplored wilderness, inhabited by fierce savages, who were either hostile to the English or of doubtful attachment."

That he failed to dislodge the French by virtue of reason alone did not disqualify the young emissary from the praise of his peers or his many future biographers. He at least did carry out his mission in impressive style. Noted Washington Irving—also a future biographer—"The prudence, sagacity, resolution, firmness, and selfless devotion manifested by Washington throughout; his tact and self-possession in treating with fickle savages and crafty white men; the soldier's eye with which he had noticed everything that would bear upon military operations; and the hardihood with which he had acquitted himself during a wintry tramp through the wilderness, through constant storms of rain and snow—all pointed him out, not merely to the governor but to the public at large, as one eminently fitted, notwithstanding his youth, for important trusts involving civil as well as military duties. *From that moment he was the rising hope of Virginia.*" (Italics added.)

On this trip, too, began what might be called the *Perils of George.* From his bout at age nineteen with smallpox, through one early episode after another—all coming before the American Revolution—he established a remarkable record of survival. The fact is, he came so close, so many times, to meeting an early and untimely end, someone else could have become the country's *Father . . .* could have given his name to the federal capital we call Washington, D.C.; the grand state of Washington, and so many little towns across the country also known as Washington.

Just hours before his plunge into the Allegheny River, an Indian guide had turned and fired his musket at George Washington and woodsman Gist at point-blank range, but he missed them both and ran off. Moving on to 1754, we find a twenty-two-year-old George back in the same frontier country and reporting the "charming" sound of bullets whistling past as he led a small force (fifty or so) of Virginia militia and friendly Indians in an ambush of about thirty Frenchmen near Great Meadows in the vicinity of the future Pittsburgh. In that episode of May 28, people were actually killed. Just weeks later, in July, he and fellow survivors from a force of 360 militia had to surrender to 600 French and Indians at Fort Necessity at Great Meadows. Washington and his men had to walk back to civilization. It could have been a lot worse.

Then, in 1755, came a watershed battle for the British and their Colonials . . . and for young George, still weak from a severe fever. To the surprise of all, it was *Lieutenant Colonel* George Washington of the militia who, at age twenty-three, emerged hero of the day as 900 French and Indians ambushed British Major General Edward Braddock, his 1,400 British regulars, and Washington's own 450 militiamen eight miles from the French Fort Duquesne (also near the site of Pittsburgh) on July 9. After foolishly deploying his men out in the open, European-style, against the well-hidden enemy,

Braddock was killed and his force routed. George Washington assumed command, rallied the survivors, organized their defense, and led the retreat. He survived two horses shot out from under him and four bullet holes found later in his hat and clothing. Overall, he spent twenty-four hours in constant activity, all after rising from his sickbed to accompany the ill-fated Braddock.

Possibly apocryphal, meanwhile, is the long-standing report of still another threatening challenge to the tall Virginian's seemingly charmed life—also in 1755, but in a location far removed from the site of Braddock's debacle. This test of George Washington's good fortune came in October as he and a handful of companions rode their horses northward from a tour of colonial forts near the North Carolina line. None in the party were aware that several hostile Indians were lying in wait ahead, with a few unwary white settlers already being held as their prisoners.

The leader of the Indians left for a short while—after telling his braves to ignore anyone traveling north, for fear of giving warning to his intended southbound victim. Washington and his companions were doubly lucky as they passed the ambush site minutes later—not only were they proceeding north, but their rain-soaked firearms would have been useless in case of attack.

George Washington soon would turn to marriage and stewardship of his Mount Vernon estate on the Potomac River, along with service in the Virginia House of Burgesses—in short, no more military confrontations, no more frontier adventures to speak of. Like anyone else of his day and age, however, he still had to survive the vicissitudes of an often harsh eighteenth-century existence (no hot running water, no central heat or air conditioning, no antibiotics, no electricity, no motorized vehicles, no aspirin for a simple headache, and so on). But survive he did, until thrust at the very center of the Revolutionary War in the 1770s as overall military commander for the rebelling Colonials. And now, as might be expected, the perils of George really did mount up . . . but more on that a bit later.

Additional note: Did George Washington, *our* George, touch off the French and Indian War with his own small war against the French in the Ohio Valley, which, in turn, fed the flames of the worldwide

Seven Years' War (1756–1763)? Remember Washington's ambush of the French in May 1753, followed by defeat at his Fort Necessity that summer at Great Meadows? French philosopher Voltaire clearly had Fort Necessity in mind when he later said, "Such was the complication of political interests that a cannon shot fired in America could give the signal that set Europe ablaze." (India and other hot spots around the globe were "set ablaze," too.)

Was it really George Washington, with match in hand, who touched off the fires of war? Well, yes and no. He certainly was the figurehead who confronted the French in the North American wilderness, first as diplomatic emissary, then as soldier willing to fight. Certainly, too, as Louis Koontz wrote in his book *The Virginia Frontier, 1754–1763,* "the first hostile forces sent out were Virginians, and the first blood was shed by Virginians."

Like a good soldier, on the other hand, young George was acting on orders from his royal governor, Robert Dinwiddie, who in turn had acted on behalf of King George II, who explicitly did order Dinwiddie to warn the French against encroachment, and if that failed, then to use force.

After his return from the frontier lands in 1753, meanwhile, George Washington was unhappy to learn that Governor Dinwiddie was displeased with his performance at Fort Necessity and might even demote him. Stung, the young officer resigned from his militia posting, only to reappear in uniform in 1755 when the ill-fated General Braddock asked him to join his staff as an aide. It was that informal arrangement that placed Washington at Braddock's side for the British general's disastrous defeat near Fort Duquesne.

Now, Governor Dinwiddie rallied and appointed George Washington commander of all Virginia military forces, as a full colonel in rank. Thus, a still-young George Washington was able to play a leading role (with John Forbes) in seizing Fort Duquesne from the French in 1758. The British then settled the war of the Ohio Valley in their favor by capturing Quebec the next year and gaining control of Canada as a result.

George Washington, meanwhile, was destined to remain at his beloved Mount Vernon, more or less undisturbed by outside events, for the next decade and a half. The Seven Years' War, meanwhile, was officially ended with the signing of the Treaty of Paris in 1763.

Meanwhile, Another George

GEORGE III, THE THIRD OF the Hanoverian line to rule England, chose a difficult time to be king of England. Before being set aside by insanity in 1811, he would be confronted by the American Revolution, the French Revolution, the Napoleonic Wars of Europe, and even an Industrial Revolution that changed the face of England.

During King George's lengthy tenure of sixty years, officially 1760 to 1820, England's population would double, its monarchy would weather the revolutionary storms intact, the outlines of the Victorian Empire would come into focus . . . but Great Britain would lose her American colonies.

His reign began on a faintly ridiculous note and for a time continued that way.

With his father, Frederick, succumbing to an injury received in a game of cricket, thirteen-year-old George suddenly found himself in line to succeed his grandfather, King George II, who in turn was the son of King George I, first of England's German kings.

Their ascension to the English throne, in fact, is a story deserving quick review here. It goes back to the death of Queen Anne in 1714 without a single one of her seventeen children still living (most died in infancy). Thus, no purely English heir stood in line to succeed her. The German-born and -raised George I came to the vacated throne as a great-grandson of England's James I. He never learned English, a failing that allowed Sir Robert Walpole to dominate at council meetings, thus becoming the country's first "prime" minister.

The unloved, Hanover-born king was notorious for having imprisoned his wife, Sophia, for thirty-two years for her suspected adulterous affair with a Swede, Philip von Konigsmark—who mysteriously disappeared, never to be seen again, and may have been murdered by the furious husband.

With George I's death in 1727, his son George II took over the regal reins. The younger George had despised his father and had once tried to swim a castle moat to see his imprisoned mother. Also raised in Hanover, Germany, he spoke English with an accent. Though never popular, he did briefly impress his English subjects for personally taking part in the Battle at Dettingen in 1743—the last English monarch to lead troops into battle. Unfortunately for the imperial image, when he died at Kensington Palace after a morning cup of hot chocolate in 1760, it was in the bathroom—"a martyr to constipation," is the way a modern British publication describes his passing. He was seventy-seven.

His grandson, George, Prince of Wales, heir to the throne at age twenty-two, was much more "English" than the two Georges before him but at first a bit immature and not taken too seriously by his subjects—nor by his intimates in court and government. He didn't help his image by his early infatuation with fifteen-year-old Lady Sarah Lennox, a fellow "royal" (great-great-granddaughter of Charles II and a mistress) who apparently flirted with him but turned down his offer of marriage. He then married seventeen-year-old Princess Charlotte of Mecklenburg-Strelitz.

Onlookers considered it a bad omen when the large diamond in George III's crown fell out on their wedding day in 1761—some, aided by the virtues of hindsight, thought it presaged the loss of the American colonies.

It may be apocryphal that George's mother, the Princess Augusta, told her young son, "George, be a king," but he did ascend the throne with fixed monarchial ideas. One of them was his determination to reassert royal authority over Parliament, the very institution that had placed the Protestant "royals" from the German Duchy of Hanover on the English throne to begin with. Before his premature death, George's father had written down his earnest hope that, as king some day, young George would "retrieve the glory of the throne." And this he apparently was determined to do.

Even before becoming king, George himself once said, "Though I act wrong in most things, I have too much spirit to accept the crown and be a cipher."

A critic of his own grandfather, George II, the new King George taking the throne in 1760 held a shockingly low opinion of the late monarch's famous secretary of state, William Pitt, the "Great Commoner." It was under Pitt that the British had destroyed French power in India, Africa, the West Indies, and North America. So great were the British triumphs that the year 1759 was known as the "Year of Miracles." Said popular pundit Horace Walpole (son of

Robert): "Victories come so tumbling over one another from distant parts of the globe that it looks like the handiwork of a London romance writer."

And yet, to the incoming King George III, Pitt was "a true snake in the grass," the "blackest of hearts," and the "most dishonorable of men." The new king, England's youngest incoming monarch since Queen Elizabeth took the throne in 1558, shared these views with a small circle of intimates, chief among them his longtime Scottish tutor, John Stuart, Earl of Bute—who considered the late king an inept tool of his cabinet and encouraged the new king at every opportunity to reassert his royal authority.

George III had to temper his critical view of Pitt the very night of King George II's death. In a full cabinet meeting held that evening, the new monarch tried out a statement—composed by Bute, it so happens. It began innocently enough with George's pledge of "tenderest affection for this my native country." He also promised to "preserve and strengthen the Constitution." The rub came when he expressed hopes that the highly successful Seven Years' War (known in America as the French and Indian War) would soon be ended. When the new king called it the "bloody and expensive war," however, Pitt objected and insisted upon a change of language citing the "expensive but just and necessary war."

That done, history marched on. Young George was off to his lengthy reign, during which he at first was hampered by his reliance upon the politically inept Bute, as prime minister. One result was a revolving door of ministries. In time, though, George III learned to leave most policy decisions to his ministers and even, in the case of the American Revolution, to defend Parliamentary authority over the American colonies, rather than his own monarchial authority. Indeed, after the Boston Tea Party defied Parliament's authority over colonial affairs in no uncertain terms, George III described himself as "fighting the battle of the legislature."

In the war that soon followed, he was without doubt committed to stamping out the colonial insurrection. He followed the military events closely, he consulted often with his ministers and offered his advice, but his cabinet made the big decisions. Toward the end, he was obviously reluctant to admit the war was lost. But once it was over, he was perfectly willing to be friends with the new nation across the Atlantic.

As he once told John Adams, he only had acted during the conflict by "what I thought myself indispensably bound to do by the duty which I owed my people." He said that he had been the "last to consent to the separation," but now, "the separation having been made, and having become inevitable, I have always said, as I say now, that I would be the first to meet the friendship of the United States as an independent power."

Additional note: Despite the loss of the American colonies, George III actually became a popular king in England, but his years ahead would be troubled ones. In 1786, a woman tried to stab him at the garden gate of St. James palace in London. In 1788, his mental illness first made its presence known. A shaken Queen Charlotte told a confidante that he had foamed at the mouth; the king's doctors sometimes restrained him in a straitjacket or tied him to his bed. He seemed to recover and was perfectly composed after another would-be assassin took a shot at him during an opera performance at the Drury Lane theater in London in 1800.

His mental illness reasserted itself the very next year—the queen and his doctors conspired to isolate him at the White House in Kew, from which he signed Parliamentary acts into law, corresponded with his ministers, but objected strenuously to his status of near-imprisonment.

As the nineteenth century succeeded the eighteenth, he went blind, he suffered a hostile relationship with his two eldest sons, and was stunned by the early death of Princess Amelia, his youngest and favorite daughter. He and Queen Charlotte had produced a total of fifteen children—nine of them sons once described by the Duke of Wellington as "the damnedest millstones about the necks of any government that can be imagined."

His madness erupted one final time in 1811, at which point his least favorite son, soon to be King George IV, took the royal reins as regent while George III was relegated to an empty life in Windsor Castle—"persuaded that he is always conversing with angels," according to diarist Fanny Burney, a court intimate and Joint Keeper of the Queen's Robes.

When he died in 1820, wrote another diarist of the day, Mrs. John Arbuthnot, wife of a cabinet official, the man "sunk into an honoured grave" had been "the best man & the best King that ever adorned humanity."

She was consoled in her grief by the fact that "such a sovereign was followed to his last home by countless thousands of affectionate subjects." The crowds, she also asserted, were "drawn to the spot by no idle curiosity to view the courtly pageant, but to pay a last tribute of respect & to shed the tear of affection & gratitude over the grave of him who, for sixty long years, had been the Father of his people!"

To continue the story of England's four sequential Georges, the next and final royal George in the string only held the crown until his own death in 1830, to be succeeded by his brother William IV for an even briefer reign of seven years, also ended by death. Next in line was William's niece, an eighteen-year-old girl named Victoria . . . but there begins an entirely different story.

To Pay the Bills

ONE BOMBSHELL AFTER ANOTHER CAME from across the Atlantic. Just count 'em up. Navigation Acts. The Stamp Act. The Townshend Acts. The Tea tax. The Coercive or Intolerable Acts. The Boston Port Act. The Quebec Act.

Didn't they, didn't anybody back in England, realize?

Applying one aggravation after another, the British hardly could have dreamed up a series of dictates and actions so punitive in appearance, so likely to stir up resentment, even revolution, among their American colonists. In actual fact, the Mother Country sometimes wanted to be punitive, but at other times simply didn't realize the full ramifications of her actions.

Occasionally, too, "Mother" England had her own crying needs to be taken care of.

Consider the world situation in 1763 as the Treaty of Paris closed out the French and Indian War in North America (known world-wide as the Seven Years' War). For Great Britain and her American colonies, the future looked rosy indeed. Great Britain had emerged the dominant power in Europe, the colonial master of India, the West Indies, and North America (even including Spanish Florida). In North America, not only were the French swept out of power in Canada and the Ohio Valley, but their more aggressive Indian allies, pushed westward, past the Appalachian Mountains, were left on their own.

For Virginia, especially, 1763 seemed to herald a golden age similar to the boom times of 1720 to 1750, right before the just-concluded war. Virginia in 1763 was the largest and most populous of the American colonies—up from just 88,000 souls in 1720 to an amazing 350,000 (but 140,000 of them were slaves with little to no prospect of sharing in the next round of good times). Here, too, was the original font of tobacco and still a great center of trade in the golden leaf—so valuable a commodity that it had served for a time in Virginia as legal tender, as money.

For all these wonderful tidings, though, there was a price to pay . . . wars are expensive; armies and navies cost money to feed and equip. Somebody would have to pay. In England, taxes already were levied on imports and exports, on all kinds of specific items such as windows or carriages; on newspapers, cards, and dice; on services such as advertisements, and, that old bugaboo, on land. Just consider the sapping effect of a real estate tax of $20,000 for a land parcel worth $100,000! But that's what the land tax was—20 percent of value.

Rather than ask the English in England to take on even greater burdens, wouldn't it be reasonable to assess the English colonies for a greater contribution to their own upkeep and protection in the future? Indeed, that was the thought in the Mother Country. It did seem reasonable to them. Especially with a national debt of many millions to retire.

Now, quite true, there was little poverty to be found in the American colonies. True also that Englishmen visiting Virginia were startled to find "settler" after "settler" living in homes and enjoying fashions that mirrored the lifestyles of the country gentry and wealthy merchants of England. Except for those hardy souls hacking out new homesteads on the frontier to the west, these in fact were no settlers at all. In composite, they made up a contradiction—a mirror image of Mother England herself, and yet another country altogether.

If it appeared they could well afford to pay a greater share of the

Mother Country's bills, however, it turns out they had a mind of their own. They had their own legislatures, their own laws, their own practices and needs. As summed up by a twentieth-century Virginia guide for history teachers: "They [the colonies] paid little attention to parliamentary laws and the Navigation Acts; they smuggled extensively and bribed customs officials; and they traded with the enemy in wartime."

More insidious yet: "Legislatures ignored the king's instructions, often refused to support the [recent] war efforts until they had forced concessions from the governors, and had taken royal and executive prerogatives unto themselves."

In Virginia specifically, recent royal governors such as Robert Dinwiddie and Francis Fauquier had "yielded to the demands of the House of Burgesses and accepted laws explicitly contrary to their royal instructions." Instead of the imperial colonial system "as set forth in the creation of the Board of Trade in 1696 . . . in its place there had been substituted, quite unnoticed by British officials, the House of Burgesses, which thought of itself as a miniature House of Commons."

In sum, with the advent of peace in 1763, Mother England suddenly awoke to the liberties the American colonists had taken unto themselves. And as the next few years would demonstrate, the colonists had no intention of giving up a single one of their new-found freedoms.

Another troublesome factor that came with the end of war was England's own political upheaval. A once-solid and dominant Whig coalition in Parliament now split into quarreling factions. At the same time, a new and uninspired king (George III) would try out one set of ministers after another before finally settling upon the administration of Lord North and the Tories, destined to hold power from 1770 to 1782.

Long before this point, however, the colonists had an old quarrel to settle in the form of the Mother Country's widely ignored Navigation Acts, a series of laws that had been in effect since the previous century to give English merchants and shipowners dominance in trade with the colonies and to shut out their European rivals. The first (1651) of these acts, for instance, stated that only English ships could carry goods shipped from the colonies to the Mother Country. The last (1696), significantly, established English-supervised customs houses in America.

But now, after the midway point of the eighteenth century, would come a series of ill-considered actions by the British that only hastened the separation of colonial America from England.

In 1765 came the infamous Stamp Act, which called for payment of a tax on purchases of newspapers, magazines, commercial papers, legal and other documents. The act produced an immediate uproar in the colonies, marked by riots, a famous declaration of defiance by Patrick Henry in the Virginia House of Burgesses and, meeting in New York, a Stamp Act Congress of twenty-seven delegates from nine colonies. This first American congress, gathering in September 1765 at the behest of the Massachusetts House of Representatives, adopted a statement of grievances and rights to send across the Atlantic to the attention of both the Crown and Parliament. The statement complained that the tax would "subvert the rights and liberties of the colonies." The hated Stamp Act was then repealed.

Next, in 1767, came the punitive acts named for Charles Townshend, Chancellor of the Exchequer, and intended to replace the Stamp Act revenues. The Townshend Acts imposed duties on tea, paper, lead, and paint colors but also were intended to demonstrate Parliament's powers to tax the colonies as it saw fit. Again, the colonial response was strong opposition, resentment, and rebellious thinking—by early 1770 most of these laws would also be repealed.

Now, in 1770, came an unplanned and accidental incident that played right into the hands of the more extreme propagandists critical of Mother England's policies. It was the Boston "Massacre," in which a group of British soldiers on sentry duty at the customs house fired into a rowdy and harassing crowd of four hundred or more. Pelted by snowballs and chunks of ice, the rioters pressing close and even knocking down one soldier with a club, the handful of troops finally let loose a scattering of shots into the unruly crowd. The result was five men killed and several others wounded. The thoughtful, widely respected Patriot leader John Adams led the legal defense for the eight soldiers and their commander, winning acquittal for all but two soldiers found guilty of manslaughter.

For some Americans, the incident only fanned the flames of resentment against Mother England. But it also gave pause to other Patriots who realized that mob actions were dangerous, wrong in principle, and likely in the long run to give their crusade for greater freedoms a bad name.

Next, with outright rebellion already brewing, Parliament gave the East India Company exclusive rights to ship tea into the American colonies, a fresh action taken against colonial will. This resulted, late in 1773, in the Boston Tea Party—staged by a group of Boston rebels disguised as Indians. To prevent delivery of freshly imported tea, they boarded the arriving ships and dumped the contents from 342 chests of tea, a cargo worth $90,000, into the harbor waters. Other symbolic "tea parties" were staged elsewhere in the American colonies.

Outraged at such colonial intemperance, Parliament now, in 1774, passed the collection of punitive laws known in America as the Intolerable Acts. One, the Quebec Act, extended the boundaries of Quebec Province in Canada to the Ohio River, thus seeming to snatch away the frontier gains the American Colonials had helped to win from the French in the recent French and Indian War.

Another, even more galling, measure in this decidedly punitive package was the Boston Port Act, which closed the port of Boston, shifted its customhouse to Salem, Massachusetts, and placed British warships in Boston Harbor as an obvious counter to possible disorder or insurrection. This blockade of Boston would be removed only when the colonists paid for the tea destroyed in the recent "Tea Party" . . . and when it became clear the colonists would pay future duty fees as ordered by the Crown.

This measure provoked a flurry of sympathetic actions by the other colonies in support of Boston and Massachusetts. By far the most significant and—for Great Britain, ominous—development was the call echoing through all the colonies to send delegates to a Continental Congress meeting in Philadelphia to develop concerted plans and actions on behalf of all the colonies.

Take This Job And . . .

TO BE A STAMP ACT commissioner in the colonies turned out to be dangerous work. It wasn't thought so at first, since at first even the colonial agents lobbying in London for their respective colonies anticipated little objection to Prime Minister George Grenville's latest revenue-raiser.

Parliament had gone along with him by lopsided vote. To be sure, the colonial agents, Pennsylvania's Benjamin Franklin among them, had objected to imposition of the stamp tax on all sorts of documents, but once the deed was done, few in London, English or American, expected to hear more than a murmur of protest.

So mesmerized on this one issue were the agents that they happily complied with the PM's proposal that they, themselves, should name the American-based commissioners who would distribute the stamps and collect the tax fees, while keeping a handsome percentage for themselves. Franklin, for one, appointed old Philadelphia friend John Hughes.

Imagine Franklin's surprise to hear from Hughes just weeks later that he was holed up in his house with an angry mob outside demonstrating its abhorrence of the Stamp Act levies.

In Boston, protestors hanged, beheaded, and burned in effigy stamp commissioner Andrew Oliver. A mob broke into his house and sacked its interior. A few days later, angry Bostonians broke into the home of Oliver's brother-in-law, Chief Justice Thomas Hutchison, and completely wrecked it as well. His furniture, books, clothing, and chinaware all carried off, the mob left him nothing but an empty shell.

Governor Francis Bernard, retreating to the island fortress of Castle William in the harbor, complained that he had "no force to oppose" such rioters.

Royal officials in New York hardly fared any better—not even the commander of the 130 redcoats garrisoned at Fort George in Manhattan. Major Thomas Jones probably should have known better than to threaten dire action to make the colonists adhere to the

Stamp levy. What he got in return was a mob of two thousand sacking his house and the burning in effigy of Acting Governor Cadwallader Colden—who not long after quietly turned over his colony's supply of stamps to the Sons of Liberty.

So it went, up and down the eastern seaboard of North America—nobody but a few royal officials was willing simply to grumble, yet put up with the Stamp Act tax. In Virginia, a calm but concerned George Washington called it an "unconstitutional method of taxation." He predicted it would force many of his fellow Americans to do without English luxury goods and thus prove painful to British merchants.

Far more passionately, fellow Virginian Patrick Henry, recently elected as a member of the House of Burgesses, denounced the Stamp Act in fiery terms while proposing his incendiary Stamp Act Resolves (also known as the Virginia Resolves), which asserted that only the General Assembly of Virginia had the right to tax Virginians.

Oddly, while it adopted Henry's defiant resolves, Virginia would not be represented in the Stamp Act Congress that soon met in New York at the behest of Massachusetts—the Virginia House of Burgesses was not in session at the right moment to name delegates. In any case, Patrick Henry's Stamp Act Resolves, widely circulated (and often even intemperately amended by other firebrands) had already made Virginia's position clear.

In the Virginia capital of Williamsburg that same May of 1765, an onlooking college student with an interest in political philosophy had watched newcomer Henry's performance and realized: "By these resolutions Mr. Henry took the lead out of the hands of those [who] had heretofore guided the proceedings of the House. . . . These were honest and able men, who had begun the opposition on the same grounds, but with a moderation more adapted to their age and experience. Subsequent events favored the bolder spirits. . . ."

Bolder spirits, that is, such as Henry and his future allies, among them the onlooking student from the College of William and Mary, one Thomas Jefferson.

By the time the new Stamp Act took effect on November 1, 1765, most, if not all, of the would-be stamp commissioners in the colonies had heard the message of their fellow colonists loud and clear—and found other ways to occupy their time.

Virginia's appointed stamp commissioner was plantation owner Colonel George Mercer, a close friend to George Washington, it so happened. He arrived in Williamsburg from London just a day or two before the tax was to take effect, only to encounter a large, restless crowd demanding he step down as stamp commissioner. He asked for time to consider the crowd's plea, then hurried over to a nearby coffeehouse to consult with Royal Governor Francis Fauquier—who later said he would have called the protesting crowd a "mob," except that it was "chiefly if not altogether composed of Gentlemen of property in the Colony, some of them at the Head of their respective counties, and Merchants of the country, whether English, Scotch, or Virginia."

The next morning, Mercer arose to find an estimated two thousand persons awaiting him . . . and his answer. Deciding that discretion should rule in the face of such numbers, he promptly resigned as stamp commissioner.

Early Internet

SO THERE WERE THE BOSTON Massacre and the Boston Tea Party. But, in between, there also was the *Gaspee* Incident.

The *Gaspee,* a British armed schooner, was on customs duty and chasing smugglers in Narragansett Bay one night in June of 1772. Unfortunately for ship and crew, it ran aground. At which point a crowd of Rhode Islanders, some of them prominent citizens of the Providence area, stormed the ship and burned it to the water line.

This seemingly rash act came during a relatively quiet period for the uneasy relationship between the colonies and the Mother Country. Thanks to the repeal of the Townshend Acts, the quarrels had abated for the moment. In North Carolina, all attention recently had been focused upon the minor war between uplanders and lowlanders, with Royal Governor William Tryon and his planter allies of the lowlands roundly defeating the upland "Regulators," as they were called, in the Battle of Alamance Creek. In Pennsylvania, would-be settlers from Connecticut tilted with Pennsylvanians over land in the Wyoming Valley, while to the north others hungry for land argued over claims in the Hampshire Grants, located between New York and New Hampshire.

The *Gaspee* Incident, however, shifted the colonial focus back to relations with Mother England. While moderate Patriots were aghast at the outright attack on an armed British ship, local efforts to unearth the perpetrators were not taken seriously. But then London sent a royal investigating commission—with stern promises of trial in England for the guilty parties, probably followed by hangings. The commission, though, failed to find a single person to prosecute. With such mockery made of royal authority, Rhode Island's Collector of Customs could only moan, "There's an end to collecting a revenue and enforcing the acts of trade."

From the Patriot point of view, on the other hand, there was the danger that royal use of an investigatory commission in one case could be a precedent for the intrusion of like bodies in all kinds of other colonial affairs.

For all the Royals and Loyalists in North America, meanwhile, there was worse news than the failure of the *Gaspee* commission, far worse, yet to come. In Massachusetts, Governor Thomas Hutchison put out the word that starting in 1773 he and the colony's judges would be paid their salaries by the Crown, meaning, according to the onlooking Patriots, that colonial officials would be beyond local control. In no time, reinvigorated Committees of Correspondence were back in action in Boston and throughout the colony. Their stream of resolutions, pamphlets, and news items led to the formation of more such committees in town after town, matched by a similar eruption of revolutionary cells in colony after colony.

In the end, through organizations such as the Sons of Liberty and the multitudinous committees of correspondence springing up all over, the Patriots of North America had formed an interlocking "Internet," providing one another with the latest in revolutionary words and deeds.

In Virginia, for example, the House of Burgesses in March of 1773 formed a colony-level Committee of Correspondence specifically to look into the *Gaspee* Incident and its ramifications. The empowering resolution, adopted on a motion by Thomas Jefferson's brother-in-law, Dabney Carr, asked the legislatures of Virginia's sister colonies to appoint one or more persons of their own membership as like committees "to communicate from time to time. . . ."

In the Virginia capital of Williamsburg the very next day, the local *Virginia Gazette* carried an explanation by an unnamed "Gentleman of Distinction," probably a Burgesses leader. The item said in part: ". . . [W]e are endeavoring to bring our Sister Colonies into the strictist union with us; that we may resent, in one Body, any Steps that may be taken by Administration to deprive any one of us the least Particle of our Rights and Liberties."

While not the first such example to be seen or heard in these revolutionary days, these were the code words on the tongues of Patriots far and wide. *Colonies in a Union. Our rights. Our liberties.*

Up in New England, instead of Web sites spreading the word of this early "Internet," it often was horseback riders galloping into far-flung towns and villages with the latest news or Patriot propaganda. "Selected riders carried the writings . . . deep into the Berkshire hills, to the green shores of Rhode Island, down through the rolling Connecticut fields, far over the New Hampshire border," wrote Bruce Lancaster in his history, *The American Revolution.*

In this regard, he also noted, "No horseman was busier than silversmith Paul Revere, who might have a mass of pamphlets or letters or only a scrap of paper bearing the single line: 'Mr. Revere will give you all the news. J. Adams.'"

John Adams, naturally.

America's Man in London

He had known that taking on the role of London agent—i.e., lobbyist—for his native Massachusetts would endanger his many connections in England. For all her faults, he loved the Mother Country. And he was quite a well-known figure there. He enjoyed a Crown salary as deputy postmaster general for America. He was a recipient of British scientific honors, he had many friends in high and low places . . . he had even talked a number of them into joining him in plans to found a twenty-million–acre western colony in lands later to comprise the state of Illinois.

Despite the opposition of Lord Hillsborough, secretary of state for America, the truly high and mighty Privy Council had approved the scheme; the chagrined Hillsborough had then resigned. Benjamin Franklin, together with his son William, also a committed Anglophile, had the "right people" behind him and stood poised to reap a fortune.

But the Boston "Massacre," an outgrowth of protests over the latest British decision to quarter troops in Boston, rankled and deeply offended. Never mind that a handful of British soldiers had been hard-pressed by an angry, dangerous-looking mob of about four hundred Colonials. For Ben Franklin, the street mob wasn't the real issue. The issue, he said in a letter to a friend back in Massachusetts, was that it was unconstitutional for the British to keep "a standing army . . . among us in time of peace, without the consent of our assemblies." Not even the king, Franklin argued, could do the same in England without the approval of Parliament.

And so, putting aside all risks, when the Massachusetts legislature ignored acting Governor Thomas Hutchison's objections and decided to choose its own agent, Ben Franklin agreed to be the colony's man in London.

Franklin's stint in England started out well enough, but not quite three years later, with violent revolution stirring in America, the erudite Franklin came across a set of potentially incendiary letters that Hutchison had penned back in 1768 and 1769, during the riots that had greeted the punitive Townshend Acts.

In the course of communicating with a Treasury official named Thomas Whatley, Hutchison had called for the deployment of British troops to discourage the mobs on Boston's streets. Worse, he had stated, "There must be some abridgement of what is called British liberty." Franklin sent the letters back to Boston to show, he later said, that not all the troublemaking could be blamed upon the British—there were also ill-advised Loyalist friends and agents, like Hutchison.

When the gist of the governor's remarks became public, a double furor arose. "From Worcester to Boston indignant citizens demanded Hutchison's ouster as governor," wrote historian Thomas Fleming in his book *Liberty! The American Revolution*. "As the story spread to other colonies, Hutchison was burned in effigy in several cities and compared to Judas Iscariot, Nero and other villains of history." Franklin soon received a petition from the Massachusetts legislature requesting that Hutchison be removed as governor.

It would now be agent Franklin's delicate job to see that the petition reached the desk of King George III, after traveling through the hands of Lord Dartmouth, the new secretary of state for America.

Of course, wasn't it Ben Franklin himself who first obtained the letters and sent them back to America? Where they became public and thus brought about the framing of the petition? Wouldn't it seem—in England, anyway—that he somehow orchestrated the entire affair?

Keep in mind, too, that Ben Franklin was a very public figure in the Mother Country. Not only was he active socially, he knew how to get his name—and his American point of view—in the newspapers. "In London," wrote Fleming, "Benjamin Franklin jousted with anti-Americans in the press, but his wit seemed to make the dispute almost good-natured. 'Rules By Which A Great Empire May Be Reduced To a Small One' skewered the government's American policies. 'An Edict By The King of Prussia' declared England to be a Prussian colony, because the first settlers had been Germans. In Franklin's satiric scenario, the king of Prussia proceeded to announce taxes and duties similar to the ones England had imposed on America, warning that anyone who opposed them would be guilty of high treason."

Where Franklin obtained the Hutchison-Whatley correspondence is still not known for sure, but the deceased Thomas Whatley's brother William accused Franklin's fellow American John Temple of stealing the letters. Temple then fought a duel with William Whatley and wounded him. Franklin, shocked at these events, hurriedly placed a notice in the *Public Advertiser* saying, "I alone am the person who obtained and transmitted to Boston the letters in question." He also asserted that the letters "by public officers to persons in public stations" were not really private and, in fact, were well known to various officials in England.

Then came a summons for Franklin to attend a hearing before the august Privy Council on the petition to remove Governor Hutchison of Massachusetts—on January 29, 1774, Ben Franklin would be standing in the "Cockpit" before England's most powerful men, other than the king himself.

The *Cockpit*? Once the site of cockfighting and located in a section of Whitehall, noted Fleming, it was now a meeting place for the prime minister and his cabinet. And the rumor in London was that certain parties were out to skewer colonial America's best-known spokesman in England.

As if Ben Franklin didn't have enough to worry about while he—and the two lawyers he hired—prepared for the crucial confrontation, there now came, by ship, a startling bulletin from the American colonies. It was news of the Boston Tea Party and related acts of defiance in America. Here was added trouble . . . or could it be unexpected opportunity for the clever lobbyist?

As Fleming also noted, the latest news from America presented the issue in simple terms. "The King's ministers, face to face with the one American in London who could speak for all the colonies, could prove they wanted to settle the quarrel peacefully by letting Benjamin Franklin explain why Thomas Hutchison's talk of abridging British liberty was at the heart of America's grievance against England."

Unfortunately, Franklin would be pitted against newly appointed Solicitor General Alexander Wedderburn, whose sense of conscience even Prime Minister Lord North called "accommodating." King George III once echoed North's opinion by noting the "duplicity that often appears in his [Wedderburn's] political deportment."

In anticipation of a bloodletting, a rare total of thirty-six English lords crowded into the chamber chosen for what would amount to a prosecutorial attack on Ben Franklin by Wedderburn. "They sat at a long table in the center of the spacious chamber, built in drawing-room style with a fireplace at one end," wrote Fleming. "Through the windows at that end loomed St. James palace, the King's residence."

So crowded was the room that Lord North, arriving late, couldn't find a seat and had to stand beside the seated council president. Then, after Franklin's two lawyers presented the argument for removal of Governor Hutchison, Wedderburn advanced to the table and launched a scathing personal attack upon Ben Franklin.

Governor Thomas Hutchison had only acted, only spoken, as a loyal minion of the king, argued Wedderburn. If he had lost the confidence of the so-called "people," that was Franklin's doing. What's more, Franklin was a thief! "I hope, my Lords, you will mark and brand that man, for the honor of this country, of Europe, of mankind," shrilled the Scotsman Wedderburn.

The solicitor general indulged in his tirade for almost a full hour, and all the while Ben Franklin stood quietly, said an onlooker later, "like a rock, in the same posture, his head resting on his left hand, and in that attitude abiding the pelting of the pitiless storm."

In the meantime, added Fleming's account, "the Cockpit rocked with laughter at Wedderburn's sallies and the lords of the Privy Council studied him [Franklin] with mocking, haughty eyes."

Finally, thankfully, the storm of abuse ended, unanswered—at the moment—by its victim. Ben Franklin of course left the chamber deeply humiliated, but at the same time the scales had dropped from his eyes. Clearly, there could be no real accommodation between the Mother Country and her restless, freedom-seeking Colonials. "The deep affection he had acquired for England and Englishmen had been demolished in front of his eyes," wrote Fleming. "That these great lords, most of whom he knew personally, could allow him to become the target of a man as despicable as Alexander Wedderburn was almost beyond belief. A profound, even immense personal resentment multiplied his rage."

It may or may not be true, but there is a postscript to relate here as well. While the Revolution would later prove the ultimate satisfaction for Ben Franklin's wounded feelings, he allegedly was able to take Wedderburn by the arm as the crowd in the Cockpit broke up and left the bloodied chamber, and Franklin was able to whisper into the Scotsman's ear this prophetic promise: "I will make your master a little king for this."

True story or not, in the coming years that would be an outcome to which Ben Franklin himself would contribute in great measure.

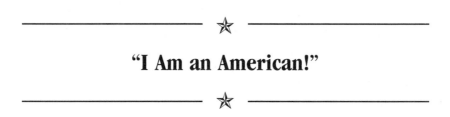

"I Am an American!"

It was a farewell dinner to remember. There was the Massachusetts firebrand Samuel Adams, rough, tough . . . and dressed in a wine-colored suit, a gift from the Sons of Liberty. There, too, was Virginia's tall, imposing Colonel George Washington, rather stunning in blue and gold braid. John Adams, for that matter, wore blue and canary, looking handsome in his wig.

The site was the City Tavern on Philadelphia's Walnut Street. The occasion, on October 20, 1774, was an end ... and a beginning, really. It was a farewell dinner for the fifty-six members of America's first Congress but a prelude also for those future Continental Congresses that would authorize creation of a national army, declare independence from England, and make war, revolutionary war.

Not that it was the very first congress ever held in the colonies. In fact, two such gatherings had preceded it. The first, attracting representatives from New England, New York, Pennsylvania, and Maryland, had met in Albany in 1754 to consider a concerted approach to Indian relations—and to hear Benjamin Franklin's discussion of a colonial union. Next, in 1765, came the Stamp Act Congress, a three-week meeting in New York of delegates from nine colonies. They sent George III a petition calling for repeal of the Stamp Act, an action eventually taken.

Just nine years later, in 1774, the stubborn Colonials were at it again, this time in response to the Coercive or Intolerable Acts passed by Parliament, specifically the measure closing the port of Boston to all shipping except for military supplies and essential foodstuffs. That legislative action was taken in England on March 31, but America wouldn't receive word of the blockade until the docking of the first ship to cross the Atlantic from England.

Once the bitter news reached America, however, Patriot organizations in the various colonies wasted little time in agreeing to concerted action. As early as May 17, Providence, Rhode Island, issued a call for a colony-wide congress to discuss the latest British restrictions on colonial freedoms. Philadelphia chimed in on May 21 and New York followed suit May 23.

In Williamsburg, Virginia, Royal Governor Lord Dunmore had dissolved his obstreperous Virginia Assembly, but no great matter—members of the House of Burgesses met in Raleigh Tavern on May 27 to issue their own call for a Continental Congress. It should develop "a general and uniform plan for the defense and preservation of our common rights," the Virginians resolved.

Thus it would be, and from June to August of that year, the various colonies—Georgia excepted—went about the business of choosing the men (for they *were all* men) who would represent them at this greatest, most important colonial congress yet.

The newly chosen delegates would be traveling to Philadelphia, the meeting place suggested by the Massachusetts Assembly when it acted on June 17 to join the stampede toward a congress. As events turned out, forty of the original fifty-six convened as a single legislative body on September 5, 1774, in the city's newly constructed Carpenters' Hall. Their remaining brethren would be filtering into town shortly.

Church bells in the city of thirty thousand had rung out in greeting, and now, in their first legislative hall, the delegates would be hearing the repeated peal of clarion calls to action. First, though, the housekeeping preliminaries allowed one and all to look about and gauge their fellow delegates, in many cases for the first time. "Big, dark John Sullivan, lawyer and militia major from New Hampshire, could soon pick out Roger Sherman of Connecticut and Matthew Tilghman of Maryland, George Read of Delaware and Christopher Gadsden of South Carolina," wrote Bruce Lancaster in *The American Revolution.* "Gray old Stephen Hopkins of Rhode Island, veteran of that first, feeble Congress in Albany in 1754, sat near the dais, listening to John Dickinson of Pennsylvania and Caesar Rodney of Delaware."

Peyton Randolph of Virginia was chosen presiding officer, while Charles Thomson, a Philadelphian (and not a delegate), became secretary. The first speaker of the session would be New Hampshire's Sullivan, it turned out. He reported his constituency's desire for measures securing colonial rights but also restoring "that peace, harmony and mutual confidence which once subsisted between the parent country and her colonies."

In the days ahead men of many views and backgrounds spoke, argued, cajoled, pleaded, thundered, even "shook their fists in angry debate," noted historian Lancaster.

From Edward Rutledge of South Carolina came words expressing the common concern of all, "That the Acts and Bills of Parliament in regard to Massachusetts Bay affect the whole Continent of America." Gradually, however, two competing streams of political thought emerged. There were those who argued American rights were based upon legal precedent such as English common law, the British constitution, and the original colonial charters. Others would add, above all else, the laws of nature to those legal foundations as the true basis for human rights.

It was the latter view that finally prevailed as a subcommittee busily set to work composing the Declaration of Rights destined to be adopted by the full Congress on October 14, 1774. Stating that the Colonials were still loyal subjects of the king, this document asserted that only the colonies could tax the colonies, that only they could legislate their own internal affairs. It took Parliament to task for the so-called Intolerable Acts, the Quebec Act, and the quartering of British troops in a peaceable America. It objected strenuously to the various revenue acts imposed upon the colonists since the end of the Seven Years' War in 1763. Further, it claimed for all Americans the rights to "life, liberty and property."

A good part of the Rights statement could be attributed to the flurry of excitement created by news of the "Suffolk Resolves," a stern declaration of colonial rights written by Dr. Joseph Warren, a leading Massachusetts Patriot, and adopted by his colony's Suffolk County on September 9. It was the ubiquitous rider Paul Revere who galloped into town on October 6 with this condemnation of the Intolerable Acts as "murderous."

Soon endorsed by the assemblage in Philadelphia, the Suffolk Resolves went so far as to urge Massachusetts citizens to place their tax payments in escrow in anticipation of later, more lenient treatment by England—but in the meantime, prepare for possible war.

Now, though, came a jolting debate as conservatives led by Pennsylvania's Joseph Galloway proposed a new form of colonial government called "The Plan of Proposed Union between Great Britain and the Colonies." Joining future Loyalist Galloway in this venture were some "big names" from the delegate ranks, such as South Carolina's Rutledge and John Jay of New York. (Jay, incidentally, goes down in history as the delegate who resolved an earlier hot debate over the issue of voting representation in the Congress. His simple expedient: Each colony's delegation would have but a single vote to cast.) Galloway's plan, calling for an American Parliament more or less matching the English Parliament in powers and an American president-general appointed by the king, eventually was tabled and thus killed by a close six-to-five vote.

Before turning for home late in October, the delegates agreed upon a boycott of trade with England. They established a Continental Association (to be complemented by local Association committees) to enforce the cutoff of imports from England and like economic sanctions—all hopefully pending a change of heart by the Mother Country.

So they had come together, these first members of a real

American Congress, disparate men from disparate backgrounds.

As all had known from the start, had hoped and prayed, their work had been to one concerted purpose—joint actions, joint declarations on behalf of all the colonies. History might note what they said and did before going home, but more significant was the very fact that they met at all, and then presented a united front.

Whatever they actually accomplished, it may have been Patrick Henry of Virginia who expressed the historical import best when one day in Carpenters' Hall he shouted: "The distinctions between Virginians, Pennsylvanians, New Yorkers, New Englanders are no more well-suited. I am not a Virginian, but an American!"

The Well-Suited Cat

LIFE ALWAYS *DOES* GO ON, even on the eve of a world-shaking revolution, and so it was one eighteenth-century day that a young tailor's apprentice in the Carolinas found himself alone in his master's house without much to do . . . except perhaps to stare at the large family cat "that generally lay about the fire."

It was close to the Christmas after Lexington and Concord to the north, or perhaps it was the year before. James P. Collins, born in 1763, couldn't be sure when writing his autobiography decades later, but he estimated his age as "about twelve" when he was "bound" to a tailor to learn the clothing trade. Two months later came Christmas, and one day the tailor and his wife left the young apprentice alone in their home to attend a party.

Alone, that is, except for the cat. And it was the cat that would give young Collins something useful to do.

"In order to try my mechanical powers," he wrote years later as an old man, "I concluded to make a suit of clothing for puss, and for my purpose gathered some scraps of cloth that lay about the shop-board, and went to work as hard as I could."

It was late afternoon before he finished, but when he did, he had created an entire suit—"coat, vest and small-clothes." Then he had to catch the cat. He succeeded and buttoned "all on tight," then set down the cat "to inspect the fit."

The fit was just fine, but now came the unexpected: "Unfortunately for me, there was a hole through the floor close to the fireplace, just large enough for the cat to pass down."

Well, guess what? After various gyrations intended to shake off the fine new suit, the frustrated feline disappeared down the hole in the floor. "The floor was tight and the house underpinned with brick, so there was no chance of pursuit."

Young Collins, soon to be a teenage militiaman fighting the British and their Loyalist allies, could only hope the cat would come out of its own accord.

But it was not to be—at least not right away. Indeed, "night came and I had made a good fire and seated myself for some two or three hours after dark, when who should make their appearance but my master and mistress and two young men, all in good humour, with two or three bottles of rum."

Now the cat, secreted under the floor boards, apparently had second thoughts. After all, instead of the new apprentice with his infernal ideas of dressing up felines, those above were the familiar voices of Master and Mistress. With all comfortably seated about the fireplace, "who should appear amongst us but the cat in his uniform."

By his own account, the young apprentice "was struck speechless." Further, "the secret was out and no chance of concealing; the cat was caught, the whole work inspected and the question asked, is this your day's work?" Young Collins, his heart in his mouth, of course answered yes. "I would then have been willing to have taken a good whipping and let it stop there. . . ."

But on the contrary, to complete his "mortification," the cat's suit was carefully removed and "hung up in the shop for the inspection of all the customers that came in."

Obviously, the tailor had liked his apprentice's suit design for the family cat . . . and approved of young James himself, who stayed on with the tailor and his family for another two years and two months, by which time "the revolutionary war began to make some interruption in the South."

Soon young Collins, despite his still-downy cheeks, would have more serious matters on his mind, such as spying on Tory partisans on behalf of his own Patriot militiamen, and fighting in the Battle of King's Mountain. For now, though, it was almost Christmas, and he was more concerned with the glad tidings of the season—and his well-suited cat.

II. 1775:
Lexington, Concord,
and Menotomy

Orders from General Gage

FROM LIEUTENANT GENERAL THOMAS GAGE, military governor of the Province of Massachusetts Bay, to Lieutenant Colonel Francis Smith, Tenth Regiment of Foot (a true copy):

Boston, April 18, 1775
Lieut. Colonel Smith, 10th Regiment 'Foot,

Sir,

Having received intelligence, that a quantity of Ammunition, Provision, Artillery, Tents and small Arms, have been collected at Concord, for the Avowed Purpose of raising and supporting a Rebellion against His Majesty, you will March with the Corps of Grenadiers and Light Infantry, put under your Command, with the utmost expedition and Secrecy to Concord, where you will seize and destroy all Artillery, Ammunition, Provisions, Tents, Small Arms, and all Military Stores whatever. But you will take care that the Soldiers do not plunder the Inhabitants, or hurt private property.

You have a Draught of Concord, on which is marked the Houses, Barns, &c, which contain the above military Stores. You will order a Trunion to be knocked off each Gun, but if it's found impracticable on any, they must be spiked, and the Carriages destroyed. The Powder and flower [flour] must be shook out of the Barrels into the River, the Tents burnt, Pork or Beef destroyed in the best way you can devise. And the Men may put Balls of lead in their pockets, throwing them by degrees into Ponds, Ditches &c., but no Quantity together, so that they may be recovered afterwards.

If you meet any Brass Artillery, you will order their muzzles to be beat in so as to render them useless.

You will observe by the Draught that it will be necessary to secure the two Bridges as soon as possible, you will therefore Order a party of the best Marchers, to go on with expedition for the purpose.

A small party on Horseback is ordered out to stop all advice of your March getting to Concord before you, and a small number of Artillery go out in Chaises to wait for you on the road, with Sledge Hammers, Spikes, &c.

You will open your business and return with the Troops, as soon as possible, which I must leave to your own Judgement and Discretion.

I am, Sir,
Your most obedient humble servant
Thos. Gage

Alarums in the Night

IT WAS AFTERNOON ON APRIL 18, 1775, and in Massachusetts something was brewing, some kind of British action. A stone tablet today marks the spot on Massachusetts Avenue in Arlington where the Black Horse Tavern once stood—members of a British patrol stopped and ate there the afternoon of April 18.

That very morning, the Patriots had moved four 6-pounder cannon from Concord to Groton, eighteen miles to the northwest. The Patriot Committees of Safety and Supplies not only ordered the precautionary move, but had made plans to hold their next meeting at the Black Horse Tavern.

In Boston the afternoon of April 18, meanwhile, a stableman at Province House, the residence of Military Governor Thomas Gage, heard someone say there would be "hell to pay tomorrow." Others in Boston heard the British were about to march.

In Lexington that evening, a local man returning from the markets in Boston reported he had passed the British patrol on the road to Lexington and Concord. His report was buttressed by a rider from Menotomy—at the time, the name for the future Arlington—carrying news for John Hancock, head of the Massachusetts Provincial Congress, that the British patrol had been in Menotomy, site of the Black Horse Tavern.

In fact, both John Hancock and the fire-eating rebel Samuel Adams were staying in Lexington at the home of local minister Jonas

Clarke. The Provincial Congress, in fact, had just adjourned its latest session three days before, on April 15—at Concord.

But back to the eighteenth: Apprised of the British patrol, Sergeant William Munroe of the Lexington Minutemen, himself a tavern-keeper, hastily made arrangements to post an eight-man guard at the minister's house—the Hancock-Clarke House, still standing today and open to the public as a historical site.

That was at 7 P.M., and at 8 P.M. the mounted British patrol actually rode through Lexington and continued on the road to Lincoln, between Lexington and Concord. In short order, members of the Lexington Minuteman Company began to gather in Buckman's Tavern, next to the Common, or green, in the center of town.

By 8:30, the British patrol had passed Lincoln Minuteman Samuel Hartwell's farmhouse on the road to Concord. Shortly after that, however, the horsemen turned back toward Lexington. In Lexington, meanwhile, three men from the Minuteman Company saddled up and rode out on the trail of the mysterious British horsemen to see what they were up to.

To their regret, the three scouts found out all too well ... but would not be able to report their findings until too late. In a joint affidavit, they later said that while riding the road to Concord about ten o'clock that night, they were "suddenly surprised by nine persons whom we took to be regular [British] officers, who rode up to us, mounted and armed, each holding a pistol in his hand, and after putting pistols, to our breasts, and seizing the bridles of our horses, they swore that if we stirred another step we should all be dead men."

At this point, and for the next four hours or so, the three scouts were prisoners of the British patrol—whose members questioned them about the stores held at Concord and the potential guard force to be encountered there, then announced that "four or five regiments of regulars would be in possession of the stores soon."

In Boston at ten o'clock, those "regulars," seven hundred to eight hundred strong, were just being alerted and ordered to prepare for a lengthy night's march under Lieutenant Colonel Francis Smith. At 10:30, the men quietly assembled at the foot of the Boston Common, then started boarding boats to cross Boston's Back Bay to Lechmere Point on the opposite shore. Their expedition was still supposedly a secret, but Paul Revere and William Dawes Jr. were already on their way to warn their fellow Patriots on the road to

Lexington and Concord. Departing by way of the north section of Boston, Revere crossed the Charles River in a boat rowed by two friends, the oars muffled with a petticoat.

By prearrangement, two signal lanterns in the steeple of Boston's Old North Church (today's Christ Church) alerted Revere confederates that the British initially were moving by water—one lantern would have meant a longer march by land alone. The signal lanterns would have been vital if Revere had not been able to skirt the British man-of-war *Somerset* in the Charles River . . . but he had.

A helpful chronology of events compiled by the Concord Chamber of Commerce reports that Revere came to shore at a wharf in Charlestown "off Water Street, just north of the present Charlestown Bridge and near City Square." Borrowing a horse from his awaiting Patriot comrades, the Boston silversmith then hastened off for Cambridge and points beyond by way of today's Main Street.

Also galloping up the road to Lexington with the grim message that the British were coming was Dawes, a tanner by trade, and he would be taking a somewhat longer route through Boston Neck, Roxbury, Brookline, Cambridge, and Menotomy.

In Boston about this time, Lord Hugh Percy heard a man on the Common say, "The British have marched, but they will miss their aim." When he asked what "aim," the man said, "Why, the cannon at Concord." (Percy didn't know it yet, but he himself would be on the road to Lexington the very next morning with one thousand men and two light field cannon as welcome relief for the British column just now setting off for Concord.)

Revere, at about 11:30 P.M., had to change course after encountering two mounted British at the site of the future Sullivan Square. Eluding them, he continued on toward his goal. He stopped at Medford to warn a Minuteman officer, then passed through Menotomy, frequently pausing to knock on a door and shout the alarm to those inside. He arrived in Lexington about midnight.

There, tavern-keeper (and Sergeant) Munroe allegedly barred Revere entry to the minister's home where Hancock and Adams were staying, saying his arrival would create too much noise. "Noise!" Revere reportedly exclaimed. "You'll have noise enough before long. The Regulars are coming out!"

By 12:30 A.M., Dawes also had ridden into town. Having alerted Lexington, he and Revere hurried on toward Concord, several miles beyond. About the same time, a belfry on the Lexington Common sounded the alarm and summoned members of the local Minuteman Company. In minutes, too, Concord resident Samuel Prescott, a physician, also set out for Concord—he had spent the evening in Lexington courting a young lady named Mulliken.

In a short time, he overtook Dawes and Revere. At the Lexington-Lincoln line, they passed the word to another courting couple, Nathaniel Baker of Lincoln, also a Minuteman, and Miss Elizabeth Taylor, visiting in Lincoln from her home in Concord. Baker then rode off to warn his own neighbors.

Still on the road to Concord, Revere, with Dawes and Prescott riding about two hundred yards behind him, was surprised by the British patrol that had seized Lexington's three scouts earlier in the night. "I saw four of them, who rode up to me, with their pistols in their hands, [and] said . . . if you go an Inch further, you are a dead Man," Revere later related.

Dawes managed to turn quickly and gallop off in the direction of Lexington. Doctor Prescott came up to where the British officers had stopped Revere in the road and seemed docile enough as the British forced both men to turn into an adjacent pasture. But the good doctor had other intentions entirely, it turned out.

As Revere later told the story, "[W]hen we got in, Mr. Prescott said put on. He took to the left, I to the right." Revere tried to break away and reach a woods at the pasture bottom, then abandon his horse and flee on foot. "Just as I reached it [the woods], out started six officers, siesed [sic] my bridle, put their pistols to my Breast, ordered me to dismount, which I did," Revere added.

Prescott, however, was more successful. Before the British could stop him, he and his horse jumped a nearby stone wall and disappeared into the night. Prescott then hurried on toward Concord by way of a farm lane, with a stop en route at the home of Lincoln Minuteman Samuel Hartwell. Mrs. Hartwell then carried the message to a nearby Minuteman officer's home—as a result of all these warnings, Lincoln's two Minutemen companies would be the first from outlying towns to reach beleaguered Concord later that morning.

In Lexington, meanwhile, the Minutemen who had formed up on the Common earlier were dismissed, but told to stay close by and respond immediately if they heard a warning drumbeat. It was now about 1:30 A.M. on April 19. The British, oddly enough, were not yet on the march—they had been delayed for nearly three crucial hours awaiting provisions and ammunition after disembarking from their boats in East Cambridge.

At 2 A.M. or thereabouts, Prescott rode into Concord and gave the alarm. At the summons of the Town House bell, the first man to respond was local minister William Emerson, destined to be the grandfather of Ralph Waldo Emerson. As the town's Minutemen then gathered at Wright's Tavern in a central square, frantic efforts were made to finish carrying off or hiding the military goods that had not yet been sent away.

The British, meanwhile, at last began their fateful march. They passed through western Charlestown (today's Somerville) and soon hit the road to Menotomy on the northwest edge of Cambridge.

At 2:30 A.M., Revere and the three Lexington scouts were released after their horses were either chased off or, in Revere's case, commandeered by the British. Revere hastened toward Lexington on foot, determined this time to convince Hancock and Adams to flee the town.

In Menotomy, local residents heard the measured tramp of the marching British soldiers or saw the gleam of their bayonets in the moonlight. Three leading Patriots spending the night at the Black Horse Tavern stealthily watched the column filing by until they saw a search party break off and approach the tavern itself. One of the Patriots, Eldridge Gerry, unaccountably started to open the front door, but desisted when the landlord cried, "For God's sake, don't open that door!"

The three Patriots then fled into the night from a back door, plunging into a cornfield. Here, Gerry tripped and fell heavily. The other two followed suit more deliberately, and all three successfully hid in the corn stubble until the British had moved on. (Gerry may also be remembered today as a signer of the Declaration of Independence, as an early governor of Massachusetts, as vice president of the United States under President James Madison—and as the political figure for whom the term "gerrymander" was coined, in a dispute over the drawing of voting districts in Massachusetts.)

Take You There

Try to picture it. You're a reservist, a National Guard member . . . a militiaman of times past. Tense times, too. And outside the house one night, about two in the morning, the sound of unaccustomed "traffic"—in this case, the clip-clop of horses' hooves on the dirt road by the house.

You emerge from the house and in the dark shout at these dimly seen strangers: "Have you heard anything about when the Regulars are coming out?"

That's the way it happened to one Josiah Nelson, a Minuteman from Lincoln, Massachusetts, the eventful night of April 18–19, 1775. He shouted, they answered . . . but not exactly the way he expected. Or wanted.

Today, more than two centuries later, those shots at Lexington and Concord tend to be remembered in the abstract, the people and events of that distant day only dimly perceived . . . their emotions hardly ever felt. To Nelson and other actors in the great drama, however, there was nothing in the abstract about it all. It was happening, second by second, all around them . . . to them.

He came out of his roadside house in the dark, asked the strangers about the "Regulars"—the British troops expected to show up any day now—and received a rough reply for his troubles. Still three hours before the historic exchange of shots on the Lexington Green, the mounted passersby *were* the Regulars!

They were British army officers. They, in fact, were escorting four prisoners back to Lexington—Josiah Nelson, you see, lived between Concord and Lexington, and the Regulars before him were the same who a short while earlier had captured Paul Revere and Lexington's three scouts.

Josiah Nelson wouldn't fare so well at their hands, either. "We will let you know when 'they' are coming," one of the officers declared, while angrily swiping at the American with a sword and opening a lengthy gash on his head. With that, the British added Nelson to their string of prisoners.

By 2:30 A.M., however, the British had released all five Colonials—without their horses. Nelson briefly returned home, where his wife bound up his head wound, then he set off on horseback to warn citizens—and fellow Minutemen—of nearby Bedford that the British were on the prowl.

On foot now, Revere hurried toward Lexington, crossing a "burying-ground and some pastures" on the way, he later wrote. He was anxious to reach the local minister's home where the two Patriot leaders John Hancock and Samuel Adams were sequestered. With the British marching out from Boston in strength and obviously in no accommodating mood, those two must be moved out of harm's way immediately!

Thanks to his timely arrival, they did move on, first to a friendly home in Woburn (now Burlington) about two miles away, then somewhat farther afield, to the home of another minister's widow. Still later, they wound up at Billerica, about four miles from Lexington. Meanwhile, Revere and Hancock's clerk had returned to Lexington—"to enquire the News," Revere later explained.

At Buckman's Tavern in town, right by the central green, wrote Revere, "a man who had just come up the road told us the troops were within two miles." Even so, Revere and Hancock's clerk were supposed to pick up a trunk full of Hancock's papers left at Buckman's Tavern.

Going upstairs to retrieve the trunk, Revere looked out the window and, "I saw the Ministeral [British] Troops from the Chamber window coming up the Road."

As Revere and his companion rushed off to the minister's house with the trunk, they went right past the Lexington Minutemen, drawn up on the green for their historic encounter with the oncoming British. "We made haste & had to pass thro' our Militia, who were on a green behind the Meeting house to the number I supposed about 50 or 60." So close was Revere that he heard the militia commander tell his men, "Lett the troops pass by, & don't molest them, without they begin first."

Now came the British troops, appearing just a short distance away. "They made a short halt, when a gun was fired. I heard the report, turned my head, and saw the smoake in front of the Troops, they imeaditly gave a great shout, ran a few paces, and then the whole [body] fired."

It now was still only about five o'clock, daylight edging out the night, that fateful morning in Lexington, Massachusetts.

At the moment all was confusion—events were not totally clear even to the participants. For instance, who had fired first? That is a question that was never completely cleared up, although by most historical accounts the blame has been placed on the British—one of whose officers already had shown no hestitation in slashing Josiah Nelson across the head with a sword earlier that night.

Not even Paul Revere as a witness could clear up all the uncertainties. As he explained: "I could first distinguish Iregular fireing, which I suppose was the advance Guard, and then the platoons [all British].At the time I could not see our Militia, for they were covered from me, by a house at the bottom of the Street."

Additional notes: While it's never been proven who fired first at Lexington, many American participants and witnesses said in sworn statements that it was the British—whether by passion or calculation—who fired first.

Captain John Parker, commander of the Lexington Minuteman Company, later said that upon the "sudden approach" of the British regulars, "I immediately ordered our militia to disperse and not to fire." The redcoats, on the other hand, "rushing furiously, fired upon and killed eight of our party, without receiving any provocation therefor [sic] from us."

In another sworn statement, Simon Winship of Lexington said he was stopped by a body of British troops just outside of Lexington around four in the morning on that April 19. They demanded to know if he had been riding about the countryside to give warning of their approach, but he said no, he was merely returning to his father's home. Then, forced to march toward Lexington with the British troops, he watched as they stopped a quarter mile outside of town to prime and load their muskets.

Minutes later, they marched to "within rods of Capt. Parker and company, who were partly collected on the place of parade [the common]." At that point, Winship saw and heard a British officer "at the head of said troops, flourishing his sword and with a loud voice giving the word fire, which was instantly followed by a discharge of arms from said regular troops." Said Winship: "There was no discharge of arms on either side, till the word was given by said Officer as above."

Another eyewitness, Thomas Rice Willard, was watching events on the common from his window. He later swore that the Minutemen had already dispersed when a British officer shouted at them: "Lay down your arms, damn you, why don't you lay down your arms?" According to this Lexington resident, "There was not a gun fired till the militia of Lexington were dispersed."

Others who said the British fired first, with no provocation, included thirty-four of the Lexington Minutemen who had been on the common that morning and who swore "whilst our backs were turned on the [British] troops, we were fired on by them." Another fourteen of the Minutemen who still were facing the British separately swore the redcoats fired first.

But now, a final and last word on the subject from one John Bateman, soldier, fifty-second Regiment, Great Britain. Sworn on April 23, 1775, at Lincoln, Massachusetts, he saith:

"Being at Lexington, in the county of Middlesex, being nigh the meeting-house in said Lexington, there was a small party of men gathered together in that place, when our said troops marched by; and I testify and declare, that I heard the word of command given to the troops to fire, and some of said troops did fire, and I saw one of said small party lie dead on the ground nigh said meeting-house; and I testify, that I never heard any of the inhabitants so much as fire one gun on said troops."

"First Blood Drawn"

THEY DISEMBARKED FROM THEIR BOATS and were on the march by 2:30 A.M., first passing through "swamps and slips of the Sea," wrote Ensign Jeremy Lister of England's Tenth Regiment of Foot. It was "soon after" he and the troops hit the road to Lexington that "the Country people begun to fire their alarm guns [and] light their Beacons, to raise the Country."

He could have guessed right then that it was only the beginning of a long night and day for himself and his fellow soldiers of the Crown. He, for one, would survive, but not entirely unscathed.

The first action he saw was at Lexington, "the first Blood drawn in this American Rebellion."

By his written account, the Americans were drawn up before the British "in regular order." Major John Pitcairn, second in command of the British light infantry and grenadiers, "call'd to them to disperce."

When the Americans showed no sign of obeying the order to disperse, Pitcairn then told his men "to mind our space[,] which we did." That, according to Lister, was "when they gave us a fire then run of[f] to get behind a wall."

A man in his company was wounded in the leg, added Lister. "[H]is name was Johnson also Major Pitcairns Horse was shot in the Flank." That, of course, was not the end of the affair. "[W]e return'd their Salute, and before we proceeded on our March from Lexington I believe we Kill'd and Wounded either 7 or 8 Men."

Now it was on to Concord and more action there.

Arriving just before 8 A.M. April 19, some of the British immediately began searching the houses and barns for Patriot military stores. Others were posted to guard the south and north bridges, and still others were dispatched to search a suspect farm two miles out of town. Ensign Lister's light infantry company was one of those posted beyond the North Bridge.

From all around the countryside, meanwhile, American Minutemen and militia members were converging on the town. With their commander, Colonel James Barrett, stunned by news of the shooting at Lexington and yet unwilling to fire on the British first, the Americans initially made no effort to interfere as the British searched Concord for arms and munitions. By Barrett's direction, the citizen-soldiers assembled on a ridge just beyond the North Bridge and from there watched the search parties in the town below.

Most of the military stores had been removed by now or at least well hidden, but the British did find a few items—gun carriages, cartridge paper, tents, and entrenching tools. Barrett apparently still thought the British would not fire on his men if they did not fire on the British first . . . but some of his men were obviously agitated at the armed invasion of their town. They urged Barrett to order an attack on the interlopers. Aware that his numbers were on the increase by the minute but unsure of the ultimate British intentions, Barrett counseled patience.

But then the invaders piled up the recovered items and set them ablaze.

That was just too much for the onlooking Americans. "Are you going to let them burn the town down?" demanded one of Barrett's officers. Well, no, the least he could do, with four hundred men now gathered, would be to organize a show of force. Barrett ordered his men to form up and start marching down the ridge toward town— and the North Bridge in between.

And so, down they started, two abreast at first, with a fife-player from nearby Acton sounding the marching tune "The White Cockade." Up front, in fact, was an entire company of Minutemen from Acton who had been practicing their marksmanship twice a week under their leader, Captain Isaac Davis.

Now Lister: "[W]e had not been long in this situation [guarding the North Bridge] when we saw a large Body of Men drawn up with the greatest regularity and approach'd us seemingly with an intent to attack."

The British retreated across the bridge, but regrouped there, intent on holding the span. As yet, no shots fired.

The American column still came down the hill, closer and closer to the plank bridge and the massed British. Somewhere far behind would be the four companies of British light infantry that had set out shortly before to search that farm two miles away—Colonel Barrett's farm, it so happened. The bridge must be held for their use when they returned.

The Americans solemnly stepped, stepped, stepped. Colonel Barrett had achieved his show of force. The Americans obviously meant to cross the bridge, British or no British. On they came . . . almost right at the bridge.

Lister again: "I proposed destroying the bridge, but before we got one plank of[f] they got so near as to begin their Fire[,] which was a very heavy one."

Most histories say the firing began, actually, with a few British soldiers letting loose scattered, undisciplined shots into the river, presumably as a warning. But then came a full, disciplined volley by a hundred men of the King's Own light infantry. The fusillade tore through the first ranks of the American column, into the men from Acton. Their leader, Captain Davis, went down, killed on the spot. So, too, Private Abner Hosmer, while four others were wounded.

It could have been worse. The British may have fired too high. Even so, as the toll from their volley made clear, they obviously were using killing ammunition in this unprecedented confrontation. Until this moment, few Americans on the scene really had anticipated the use of deadly force.

Someone in their ranks shouted, "They're using ball [real bullets]!" Major John Buttrick, who had been marching alongside the stricken Captain Davis seconds before, turned and yelled, "Fire fellow soldiers! For God's sake, fire!"

The British soldiers massed at the far end of the bridge were easy targets for the sharpshooting Americans, who now poured their own lethal ball into the adversary's ranks. That was Lister's "heavy" fire. And now, he also recalled, "[T]he weight of their fire was such that we was oblig'd to give way[,] then run with the greatest precipitance."

British Captain Walter Laurie, by whose order the redcoats had been massed at the bridge to begin with, was furious with his retreating men. "The whole went to the right about in spite of all that could be done to prevent them," he later complained.

None on the scene would have stopped just then to contemplate their place in the history books . . . as participants in a watershed event of the American Revolution. But that's what it was, the Battle of Concord Bridge. The very battle that Ralph Waldo Emerson later would call "the shot heard 'round the world." (And, interestingly enough, his own grandfather, Concord's young minister William Emerson, had been among the first of those urging Colonel Barrett to attack the British much sooner.)

Rough Road Home

THE FAMOUS BATTLE OF CONCORD ended in desultory fashion, with the British facing a long and rough road home to Boston. First, though, the redcoats rallied in the center of town, while the Americans took cover by the North Bridge. Still at issue was the expected return of four British companies from a search of American Colonel James Barrett's outlying farm—these redcoats must return by way of the North Bridge, held by the Americans.

Two or more hours would pass with no one quite knowing what to expect next. Wrote British Ensign Jeremy Lister: "After we had got to Concord again my situation . . . was a most fatigueing one, being detached to watch the Motions of the Rebels, we was kept continually running from hill to hill as they chang'd their position."

In time, the four British companies came into view on the long downhill approach to the North Bridge—"and tho. there was a large Body of Rebels drawn up upon the hill . . . yet they let him [British Captain Lawrence Parsons and his men] pass without firing a single shot."

And that was that. Now, for the British, it was well past time to turn for home . . . but first there would be the march back to Lexington, scene of the day's first confrontation between the British and the Americans.

Recalled Lister: "[T]he Light Infantry March'd over a Hill above the Town[,] the Grenadiers through the Town, immediately as we descended the hill into the Road the Rebels begun a brisk fire but at so great a distance it was without effect."

Soon, the Americans were closer and the British grenadiers were firing back. "About that time," said Ensign Lister, "I rec'd a shot through my Right Elbow joint which efectually disabled that Arme."

From there all the way to Lexington, added Lister, "it then became a general Firing upon us from all quarters, from behind hedges and Walls." To be sure, the British returned fire at "every opportunity," but the harassment by the aroused Colonials was unabating. Lister, in fact, doesn't even begin to tell the full story.

For one thing, when the rough dirt road to Lexington reached a creek and stone bridge at Meriam's Corner, the British had to pull in their flanking parties to squeeze their column across . . . with an estimated six hundred Americans facing them at the bridge. After more American fire left more British casualties lying on the ground, the light infantrymen charged and chased off their tormentors. Half a mile long, the column hastened on down the road to Lexington, where reinforcements with two light cannon would be awaiting the beleaguered troops.

First, though, there would be even more severe punishment in store. As an estimated 1,500 armed Americans swarmed about the fields on just one side of the road, the British stumbled onto Hardy's Hill, where five companies of Minutemen greeted them with withering fire. More redcoats went down.

Just beyond, at a crook in the road destined to be known as "Bloody Angle," lurked Woburn's Minutemen. The booming crack of a single volley took down thirty-one redcoats in an instant, eight of them dead, the rest wounded. The column was held up for thirty minutes clearing this one spot on the road.

Buffered by natural obstacles alongside the road—swamps, creeks, and the like—the British this time moved on at a trot, with Lexington and relative safety just ahead. First the British had to pass a small woods and cross yet another bridge, then climb three hills to reach the town center.

Waiting in the woods were the Minutemen from Lexington victimized by the very same British just hours before. To be sure, the Lexington men were spoiling for a fight this time—their lethal volley came as the British began crossing the small bridge. As a nasty fight at close quarters ensued, the delay allowed the Americans pursuing from the countryside to reach the tail end of the column and join in the attack once more.

Seeing the column being picked to pieces, Major Pitcairn organized a line of defense on the first hill ahead. With his marines barely holding on for a few minutes' delay of the swarming Americans behind, the rest of the column streamed ahead, only to encounter a fresh blast of fire from Minutemen hidden in the woods crowding the road at the second hill ... hidden in nearby houses and barns as well.

By the time the surviving fragments of the British column cleared the crest of the third and final hill, recalled one British officer later, "We began to run rather than retreat in order."

There was a pause just beyond Lexington, where Brigadier Hugh, Lord Percy, was waiting with his two cannon and a brigade of troops. Here at last, it seemed, was salvation for Ensign Lister and his shattered column. As Percy himself later said, "I had the happiness of saving them from complete destruction."

For Lister now, a few bad moments. A surgeon's mate extracted the musket ball from his arm, "it having gone through the Bone and log'd within the Skin." He blamed the long march, his loss of blood, and the fact he hadn't eaten (or slept, for that matter) since the day before for his suddenly feeling faint.

Recovering, he borrowed a horse, begged a mouthful of "Bisquet and Beef" from a soldier, and doused his head with a hatful of cooling water a grenadier obtained from a nearby horse pond. He felt greatly refreshed as the strengthened British column now turned for Bunker Hill and Boston itself, another thirteen miles down the road.

The redcoats had hardly left Lexington when they met the same stinging harassment as before, with concurrent casualties. Said Lister: "When I had Road [ridden] about 2 Miles I found the Balls whistled so smartly about my Ears I thought it more prudent to dismount and as the Balls came thicker from one side or the other so I went from one side of the Horse to the other for some time."

But then a horse close by was shot dead. The animal had been carrying a wounded man on its back, with three more "hanging by his sides." When they asked Lister for his horse, he readily complied.

After a major battle at the village of Menotomy (now called Arlington), perhaps involving as many as 5,500 men from both sides, the British column at last staggered onto Charlestown peninsula, a neck of land next to Boston that lay under the cover of the naval guns aboard British warships. It was about 7 P.M. as the survivors of the daylong fracas reached this safe territory. By now, British losses amounted to 73 men killed, another 174 wounded, and 26 missing— 373 all told. The American casualties numbered 49 known dead and probably 2 or 3 times that number wounded.

The British wounded included Ensign Lister, who was greatly relieved to reach Bunker Hill on the Charlestown peninsula without further personal harm. At that point, though, he began to feel faint again. Unable to exercise command over his company's surviving men, he was taken over to Boston by boat. He then made his way "through the Town" to his lodgings—"where I arrived about 9 oClock after a March in the whole of about 60 Miles in course of 24 Hours, about 24 Miles after I was Wounded." In all that time, too, he had had no sleep and only a mouthful of food, back in Lexington.

Unsurprisingly, the young English officer was exhausted by now, but when he arrived at his lodging place he asked for a spot of tea. A Loyalist couple named Funnel who had been driven into town by the rebels was staying at the same house. Others were visiting as well. They noticed that Lister was "light Headed" and urged him to go to bed immediately. But he insisted upon having his tea first, "notwithstanding I was interrupted with a Thousand Questions."

Additional note: Ensign Lister was a chance volunteer for the historic expedition to Lexington and Concord. He took the place of a Lieutenant Hamilton, who had feigned illness to stay behind in Boston rather than venture into the Massachusetts countryside with his troops.

His Aim Was Death

MANY AMONG THE REDCOATS STAGGERING back to Boston April 19, 1775, after their punitive raid on Concord and Lexington, saw the man on a white horse and wondered from that day forward who was that man on a white horse. Perhaps they even wished they had never seen that man on a white horse.

All the way back on the road from Concord, they repeatedly had to warn one another, "Look out, there is the man on the white horse."

If any of them could have stuck around for about ninety years, they would have learned a bit more from West Cambridge's Rev. Samuel Abbot Smith, a local historian who pieced together the story of the major battle fought that fateful April 19 in his own town, then named Menotomy, later West Cambridge, and finally, its present-day name, Arlington. Part and parcel of the Menotomy story is the running fight the British encountered all the way back to Boston after their raid on Concord, six miles beyond Lexington . . . where they first exchanged fire with the Patriot Minutemen about sunrise that day.

It was hours later, of course, when the redcoats turned for home from Concord, harassed from both sides of the lone dirt road that had to be their route back to Boston.

And it was from Concord on that the redcoats saw and learned to fear the man on the white horse.

"He was an old, grey-haired hunter, named Wyman of Woburn,

and he rode a fine white horse," wrote the Reverend Smith in 1864—during the Civil War. "He struck the trail as they [the British] left Concord, and would ride up within gunshot, then turning the horse throw himself off, aim his long gun resting on the saddle, and that aim was death." The man on the white horse mounted up again, then he just kept on following the tattered column of redcoats.

Smith may have lived during another century, another cataclysmic war, but he was able to interview descendants of the many men and women alive during the Revolution. Smith obtained this glimpse of Old Man Wyman under pursuit by the British flankers who sometimes succeeded in clearing the sides of the long route home.

"James Russell, the father of James Russell, Esq., then a boy of a dozen years, from behind a house on Charlestown street, saw him gallop across the brook and up the hill, pursued by a party of the flank guard who kept the plains [clear] midway between Charlestown and Main streets.

"He turned, aimed, and the boy saw one of the British fall.

"He rode on, and soon the same gun was heard again, this time also with deadly effect."

(The Reverend Smith's account of the Battle of Menotomy appears as a facsimile booklet published by the Arlington Historical Society under the title *West Cambridge 1775*. The original, composed as a lecture, was published in 1864. At the time, Smith was minister of the First Congregational Parish Unitarian Church in West Cambridge, now Arlington.)

Biggest Battle of the Day

IN LITTLE MENOTOMY ABOUT TWO O'CLOCK the morning of April 19, the townspeople heard the tramp, tramp, of passing soldiers. They heard and felt the measured tread of hundreds of feet. In one house by the road running through town, the rattle of pewter plates on a dresser awoke a man and sent him scurrying to his window. He saw the British . . . out of Boston and on their way to Lexington and Concord.

The redcoats didn't stop. Off in those distant towns, they would trigger the opening shots of the American Revolution. As a result, Lexington and Concord are the names remembered today.

But later in the day, they would be coming back. They would be returning to their base in Boston, and they again would be passing through little Menotomy.

And here, in the town later known as West Cambridge and today named Arlington, Massachusetts, the British and the American Patriots would be fighting the biggest battle of the day. Here, each side would suffer its greatest number of casualties. Here, a housewife returning home after the gunfire would find twelve bodies lying side by side in a giant pool of blood, including the body of her own husband.

This was a bloody, sometimes hand-to-hand fight with gunfire and bayonet, between soldier and volunteer citizen-soldier, even between soldier and old men.

After the first British column marched through in the dark hours of early morning, there would be three more British incursions at Menotomy. Between nine and ten o'clock that morning, Lord Hugh Percy's relief column of one thousand men came tramping through town to meet the original expedition as it fought its way back to Lexington from Concord beyond. Eight-year-old Ephraim Cutter watched in awe—and many years later told his grandchildren that the marching men, their bayonets glittering in the sunlight, looked like a river flowing through the small village.

The solemn symmetry was spoiled for one moment, however, as a cow left the roadside and ambled across, right through the serried British ranks. A small girl minding the cow for her mother ambled along beside the animal unscathed. According to local lore, the nearest soldiers said, "We will not hurt the child." The British column moved on, sometimes marching to the spirited tune of "Yankee Doodle" in a calculated insult to any pretentious rebels who might be listening.

Next to come along, also headed outbound, would be Percy's supply train . . . fated, as events turned out, never to catch up with him and his troops. And finally, late in the afternoon, would come the two British columns seen earlier, but returning to base now, badly battered, many of the men exhausted, others wounded, and all fight-

ing their way home through the swarms of angry militiamen harassing them from both sides of the road.

But first, the fate of that supply train. It at one time had been
close on the heels of Lord Percy's marching troops and two accompanying field pieces, but all had been forced to a brief halt at
Brighton Bridge because the bridge's planks had been removed by
area rebels. With the missing boards simply left on the far side, it
didn't take the redcoats long to replace them and cross over.

However, the supply train and its cumbersome wagons did not
have such an easy crossing. That was one delay separating the two
segments of the relief column. Another was a mistaken direction
taken by the wagoners. As a result, the supply train was reported
approaching a fully alerted Menotomy long minutes after Lord Percy
and his men had marched through the village on their way to
Lexington.

An alerted Menotomy at this hour did not necessarily mean a
Menotomy in full fighting fettle, since most of the town's young
men, its Minutemen, had galloped off in the direction the British had
taken, both during the night and again in mid-morning. Those
remaining, aside from the women and children, were the so-called
"old men" of town—who were certainly older and exempt from
militia duty but in some cases combat-baptized veterans of the
French and Indian War.

Several of these old men met at Cooper's Tavern, on the corner
of the Medford and Charlestown roads, and decided to ambush the
supply train as it passed through the very center of the village. They
elected David Lamson, described as part Indian, as their leader, then
took cover just down the road from their meeting place.

When the supply convoy drew abreast minutes later,
Menotomy's "old men" rose with their firearms aimed at the
horses—Lamson shouted orders to stop and surrender. But the
teamsters instead urged their horses ahead. A crackling volley of
rebel fire brought down several horses in their traces—and may
have killed two of the British. The result was capture of all the supplies and provisions, an unexpected windfall for the area's
militiamen.

The remainder of the drivers and guards, it is said, then fled to a
nearby pond and threw their weapons into the water. The local
story is that they gave themselves up to an old woman digging dan-
delions nearby. She turned them over to a group of local men at the

home of Captain Ephraim Frost on the Watertown Road, telling them: "If you ever live to get back, you tell King George that an old woman took six of his grenadiers prisoners."

They later were exchanged, and the story, if not all six men, did get back to England. It appeared in various newspapers with the line: "If one old Yankee woman can take six grenadiers, how many soldiers will it require to conquer America?"

What happened the rest of the day in Menotomy, however, was no joke for anyone involved. It was nearly 4:30 P.M. when the returning British, now formed into one column, negotiated Pierce's Hill west of town (today's Arlington Heights), then plunged down the other side to the lower "Foot of the Rocks." This was now a truly tattered British column under nearly constant militia fire from the sides of the road. Probably 1,700 men from 35 village militia companies were on hand as the weary redcoats passed from Foot of the Rocks into the center of Menotomy on the road known today as Massachusetts Avenue. Some of the rebels ventured so close, they and their adversaries fell into hand-to-hand struggle.

In one such case, an American doctor from the Brookline and Roxbury companies, Eliphalet Downer, found himself under deadly threat from a redcoat employing the bayonet. No expert in this kind of fighting, the doctor reversed his grip and swung the butt end of his musket as a club. After knocking down his foe, Dr. Downer then made the intended use of his own bayonet.

Just past the Rocks, meanwhile, Lord Percy halted his men long enough to fire his cannon and scatter their incessant pursuers—but only briefly. Then on into Menotomy proper and a burst of eighteenth-century street fighting. Before the British could emerge from this gauntlet in their path an hour or so later, forty or more of their troops were killed, along with at least twenty-five Americans. Houses were set on fire, ordinary civilians were shot, others bayoneted.

On the western edge of town was the home of Jason Russell, fifty-eight and lame. He had sent his wife and children to safe refuge earlier, then saying, "An Englishman's home is his castle," insisted on staying at the house and, if need be, defending it. He had hardly barricaded his gate when a group of Minutemen were surprised nearby by British flankers and ran for cover in Russell's house. He turned to join them, but was last to reach his own doorway and fell with two musket balls lodged in his body. He also would suffer eleven bayonet wounds at the hands of the onrushing redcoats, who now burst through the door in pursuit of the Minutemen. Inside the house, the redcoats shot or used the bayonet on anybody else they could find—but they balked at going down the cellar steps when the armed Americans hiding below threatened to kill anyone coming down the stairs.

One redcoat did try, and he was shot. Another apparently was killed in the melee upstairs. Before leaving, the British looted the house. Mrs. Russell later found her dead husband and eleven other bodies laid on the bloody floor of her home's south room.

In another soldier-civilian encounter, the British stormed into a church deacon's house and found his wife and newborn infant on a bed. Unaware that five more children were hiding under the bed, they ordered her and the baby out of the house and announced they would burn it down. According to the account pieced together by local minister Samuel Abbot Smith nearly a century later, the children under the bed watched the feet of the intruders as they looted the room. One boy, just nine, peeked out for a better look and was seen by a soldier.

"Why don't you come out of there?" said the soldier.

"You'll kill me if I do," answered the boy.

Not so, replied the soldier. As a result, the child crept forth and followed the redcoats around as they vandalized the house. Finally, they came to his father's communion service.

Until now, young Joel Adams had kept silent as the soldiers took his mother's spoons and other items, reported the Reverend Smith in 1864. "[B]ut when they proceeded to take posssesion of the sacred utensils, he could restrain himself no longer, and in horror and indignation cried out, 'Don't you touch them 'ere things! Daddy'l lick you if you do.'"

The boy's warning would have little effect. The soldiers not only took the communion service and other valuables, they also set fire to a pile of chips and broken chairs inside the house, then left Joel and his siblings to their devices. Fortunately, the children quickly doused the fire by pouring home-brewed beer and water on it—but not before pewter plates on a nearby dresser melted in the heat. Months later, after the British had evacuated Boston, a silversmith in the city informed Deacon Joseph Adams that the communion service had been pawned in his care and he was more than willing to return the looted items.

Meanwhile, the distance from the Jason Russell house on the

western outskirts of town to Cooper's Tavern in the center was about half a mile. Here, at least forty British and Americans died in the raging, running fight—the bloodiest half mile on the entire route known to historians today as the Lexington-Concord Battle Road.

In the tavern, incredibly enough, two men were sitting over their drinks (by some accounts) while tavern-keeper Benjamin Cooper and his wife, Rachel, were at the bar mixing a drink called flip. When the British started shooting through windows and doors, the Coopers made for the cellar, but their two customers, both unarmed, had lingered too long. They were killed (and by some accounts badly mutilated) by the combat-maddened redcoats bursting into the taproom.

Not far away, eighty-year-old Samuel Whittemore, a militia officer many years earlier, had been lying in wait behind a stone wall. When the redcoats appeared on the road in front of him, he began firing his musket. He probably had gotten off half a dozen shots before he heard a noise to his rear, turned, and saw five men from the British flanking force hurrying toward him—"shoulder to shoulder," according to the Rev. Smith's account.

The old-timer didn't hesitate. "With his musket he shot one of the soldiers, and, instantly drawing his pistol, fired at another. He aimed the second pistol and discharged it just as they fired at him; one of the soldiers was seen to clap his hand to his breast. As he [Whittemore] fired the third time a ball struck him in the head, and he fell senseless. The soldiers beat him with their muskets, bayoneted him, and left him for dead."

Sure that it was a hopeless errand, the old man's neighbors from Menotomy carried his near-lifeless body to Cooper's Tavern, now vacated by the British and serving as a shelter and surgery for the wounded. There, a Doctor Tufts from Medford took one look and said there was no use even in dressing his wounds—Sam Whittemore had little time to live. But Dr. Tufts did apply the bandages and clean up the elderly hero . . . who then proceeded to live another eighteen years!

An informant in Boston overheard some British soldiers talking about their battle on the road to Concord the next day, April 20. "We killed an old devil there in Menotomy," said one of the soldiers, "but we paid most too dear for it,—lost three of our men, the last died this morning."

The fact is, the British paid "most too dear" for the entire expedition to Lexington, Concord, and Menotomy. The move toward future American independence was under way in any case, but the events of April 19, 1775, triggered instant revolution rather than any gradual, negotiated process. The hornet's-nest reaction of the Massachusetts citizen-soldiers, even her Patriot civilians, also served as an eye-opening warning for any British paying attention.

One British official who *was* taking heed was none other than Lord Percy, rescuer of the beleaguered Concord-Lexington column. He had once described the restless Colonials as "timid creatures" and "cowards." But no longer. Now, the very next day, he composed a report saying in part: "[M]any of them [the Americans] concealed themselves in houses & advanced within 10 yds. to fire at me and other officers, tho' they were morally certain of being put to death themselves in an instant."

The "insurrection here," he also wrote, will not be so "despicable as it is perhaps imagined at home." He also admitted to being startled by the previous day's events. "For my part, I never believed, I confess, that they wd have attacked the king's troops, or have had the perserverance I found in them yesterday."

Additional notes: The Jason Russell House, moved a short distance from its original location and preserved by the Arlington Historical Society, stands today close to the intersection of Jason Street and Massachusetts Avenue.

A summary of the facts that *should* render Menotomy equally as famous as Lexington and Concord:

- The twelve men found dead in the Jason Russell House constituted the greatest number of men, either British or American, killed at a single site, at roughly the same moment, all day long that April 19.
- Menotomy was the site of the bloodiest half-mile segment—from the Jason Russell House to Cooper's Tavern—of the entire Battle Road from East Cambridge to Concord and back to Charlestown Neck and Bunker Hill.
- The fighting at Menotomy cost each side more soldiers than any other town involved in the events of April 19, 1775—forty British and twenty-five Americans dead.

- With the attack on Lord Percy's supply train, the "old men" of Menotomy accomplished the American Revolution's first forcible capture of enemy provisions and military supplies.

Tar and Feather

BRITISH SOLDIER GEORGE WALKER EITHER was foolhardy or badly misinformed as to the mood of the local Colonials one day in August 1775. It is safe to assume, too, that up to this point in his life, the term "tar-and-feather" was a concept known to him strictly in the abstract, rather than as personal experience.

Clearly enough, it was a stubborn sense of loyalty that made him refuse to drink "damnation" to his king.

Who even today could decry such an understandable impulse for one of the king's own? Without a doubt, it was asking a lot . . . but then, George Walker's defiant reaction was one that bode little good for his personal well-being in the colorful, busily teeming port city the Colonials had created on the Atlantic seaboard.

It was called Charles Town at the time, it's Charleston, South Carolina, today. Either way, it was no place for George Walker to be in 1775, the eve of the American Revolution . . . no place, indeed, for any Loyalist or British soldier, sailor, or official.

The restive citizens of Charles Town hadn't even heard about the shooting at Concord and Lexington, Massachusetts, when they seized British arms and ammunition from two magazines and the State House. Asked to investigate such bold, rebellious conduct, the Commons House of the Assembly blandly reported to William Bull, acting royal governor, that the necessary "intelligence" wasn't available. Oddly enough, some members of the Assembly's House themselves had helped seize the missing arms.

Loyalists, suspected or known, were harassed on the street or ordered to stay at home that summer. One local planter was banished from the colony, then shipwrecked and drowned when he complied, reports Walter J. Fraser Jr. in his book *Patriots, Pistols and Petticoats: "Poor Sinful Charles Town."* Says Fraser: "Two avowed Loyalists to the crown were taken by a mob, stripped, tarred and feathered, and then carted through the streets as a example to others."

Who were the tormentors making life miserable for the Tories and their British friends? They were not moderates such as Henry Laurens, newly elected president of the South Carolina Provincial Congress and future confidant to George Washington. Nor were these more thoughtful Patriots able to control events around them. A "crown officer" lamented the "numerous body of the low and ignorant" who followed the lead of "a few incendiaries and some hotheaded young men of fortune" in the sometimes violent street actions. Among the latter was wealthy young planter William Henry Drayton, who joined members of the Committee of Safety as they "prowled the streets" in search of any unfortunate considered "inimical to the Liberties of America," reports Fraser.

It was in this hothouse atmosphere that British soldier George Walker refused the demand to join a toast offering damnation to his king. The response of the American colonists taunting him was immediate—and rough.

As Fraser puts it, they first "jostled" him through the streets, stopping only to toss a bag of feathers onto the balcony of a Crown official's home and to shout imprecations in that direction as well. The mob, equipped with tar and more feathers, next "pushed and shoved" the hapless Walker along Broad Street until reaching Charleston's famous Exchange Building, still standing today.

"Here," adds Fraser's account, "a kangaroo court 'condemned' him for being 'a Tory and an enemy to the country.' He was sentenced to be 'stripped naked, tarred and feathered all over his body.'"

For George Walker, the abstract now became the reality—and painfully so. He indeed was tarred and feathered. Additionally, he was stoned, "doused repeatedly with water," and finally thrown into the Cooper River. He was fortunate enough to escape drowning, thanks to a passing boat that gave him sanctuary. Even so, his searing experience cost him an eye for life, along with two broken ribs.

Back in town, says Fraser, the Loyalist contingent certainly could take no solace from the latest mob action. "A loyalist sympathizer in Charles Town declared that the King's friends are despondent, 'expecting every moment to be drove from their occupations, and homes and plundered of all they have.'"

Additional note: The not-so-quaint custom of tarring and feathering as a punitive practice can be traced back to the English fleets of the Middle Ages and to mob actions in London. There the victim was often carried to the Strand and left bound to a Maypole. Tax collectors and bailiffs were frequent targets of the mob wrath.

Also on the eve of the American Revolution, British soldiers in Boston one day in 1775 very publicly resorted to the same cruel treatment of a peddler—then marched him through town accompanied by fife and drums. In the months ahead, the rebellious Sons of Liberty often would pay the same "compliment" to known Loyalists and other perceived enemies of the Revolution.

Start to Famous Career

AT AGE THIRTY-FOUR, HE WAS an apothecary, a merchant, and fire-eating commander of a militia company in New Haven, Connecticut. His Governor's Foot Guard was a showcase outfit, every man decked out in striking uniform of white, black, and scarlet red.

So far, so good, it would appear.

But he could be brash, he could be troublesome. After Lexington and Concord, the town fathers balked at allowing him access to the local powder magazine. His reaction? Pass along those keys, or he and his men would break in and help themselves to the powder and ball to be found inside.

The selectmen complied, and the militia commander was soon marching his men north to Massachusetts to join in the fighting. "None but Almighty God shall prevent my marching," he declared before setting out.

None did, but, to give him credit, there were those who placed obstacles in his intended path to fame and glory. Acts of God or nature intervened as well.

On his way to the American siege lines in Cambridge outside

Boston, he encountered a returning Connecticut militia officer, Colonel Samuel Parsons, who told him the Americans were greatly lacking in cannon. The captain of the Foot Guard suggested that the guns lying fallow at the lightly garrisoned Fort Ticonderoga on Lake Champlain could be captured with relative ease. He laid the same proposal before the Massachusetts Committee of Safety at Cambridge and won its approval to mount an expedition forthwith to seize Ticonderoga and its cannon and stores.

He had to recruit more men for the task, but he rode ahead to Stockbridge in western Massachusetts, a rallying point where he began to organize his campaign while awaiting his added troops. There, he discovered that Connecticut had dispatched its own expedition . . . based upon the information that he, himself, had provided Colonel Parsons of the Connecticut militia just weeks before. Not only was the rival force already on its way to Lake Champlain, but arrangements were under way for it to link up with Ethan Allen and his Green Mountain Boys of the New Hampshire Grants, with the hulking backwoodsman Allen taking overall command for the assault on the British fort.

Accounts vary as to the details, but the officer from New Haven—diminutive in size next to the giant Ethan Allen—caught up to the rowdy Green Mountain Boys and their chief and tried to press his claim to leading the raid on Ticonderoga. Openly scorned, he was allowed to go along—strictly at Allen's forbearance—and even to enter the British fort side by side with his rough-hewn rival.

As events turned out, the fort indeed was taken with ease. The two command disputants did enter the premises together, as agreed—as Allen dutifully reported to New York officials. Before he could report to Massachusetts, however, the irksome militia officer from New Haven demanded recognition as commander. Allen then turned in a report leaving out his counterpoint's role altogether.

The apothecary-turned-officer was especially annoyed by another citizen-officer, Colonel James Easton, who had been present for the Ticonderoga raid and had been appointed to carry word of the victory back to Massachusetts. Convinced that Easton had misstated the true facts of the situation, the New Haven officer became so incensed, he challenged Easton to a duel and, when that "offer" was refused, allegedly kicked the colonel.

Perhaps he was still smarting from his own rough treatment at the hands of the Green Mountain Boys, who allegedly—and drunkenly—jeered him after the Ticonderoga victory and even took shots at him.

Meanwhile, the dispute over who did what at Ticonderoga reached such proportions that the Massachusetts Provincial Congress sent a delegation to investigate the situation. Taking further umbrage at such lack of faith in his protestations, the peacetime apothecary resigned from military service.

Soon, another dispute flared up—Massachusetts would not accept and pay all his reported expenses. That imbroglio was fated to go all the way up the line to the Continental Congress before it would be settled—with the Congress finally agreeing to pay what funds Massachusetts refused to pay.

And so it went. One thing after another, again and again. Troubles of this sort—bad luck, betrayals, criticisms, fair and unfair, his own egocentrism—all amounted to a constant cloud over his head. Before the Revolutionary War ended, he would be the center of repeated controversy, argument, personal quarrel, wounded feelings, and dispute. He would also commit one indisputably unforgivable act.

Though arrogant and headstrong, he was also a brave, resourceful officer who often won the praise and respect of his fellow officers, George Washington foremost among them. Largely at Washington's instigation, he was given a commission in the Continental Army—and in no time, he was elevated to the rank of brigadier general. Indeed, in the next two years or so, he would become widely known as the hero of Quebec, Valcour Island, and Saratoga.

All that, of course, came after he rushed home from his Ticonderoga adventure in response to news his wife was deathly ill, only to find that she had died before he could reach her side. A sad moment for the embattled husband, but then, there was much to his life, both before and after, to evoke sympathy from any objective observer . . . up to a point.

While he was the descendant of a colonial governor of Rhode Island on his father's side and a wealthy, aristocratic family on his mother's side, he was *not* blessed with a happy childhood in his native Norwich, Connecticut. His father failed in business and drank heavily. Yellow fever struck the family, taking four of the six children as its victims.

The surviving boy had to leave school for financial reasons. A leader among his peers, he was so rebellious that one Thanksgiving he threatened to fight a constable intervening as he and his friends prepared to build a huge bonfire on the village green.

His despairing mother at last persuaded cousins Daniel and Joshua Lathrop to take in her son as an apprentice in their drugstore. The experiment worked—he was with them for several years, with time out only for brief military service during the French and Indian War of the 1750s. The young man moved on after his apprenticeship to operate his own apothecary in New Haven, a vocation supplemented by his financial interest in various merchant ships. He occasionally—like many colonial merchants—also "worked" as a smuggler circumventing British customs laws.

Married in 1767, he and the former Margaret Mansfield, daughter of New Haven's sheriff, had three sons, lived in a stoutly built home of their own creation, and boasted a stable of horses. Margaret's husband, popular in the community's more radical political circles, cut a fine figure in his gentlemanly dress, offset by dark skin, dark hair, and contrasting eyes of light blue, though he was a bit short by the standards of the day.

It no doubt was a sad day when he returned from the wars to the north—wars both with the enemy and presumed friends—and found his wife already beyond earthly reach. To make matters worse, he himself fell prey to a difficult siege with the gout. Fortunately, his one surviving sibling, his sister Hannah, was on hand to help care for him and his three sons, Richard, Henry, and Benedict.

The last, of course, was an enduring family name. That early governor of Rhode Island bore the name Benedict, as did the militia captain's own hard-drinking father, as, now, did his son in Hannah's care. All Benedicts. All Arnolds. All of them, Benedict Arnolds.

Gentleman from Georgia

COMING TO ORDER IN THE Second Continental Congress sessions of 1775 were the assorted—indeed, the distinguished—delegates sent to the rebel legislative body in Philadelphia by . . . well, not quite all thirteen of the original American colonies, but only twelve of those historic entities.

Delegates, that is to say, from twelve of the colonies . . . and a single, fervent Patriot representing a single, county-size parish in that one remaining sister of the original sisterhood, Georgia.

He was Lyman Hall of St. John's Parish on the Georgia coast—physician, former minister, and a transplanted Connecticut Yankee at that. From May 13, 1775, through the next four months, he alone would be Georgia's contribution to the deliberations of the revolutionary body convened in Philadelphia in the name of all the American colonists.

By the history-making days of July 1776, however, Georgia could claim full representation at the Philadelphia gathering by three delegates who, along with their brethren from the other twelve colonies, would be signers of the Declaration of Independence—and what an unusual threesome they were!

Lyman Hall himself was a rarity, not only as the lone delegate in Congress from one of the Original Thirteen, but also as one of only five physicians destined to be signers of the Declaration. A second Georgian attending the historic Philadelphia sessions of 1776 was George Walton, at age twenty-six one of the youngest of the great document's signers. The last of the trio, Button Gwinnett, sadly enough, would not live to see the revolutionary Spirit of Seventy-Six prevail. His unfortunate destiny, fulfilled in 1777, was to be fatally wounded in a duel with a fellow Georgia Patriot.

Why was Georgia such a latecomer to the revolutionary movement? The fact is, Georgia, the last of the colonial sisterhood to be established upon the Atlantic seaboard, definitely was lukewarm at first to any notion of breaking with its recent benefactors and founders from across the Atlantic. Stated another way, Georgia, baby of the colonial brood, still clung to Mother England's apron strings. The colony's leaders felt, moreover, that they and their people had been relatively well treated. And most were happy with the diligent, even-handed performance of Royal Governor James Wright.

Once Georgia did jump into the revolutionary fray, it was with not one, but two Whig factions seeking redress against the Crown, each by its own lights, each in its own image. The unfortunate Gwinnett, second president of the Georgia Council of Safety, was both a victim and an advocate of that sharply, even murderously, divided house of rebels.

Murderously? Well, there was, of course, Gwinnett's own unhappy and highly visible fate in the spring of 1777, less than a year after he signed off on the document declaring independence from Great Britain. Just weeks beforehand, furthermore, his predecessor as Council president, Archibald Bulloch (an ancient ancestor to Eleanor Roosevelt), died quite suddenly. *Poisoned* was the never-proved, possibly unfounded, but nonetheless prevalent rumor.

When Gwinnett, as a fellow Council member, succeeded Bulloch at the body's helm, it was by virtue of a solid membership vote—with only one negative vote registered against him. That vote came from an old political enemy symbolic of the Whig factions in Georgia, one George McIntosh. And it was George's brother, militia General Lachlan McIntosh, who would wound Gwinnett fatally in their duel by pistols not three months later ... after Gwinnett in the meantime had been instrumental in putting George McIntosh in irons as an alleged traitor.

To sort all this out, it helps to look at Georgia a bit earlier, on the eve of the Revolution. For at that moment in time, as a symbol of the old order, there was a strong, largely well-intended royal governor seated in Savannah. And not all that dissimilar in their authoritarian views were the aristocratic Whigs of Christ Church Parish, also Savannah-based. And finally, as the third corner of the triangle, there was the far more radical, populist-leaning Whig faction of St. John's Parish, located on the Atlantic Coast.

It was the latter group that produced the restless Lyman Hall, a rice-grower and physician living near Georgia's port city of Sunbury at the mouth of the Medway River. Hall, born in Wallingford, Connecticut, in 1724, was educated at Yale and had once been a Congregationalist minister. He had joined fellow New England Congregationalists in migrating south, first to South

Carolina, then to Georgia, then back again to South Carolina, and finally to Georgia one more time, as part of the New Englanders' Medway settlement in St. John's Parish. His rice plantation, "Hall's Knoll," was but one occupation, since he also spent time doctoring the sick and the dying among his neighbors.

He had a preoccupation, as well: revolutionary politics. In this regard, he and his fellow New Englanders of Puritan stock were way ahead of their fellow Georgians. As late as 1774, many Georgians were fairly satisfied with the annual grants that Parliament bestowed upon their colony—and with the lucrative trade in rice and indigo they enjoyed with the Mother Country. They were aware of the mounting disquiet among their brethren to the north, of course, and some Georgia settlers outside of St. John's Parish also were paying close attention. Indeed, Savannah could boast its own "chapter" of the Sons of Liberty, and the conservative-dominated Assembly had gone so far as to protest the increasingly restrictive British policies toward the American colonies.

Even so, Georgia as a whole failed to respond to the call in 1774 to join in the formation of the First Continental Congress in Philadelphia. The more restive settlers from all over Georgia did assemble at Tondee's Tavern in Savannah to discuss the summons from the north—and, indeed, to rail against the latest British mea-sures—but they balked at sending delegates to Philadelphia.

The participants from St. John's Parish were far from satisfied with that result. They went home, continued their agitation and, at further meetings, decided to send Lyman Hall to the Philadelphia gathering on behalf of Georgia. He declined the honor at first, but later a threat by the Patriots assembled in Philadelphia to boycott uncooperative colonies—i.e., Georgia—stirred St. John's Parish anew. There was talk of seceding from the rest of Georgia, there was an attempt to align with Patriot groups in Charleston, South Carolina, immediately to the north (which was rebuffed), and there was general consternation over the prospect of losing trade with the outside world.

This time, shortly after the shooting had begun at Lexington and Concord, Lyman Hall agreed to travel north ... but primarily to carry his community's appeal against the Patriot-ordered trade embargo. He took two hundred barrels of locally grown rice with him, a dona-tion for the Patriots in the north.

As a result, on May 13, 1775, the Second Continental Congress

(rather than Georgia itself) recognized him as a delegate to the Philadelphia proceedings. No honorary onlooker, he shared official duties with delegates from all the remaining colonies—he served on one committee with Virginia's fiery Patrick Henry, with Pennsylvania's legendary Ben Franklin, with the great mover from Massachusetts, John Adams.

By now, events were moving rapidly and irrevocably, even back home in Georgia. There in early 1776, local Patriots arrested Royal Governor Wright, then gave him parole that allowed him to flee to the British warships in the Savannah River. A battle erupted in the river over British attempts to seize Georgia-grown rice. A Georgian provincial congress chose Hall, his neighbor and occasional patient from St. John's Parish, Button Gwinnett, and young Savannah lawyer George Walton as the colony's three delegates to the Continental Congress in Philadelphia.

As destiny would have it, they would be on hand for what John Adams would call "the greatest debate of all"—the session in July devoted to considering the proposed Declaration of Independence.

That was the very phrase Adams used in a letter he wrote on July 1, 1776, to Archibald Bulloch, president of Georgia's provincial congress. Adams wrote: "A declaration, that these colonies are free and independent states, has been reported by a committee appointed some weeks ago for that purpose, and this day or to-morrow is to determine its fate. . . ."

Adams assured Bulloch that Georgia finally would be well represented in the deliberations of the historic Patriot body assembled in Philadelphia. He didn't mention the Savannah-based Walton, but he did write Bulloch that his colleagues Hall and Gwinnett "are here in good health and spirits, and as firm as you yourself could wish them."

Additional note: The Second Continental Congress that gathered in Philadelphia in May of 1775—after Lexington, Concord, and Menotomy—shifted its meeting place from the tight-fitting Carpenters' Hall to the grander Pennsylvania State House, known today as Independence Hall. The Second Congress counted some now-famous faces among its newer members—Thomas Jefferson, Benjamin Franklin, and John Hancock, to name a few.

Early housekeeping steps included the resignation of Virginia's Peyton Randolph as presiding officer, to be succeeded in that post by Hancock of Massachusetts. The major policy issue overriding all considerations by this Congress, now that shooting had actually erupted, would be a choice between declaring full independence or seeking reconciliation with Mother England.

Before addressing such a momentous decision, however, this Congress had to act quickly in several areas. Thus it issued a call for all the colonies to prepare for possible war, appropriated funds to buy military supplies, announced the raising of six rifle companies from Virginia, Pennsylvania, and Maryland to reinforce the New Englanders holding Boston under siege and, last but far from least, appointed Virginia's George Washington as commander of the tiny, newly created Continental Army.

The Congress of colonists also named four men with extensive military experience as his chief subordinates for now and gave each the rank of major general—Charles Lee, Israel Putnam, Philip Schuyler, Artemas Ward. Eight more men were appointed as lesser-ranking brigadier generals, some of them easily recalled today, most not. The best known of this lot were John Sullivan, Nathanael Greene, and Richard Montgomery. In related action, Congress named Horatio Gates as adjutant general.

On other fronts, Congress urged British-controlled Canada to join in the American crusade for greater freedoms while also, on the now-inauspicious date of July 5, 1775, adopting John Dickinson's so-called "Olive Branch Petition," addressed to King George III and seeking reconciliation. The legislative conclave next took up and adopted the Declaration of the Causes and Necessity for Taking Up Arms, a manifesto written by Pennsylvania's Dickinson and Virginia's Thomas Jefferson. The document accused Parliament of using force to enslave the colonies and sought to justify their use of force to meet force.

This same action-oriented Congress soon created a colonies-wide postal system, with Ben Franklin appointed as the future nation's first postmaster general. Before briefly adjourning on August 2, the body rejected as inadequate an early British effort at conciliation, which had been received on May 26 from King George's latest prime minister, Lord Frederick North.

Resuming its deliberations in Philadelphia five weeks later, Congress could now greet a newly named Georgia delegation of three members, Lyman Hall among them. Two months later, on November 19, Congress was informed that back in August King George III not only had turned aside its Olive Branch Petition, but had declared the colonies to be in a state of rebellion.

Still seeking reconciliation, Congress moved on December 6 to send the Mother Country yet another statement of loyalty to the Crown—but not to Parliament.

Even so, as the year ended, momentum was building in the direction of real independence rather than accommodation of any kind. Soon, there came a new edict from King George ordering the closure of American ports to normal commerce. That only intensified the American mood in favor of total and irrevocable separation from England.

Two Hills Known as One

OUTSIDE OF BOSTON, THE AMERICAN militiamen besieging General Thomas Gage and his redcoats in the port city moved during the night to a key hill and began fortifying it for the British assault sure to come.

Right idea, but wrong hill. Or was it?

Their orders said Bunker Hill, but the smaller knob they decided to fortify—in the dark and on the spot—was Breed's Hill, just forward of the intended Bunker Hill. The two were connected by a long ridge called Charlestown Heights, a substantial rise on the Charlestown peninsula across the Charles River from Boston proper, which in June 1775 was a port city of sixteen thousand. Whoever held the Charlestown high ground and armed it with artillery could bombard the northern end of the city and control access to the river passageway into Boston's Back Bay.

Supplied by sea, the British figured they could hold out in Boston until the amateurish American militiamen wearied of their insurrectional activity and returned to farms and shops scattered throughout Massachusetts and adjoining New England colonies. The hot tempers that flared up in the unfortunate Lexington-Concord-Menotomy fracas in April might even cool down; negotiation might yet restore a peace of sorts, albeit an uneasy one.

First, though, it would be essential for the British to hold both the Charlestown Heights across the river to the north and Dorchester Heights to the south. Otherwise, the errant colonial leaders might bring heavy artillery into play—a dangerous possibility for the British force quartered in the city between the heights north and south.

Charlestown, town and peninsula, already had figured in the maneuvering of the two sides in the weeks since real shooting had broken out April 19. Retreating from the aroused militia swarming out of the Massachusetts countryside that unforgettable day, the British had briefly paused on the peninsula and had even spent time placing light fortifications on Bunker Hill. But Gage then pulled all his men into the city itself.

Barely a month later, Gage's American spy, Dr. Benjamin Church, reported that the Patriots planned to take over both the Charlestown and Dorchester Heights. Gage should have moved immediately to counter them, but he didn't. He remained strangely inert in the city.

His secret? He was expecting significant reinforcements from England, led by a trio of British major generals destined to win historical fame, if not outright fortune, in the Revolutionary War years ahead—Sir William Howe, Sir Henry Clinton, and John ("Gentleman Johnny") Burgoyne.

On May 13, true to Doctor Church's warning, three thousand American militiamen moved onto Charlestown Heights, but then, like the British before them, pulled back . . . cleared out.

For the British, meanwhile, the newcomer generals arrived aboard the *Cerberus* May 25, and for the next three weeks they consulted with Gage over various schemes to seize the initiative from the loosely organized militia surrounding them on three sides. No real surprise, the strategy that emerged was to march on the two sets of high ground, north and south of the city, as well as the American center at Cambridge. In detail, the plan was to assault the Dorchester Heights first, then swing through nearby Roxbury while another force crossed the Back Bay by boat and struck out for the Cambridge center.

Through their own spies, the Americans heard about the British forces' intentions right away and moved quickly to forestall them . . . in part. Lacking cannon and the manpower to defend both heights, the Americans decided to rush back onto the Charlestown peninsula and fight for possession of the high ground there. Doctor Church, busy delivering dispatches to the Continental Congress in Philadelphia, this time was out of the picture—the Americans surprised the British by moving back onto the peninsula in force before Gage and his generals could launch their own operation.

For the Americans, it was cautious Major General Artemas Ward, in command of the New England militia, who dispatched 1,500 to 1,600 men under Colonel William Prescott on the night of June 16. The colonel marched off with three Massachusetts regiments, 200 Connecticut men, a small number of New Hampshire militia, and the legendary Colonel Israel Putnam of Connecticut by his side. Their orders were to filter through the abandoned town that gave the peninsula its name, then to build fortifications on Bunker Hill.

At the urging of Putnam, like Prescott a hero of the French and Indian War, the Americans instead set to digging furiously on smaller Breed's Hill, closer to Boston proper. From there Prescott's light artillery could reach into the city. The position on this rise—sometimes itself called Bunker Hill—was so close to the British, in fact, that they would have to react to it and thus ignore Dorchester and Roxbury for now.

The British in the city and aboard ships indeed were startled by the next dawn's light to see the major earthworks the Americans had thrown up on Breed's Hill during the night. Highly visible from Boston, their redoubt was 160 feet long and 80 feet across, with protective walls of dirt piled 6 feet high. And they were still digging their entrenchments.

With supporting fortifications added on Bunker Hill, it appeared, and rightly so, that the Americans could inflict severe punishment on any attacking force.

They didn't have long to wait, either. With the first light of day, two nearby British warships began a steady bombardment of the earthen fort on Breed's Hill—soon joining in was a battery on Copp's Hill. The solid walls proved effective at smothering most of the cannonballs before they could do real damage, but the cannonade did lead to one gruesome incident. To the horror of every onlooker, a random cannonball took off a militiaman's head.

Prescott reacted quickly. He ordered the body buried, then sought to rally his green and jittery troops by parading back and forth on the parapet in front of them . . . under fire, of course. And it undoubtedly did encourage many to see him eventually step down unharmed.

In Boston, meanwhile, the British generals had hurried into conference to decide their best response to the radically altered situation. Their assault on Dorchester, Roxbury, and the American center at Cambridge would have opened the next day, a Sunday. What to do for now, a bright and warm Saturday?

Howe urged an amphibious landing on the Charlestown peninsula that very afternoon, before the Americans could consolidate their new position. In fact, he and his fellow brass decided, they now should turn their original plan on its head—they now would overwhelm the Americans on the high ground to the north (at Breed's Hill), next mount their assault on the center at Cambridge, and then go after Dorchester Heights to the south last, instead of first.

But Howe would have to scramble to line up boats and fully equipped personnel, if he was to make good use of the day's high tide, due at 2:30 P.M. As events turned out, he indeed did manage to move his first wave of one thousand grenadiers and light infantry across the Charles River on the favorable tide. They came ashore at Moulton's Point at the tip of the peninsula, beyond reach of the American guns.

When Howe saw the extent of the American defensive lines shortly after he stepped ashore, he called for even more men. In a short time, he had almost 2,200 redcoats on the ground and at his disposal. For the first head-to-head battle of the American Revolution, most of the British soldiers wore full gear and packs weighing fifty to one hundred pounds, by various estimates available today. With some of Howe's light infantry beginning a flanking movement to the American left, along the Mystic River shoreline to the rear, the redcoats assigned to a frontal assault wave formed their traditional close ranks and stepped out.

When newly fortified Breed's Hill rose in front of them, no great matter. They simply marched onward in the hot June sun and started up the incline. But not for long. The first ranks were struck down by sheets of musket and light-artillery fire from the entrenched rebels. The survivors reeled back, leaving inert forms on the ground.

In short order, the ranks closed up and a fresh assault went forward . . . in the old, European style. Again the crashing waves of Patriot gunfire took their toll and sent survivors reeling back.

Now, with the Americans running low on powder, came General Sir Henry Clinton with four hundred to five hundred fresh men to join in the fight. And now came a third and final British assault, with heavy packs thrown aside, bayonets fixed. This time it was the outnumbered Americans who had to give way, first at Breed's Hill, next at adjoining Bunker Hill as well.

In the end, the Americans would have to retire from the field. First, though, the British left had suffered from snipers firing from the vacated houses in Charlestown itself. Then, fiery-hot shot lobbed from the ship cannon had set ablaze the entire town, about three hundred homes, an event shocking the Bostonians watching the battle unfold from their own windows and rooftops.

As they and their fellow Colonials would soon learn, they had witnessed a historic American defeat . . . and yet not entirely a defeat.

True, the British had gained possession of the high ground, but Howe had only pursued his enemy to the base of the peninsula, then stopped. The redcoats now held the Charlestown peninsula as hoped, but they had lost in the numbers game accompanying any battle—in casualties. Overall, out of 1,600 American men deployed, 140 had been killed, an estimated 271 wounded, and 30 captured. The British, on the other hand, could count 226 killed and a total casualty list of 1,054, nearly one-half the force of 2,200 they had deployed. Many of the British killed or wounded were officers, prime targets for the sharpshooting Americans. Among the fallen officers on this day in June was Marine Major John Pitcairn, whose troops had fired the first shots of the Revolutionary War on the Lexington Common back in April.

Every battle has its difficult moments for either side—sometimes its inspiring moments, too. On Breed's Hill that morning, Colonel Prescott certainly had been the inspiring hero for his virginal Americans, new as they were to set-piece battle. Before he leaped to the top of the earthen wall, however, the otherwise ineffective fire from the British warships *Lively* and *Somerset* had so shattered the nerves of Prescott's militiamen that two of the Massachusetts regiments had withdrawn, decamped. Their officers and men explained they were exhausted by the night's labors—after their leave-taking, Prescott for a time was left with only five hundred men.

But Israel Putnam was back in Cambridge, where he successfully talked the timid Ward and the Massachusetts Committee of Safety
into sending reinforcements over to the Charlestown high ground.
Later in the day, Putnam and New Hampshire's John Stark commanded sharpshooting Americans placed behind hastily erected barricades to halt British General Howe's attempted flanking movement along the Mystic River shoreline on the northeast side of the
peninsula. "Don't fire until you see the whites of their eyes," Putnam
told his compatriots behind a rail fence blocking Howe's path.
Putnam, incidentally, had been with the British when they failed in
an attempt to seize Fort Ticonderoga from the French in 1758, an
action costing the British a ranking officer who had died in
Putnam's arms. The officer was George Howe, older brother of
General William Howe, who was now attacking Putnam and his
American compatriots outside of Boston.

In the end, the British flanking movement was beaten back, but
the outnumbered and poorly supplied Americans on the two hills
simply couldn't hold out against the repeated frontal assaults—
many of their casualties for the day in fact stemmed from their withdrawal, even though it was an orderly one considering the circumstances and their inexperience. "My God, how the balls flew!"
exclaimed Connecticut Lieutenant Samuel Webb. "Four men were
shot dead within five feet of me."

As details of the day's battle spread, it was obvious to most that
the moral victory, at least, lay with the Americans. That was the message quickly grasped by Nathanael Greene, Rhode Island's neophyte
brigadier general. "I wish we could sell them another hill at the same
price," said Greene, who was destined to become possibly the most
brilliant of George Washington's subordinates.

The British, of course, were well aware that they had failed to
break the siege, that they had seen nearly a third of their force in
Boston become casualties . . . and that the Americans were prepared
to fight and die for their cause. The flashpoint events of Lexington,
Concord, and Menotomy on April 19 could no longer be written off
as some sort of accidental friction between angry men armed with
guns.

Letter to Martha

UPON HIS APPOINTMENT AS COMMANDER IN CHIEF of the newly created Continental Army in June 1775, a humble, almost chastened George Washington wrote to his wife, Martha:

MY DEAREST,—I now sit down to write to you on a subject which fills me with inexpressible concern, and this concern is greatly aggravated and increased when I reflect upon the uneasiness I know it will give you. It has been determined in Congress that the whole army raised for the defence of the American cause shall be put under my Care, and that it is necessary for me to proceed immediately to Boston to take upon me the command of it. You may believe me, my dear Patsy [his pet name for her], when I assure you, in the most solemn manner, that, so far from seeking this appointment, I have used every endeavor in my power to avoid it, not only from my unwillingness to part with you and the family, but from a consciousness of its being a trust too great for my capacity, and that I should enjoy more real happiness in one month with you at home than I have the most distant prospect of finding abroad, if my stay were to be seven times seven years. But as it has been a kind of destiny that has thrown me upon this service, I shall hope that my undertaking is designed to answer some good purpose. You might and I suppose did, perceive from the tenor of my letters, that I was apprehensive I could not avoid this appointment, as I did not pretend to intimate when I should return. That was the case. It was utterly out of my power to refuse this appointment without exposing my character to such censures as would have reflected dishonor upon myself and given pain to my friends. This, I am sure, could not, and ought not to be pleasing to you, and must have lessened me considerably in my own esteem. I shall rely, therefore, confidently on that Providence which has heretofore preserved and been bountiful to me, not doubting but that I shall return safe to you in the fall. I shall feel no pain from the toil or the danger of the Campaign; my unhappiness will flow from the uneasiness you will feel from being left alone. I therefore beg that you will summon your whole fortitude, and pass your time as agreeably as possible. Nothing will give me so much sincere satisfaction as to hear this and to hear it from your own pen. . . .

A Feat Like Hannibal's

Fort Ticonderoga, that fiercely named bastion of the English during the French and Indian War, lay far off, at a conjunction of Lakes George and Champlain in northern New York, up there near Canada. Dorchester Heights, on the other hand, overlooked Boston from the southeastern side of a bay.

In the summer of 1775, the British held the city and its port facilities, along with the knob known as Bunker Hill, to the north. The aroused colonists of Great Britain, the Patriots, held the countryside all around. They held Boston in their grip, down there, below a ring of hills.

This was the scene that greeted the newly appointed commander in chief of the Americans when he arrived that summer, fresh from Philadelphia and the rebel Congress that had named and dispatched him to direct the siege of Boston.

But truly, was it much of a siege? Or merely a stalemate? George Washington's own men, twice the number of the British inside the Patriot ring, were themselves wondering. For many enlistments soon would expire—Washington's restive army could simply melt away. The British, easily resupplied by sea, could simply wait . . . and wait.

If only the Americans, unprepared for war with a great world power, had some artillery!

And, yes, there was the key. Move a few pieces to the top of Dorchester Heights, and the Patriots would have the city below at their mercy. But where . . . where could they find the necessary guns?

Heavy guns, real cannon . . . that was what was so badly needed.

Enter now a young, overweight, inexperienced bookseller from Boston itself, one Henry Knox, twenty-five, member of the colonial militia—and proprietor of Boston's ironically titled London Bookstore.

Soon introduced to the new commander from Virginia, the bookseller was also a book-*reader* and self-appointed student of military affairs. As John Adams explained to George Washington, young Henry Knox, self-tutored or not, really knew his artillery. He, in fact, could be appointed a colonel in charge of the fledgling army's artillery. Could be, should be . . . and was. But still, *what* artillery?

It was Knox, himself, who said the solution to the problem was the recent capture of Fort Ticonderoga (in May of 1775, the feat engineered by Ethan Allen and Benedict Arnold). There the Patriots had come into possession of cannon that could serve as siege guns for the force surrounding Boston.

The only trouble was that the sixty or so most-serviceable guns, weighing more than 120,000 pounds, were a good three hundred miles away, separated from the American army at Boston by a combination of mountains and untracked wilderness. Hercules was not available, but Knox, a "can do" young man if there ever was one, not only was available but was volunteering to undertake the seemingly impossible task of hauling the Ticonderoga guns to Cambridge and Boston.

It was an offer the hard-pressed Washington could not refuse. Hoping for the best, he urged Knox on with the project and ordered that "no trouble or expense must be spared to obtain them [the guns]." With that endorsement, Henry Knox and his brother William set off for Ticonderoga in late November of 1775—already wintertime in New England and upper New York.

It took them a mere four days to reach Ticonderoga, but it would be a much longer trip coming back. First, quite naturally, Henry Knox had to determine how great a treasure trove he might have . . . and, yes, he discovered, it would be an artillery assemblage well worth the effort to be expended on the arduous journey back to Boston.

After discarding guns that were broken or worn out, Knox counted fifty-nine usable pieces, from little four-pounders all the way up to big twenty-four-pound cannon, along with assorted mortars and howitzers.

And now came the hard part . . . all in stages, and no comfort to the impatient. Stage One, after dismantling the guns, was carrying their pieces across a peninsula—consisting of both swamp and woodland—to three barge-like boats that were waiting on the waters of Lake George.

That done, the boats, with William in charge, navigated thirty or more miles down the narrow lake to Fort George, despite the ice rimming the lake shoreline a mile out and the grounding of one boat, a scow, that forced a redistribution of its cargo.

That was the easy part, actually. Now, with various river and lake crossings en route, would come the overland part of the trip, including treks up and down mountainsides. For this task, Henry Knox had gone ahead and assembled a "fleet" of forty-two great sledges to be hauled by eighty horses and oxen. They, together with a mixed force of Revolutionary soldiers, teamsters, and other civilian volunteers, were assembled at Fort George to take the guns on from there.

At the river crossings lying ahead, Knox had to hope for open water—to accommodate scow or barge—or for ice solid enough to hold his men, their animals, and the enormously heavy sleds carrying the dismantled guns, plus a goodly store of muskets and cannonballs. Any in-between conditions, such as a river partially iced over, would only delay his progress.

By early January of 1776, however, he and the artillery train had reached Albany, New York. He crossed the Hudson River and inched on southward to Claverack, where he turned onto an old Indian trail—today's U.S. Route 23, actually. It ran eastward, through the southern Berkshire Mountains, past Great Barrington, Massachusetts, to Monterey. By then, Knox later wrote, his caravan had climbed mountains "from which we might almost have seen all the Kingdoms of the Earth."

Next came a difficult stretch of unspoiled pine forests, on to Blandford and today's Westfield Mountain, notable during the tedious winter journey of 1776 for the fact that the teamsters with Knox had to take great care going down the mountain—take care that the heavy sleds would not careen downhill upon the men and oxen ahead.

Advancing cautiously and gingerly, they employed tricks such as restraining lines fastened to trees alongside, check poles thrust under the runners, and drag chains, all of which conspired to bring the heavy loads slowly and safely down the mountainside.

A bit more prosaically, the artillery train soon after crossed the Connecticut River at Springfield, Massachusetts, on ice but then, caught by a sudden warming trend that softened the ground, became stuck in mud.

Rarely discouraged, Knox simply waited for the weather to turn cold again, then moved his sledges on, over once-more frozen ground.

From there, his artillery train was able to grind its tough way to Framingham, outside of Boston. At this point, Knox transferred the lighter, more mobile guns to Cambridge and left the heavier, slower-moving cannon for a later but still-imminent day.

All in all, it had taken him about six weeks to move the guns from Ticonderoga to George Washington's side at Cambridge. Moreover, Knox arrived with his shipment just about intact—when on occasion one of his sleds had broken through thin ice, his men had been able to recover the artillery pieces aboard. Overall, it had been an amazing operation, a feat not unlike either Hannibal or Napoleon and their armies crossing the Alps to take their respective enemies by surprise.

Knox and his "noble train of artillery," as it is often called, arrived in early February. The Patriot bombardment of Boston began on March 2, even as many of the guns were still being moved to the Dorchester Heights. Before all of the new guns had even unleashed their shot and shell, however, the British left the city on March 17, evacuating the port by sea. Fittingly, when George Washington rode into the newly abandoned town at the head of his momentarily triumphant Continental Army, Henry Knox, the onetime bookseller, was riding beside him.

Son Unlike Father

WHAT'S THIS? BEN FRANKLIN'S SON William accused of treason by the Patriots? Arrested, booted out of New Jersey, and thrown into jail in Connecticut?

Obviously, there's been a mistake here. Why else would George Washington consider William Franklin an enemy to the cause? Why, even a year later, would he refuse the younger Franklin permission to visit his dying wife in British-occupied New York?

But no, there was no mistaking the clear-cut loyalty of the royal governor of New Jersey—Ben Franklin's illegitimate son, William—to the British Crown.

It really did happen that way.

Once upon a time, they were a close father and son. Those experiments by Ben Franklin to see if lightning packed an electrical wallop? By some historical accounts, son William held the kite string during the thunderstorm.

Young William, born in 1730 or 1731, eventually would be honored with a doctorate from Oxford University for the role he played—starting as a teenager—in his father's scientific experiments, but that recognition would come only when he and his father traveled to London together shortly before George III's ascension to the throne of England in 1760.

Before undertaking the Atlantic crossing with his father, William had quite a few accomplishments to his credit—or were they products of his father's political influence? One may ask, but the fact is, while he "read the law" as a student of the legal process, young William served as postmaster of Philadelphia. Then, too, since he had been a useful aide to his activist father in the art of politics as well as in scientific experimentation, no surprise that William should appear for a time as clerk of the Pennsylvania Assembly. As a matter of fact, young "Billy" was only following in his father's footsteps in both of these politically appointed jobs.

The young man also put in time soldiering in the French and Indian War, even to the extent of leading a small force into the Ohio Territory.

During all these highly visible activities, separately and together, Benjamin Franklin never denied fathering William, raised as his eldest son. William may or may not have been a premarital infant born to Benjamin Franklin and his common-law wife, Deborah Read. The situation simply comes down to us today as a muddled one ... and it no doubt was rankling at moments to all in the immediate family. Oddly enough, William in time would produce an illegitimate son of his own. And the son would produce an illegitimate daughter of *his* own, as well.

But first, with his venerable father known as the American Revolution's unofficial ambassador to one and all in Europe, how and why did son William wind up as royal governor of rebellious New Jersey? The ironic contretemps stems in large part from the joint trip to London undertaken by father and son before the French and Indian War was concluded.

By strange historical alchemy, they were in London at the very moment young George III and his new bride, Princess Charlotte of Mecklenberg-Strelitz, were crowned in Westminster Abbey. Interestingly enough, it was Billy Franklin who sat inside the grand abbey for the event, in a VIP seat costing ten guineas, while his father, Ben, contented himself with a view of the royal procession from a curbside wooden booth.

The father-and-son pair was in London for more than one reason, not so incidentally. For one thing, Ben Franklin, already famous for his scientific experiments, had seen his conclusions published in the proceedings of England's most prestigious assembly of scientists, the Royal Society. "He had been made a member of this select body," wrote historian Thomas Fleming in his book *Liberty! The American Revolution,* "and from the moment he came to England, the cultured and sophisticated members of English society had virtually adopted him. England's Oxford and Scotland's St. Andrew's Universities gave him honorary doctorates. Oxford threw in a master of arts for William because he had assisted his father in many experiments—notably the risky feat of flying a kite in a thunderstorm."

As Fleming noted also, they both loved the "Mother Country," and for handsome young Billy, still only thirty years of age, there was one further pleasure—"In London he met none of the social rebuffs he frequently encountered in provincial Philadelpia because he was illegitimate."

Indeed, Billy won such acceptance that he was able to resume his law studies at the Inns of Court, meet the king's new prime minister, Lord Bute, and even, in 1762, marry Elizabeth Downes, a devotee to the Crown originally from the West Indies.

He and his father, in the meantime, had achieved a major coup in a long-standing dispute with Thomas and Richard Penn, sons of William Penn, founder of Pennsylvania. As historian Fleming explained the situation, "As proprietors of the colony, the Penns owned huge swaths of the countryside. With a greed that made it clear they disdained their saintly father's Quaker faith, they instructed the governor, whom they appointed, to forbid the legislature to tax their lands."

The two Franklins made it their business to petition the Privy Council for relief—but Ben Franklin ran into a buzzsaw when he approached council president John Carteret, Earl Granville, a brother-in-law, it so happened, to Thomas Penn. "You Americans have wrong ideas on the nature of your constitution," he grandly stated. "The King is legislator for the colonies."

Not quite, argued the wily elder Franklin. "As the [colonial] assemblies cannot make permanent laws without his [the king's] assent," he retorted, "so neither can he make a law for them without theirs."

Well, Lord Granville certainly couldn't accept that notion, and Ben Franklin retired to his lodgings with nothing to show for his petitioning effort thus far. Clearly, a new strategy was needed.

Putting their heads together, the two Franklins—and a British attorney they hired—came up with a typically American ploy, a publicity campaign. Fleming again: "It began with a full-length book on the history of the government of Pennsylvania, which William Franklin researched and [Attorney Richard] Jackson wrote. The most important thing about it was the motto on the title page, which was Benjamin Franklin's contribution: 'Those who give up essential liberty, to preserve a little temporary safety, deserve neither liberty nor safety.'

"Simultaneously, Jackson lobbied . . . on Franklin's behalf. Franklin's friends, who included Dr. John Pringle, Lord Bute's personal physician, also spoke up on his behalf at St. James's Palace. The coup de grace was a direct appeal to William Pitt himself. The Great Commoner sided emphatically with the Americans. The Penns were soon practically pleading for mercy, and in a final showdown before the chief justice of the King's Bench, they feebly surrendered all their objections and agreed to let their lands be taxed."

Next, another coup, but a controversial one on both sides of the great water, the Franklins returned to America with Billy Franklin's appointment as royal governor of New Jersey fresh in hand. He took office in 1763. Another chapter, another life thus began for the younger Franklin . . . but it also was a pathway eventually leading to estrangement from his father.

As an early indication of the pending split, Royal Governor Franklin of New Jersey took occasion in the midst of colonial outrage against the infamous Stamp Act in 1765 to express his own umbrage over the "outrageous conduct" of the violent mob actions in Boston. While many a thoughtful citizen might have agreed, the fact is that Billy Franklin was already parting company with his famous father, now back in London.

When the elder Franklin returned to the turbulent colonies in 1775, the year after his wife Deborah's death, daughter Sarah greeted him with the bald statement: "Billy is a Tory!" Benjamin apparently had held hopes his son would have resigned his royal post in support of the long struggle for colonial liberties. But no, Sarah and her husband, Richard Bache, told Franklin, despite his advocacy in London, despite the recent fighting in Lexington and Concord, William's loyalty was to Lord North and the Crown of England.

Immediately made a member of the Pennsylvania delegation to the Continental Congress, Ben Franklin met shortly afterward with his son and Joseph Galloway, an old friend who refused to join the revolutionary body. It was a long meeting, during which William and Galloway would "denounce both sides in the dispute," Fleming has noted.

When Ben Franklin told them he was "for independence," wrote Fleming in *Liberty,* "The two younger men could only gasp and shake their heads." In their view, "the Continental Congress was as wrong-headed as Parliament, with the worse handicap that the Congress had no legal right to exist." They were stunned to learn that the elder Franklin, until now "a symbol of moderation and rational moderation," could espouse "this radical idea [independence], which thus far only a few extremists dared to whisper in private."

In the Congress, assembled in Philadelphia, meanwhile, there were men as eminent as Virginia's Richard Henry Lee who were suspicious of Benjamin Franklin's sincerity, due to the fact that his own son remained a royal governor—of next-door New Jersey, for that matter. Shortly, too, William alarmed all his father's fellow Patriots by talking his New Jersey legislators into endorsing a petition to the British king that, in Fleming's words, "threatened to unravel the fragile American union." A visit to Trenton by members of the Continental Congress "barely" managed to end that threat.

As in her sister American colonies, the governing circles of New Jersey were in turmoil in any case. Governor Franklin, after firing the colonial treasurer in 1774 in a matter of theft, had been at odds with his legislators ever since. In early 1775, they tried to cut back his salary and the rental payments on his home unless he moved away from the capital. He, in turn, dissolved the assembly session.

Then came bombshell news—ever since May of 1774, William Franklin had been sending informational reports to Colonial Secretary Lord Dartmouth, along with offers to serve as a peacemaker between the Mother Country and her colonials. Why this should have been surprising to anyone of the time is a mystery today, but the news was greeted as a final turning point, both by Franklin's long-standing enemies and by more neutral observers. It didn't help that he accused his critics of being "actuated by unmanly private resentment, or by the conviction that their whole political consequence depends upon a contention with their Governor."

He once more cut off the New Jersey Assembly's session on May 23, 1775, with a call to meet again in a month. Only three days after his legislators went home, however, Franklin's rule in New Jersey effectively and abruptly ended. A Provincial Congress of New Jersey assembled at Trenton on May 23 and took over the reins of government in all but name. William Franklin more formally was bereft of office when the Patriots adopted a state constitution in July and installed William Livingston as their new governor.

For Ben Franklin's son, events now only went from bad to worse. Charged with treason and arrested when he refused to live under parole, he was "exiled" to Connecticut, where he was confined for a time in the Litchfield jail. George Washington was somewhat agitated to learn that the guards escorting this enemy of the Revolution had allowed him a stop at Hackensack on the way out of New Jersey.

Franklin's wife, in the meantime, took up residence with the Loyalists and occupying British forces in New York. When she was suffering the next year from a terminal illness, George Washington would not relent in his enmity for William Franklin and permit him to visit the dying woman. She succumbed in August of 1777.

In a prisoner exchange not long after, Franklin was allowed himself to take up residence in New York for the remainder of the war. But he wasn't quite ready to sit out the hostilities quietly. Still an active apostle of the British Crown in 1780, he formed the militia group known as the Associated Loyalists to conduct guerrilla-like raids against Americans in New Jersey and Connecticut. As one action led to reprisal, and reprisal led to more reprisal in this bloody side war, Franklin's militiamen outraged George Washington, Tom

Paine, and Patriots in general by hanging a captured American officer in retaliation for the earlier shooting of a Loyalist. George Washington called the Loyalist action an atrocity and ordered the execution of a British prisoner as yet another reprisal. In the end, fortunately, the man picked for the hangman's noose was spared and, on the British side, the controversial Associated Loyalists were disbanded.

With the hostilities at last ended by treaty in 1783, William Franklin soon moved on to England, where he saw his venerable father for the first time in a decade. Theirs was only a lukewarm reconciliation, by most accounts. For one thing, according to historian Fleming, "[Ben] Franklin could not forget that William was wanted in America for murder and other crimes committed by the Associated Loyalists. . . ."

Further, by Fleming's account again, the elderly Ben handed his son a bill for 1,500 pounds—loaned years before to help William keep up his lifestyle as royal governor of New Jersey. Other accounts say that Ben forgave William his debts—in any case, Ben Franklin did leave his son some land in Nova Scotia, but it's not clear that the title was definitive enough to be fully valid.

While his father returned to America in that same year of 1785 (and died there in 1790 at the age of eighty-four), son William passed his remaining years in England. After a protracted struggle to assure the Loyalist Claims Commission of a loyalty to the Crown unfettered by ties to his father, William finally was granted 1,800 pounds sterling in compensation for properties he lost in America. Also winning a government pension, he lived in London until his death in 1813—like his father, he died in his early eighties.

William's illegitimate son, William Temple Franklin, in the meantime, had spent years in France with grandfather Benjamin as a confidential secretary and aide, much as William once had done as an equally young man. By some accounts, Temple also fathered an illegitimate child—a daughter named Ellen. It was to her that William Franklin, son of Benjamin Franklin and onetime royal governor of New Jersey, left his estate.

"Most Arbitrary Usurpations"

THEY NEVER SHOULD HAVE BELIEVED their man in Carolina when he said just to send a few troops. Send them, he vowed, and the Loyalists of North Carolina would rise up against those infernal rebels and crush them! Not only North Carolina, but the entire South would be saved for the Crown. Just send the troops. Send them quickly!

Back in London, it sounded reasonable enough. All those Scottish Highlanders over there—now considered absolutely loyal to the Crown they had fought in the past. There were other loyal subjects of His Majesty in the colony who surely would join the fight, and with one blow they all together would smite those presumptuous Colonials who had dared to raise their fist. And so . . . send the troops they, the managers in London, indeed would.

Now it was Royal Governor Josiah Martin's turn. He would send out the call, raise his army of adherents to the king, and all would be well. They had only to march, to meet the soon-arriving troops, and then turn their combined, righteous might against the ill-led, ill-clothed, ill-organized, ill-trained rebels.

It was true, of course, that Governor Martin had been forced a bit earlier to abandon the traditional colonial capital of New Bern. Spiking the palace guns and burying the royal powder beneath the cellar floor and in a cabbage patch, he had slipped away from the capital under the cover of darkness one night late in May 1775. He briefly took up residence in not-so-stout Fort Johnston on the Cape Fear River below Brunswick. And there he would have stayed for a while, except that the normal caretaker garrison of twenty-five men was down to less than half that number—except, too, that the pesky rebels served notice they would be coming any day to seize the fort's guns.

Martin then felt obliged to move on once more, this time to the Royal Navy's offshore sloop *Cruizer.* And a good thing, too, since the rebels burned down the fort shortly afterward, on July 18, 1775. As a result, Royal Governor Martin was reduced to directing a shadow government from the only British warship in the vicinity.

For a retired army officer tracing his lineage back to a follower of William the Conqueror, it was a damnable situation to be in ... but by now not an entirely new one for the fifth and last of North Carolina's royal governors. Hardly new, in fact.

In the short four years since Josiah Martin had succeeded William Tryon as royal governor in 1771, the newcomer at New Bern had been subjected to the same steady erosion of authority experienced by virtually all the royal governors in the tumultuous 1770s.

The very year of Martin's arrival, the North Carolina Assembly, still a legitimate and royally sanctioned body, rescinded an unpopular colonial tax imposed since 1748. Martin, disagreeing in principle, vetoed his legislature's action. The tax, for the moment, still stood.

The Assembly quickly retaliated with instruction for the various county sheriffs to ignore their tax-collection duty, whereupon Martin, as royal governor, dissolved the Assembly. But he was foiled there, too. House Speaker Richard Caswell still managed to send out word instructing the sheriffs against collecting the controversial tax.

More frustrating for the new governor, he issued a proclamation ordering the sheriffs to go ahead and collect the tax anyway, only to see his edict widely ignored.

That was only the beginning of the downhill slide in Josiah Martin's authority as royal governor, a descent ending with his lament in 1775 that "nothing but a shadow" of royal authority was left in North Carolina.

After the sheriffs debacle of 1771, Martin had waited until January 1773 to call a new Assembly into session. The burning issue keeping the royal governor and the colonists at odds this time would be a courts-related measure allowing the Carolina colonists to seize local assets of nonresidents who owed local debts—that is to say, debtors safely located in distant England.

With no agreement reached on the issue, a renewable law providing the foundation of the colony's court system was left unrenewed—North Carolina found itself with no judicial system, other than lower magisterial chambers for petty crimes and small civil cases. When Martin tried to create emergency criminal courts by executive fiat, the Assembly refused to fund them. And so he had been foiled again.

During the same period, both governor and citizens of North Carolina were reacting predictably to the larger pre-Revolutionary issues gripping all of colonial America—the Boston "Tea Party" was

matched in North Carolina, as in other colonies, by public protest
and boycotts of British tea. At the end of 1773 also, North Carolina's
Assembly joined Patriot leaders of other colonies in establishing
Committees of Correspondence as a means of exchanging information with one another.

For North Carolina, the most dramatic showdown yet came in
the summer of 1774, when Martin refused to allow his Assembly to
meet and choose delegates for the predictably hostile Continental
Congress of Colonials soon to convene in Philadelphia.
Undeterred—and now taking matters into their own hands with no
legal authority to do so—North Carolina's colonists held a mass
meeting in Wilmington to sanction by their own fiat a gathering in
New Bern the next month, a gathering they boldly termed a "provincial congress independent of the governor." The provincial body
accordingly did meet, and they did choose three Carolina delegates
to the First Continental Congress.

By spring of the next year, Patriot militiamen had made their
appearance in North Carolina, and Martin found his authority further eroding as he called his Assembly into session at New Bern on
April 4. The defiant colonial leaders responded by convening their
Second Provincial Congress in New Bern the day before—with all
but one of the fifty-two legally constituted Assembly members also
counted as Provincial Congress members.

It was no surprise, then, to see the "legal" Assembly play exact
copycat to the extra-legal provincial body before a thoroughly frustrated Royal Governor Martin once again dissolved an Assembly session—dissolved it and despairingly wrote to his superiors in London
that he was in a "most despicable and mortifying" position.

He also took the time, incidentally, to add one of the most striking paeans to the British Crown to come out of the revolutionary
period. Providing unwitting view of the loyalist motivation at its
most pure, Josiah Martin wrote a statement of fidelity, almost of love,
as he deplored the sight of "the Sacred Majesty of my Royal Master
insulted, the Rights of His Crown denied and violated, His
Government set at naught, and trampled upon, his servants of highest dignity reviled, traduced, abused, the Rights of His Subjects
destroyed by the most arbritrary usurpations, and the whole
Constitution unhinged and prostrate. . . ."

None of which is to say that Royal Governor Martin was ready
to furl his flag and abandon the field—not at all, not even while rel-

egated to a government "headquarters" aboard a wooden sailing ship plying a North Carolina river. No sir, so far as he was concerned, those "motley mobs," those "promoters of sedition," would yet rue the day.

The Josiah Martin plan, proposed in June of 1775 and quickly approved in London, was this: Governor Martin himself would raise an army of 3,000 Scottish Highlander Loyalists who had settled in North Carolina in recent years. Next, British General Thomas Gage up in Boston would send Martin and his Highlanders guns and ammunition. Further, 2,000 troops would be sent southward from Boston, to arrive at Wilmington on the Cape Fear River in February 1776. And, finally, Mother England herself would dispatch a new force of seven army regiments transported in seventy-two ships, the redcoats to be commanded by Lord Charles Cornwallis.

That latter officer and gentleman of course did come to America, together with 2,500 troops—but he wouldn't be arriving quite on time, and even then it would be to join British forces attacking Charleston, South Carolina.

General Gage, on the other hand, was quick to take a small step in fufilling his part of the bargain—by sending two officers, both Highlanders themselves, to help recruit Martin's homegrown army of Carolina Loyalists. Gage's two officers arrived on the scene before the end of July 1775—not all that long after the first fighting of the war had broken out in Massachusetts. Martin, in the meantime, had received London's approval of his plans, along with instructions from Colonial Secretary of State Lord Dartmouth to "lose no time" in recruiting a Loyalist army.

But there, unfortunately for Martin and his allies, was the problem. The Scottish Highlanders at the hub of the plan were not nearly as well disposed toward the Crown as everyone had thought.

It had seemed so made to order, too. The Highlanders, the Irish and fellow backcountry settlers had it in for the haughty planters of the coastal lowlands, didn't they? Weren't they neighbors, friends of the backcountry "Regulators"... in some cases even mixed with that same crowd who fought the lowlanders in the Battle of Alamance Creek back in 1771? And weren't the arrogant planters of that day now, in 1775, the leading rebels of the colony?

All true facts, all logical-seeming expectations, but in the actual event, only about 1,400 Highlanders responded to the royal governor's urgent call, barely 500 of them armed for actual battle. As for the Regulators, 2,000 to 3,000 strong for their crushing defeat at Alamance Creek, it appeared they had no stomach for this fight. Only another 100 or so backcountry settlers joined the Highlanders gathering at Cross Creek. Perhaps such a lukewarm attitude could have been expected, given the fact that William Tryon, Martin's immediate predecessor as royal governor, had led the destruction of the Regulators at Alamance Creek, a debacle followed by the execution of six of their leaders.

Whatever the possibilities, as late as January 1776, Martin expected Cornwallis to be arriving at the mouth of the Cape Fear River, but that also was not to be, since the Cornwallis force at the last moment was directed to Charleston instead.

Under eighty-year-old Brigadier General Donald MacDonald, meanwhile, the Highlander-dominated Loyalists struck out for the coast on February 18 along the south side of the Cape Fear, but they soon were pursued by a Patriot force directed by Colonel James Moore. After some days of near-encounters, the two forces finally met at a bridge on a stream called the Widow Moore's Creek, eighteen miles northwest of Wilmington.

Still plagued by misfortunes or outright miscalculations at nearly every step of the campaign originally envisioned by Royal Governor Martin, the 1,500 Loyalists now lost the services of the elderly MacDonald, who had been rendered ill and exhausted by the tough march. Meanwhile, the Patriots reached the Moore's Creek Bridge on February 26, just hours before the Loyalists camped for the night six miles away.

The Patriots, 600 militiamen under Moore's subordinate Richard Caswell, established their defenses at the swampy bridge site in hopes the Loyalists would be crossing it the next morning. New Loyalist commander Alexander McLeod obliged by deciding the moment had come to face the Patriots in outright battle rather than continue trying to elude them. The die was cast.

Unfortunately for the Loyalists, their hopes of achieving *some* element of surprise meant slogging through unfamiliar swampy terrain in the dark from one o'clock in the morning until dawn. Their stamina already sapped by that struggle, they foolishly mounted an immediate charge against the Patriots holding the primitive span at Moore's Creek.

In the half-light of dawn, they didn't realize the Patriots had removed much of the bridge flooring and greased the narrow supports remaining. Worse, Caswell and his men were waiting with rifles and even two cannon at the ready. Once the deadly fire struck the floundering, exhausted Loyalists, the battle lasted only minutes.

Among the 850 Loyalists taken prisoner was the elderly MacDonald, and among the 30 or so Loyalists killed was his unfortunate successor as commander, Alexander McLeod. The result, for the time being, was Patriot ascendancy in North Carolina, but this was only a beginning to years of bloody civil war among Patriots and Loyalists in both Carolinas. The British, seeing the futility of Martin's scheme of preserving North Carolina as a base for saving the South, now diverted their attention from his Cape Fear region to Charleston to the south.

III. Generally Speaking

Personal Glimpse: Tom Jefferson

THE YOUTH ARRIVING IN COLONIAL Virginia's capital of Williamsburg at the age of seventeen was tall, red-haired, shy of speaking before groups, and even given to occasional stammering.

He was there, in 1760, to begin his studies at the College of William and Mary, and the academic process indeed was one fascination for this truly eager student. Another, however, was the political caldron known as the Virginia House of Burgesses.

Later in life, after he was fully grown to six-feet-two, it would be seen that both centers of interest had left their permanent mark on the youthful Tom Jefferson—he would be founder of the University of Virginia and chief author of the Declaration of Independence.

The teenager from tiny Shadwell in Albemarle County, Virginia, arrived in Williamsburg already well-tutored in Greek, Latin, French, and the classics. At William and Mary, itself tiny by today's standards (only six professors), he quickly fell into the orbit of William Small as his primary instructor.

This perpetually inquiring Scotsman was able to add considerably to Jefferson's knowledge of mathematics and natural philosophy . . . and to become a lifelong friend who, Jefferson once said, "fixed the destinies of my life." Through Small, Jefferson met two more influential figures: his future mentor in the law, George Wythe, and the urbane, highly affable Francis Fauquier.

Ironically, Wythe would later be a signer of Jefferson's Declaration, and Fauquier would fade from the scene as one of Virginia's last royal governors.

It was the privilege of all three older men to dine quite often in the governor's palace with no one else but themselves and the gangling youth from Albemarle County . . . and, to be sure, it was his unusual privilege to be in their company as well.

Also a formative influence for the fast-maturing "Man for all Seasons" was the nearby House of Burgesses, where, it so happened, some of the future nation's Founding Fathers were grappling with the major issues of the day on a frequent, if not a daily, basis . . . and in an open forum that drew the young Jefferson as a spellbound onlooker.

Remaining in Williamsburg off and on for several years, he also could be a college kid. He belonged to a secret society of six students called the "Fat Hat Club." He visited Raleigh Tavern and like watering holes, went on long walks or runs, and attended dances with a young woman named Rebecca Burwell, who later rejected his proposal of marriage.

Aware of the temptations in such an urbane town as Williamsburg, he nicknamed the capital city "Devilsburg."

As another of the young man's early accomplishments, he played the violin, well enough, in fact, to appear in chamber ensembles. He also liked to sing on outings with his college chums, and it goes without saying that he was a spirited, knowledgeable conversationalist.

He completed his undergraduate studies and graduated from William and Mary in 1762. He then began his law studies under Wythe, often traveling the ninety or so miles between Shadwell and Williamsburg, a program he followed until admitted to the bar in 1767. He then practiced law in Williamsburg as well.

In the meantime, since his father had died when Tom was only fourteen, he came into his inheritance at age twenty-one—a legacy that included twenty-five slaves. In 1769, still in his twenties, he began building his villa-like "little mountain" home overlooking Charlottesville, Virginia—the famous Monticello, well known today for its striking architecture and inventive devices designed to improve efficiency.

Seventeen sixty-nine would also be the year that Jefferson became a member of the Virginia House of Burgesses, thus joining the distinguished company that included George Washington, Patrick Henry, Richard Henry Lee, Peyton Randolph, and others who would soon be luminaries of the Revolution. The onetime college kid who would drop in and watch the proceedings of the Burgesses would soon be as well known to the world—and to history—as any of them.

Before traveling to Philadelphia and finding that destiny as a member of the Continental Congress, however, Jefferson took one more major step in his life, as an echo of his college days at Williamsburg. The bride he brought to the one-room structure that was the start of Monticello one wintry night in the early 1770s was Martha Wayles Skelton, the young widow of his college friend Bathurst Skelton.

"Royals" of America

ONE AND ALL, THEY DID their best to stem the tide of revolution engulfing the king's American colonies—their own colonies, you could also say, since they were the king's royal governors: Sir James Wright, Lords Dunmore, Campbell, and Montagu, and even Ben Franklin's illegitimate son, William. If things had only turned out a bit differently, their names might be household words today. New Bern could be capital of North Carolina and Williamsburg capital of Virginia.

Still fairly well known is the name Thomas Gage, legacy of the British general who not only was military governor of Massachusetts, but for a while commander of all British forces in North America. It was Gage, of course, who dispatched from Boston that small yet fateful expedition that ran afoul of the aroused Minutemen at Lexington and Concord in April 1775, with battle—and outright war—quickly ensuing.

Also a soldier and a general was William Tryon, royal governor of not one, but two American colonies—first North Carolina and then New York. In 1771, he led eastern North Carolina's militia to victory in pitched battle against antiestablishment backcountry "Regulators" at Alamance Creek. Transferred to New York soon after, he would spend the better part of the Revolution as a leader of Loyalist raiding parties descending upon Patriot strongholds in New York, New Jersey, and Connecticut.

Another soldierly fire-eater was Virginia's Lord Dunmore (born John Murray), once fondly known by his Old Dominion subjects for his leadership against marauding Indians on the frontier. Taking place before the Revolution, this aggressive activity was called "Dunmore's War." A lavish spender with an eye for the right investment, he later had to flee his former colony after offering freedom to slaves who would fight for the British. He first bombarded Norfolk and fought his former subjects at Great Bridge in a losing battle.

Another who eventually fought his own people was the thirty-four-year-old soldier who succeeded Tryon in North Carolina: Josiah

Martin. But it is Tryon's palace that is a popular, lovingly restored historic site in New Bern today, rather than any major memorials to the obscure Martin. Almost equally—and surprisingly—invisible today are reminders of the American-born William Franklin of New Jersey, who served on the opposite side of his famous father, Benjamin. The same obscurity cloaks John Wentworth, the third New Hampshire Wentworth to serve as royal or lieutenant governor on behalf of the Crown. All three of the foregoing, even the two native-born governors, shared the usual fate of fast-emerging America's royal governors—they eventually had to relinquish their posts and flee their royal capitals.

The Patriots were happy to see them go, while the colonial Loyalists sorely missed their protective influence. As one exception to the rule, however, Lord Montagu of South Carolina turned over his governorship to a successor, stuck loyally with the British throughout the Revolutionary War . . . and yet was destined to be honored in death by a Patriot monument erected at his grave.

Meanwhile, the situation of Georgia's stubborn Sir James Wright offers quite a contrast. Wright was a dedicated man who loyally resisted Patriot pressures for years. While his powers were gradually whittled away, Wright repeatedly begged his superiors in England to send troops, send ships . . . send help! Little did he know that at one point his Patriot enemies had made him the victim of a "disinformation" ploy: a forged letter supposedly sent by Royal Governor Wright to British Vice Admiral Samuel Graves to say *no help needed after all.*

After more than fifteen years of faithful service to the Crown, Sir James finally, in 1776, had to flee his royal seat at Savannah, taking refuge aboard the twenty-gun British warship *Scarborough*—the same vessel, oddly, that would provide New Hampshire's refugee Governor Wentworth his sanctuary as well (different time, different place, of course). Wright would be back for a brief interregnum after the British seized Savannah at the end of 1778, only to abandon their prize in 1782.

In South Carolina, meanwhile, two British lords took turns as royal governor with native-born William Bull II temporarily serving between them as acting governor. To wit: Lord Charles Montagu, leaving the office in 1773, was followed by Lord William Campbell—whose departure months later, in 1775, was somewhat ignominious. After raising Patriot hackles by a series of actions, especially the favoritism he showed toward backcountry Loyalists, Campbell secretly slipped out of his house one night. He crossed his rear garden to a creek where he boarded a small rowboat that carried him quietly along the waterway into Charleston Harbor to the awaiting British sloop-of-war *Tamar.*

His predecessor, Lord Montagu, in the meantime, had not abandoned his own royal governorship all that willingly either. He was forced to resign while on a visit to England—in effect, on a visit to the home office. It seems he was considered a bit incompetent.

Inept or not, Montagu would have the last laugh. Possibly a Patriot sympathizer all along, he now won many a Patriot heart when ordered to recruit both Loyalists and American prisoners for British military units based in the Caribbean and poised for action, if needed, in Central America. The net result was salvation for Patriots who might have died if left aboard foul British prison ships in the Charleston and New York harbors.

After the Revolution, Montagu and many of the onetime Patriot prisoners resettled in Nova Scotia, better known as a sanctuary for dispossessed Loyalists. When Montagu died there in 1784, the Patriots marked his grave with a monument recalling his efforts rescuing so many of them from illness or death aboard the dreaded British prison hulks just a few years before.

How Far Would They Have Gone?

"WHEN HE FELL, LIBERTY WEPT." So wrote Abigail Adams to her husband John in Philadelphia in the immediate aftermath of the Battle of Bunker Hill.

The British had suffered more casualties by far than the Americans, but the Patriot leadership of Massachusetts found one loss especially difficult to bear . . . for Dr. Joseph Warren had been one of their most active, most dedicated, most inspiring leaders from the beginning. Typical of this Patriot propagandist and political organizer, too, he had gone to a hero's death in battle.

Who knows, in that difficult birthing period of a great nation, how far he might have gone in helping to bring Patriot ideals to fruition; what ranking he might have attained in the Pantheon of Founding Fathers?

As in the case of many others who fell before the revolutionary storm, however, the promise of his presence was no longer . . . was gone. Irrevocably. "Not all the havoc and devastation they [the British] have made has wounded me like the death of Warren," lamented Abigail. "We want him in the senate; we want him in his profession; we want him in the field. We mourn for the citizen, the senator, the physician and the warrior."

Only thirty-four (and a widower at that) when he died, Warren had emerged from a Harvard education and brief career as a school-teacher to become a widely respected doctor in Boston in the early 1760s. By the 1770s, he was spending more and more time with the Boston area's Patriot leaders. Among his friends were both John and Samuel Adams, James Otis, John Hancock, and Paul Revere.

After bearing their four children, his wife of just nine years, the former Elizabeth Hooten, died in 1773. By this time, Warren himself was a recognized leader of the Patriot cause in the highly restive Boston area. Indeed, he may have taken part in the Boston Tea Party in late 1773, and it is a matter of record that earlier, both before and after the "Boston Massacre" of 1770, he made speeches protesting the presence of British troops. A leading member of the Committee of Correspondence, he worked with Samuel Adams to communicate with other colonies about the Patriot cause. And it was Doctor Warren, his medical practice all but abandoned, who drafted the Suffolk Resolves that electrified members of the First Continental Congress meeting in Philadelphia in the fall of 1774.

It also was Doctor Warren who sent Paul Revere and William Dawes on their way to Lexington the night of April 18, 1775, to warn that the British would be on the march from Boston that very night.

The next day, he rode to the scenes of battle between the militia and redcoats to treat the wounded—and to help organize harassing militia attacks on the British. It again was Doctor Warren who, as a real propaganda coup, composed a narrative of the events on that fateful April 19, combined it with sworn statements from participants and local newspaper articles, then somehow managed to deliver the entire pro-Patriot package to England for public dissemination two weeks before the official report arrived from British authorities in Boston.

Soon elected president of the Massachusetts Provincial Congress, Warren was at the center of the entire colony's post-Lexington activities and was instrumental in organizing the siege of Boston by an army of New England militia. Although he had no military experience, the Boston physician accepted appointment as a major general of the militia just three days before the Battle of Bunker Hill. He favored that role over a far less risky choice of serving as the besieging army's physician general.

When the British challenged the American occupation of Bunker Hill and adjoining Breed's Hill on the Charlestown peninsula on June 17, 1775, Warren hurried to both battle sites to volunteer his services. He wound up in the American redoubt on Breed's Hill, fighting alongside militiamen of all ranks as the British mounted their three frontal assaults that afternoon. The last march up the hill, ending in hand-to-hand combat, finally carried the day.

Doctor Joseph Warren, among the last to relinquish the redoubt, bleeding from a bayonet wound in one arm, tried to rally his compatriots for yet another stand. Who knows what else he might have accomplished? The fatal bullet took him behind the ear.

As Abigail Adams said, Liberty no doubt wept over this loss especially.

It was the night before Christmas, 1776, that George Washington's good friend Hugh Mercer had his unsettling nightmare of a ferocious bear taking him apart piece by piece. The hulking Scot, himself a bit bear-like, fought off the creature as best he could, but it was too big, too strong, too vicious.

The next night, of course, there was no dreaming—no sleeping—for George Washington's coterie of key officers—nor for the disheartened troops of his crumbling army. Christmas night 1776 was for crossing the icy Delaware, and that following morning of December 26, 1776, for attacking the Hessians at Trenton, New Jersey . . . all of which Hugh Mercer survived despite his ominous dream on Christmas Eve.

He, in fact, had another week of life left to him before he would suffer a succession of bayonet wounds in battle with the British—one vicious thrust after the other, and seven in all, much like the succession of bites by the bear of his nightmare.

Revolutionary America and George Washington lost a good and reliable friend in the death of Hugh Mercer, fifty-one, a Scots Highlander who had emigrated to the colonies some years before the Revolution. Like many another Highlander, he had taken the part of Bonnie Prince Charlie in the revolt of 1745. As a young military doctor he had been present for the Battle of Culloden, a disaster for the Highlanders marked by brutal English use of the bayonet against the Scottish rebels.

The recent graduate of the University of Aberdeen found early use for his medical training—he personally treated many of the bayonet victims before going into hiding from the English as they hunted down the last remnants of the Highlander army.

Mercer, still a very young man, crossed the Atlantic in 1747 to join the frontier settlers of western Pennsylvania. Unlike many of his fellow Highlanders, he ultimately would fight rather than defend the British in colonial America, but first he emerged a steady hand in the French and Indian War of the 1750s . . . on the side of the English. It was during this frontier war that he met and formed a lasting friendship with fellow militia commander George Washington of Virginia.

Mercer moved to Washington's boyhood hometown of Fredericksburg, Virginia, in 1761, after the frontier troubles had died down. Still the eighteenth-century physician, he also shared the operation of an apothecary shop with partners. In 1772, he bought George Washington's boyhood home, the nearby Ferry Farm, from the Virginian himself.

It was only natural that such a good friend and esteemed military veteran would find himself at Washington's side in the Revolutionary War—first in New York, then on the Pennsylvania side of the Delaware River as Christmas approached.

There still was time—brief time—to share in the heady reversal of Patriot fortunes and victory for the Continental Army at Trenton on the morning after Christmas . . . after, of course, crossing the Delaware. Mercer distinguished himself as a steady brigade commander in the defeat of the Hessians at Trenton, then was a wise and able adviser to Washington in the flanking move to Princeton that produced fresh victory for the Americans, this one against the British themselves.

It was at Princeton, however, that these two old compatriots would part company. Mercer's horse was shot in William Clark's orchard outside the college town. Mercer quickly was surrounded by British infantrymen brandishing ugly bayonets. He refused to surrender. They moved in, stabbing. One blade penetrated his body under his sword arm but left only a small wound. Carried to a private home, he told those attempting to treat him that the innocuous-looking wound under his arm would prove to be fatal.

In nine days, on January 12, 1777, he died, despite the care he received at his temporary refuge in the Thomas Clark home. There is no telling what counsel, companionship, or comfort Hugh Mercer might have afforded his old friend George Washington or their still-abirthing nation in the years ahead, given the chance.

Menace to All

THEY TOOK A COW WITH them to supply milk and ducked out of sight for seven weeks. Father, mother, and four children—all six isolated themselves inside a house in Boston. And sick? You bet! The children "puke every morning but after are comfortable," reported the mother.

One unfortunate child didn't respond too well. He had to be inoculated three times before he caught it, broke out in ugly spots, and became delerious from raging fever for two entire days.

Once they experienced—and survived—the preventative "cure," however, the people of the eighteenth century were immune to one of mankind's worst scourges: smallpox. Never mind that the primitive "inoculation" methods of the day made the recipient pretty darn sick (and contagious to others), the cure still was better than catching the disease itself.

For the leaders—and soldiers—of the American Revolution, "the smallpox" was both a deadly threat and a vexing problem. Disease of all kinds was especially common among the young men gathered in military camps, often in unsanitary conditions, after a lifetime spent in isolated rural communities, and thus lacking in immunity. Among the illnesses they now suffered, the dreaded "pox" was a real killer. And if anyone needed convincing, the proof came early in the fighting—smallpox, rather than the British enemy, took the greatest toll among the American rebels sent to attack Quebec in late 1775. Of the eight thousand men sent to fight the British, two thousand contracted smallpox.

All told, more than five thousand were lost to combat, desertion, and disease, but it was the smallpox epidemic that John Adams, for one, bemoaned the loudest. "The smallpox is ten times more terrible than the British, Canadians, and Indians together," he wrote after a visit with still-ill veterans of the Canadian campaign. "The smallpox, the smallpox, what shall we do with it!"

Adams, himself, incidentally, had undergone the risky inoculation procedure earlier—at the hands of Dr. John Warren, the Patriot leader killed at Breed's Hill in June 1775. As future President John Adams asked, his own acquired immunity aside, what were the revolutionary leaders to do?

None other than George Washington—himself the survivor of a teenage bout with the deadly pox—had to grapple with the issue from the day he assumed command of the fledgling Continental Army encamped around British-held Boston in 1775. Indeed, the smallpox incidence in Boston was one reason he held back on storming the city. "If we escape the smallpox in this camp and the country around about," he said at one point, "it will be miraculous."

The miracle he needed, of course, was inoculation preventing onset of the dread disease—but the inoculation method of Washington's day was primitive, dangerous, and most controversial. It was in Boston, in fact, that the famous colonial-era minister Cotton Mather had espoused inoculation as a means of avoiding the smallpox epidemics that repeatedly swept through the American colonies. So controversial was the preventative measure, however, that one critic tossed a bomb through his window, while another set a cooperating physician's house on fire.

All that was during the smallpox epidemic of 1721, which laid low an estimated 5,000 persons and killed 844 of them. Among the 286 who had braved the inoculation method, on the other hand, only 6 died.

The unappealing method of inoculation was to scrape up some pus from the blisters on a smallpox victim and insert the ugly stuff directly into the willing patient's bloodstream, usually through a small cut. The result in most cases would be a mild form of the disease—and afterward, blessed immunity for life!

To some critics, it was a "heathen," unnatural, immoral practice. To some patients, it was dangerous—in the extreme, even a killer. Indeed, there is reason to suspect self-inoculations as a cause of the epidemic among the soldiers engaged in the Canadian campaign of 1775-1776. No surprise, then, that the inoculation's opponents blamed the preventative practice itself for spreading the disease even more widely among the population.

Some colonies had gone so far as to enact laws forbidding the inoculation practice. Marblehead, Massachusetts, had gone through a "smallpox war" on the eve of the Revolution, with townspeople so fearful of the inoculation method that they burned down a smallpox hospital quarantined on an offshore island.

George Washington had insisted on inoculation for his wife, Martha, but as newly named commander of the Continental Army he at first bowed to local bans such as New York's 1747 prohibition of inoculations. From his New York headquarters in May 1776, in fact, he issued a fiat saying, "No person whatever, belonging to the Army, is to be inoculated for the smallpox." He soon followed up with still another, rather violent decree: "Any officer in the Continental Army, who shall suffer himself to be inoculated, will be cashiered and turned out of the Army . . . as an enemy and traitor to his country."

Fortunately for both his army and his future country, Washington reversed himself when in winter quarters at Morristown, New Jersey, just months later. Now on the opposite side of the years-long debate, he ordered wholesale inoculation of his troops. "Finding the smallpox to be spreading much and fearing that no precaution can prevent it from running thro' the whole of our Army," he explained in a letter to army doctor William Shippen Jr., "I have determined that the troops shall be inoculated."

It wouldn't be an easy road to travel, the commander in chief acknowledged. "This Expedient may be attended with some inconveniences and some disadvantages, but yet I trust in its consequences will have the most happy effects."

By now George Washington was so convinced that drastic steps were in order he also said, "we should have more to dread from it [smallpox] than the Sword of the enemy." He urged mass inoculation of his men, to begin "without delay."

Until now, the mortality rate in his army was 160 dead for every 1,000 soldiers. After his fiat of Morristown, however, the Continental Army's mortality rate associated with the ancient disease would drop to an astonishingly low 3 deaths for every 1,000 men.

George Washington had made the right decision, the wise decision, while setting precedence, historically, as instigator of the first command-wide immunization program adopted for military operations in either Europe or North America. Most important, he had guaranteed a pox-free future for many thousands of troops. Just as important, by ensuring his army a healthier future, he had taken a giant step toward final victory in the revolutionary cause itself.

Players for the Crown

AT THE TOP OF THE organizational chart, of course, was the king, George III. But who else were the chief players on behalf of the British in the great drama known as the American Revolution?

Among others, there were:

- William Legge, Second Earl of Dartmouth, philanthropist, evangelical Anglican, secretary of state for the American colonies, and stepbrother of Prime Minister Lord North. Born in 1731, Lord Dartmouth served as first lord of trade under the first Rockingham Administration of 1765–1766. He returned to high government office with the ascension of Lord North in 1770. An early proponent of repealing the hated Stamp Act, Dartmouth also sought means of compromise and reconciliation with Americans while preserving the principles of Parliamentary authority. It was by his instruction to seize rebel leaders in Massachusetts, however, that General Thomas Gage in Boston mounted his flashpoint raid on Lexington and Concord in 1775. Dartmouth didn't feel equipped to oversee the military operations that then erupted and stepped aside late in 1775 in favor of Lord George Germain. All this did not change the decision of officials at an

"Indian school" in Hanover, New Hampshire, who several years beforehand (1769) had renamed their school Dartmouth College in gratitude for his generosity to the school.

- Thomas Gage, born around 1719—general, commander in chief of British forces in North America in 1775—was also governor of the Massachusetts Bay Colony and is best known as the man who ordered the raid on Lexington and Concord. As a boy, he spent eight years at England's Westminster School where he came to know future Revolutionary War figures (all British, of course) John Burgoyne (the later general), George Sackville (the later Lord Germain, secretary of state for American affairs), and the brothers George and Richard Howe (later general and admiral, respectively). Considered too passive (sometimes called George III's "mild general"), he did allow the Colonials the initiative immediately after the war's first shots were fired—they mounted the siege of Boston that forced the British to evacuate the port city in March 1776. In the meantime, Gage was called home in late 1775, never to return to America, even though he was married to an American-born woman. One of his enemies in Lord North's ministry had been Gage's onetime schoolmate Lord Germain, who had been trying to find ways to remove Gage even before Lexington and Concord.

- William Pitt, born in 1708, Second Earl of Chatham, the Great Commoner, so named for his oratory in the House of Commons, was prime minister during the worldwide Seven Years' War. A towering figure in his day, he was in ill health and declining in influence by the time the Revolutionary War broke out. He had struggled into Parliament shortly beforehand to make a dramatic speech calling for repeal of the Stamp Act and had worked closely with Benjamin Franklin in efforts to head off war in the last months of peace. Franklin once called him "that truly great man," while Pitt, for his part, described Franklin as "an Honour, not to the English Nation only, but to Human Nature."

- Frederick North, born in London in 1732, Earl of Guilford, was the prime minister the American rebels loved to hate . . . he, in fact, succeeded to Chancellor of the Exchequer in 1767, upon the death of Charles Townshend, author of the fiercely

despised Townshend Acts. No enthusiast for those particular measures, Lord North nonetheless stood squarely behind them—and behind Parliament's right to impose taxes upon the distant colonists, while also endorsing the dispatch of troops to keep order in Boston. He became prime minister in 1770 and retained that post until 1782. His long stewardship during a stormy period has been credited to his support from King George III, his own abilities as a politician and debater before the House of Commons, his expertise in governmental finances, and a pleasing personality that often disarmed his critics. He would have preferred compromise with the Americans but felt that Britain's own economic well-being would be threatened if the Colonials controlled their own affairs. Once he heard about the Battle of Bunker Hill, however, he told his king that Britain now faced a foreign war. North suffered from bouts of depression that sometimes shut down his leadership activity for weeks at a time. The death of a child and Britain's defeat in the Battle of Saratoga, New York, triggered two such episodes.

- General Sir William Howe came to the Revolutionary War as a professional soldier who had led the way for the British climbing the cliffs of Quebec to the Plains of Abraham above—to achieve victory over the French in 1759. Arriving in Boston at age forty-six, shortly after Lexington-Concord, he was a drinker, a gambler and a womanizer popular with the troops. Whatever his faults, he was a proven and courageous fighter, and most comfortable with light infantry tactics. Soon to be commander of British forces, he was vigorous in confronting the Americans, but would suffer strategically for his habit of delay and regrouping after achieving apparent victory over the rebel forces. His older brother George, incidentally, had been killed in the assault on the French at Quebec ... with the Americans then taking part as allies of the British. Another brother was Sir Richard Howe, admiral of the British fleet sent to quell the American rebellion. *General* Howe returned to England in the spring of 1778, largely to defend his performance in America.

- Arriving in Boston with Howe in 1775, General Sir Henry Clinton was a native New Yorker, born there in 1738 as the son of a royal governor. He was considered a brave and resourceful leader, but lacking in flair and sensitive to criticism. He became senior man in America with Howe's departure but feuded with his subordinate Lord Cornwallis. With the latter at his elbow, Clinton at last succeeded in capturing the key port city of Charleston, South Carolina, in 1780. Leaving Cornwallis to a campaign all his own in the South, Clinton returned to New York. What had upset Clinton with Cornwallis in the first place was the latter's report to Howe of a disparaging remark by Clinton. Although Cornwallis later apologized, Clinton never quite forgave such "tattling."

- A third British general destined to make a name (of sorts) for himself in the rebellious colonies was John ("Gentleman Johnny") Burgoyne, fifty-three years old upon his arrival at Boston in 1775. Known for humane treatment of his troops, he came to America contemptuous of his enemy—yet at Saratoga, New York, in 1777, he would suffer one of Britain's worst defeats of the entire Revolutionary War. Perhaps he still could take some satisfaction from his modest success back home in England as a playwright.

- Lord George Germain, First Viscount Sackville, born in 1716, came to the American Revolution in an administrative role . . . as Lord North's American secretary. He had a strong interest in the military operations of the war, perhaps an echo of his own checkered military past. He had refused an order to attack in the 1759 Battle of Minden, complaining that the order was poorly conceived and that he quite properly delayed. Nonetheless, he was dismissed from the army and court-martialed, with seven of the fifteen judges calling for his execution. He survived that controversy, but his reputation was so damaged that he was kept from any major governmental post until Lord North brought him into the cabinet in 1775 to succeed Lord Dartmouth. In the meantime, a duel with Governor George Johnstone of Pensacola had tended to offset lingering accusations of cowardice at Minden, but not completely. Later, he would be among the scapegoats blamed for the loss of the American colonies.

- No listing of the major British "players" in the Revolution would be complete without prominent mention of Charles Cornwallis, Second Earl and First Marquis of Cornwallis . . . the man forever linked with the British surrender at Yorktown in 1781, the event signaling the final outcome of the war and setting peace talks into motion. Born the last day of 1738 in London's fashionable Grovesnor Square, this Peer of the Realm attended Eton before launching a long army career at the age of eighteen. As a member of the House of Lords, he was sympathetic to colonial pleas—he voted against the infamous Stamp Act. When dispatched to America in 1776, he didn't really think England could win the Revolutionary War. He took part in the failed British assault on Charleston, South Carolina, in June of that year, then participated in the Battles of Long Island, Kip's Bay, White Plains, and Forts Lee and Washington, all significant British victories. Cornwallis then led the chase after the retreating Continentals across New Jersey to the Delaware River. He and Howe had gone into winter quarters in New York when George Washington struck back at Trenton. Days later, Cornwallis allowed Washington to slip away once more and defeat the British at Princeton. Late in 1777, Cornwallis joined Howe in the campaign that resulted in the occupation of Philadelphia. Cornwallis went home for a short respite, returned for the Battle of Monmouth, New Jersey, and the summer campaigns of 1778. He then returned to England—this time to be at the side of his dying wife. Returning to the colonies in mid-1779, Cornwallis convinced Clinton to assault Charleston the next year. With that benchmark victory behind them, Cornwallis launched his Southern campaign, which, unfortunately for all of Britain's players, fetched him up at Yorktown with his back against a river the English fleet could not reach.

George Washington's Day

WITH HIS APPOINTMENT AS COMMANDER of the Continental Army in June of 1775, the master of Mount Vernon was set upon a course that would keep him away for six years, and even a bit more, with no visits home the entire time. For this sacrifice, George Washington would draw no salary.

He didn't exactly live in a pup tent, but he was with his troops in the field at nearly all times. In his first three years as their head, he left them only once for a quick visit and consultation with the Continental Congress in Philadelphia.

With his wife, Martha, only occasionally able to join him, Washington spent most of his days and nights in a dizzying assortment of private homes, and the occasional tavern. And though he did not share a crude log hut with his troops during the harrowing winter spent at Valley Forge, he was on hand in a nearby farmhouse.

As time passed, none could complain that he hung back from the dangers of battle or accuse him of abusing his position of power. He appears to have taken no advantage of the public adulation that was his by the end of the Revolutionary War.

He had left his command role with the Virginia regiment—a creature of the Crown—fifteen years before taking on his leadership role against the Crown. In that interim, he had married the wealthy widow Martha Custis; expanded his inherited Mount Vernon estate on the Potomac River by thousands of acres; acquired another sixty thousand acres of frontier lands; and had become a cattleman and manager of personal timber and fishing ventures. He also owned nearly one hundred slaves (who, in his will, were granted freedom after both he and Martha died).

The prospering gentleman farmer from Mount Vernon, born to relatively humble promise by comparison, also had held a seat in the Virginia House of Burgesses. He enjoyed his pleasures—convivial visits to a tavern for cards or billiards, and his favorite sport, fox hunting.

The Revolutionary War changed all that. After his congressional appointment in June 1775, the forty-three-year-old Washington established a hard-working, no-nonsense daily routine. He slept and worked in his many borrowed headquarters and rarely "left home to go to the office."

He usually rose about five o'clock in the morning and attacked his paperwork alone for three or four hours in whatever room, that served as his personal chamber for the moment. On occasion, he spent his time not merely "in the field," but rather in the woods or fields with the troops, occupying a special tent that has been on view at the National Park Service's Visitor Center at Valley Forge in recent years.

On a typical day, his paperwork stint was followed by exercise and recreation typical of the era—about forty-five minutes riding his horse. Then he had a light breakfast.

Now he was ready for the central business of the day. For the next four or five hours, Washington directed staff meetings, took part in conferences, greeted visiting dignitaries, made plans, decided on crucial issues . . . all the activities of a commander—especially one short on supplies, professional soldiers and, quite often, congressional support.

Then came another core event of the day: Washington's mid-afternoon dinner mess, with his officers, visitors (both military and political), aides, and even visiting officers' wives. He made sure that his younger officers—such as the headquarters' officer of the day—were included on a regular basis.

After this get-together of two hours or so, Washington went back to work until about eight in the evening. He then put aside the papers for a light supper—wine and fruit, it seems—and an evening of relaxation in comfortable company.

This routine, of course, gave way at times to the demands of battle and military campaign. Every once in a while, Washington and his staff would find the time for an outdoor picnic, a ball, a turn at wickets, or a theater outing. Martha was able to join her husband for a few weeks out of the year, usually during the non-campaigning winter months.

On the road six years, through life-and-death peaks and valleys for the struggling new republic . . . what kind of a man could carry such a load for so long?

There were those, to be sure, who called him cold, aloof, and occasionally hot tempered. His longtime aide Alexander Hamilton said that Washington was vain and "neither remarkable for delicacy nor good temper." (But then . . . wasn't it also Hamilton who turned aside Washington's apology after a minor tiff and initiated a transfer out of Washington's headquarters entourage?)

Vain? Perhaps. But perhaps not . . . certainly ambitious and strong of ego. But then, what leader of men isn't? Naturally, Washington had to be tough-minded to order men into battle—into facing death itself—even when the odds appeared to be against them.

He could be tough-minded another way, as well. Almost all who ever knew John André, the captured British spy, whether American or British, considered him a charming, outstanding, and honorable officer who simply carried out his duty to Crown and country as Benedict Arnold's contact with the British hierarchy in New York. But Washington allowed his execution by hanging to go forward with no attempt to stop it. Fortunes of war.

Neither did Washington ask any favors, whine, beg, or plead for mercy when his own fortunes of war were at a terribly low ebb, and his entire army's, as well. After forcing the British to evacuate Boston in 1776—in large part by their own decision against fighting the rebels—Washington, in the summer and fall of 1776, almost managed to lose the war with a series of bad decisions that cost him the Battles of Long Island, White Plains, Fort Washington, and Fort Lee, all within the New York-New Jersey area. Close to year's end, he and a fast-disintegrating army had been forced into Pennsylvania. That, of course, is when the worm turned and struck back—first at Trenton, then at Princeton. From then on, there would still be defeats here and there, but the fortunes of war favored George Washington and his improving army through the lynchpin victory at Yorktown in 1781.

By then, and even before, Washington was being called the Father of His Country—or derivations such as "the first of the Age," or "first Man in this World," according to historian John Ferlin, editor of the book *The World Turned Upside Down*. The famous Marquis de Lafayette went so far as to say that without Washington, "There is nobody who could keep the army and Revolution [going] for six months."

For six years rather than six months, it would be quite a journey, and quite a different life for the master of Mount Vernon. And in the end, say what they would, even his strongest critics could not deny that, at the best and worst of times in the American Revolution, George Washington was always at his post, the epitome of sacrifice and devotion to duty, for more than six years—during which he never paid even an overnight visit to his beloved Mount Vernon plantation on the Potomac.

"A Most Violent Gust"

STORMY WEATHER. DID IT HELP or hinder the Revolution?

Item: fall of 1775. Benedict Arnold's remarkable march through a northern wilderness—now the state of Maine—into Canada. Not only did cold, wintry weather come early that year, but three days of unending rain flooded the Dead River at a critical point in the difficult journey. His boats—bateaux, they called them—were swamped. Men on foot became lost in the flooded landscape.

The column's provisions were in such short supply that Arnold had to plunge ahead of his near-starving men to send back rations. They were so hungry in the interim that they boiled leather moccasins over their campfires to produce a thin soup. They also made a gruel, it is reported, from shaving soap. Thanks to the terrible weather, few game animals were left to provide meat for the six hundred or so men in his column.

Despite all obstacles, Arnold and his tattered column finally emerged on the St. Lawrence River in Canada and prepared to assault Quebec. The British had learned of his approach, however, and were rushing reinforcements from Montreal. Clearly, he should attack right away, before the enemy became too strong. But now a major winter storm struck the area and delayed his crossing for a fateful three days. By then, the British garrison in Quebec had been greatly strengthened. He had to hold back.

Even so, Arnold had reinforcements of his own on the way—a second American column led by General Richard Montgomery, who had taken Montreal, but then lost many of his men to expired enlistments. They simply had turned for home. As a result, he could add only about three hundred men to Arnold's original six hundred. Their combined ranks, ridden by deadly smallpox, were far inferior in number to the British force now quartered behind Quebec's walls. The two American leaders were still resolved to attack, but they would await one necessary ally—a stormy night.

It came the evening of December 30, and the Americans attacked, but Montgomery was killed at the outset, Arnold was wounded, Montgomery's second in command withdrew his men, and many others were captured wandering in confusion on the streets of Quebec. The attack had failed.

In the case of Arnold's expedition into Canada, the cumulative—but obviously random—effect of severe weather was helpful to the British. But there would be much more to the Revolutionary era's "weather story" . . . even if as simply a memorable, awesome phenomenon.

Item: The storm that struck New York City on August 21, 1776, the evening before the British began landing their troops on Long Island, came at sunset and lasted for three hours—a great roiling cloud that swirled round and round above the city spitting endless sheets of rain, bolts of lightning, and crashes of thunder.

"There was no end to the accounts of almost miraculous escapes of the inmates of the houses . . . ," one onlooker recalled.

A soldier walking down the street was struck and, though he displayed no external injuries, was left deaf, dumb, and blind. Three American officers were killed by a single lightning bolt, "the points of their swords melted off, and the coins melted in their pockets," said the same eyewitness. "Their bodies appeared as if they had been roasted."

This same witness also saw ten men from a Connecticut regiment killed in "a single flash" of lightning. They were buried together in a common grave.

Even plainspoken George Washington, preoccupied with the British preparation to land on Long Island the next day—a clear summer day, ironically—conceded that the storm had been "a most violent gust."

But it didn't stop the British from landing, or derail their victory in the Battle of Long Island six days later.

Another storm, though, prevented British ships from sailing up the East River and cutting off Washington's line of retreat by boat from Brooklyn to Manhattan Island.

Other storms and weather phenomena still lay ahead and would have their effects, good and bad, upon the protagonists of the Revolutionary War. What schoolchild, for instance, doesn't know the story of the American army's wintertime withdrawal and sufferings at Valley Forge, Pennsylvania, at the end of 1777? Not so well known is the fact that the winter of 1778–1779, which the Americans spent at nearby Morristown, New Jersey, was far colder. And the fact that a majority of the illnesses suffered at Valley Forge struck, not during the coldest winter months, but during the warming days just before and during the spring of 1778.

The best-known "weather story" of the American Revolution, undoubtedly, is that of the snowy Christmas night of 1776 when George Washington braved the ice floes and freezing temperatures of the Delaware River to mount his early-morning attack upon the Hessians quartered at Trenton, New Jersey. And indeed, who will ever forget the many artistic images of Washington standing stern and brave in his Durham boat as it picks its way across the turbulent river waters?

In another incident, called the Battle of the Clouds, unexpected bad weather saved Washington and his men from possibly over-whelming British attack outside Philadelphia in late 1777. Shortly after the Battle of Brandywine (September 11, 1777), British General Sir William Howe managed to uncover both American flanks with nothing but cliff-like hills behind the Patriot force. A drive on each flank—a double envelopment—would have trapped Washington with the steep South Valley Hills barring any easy retreat to the rear. Fortunately for Washington and his men, Pennsylvania's Chester County experienced a violent storm as a cold front arrived in the wake of hot, heavy weather that afternoon. The clash of weather systems produced a memorable thunder-storm, extremely heavy rain, rivers of mud, and nearly zero visibili-ty for the troops on either side. Just as well, since few weapons would have fired in any case. The British had their bayonets, true, but couldn't organize or see well enough to form battle lines. Saved by the weather, the Americans managed to slip and slide down the far side of the hills and, as the saying goes, perform an orderly withdrawal.

Two more storms late in the Revolutionary War also deserve credit for helping the American side at a critical moment, perhaps even saving the Revolution for the Americans.

October 13, 1781: With Lord Cornwallis besieged at Yorktown, a French and American army at his front, a French fleet at his back, and a dilatory British flotilla preparing to set sail from New York on a possible rescue mission, another violent and freakish storm struck the city and its environs. Savage sheets of hail drove some of the ships aground and two large warships collided. Wrote the fleet's unhappy Rear Admiral Thomas Graves: "Ships have parted their cables, others broke their anchors and three have been driven on shore; I see no end to disappointments."

For this—and a few other reasons—the rescue mission simply did not get started in time to do any good.

At Yorktown, just days later, Lord Cornwallis and his advisers thought they saw a way out of their predicament, even with the Colonials and their French allies drawn up in a ring around Yorktown. Across the York River, at the backs of the British, was another peninsula, with Gloucester Point, Virginia, at its tip. A small French garrison held nearby Gloucester Fort, but could easily be sent packing by a large British contingent . . . such as the entire expeditionary force trapped at Yorktown. Why not remove the British troops from their Yorktown entrenchments at night and secretly ferry them across the York River to Gloucester Point before the morning light would reveal the move to the Americans? Hadn't Washington secretly moved his troops across the East River from Brooklyn to Manhattan in the dead of night after the Battle of Long Island in 1776? He had, and thus had saved his Continental Army to fight another day.

Now, in October 1781, Lord Cornwallis and his advisers formed exactly the same escape plan. On the afternoon of October 16, they placed their sick and wounded in small boats heading across the wide river mouth to the northside shore.

About eleven o'clock that night, a skeletal force of Germans moved into the British trenches while the regular British infantry quietly began boarding the small boats for the river crossing that really counted. The first wave carried a thousand men across. It was a critical moment for the embattled British, but all seemed to be going well. Cornwallis, due to cross the river with the second wave, was busy writing a letter asking Washington to go easy and have mercy on the skeletal force being left behind.

However, as the empty boats of the first wave returned to the Yorktown side, disaster struck. A squall barreled down the waterway, whipping up the normally placid waters into angry waves, blowing two boats full of troops downstream, scattering many others, and lashing the area with hard rain until 2 A.M. As a result, Cornwallis abandoned his escape plan. The next day, in broad daylight and under Allied fire, he brought back the thousand men left stranded on the opposite shore. Wrote the leader of the dragoons Banastre Tarleton later: "Thus expired the last hope of the British army."

Tarleton didn't do so, but he easily could have railed against Mother Nature and her stormy weather as the chief culprits.

Black Faces in the Crowd

A MEMBER OF THE TENTH Virginia Regiment, Shadrack Battles of Albemarle County, Virginia—a carpenter in his civilian life—served his budding country well and with distinction, from the Battles of Brandywine and Germantown, Pennsylvania, in late 1777 to the fighting at Monmouth, New Jersey, and Savannah, Georgia, later on. One of at least five black men from Thomas Jefferson's home county of Albemarle to fight in the Revolutionary War, he took his honorable discharge at Augusta, Georgia. Living into the nineteenth century, he went to court in 1820 to claim his pension . . . but he was so infirm at that point that he had to be carried to the courthouse on a litter. Some researchers, noting the entry "col." in his records, concluded he was a colonel and, thus, the first black officer in the nation's history. Alas, he was only a private in rank—"col." meant "colored" in the parlance of the day, rather than colonel. Still, he was proudly able to say in his pension papers that he served as his commander Clough Shelton's "right hand man."

Always by his master's side, in war and peace—called a servant rather than the slave he really was—Billy Lee was there with George Washington at every step. He served as a personal valet, frequent hunting companion before the revolution, military orderly during the war—however needed. A slaveholder like so many of his fellow Virginia gentry, Washington purchased the then teenage "Billy" from Mrs. John Lee of Westmoreland county in 1768, on the eve of the Revolution. Until Washington's death in 1799, Billy Lee stayed with the commander in chief. In two falls in the 1780s, however, he broke both knees and, now crippled, could no longer travel extensively. He turned to shoemaking at Mount Vernon. When Washington died, Billy Lee was freed in his master's will. The former slave lived until about 1828 and, sadly, in his later years may have become an alcoholic.

The gunfire was just beginning to abate April 19, 1775. Beaten down and bedraggled by their daylong running battle through an aroused colonial countryside, the British troops, who had marched out of Boston to Lexington, Concord, and back, now reached the relative safety of Charlestown Neck. Their angry pursuers— Minutemen, militia, and others who simply picked up their muskets and joined in—wouldn't be able to pursue them into the city streets. Now, after the last flare-up of gunfire, the redcoats saw the rebels rescue a wounded black man—possibly Prince Estabrook of the Lexington Minuteman Company. Estabrook, a slave who volunteered for service, had been on the Lexington Common for the confrontation with the British early that morning. Destined to stay in the fight for freedom to the triumphant end in 1783, he indeed was wounded at some point in the first day's fighting with the British.

Peter Salem, a black American militiaman fighting the Battle of Bunker Hill and Breed's Hill on June 17, 1775, apparently fired the shot that fatally wounded British Marine Major John Pitcairn. Almost exactly two months prior to this battle, on the night of April 18–19, Pitcairn had been in charge of the redcoats who encountered American Minutemen on the Lexington Green and killed eight of them in the Revolutionary War's first eruption of real gunfire.

Jehu Grant, in his own words, "was a slave to Elihu Champlen who resided at Narranganset, Rhode Island," but ran away in August 1777 because he was afraid his master, a Tory, would sell him to the British on nearby ships. His master secretly was supplying the

British with cattle, sheep, cheese, and other farm goods. Grant fled to Danbury, where he joined the Patriot forces as a wagoner. The following June his master tracked him down and demanded his return to Rhode Island—and slavery. Fortunately for Grant, Joshua Swan of Stonington, Connecticut, bought him from Champlen several years after the war and allowed him to work for his freedom. Now located in Milton, Connecticut, with Swan, the newly freed Grant married and fathered six children. In his old age he was denied a war-services pension because he was a runaway slave at the time of his service.

Then there was that true-enough hero of the naval war, James Forten, a powder boy all of fourteen years in age when his American ship, the *Royal Louis,* was forced to surrender to three British warships. When one of the British captains took pity on the young black prisoner and offered him freedom and an education in England if he would forswear his allegiance to the United States, Forten refused. "I was captured fighting for my country," he declared. "I will never be a traitor to her."

Like his fellow captured seamen, he wound up in the British prison ship *New Jersey,* anchored in New York Harbor. There, he lost weight—and his hair—but survived.

Later in life, he stuck by his country once again, albeit under less trying circumstances. Offered the presidency of Liberia in Africa, he said no, he would rather continue being an American citizen.

Riders All

GALLOPING THROUGH THE NIGHT (OR sometimes day), pushing up hill and down dale, disregarding the prickly thorn and whiplash branch, the bent, dedicated figure in the saddle (or some other conveyance) was . . . well, not only Paul Revere, but any one of a small host of Patriots.

And yes, it was often to deliver the familiar message, The British are coming! The British are coming!

Thus, in Virginia one time, it was a young man named Jack Jouett who rode his horse for forty tough, nighttime miles through brake and brush, just in time to alert Governor Thomas Jefferson and permit his narrow escape from Banastre Tarleton's dragoons (but not quite in time to allow Virginia legislator Daniel Boone similar avoidance of the British dragnet).

In the future state of Delaware, Caesar Rodney, a delegate to the Continental Congress, learned in July 1776 that the revolutionary body would be voting the very next day on the proposal to declare the independence of the colonies—in far-off Philadelphia. He had to get to Philadelphia from his home in Dover for that crucial vote! He rode all night, through thunder and lightning, until he reached Philadelphia and its Pennsylvania State House (now Independence Hall) the next morning. He then, without even changing his mud-spattered clothes, joined his fellow delegates in their historic vote for independence.

Another time, it was George Washington's faithful aide-de-camp, Tench Tilghman, who did some hasty traveling . . . but, in his case, with good news! Tilghman, weak from a bout with fever, set out from Virginia to inform the Congress in Philadelphia that the British had surrendered at Yorktown. The difficult trip took the Marylander by boat to Annapolis, then another leg northward by a second boat, then by a relay of horses the final 130 miles to Philadelphia. He left Yorktown on Saturday, October 20, 1781; he endured the grounding of his first watery craft and the temporary becalming of the second; he slogged along muddy roads and managed two river fordings aboard his string of strange horses, all the while shaking off persistent chills, fever, and plain exhaustion. He at last reached the congressional seat of Philadelphia at 3 A.M. on Wednesday, October 24.

In between Rodney's and Tilghman's trips to the original United States capital, a number of women had their own harrowing journeys. Remember Susanna Bolling of Virginia? (That's all right, hardly anyone does today.) At home one day in 1781 when the British came and took over the Bolling house in City Point (today's Hopewell, Virginia) as a headquarters for Lord Cornwallis, the teenager overheard discussion of British plans to surprise the Marquis de

Lafayette and his small Patriot command nearby. Determined to warn the dashing young Frenchman, Susanna slipped away from the family premises that night by way of a tunnel built years before as a safeguard against Indian raids. She emerged on the banks of the Appomattox River and rowed herself across to the opposite shore. She then borrowed a farmer's horse and rode on to Lafayette's head-quarters, where she delivered her warning in person.

In another case, to the north and some time earlier, Lydia Barrington Darragh of Philadelphia tended to eavesdrop on the British officers who were using a room in her house on Second Street for their councils of war. A closet in an adjoining room allowed her to hear the British through its thin walls.

Usually, Lydia, an Irish-born mother of a young American officer on George Washington's staff, sent off her freshly gleaned informa-tion in messages sewn into covered buttons, according to Robert I. Alotta's book, *Philadelphia's American Revolution 1777-1778.*

On the night of December 2, 1777, however, she overheard plans that galvanized her into more direct action. The British were preparing to attack George Washington at nearby Whitemarsh two days later.

The next morning, braving snow, wind, rough country roads—and the ever-present chance of discovery—Mrs. Darragh left her home and walked as far as a Patriot outpost at the junction of the York and Germantown roads, far from downtown Philadelphia. "There she met Lieutenant Colonel Thomas Craig of the Pennsylvania militia, an old family friend . . . [who] was surprised to see her," writes Alotta.

The result? She gave him the information, he rushed off to alert George Washington, and the subsequent British attempt against the Continentals at Whitemarsh failed. Later, a British officer bitterly complained to Lydia Darragh herself, "The enemy had notice of our coming, were prepared for us, and we marched back like a parcel of damned fools."

A female "Jack Jouett" was sixteen-year-old Sybil Ludington, who also rode nearly forty miles over rough roads in Putnam County, New York, the night of April 26, 1777, to warn the American militia that the British were on their way to attack nearby Danbury, Connecticut. The teenager, daughter of militia officer Henry Ludington, volunteered to spread the alarm after a messenger deliv-ered the news to the Ludington home. The messenger and his own horse were too weary to undertake the task of rousing the area militia—yet it would be vital for them in defending Danbury and its Patriot military stores. Since her father had to stay and organize his men, Sybil rode off into the night to alert his outlying militiamen. She returned quite safely early the next day.

In yet another case of a teenage girl taking on a heroic role, Laodicea Langston ("Dicey" for short) heard that the notorious Tory partisan "Bloody Bill" Cunningham was about to descend upon the South Carolina community where her brother, an ardent Patriot, was in hiding. Dicey knew "Bloody Bill's" reputation. Typical was his murder of an ill, bedridden Whig officer named Steadman in the home of Charles Moore (now the Walnut Grove Plantation in the area encompassed by modern Spartanburg County). Not only did Cunningham kill the defenseless Captain Steadman, he shot two friends of the victim when they tried to escape by running from the house.

Dicey Langston wanted no such fate for her brother and his fellow Whigs, so she set out at night from the family's cabin near Traveler's Rest in today's Greenville County. In minutes, she was pushing her way along thickly wooded ground alternating with foot-sucking swampland. Miles later, she came to the Tyger River—its waters high and rushing from recent rains. She struggled across, up to her neck in the turbulent water, pulled herself up the embankment on the far side, then wearily trudged on . . . still in time, fortunately, to warn her brother and his compatriots that Cunningham's "Bloody Scouts" were on the way.

While Paul Revere may deserve every bit of the accolades, the legend, and even the Longfellow poetry associated with his historic ride, it would be no diminution of his achievement to hear an occasional cheer for the Jouetts, Tilghmans, Rodneys, Bollings, and Darraghs, Ludingtons, and Langstons of that time. And, no doubt, for quite a few others long since lost to our historical consciousness.

Personal Glimpse: Phillis Wheatley

WHAT ELSE WOULD JOHN HANCOCK sign, other than the Declaration of Independence? Many other documents and personal papers, to be sure, but few with the poignancy of the signature he (and seventeen additional Massachusetts men of note) attached to a statement of legitimacy contained in a small book of poetry published in 1773.

The book, *Poems on Various Subjects: Religious and Moral,* was written by a frail young woman named Phillis Wheatley.

Arriving in North America at the age of seven, separated at some point from her family, lacking any knowledge of the English language, she had been given a home and a last name by John Wheatley, a wealthy tailor in Boston. She worked for Wheatley's wife, lived in their home, and learned reading and writing in English from their two teenage children. Apart from when the family had guests, she ate with the Wheatleys.

In sixteen months, she conquered English and turned to Latin. She soon began writing poetry—in English. At age fourteen, she published a poem about evangelist George Whitefield that was widely read and well received.

Her health failing, she traveled to England with the Wheatleys' son and daughter and was greeted as a prodigy, striking up a friendship with the Countess of Huntington.

Phillis hurried back to Boston when she heard that Mrs. Wheatley was very ill. The older woman died in March 1774. Four years later, Mr. Wheatley and his only daughter, Mary, also died. The Wheatleys' son, John, had remained in England.

Like the day in 1760 when she had stood on a slavery auction block in Boston Harbor, Phillis was alone again.

But not for long. America's first black poetess of note soon married and bore three children, two of whom died very young. In 1784, she and her third child, an infant, fell ill. They both died.

Phillis Wheatley, born in Africa, survivor of a slave ship, was only thirty-one. Her life had been short, but she had won admiration for her poetic talent on both sides of the Atlantic. When she wrote a

poem for George Washington, he invited her to visit him. She dedicated her 1773 poetry book to her friend the Countess of
Huntington.

Incidentally, John Hancock and his Massachusetts brethren
signed their statement up front in the book to verify before the
world that a young black woman really had written the poetry contained therein.

IV. 1776:
Independence
Declared, Battles
Won & Lost

Stand Forth, Ye Patriot!

TEDDY ROOSEVELT LATER, MUCH LATER, called him "a filthy little atheist." He died a social outcast in the free nation he helped to create. His disinterred bones subsequently disappeared in England, the result of a shoddy court fight over an old enemy's estate.

But once upon a revolutionary time, the restless radical Thomas Paine was the man of the hour, the catalystic pamphleteer whose tract *Common Sense* summed up the grievances of the rebellious American colonies and laid out their future course in burning, idealistic terms.

The sober Virginian George Washington was one who read Paine's prose, pronouncing it "sound doctrine and unanswerable reasoning." Thomas Jefferson read it before settling down to his great work, the Declaration of Independence. Many other Patriots preparing for revolution also read it and applauded.

But the little pamphlet may have had its greatest effect among the people. It was, after all, on its own front cover, "Addressed to the *Inhabitants of America.*" According to various reference works, it appeared either on January 8 or January 10, 1776. The *Pennsylvania Evening Post* dated January 9 referred to its publication and availability for purchase.

No matter what the exact date, the forty-seven-page pamphlet had immediate impact on the seething colonies when it appeared under the imprimatur of Philadelphia printer R. Bell on Third Street.

Sold for two shillings a copy, *Common Sense* achieved an estimated circulation of 120,000 in three months' time, with 500,000 eventually sold altogether.

"In view of the small population of the country at the time, these figures were phenomenal," wrote the late historian and Jeffersonian scholar Dumas Malone in his book *The Story of the Declaration of Independence.*

As for the pamphlet's political effects, Malone called Tom Paine "the most important influence on the public mind" in the early months of 1776. Noting that Paine, a recent arrival from England, served as a catalystic agent for "more cautious minds," Malone added: "The chief significance of this burning pamphlet lay in its call for immediate independence. Paine skillfully marshaled practical arguments but, like most agitators, he minimized difficulties for which responsible leaders had to allow.

"In dealing with the constitutional controversy he may have made no points not already made by James Otis, John Adams, Thomas Jefferson and others; but he went beyond the specific questions at issue to make a powerful attack on monarchy as an institution, the British monarchy in particular, and to set forth in glowing language the virtues of a republic."

Also, according to Malone, "No one until then had so clearly perceived or so strikingly described the historic mission of America as the hope and asylum of free peoples."

And Malone quoted an entire passage:

> O ye that love mankind. Ye that dare oppose not only the tyranny but the tyrant, stand forth! Every spot of the old world is overrun with oppression. Freedom hath been hunted round the globe. Asia and Africa have long expelled her. Europe regards her like a stranger, and England hath given her warning to depart. O receive the fugitive, and prepare in time an asylum for mankind.

Another famous line from *Common Sense* was Paine's declaration, "The sun never shined on a cause more just." He also noted the illogic of an island (England) ruling a continent.

But the restless journalist/political philosopher's best-known single line came later, from his intermittent Crisis reports on the progress of the Revolution itself, reports that were read to the disheartened rebel troops and, allegedly, cheered them despite their physical deprivations. That line, from the first Crisis was, "These are the times that try men's souls."

As it turned out, Paine's own career and fortunes were also trying. Given a Loyalist's farm property at New Rochelle, New York, after the Revolution, Paine spent two frustrating years seeking backing for his dream of constructing iron bridges. Unsuccessful in this country, he returned to his native England, where he was able to see one of his bridges built, but at a financial loss to himself.

Still restless and rebellious, he was also an apostle of the French Revolution. His second major work, *The Rights of Man,* called upon the English people to overthrow their king and establish a republic.

Fortunately, Paine was in France when the exasperated British tried him for treason and made him an outlaw. Like Washington, Hamilton, and James Madison, he had been made a French citizen, and in September 1792, he was elected to the French Convention.

But Paine, during the guillotine's reign of terror, apparently aroused the ire of Robespierre's followers by vainly pleading for King Louis XVI's life. Soon deprived of both his Assembly seat and his new French citizenship, he was thrown into prison. "Poor Paine, outlawed in England, was now arrested in France as an Englishman," adds the *Dictionary of American Biography*.

James Monroe, the new American minister to France, came to his rescue in 1794 by claiming Paine as an American citizen.

While in prison, however, Paine had begun his third major treatise, *The Age of Reason,* which earned him a reputation as an atheist for its attacks upon Christian "mythology." Historians today, however, regard the English Quaker's son as a deist whose unorthodox views scandalized his contemporaries of the eighteenth century.

Late in life, Paine returned to America to spend his last seven years in Bordentown, New Jersey; New York City; and New Rochelle, New York. Always poor, bohemian in dress, a heavy drinker, and intemperate enough to embroil himself in one political controversy after another, he spent those years as a social outcast.

When he died in 1809, "consecrated ground was denied to the infidel," notes the biographical dictionary. So Paine was buried in a corner of his New Rochelle farm.

But not for long. In 1819, an old enemy, William Corbett, wishing to atone for his attacks upon Paine three decades earlier, "had the latter's bones dug up, and took them back to England, intending to raise a great monument to the patriotic author of the *Rights of Man,*" says the biographical dictionary.

"The monument was never erected, and on Corbett's death in 1835, the bones passed into the hands of a receiver in probate.

"The court refused to regard them as an asset, and, with the coffin, they were acquired by a furniture dealer in 1844, at which point they are lost to history."

No Retreat Really Necessary

WITH ITS MIX OF SIEGE, repeated battle, and ferocious civil war, its 137 engagements, its collection of colorful heroes and truly villainous villains, South Carolina was no place for the faint of heart during the American Revolution.

For this is where Banastre Tarleton had his start, where the partisan leaders known as the "Gamecock" and "Swamp Fox" fought and roamed, where "Bloody Bill" Cunningham and the church-burning Major James Wemyss rode the countryside as well.

South Carolina's major city, Charleston, would be one of the last bastions in America for the British, but they paid dearly for the "privilege" of coming and going.

Their first assault on the port city, launched in June 1776, came only as an afterthought and really was aimed at a single island in the harbor rather than Charleston itself. The resulting Battle of Sullivan's Island produced the Palmetto state's first heroes of the Revolution . . . and made the palmetto tree a "hero" of sorts as well.

When General Sir Henry Clinton, Lord Cornwallis, Admiral Sir Peter Parker, and their respective forces came together at the mouth of the Cape Fear River in North Carolina for a major, Loyalist-supported Southern campaign, they saw that the Loyalist masses expected to join them would not be forthcoming after all. The recent Loyalist defeat at Moore's Creek Bridge near Wilmington, North Carolina, had shattered Royalist hopes for a massive backlash against the rebellious Whigs and Patriots.

Rather than leave Southern waters empty-handed, Parker persuaded Clinton to attack Sullivan's Island on the east side of the harbor mouth at Charleston. According to Clinton's memoirs, there was no intention to assault the port city itself. As he stated, neither the time of year nor the limited manpower at his disposal nor his orders would have allowed him to extend such a major effort at that point. But Sullivan's Island and its incomplete Patriot fort looked like easy prey. "Sullivan's Island, if it could be seized without much loss of time, might prove a very important acquisition," Clinton wrote later.

So it was that fifty or more British ships, laden with troops and cannon, appeared off the Charleston bar on June 1. The alarmed Patriots of the city naturally expected Charleston itself would be the British objective. The Continental Army's Major General Charles Lee, British-born and a veteran military professional, had been stunned by the city's incomplete and totally porous defenses. He made clear his total disregard for the attempts by homespun militia Colonel William Moultrie to fortify Sullivan's Island, graphically predicting that it would be a "slaughter pen."

But South Carolina's "president," John Rutledge, wanted the key island defended, and Moultrie apparently had no qualms about facing British guns with his still-incomplete fortress walls of sand and sponge-like palmetto logs. He was also unperturbed at Lee's concern that the island outpost afforded no line of retreat. "For my part," Moultrie later wrote, "I never was uneasy on not having a retreat because I never imagined that the enemy could force me to that necessity."

In the days after the British first appeared on the horizon, Lee fanned feverish efforts to build defenses for the city while Clinton landed hundreds of troops on outlying Long Island, right behind Sullivan's Island. A narrow band of water separated the two and, to the British, looked fordable. As Moultrie well knew, it wasn't . . . and there were not enough boats available for Clinton to attempt an amphibious "leap" to overwhelm Moultrie's own men.

Moultrie naturally stationed a defensive line and a small artillery battery to the rear of his fort and across the water from Long Island to deal with any real threat from that quarter.

When contrary winds at last died down, Admiral Parker sent forward nine of his warships, carrying 270 guns, to bombard the rustic American fort on Sullivan's Island. It now was June 28.

Moultrie's defenders answered with salvos from their own twenty-one guns. The British could fire seven times faster than the Americans, but the American marksmanship was the superior of the two. Meanwhile, Clinton's two thousand troops on Long Island could only watch helplessly as the daylong artillery exchange continued. Instead of eighteen inches deep, Clinton discovered that the channel (called the "Breach") separating him from the back end of Sullivan's Island was seven feet deep—far too deep for soldiers on foot. He tried a landing the morning of June 28 with the few boats he could round up, but Moultrie's rear guard easily drove them off.

As the spectacular cannonades between ships and the fort continued, all Charleston watched from ashore. Recalled Moultrie: "Thousands of our fellow citizens were looking on with anxious hopes and fears."

The booming exchange finally ended about 9:30 that night. In the eerie silence, the dark shapes of the British ships faded away, back to their earlier anchorage three miles toward the sea.

Daylight revealed a battered, but still intact and functioning, fort on Sullivan's Island, with only seventeen Americans killed and twenty more wounded. The British cannonballs had buried themselves in the sandy enclosures or glanced off the soft, absorbent palmetto logs without real penetration. According to a Hessian soldier who took part in the later siege of Charleston, the palmetto logs could not be "razed by any gun on earth. For the point-blank shot of a twenty-four pounder strikes not even two inches into the wood and does no damage other than leaving the impression of the ball."

The fleet, in the meantime, had suffered 64 men killed and 131 more wounded; by various accounts, two of its warships had been crippled, three attempting a flank attack on Sullivan's Island ran aground, with one of them left in such bad shape that the crew set it afire on the twenty-ninth and blew it up.

While the fleet and Clinton's men on Long Island lingered for a few more days, all finally packed up and sailed away, heading back to New York to join General Sir William Howe's operations in the summer and fall of 1776. Charleston had been given a respite from British attack that would last for four years. The heroes of the day were Colonel Moultrie, later to be General Moultrie, and all of his men who stuck to their guns under the terrific British bombardment. One in particular, though, was to be honored by the Charleston citizenry—Sergeant William Jasper of Moultrie's Second Regiment, who left the protective walls of the fort to retrieve the regimental flag after it had been shot away by the British. He then again raised the flag—consisting of a blue field behind the South Carolina crescent—on an artillery sponge staff.

Also honored was Moultrie . . . by having the fort on Sullivan's Island named after him: Fort Moultrie.

Torturous Path to Allegiance

A BRIGHT YOUNG MAN, a real comer in Philadelphia and Pennsylvania politics, was the attorney Joseph Galloway, a great friend of Benjamin Franklin. Born about 1730, Galloway grew up not only to marry the daughter of the Speaker of the Pennsylvania Assembly, but later to become Speaker himself.

He was Franklin's close ally in pre-Revolutionary efforts to turn Pennsylvania from the proprietorship of the Penn family to a royal colony. Taking an Assembly seat in the early 1760s, Galloway soon became a leader in the legislature—during Franklin's lengthy sojourns in England, Speaker Galloway proved an effective leader of the Franklin forces on behalf of their absent mentor. He also was a close friend to his former law student, now royal governor of New Jersey, William Franklin, Ben's son.

Galloway had taken strong exception when mob violence broke out in reaction to the notorious Stamp Act. So strong, in fact, that he gathered an unofficial militia in Philadelphia to quash street demonstrations. But he also was an articulate voice that urged the British to recognize colonial aspirations to a greater role in their own governance.

Therefore, he also would be a leading voice in the newly installed Continental Congress, meeting, it so happened, in his hometown of Philadelphia.

Eventually he would be appointed to the committee struggling to define the rights of the colonies. It followed also that he should remain among the founders of America who were just then emerging in all the political turmoil swirling about on the eve of the Revolution . . . that he should have remained one of them, and yet he did not.

Instead, in just two or three years, he would be a hated Loyalist and "superintendent" of British-occupied Philadelphia. His "Galloway's Police" would be notorious for stifling attempts to send supplies to Washington's starving army at Valley Forge during the winter of 1777–1778.

What had happened? Who now can exactly say? At least part of his change of heart goes back to a single, one-vote defeat in the First Continental Congress.

At issue was Galloway's proposal to ease the cross-Atlantic tensions—a plan, hopefully, to solve the crisis altogether. Called the "Plan of Union," his scheme envisioned an American parliament to balance the traditional Parliament of England. No legislation affecting the colonies could be rammed through either legislative body without the approval of its sister body on the opposite side of the Atlantic. Then, in America, there would be a "president-general" representing the king back in England.

Was this plan so crazy? Well, in the First Congress his proposal, offered on September 28, 1774, failed to clear the neophyte American legislature by just one vote. Later, the British Commonwealth made wide use of a similar dominion status for member states such as Canada.

According to prevailing historical views, the revolutionary momentum had gone too far by the time Galloway tried to find a compromise that would avoid an outright break with the "Mother Country." Indeed, Ben Franklin wrote from England to advise his old political ally and friend that his proposed union could be compared to "coupling and binding together the dead & the living."

One has to wonder how the inner Galloway reacted to that critique, since this hard-driving, obviously ambitious man strikes historians as vain, domineering, and suspicious of conspiracy. And he no doubt held aspirations of obtaining a Speaker-like role in the Continental Congress. Indeed, if his "Plan of Union" had succeeded, it might be Galloway that Americans honor today, rather than Franklin, Jefferson, and their compatriots. In any case, his plan foundered for lack of a single vote, with no minutes available for the congressional debate he triggered, other than personal notes jotted down by John Adams of Massachusetts.

Galloway remained in Patriot ranks for another year or so, but only as a lukewarm adherent—worse, even, than a "sunshine Patriot." He met with his two Franklin friends—father and son—when Ben returned from England in 1775 and, like William, was stunned to hear the elder Franklin say that he now favored a total break with England—that he now was for independence.

The final straw for Joseph Galloway came when the Congress declared independence in July of 1776. At that point, he openly took the British side as an avowed Loyalist.

For his onetime Patriot friends, he proved a spiteful enemy—as an enthusiast of the British occupation of Philadelphia, as the occupied city's so-called superintendent, and as chief of his own anti-Patriot band of "police." He also tried to enlist British support for plots to capture New Jersey's rebel legislators—even the Continental Congress itself—but to no avail in either case. When the British left his hometown in 1778, he, of course, went with them ... he went all the way to England, in fact, leaving behind the bitter comment, "I call this country ungrateful, because I have attempted to save it from the distress it at present feels, and because it has not only rejected my endeavors, but returned me evil for good."

In London, he didn't offer much comfort to his new allies. Testifying before the House of Commons, he asserted that the Revolution could have been nipped in the bud if only Britain's leadership had capitalized upon the deep residue of loyalty still remaining among Americans in 1775. He later wrote pamphlets explaining his views, including his Plan of Union.

He stayed in England, where he died in 1803 at the age of seventy-two or seventy-three—but not before he fought another quarrel, and wrote another pamphlet, because the Loyalist Claims Commission was suspicious of his true sentiments, and only would grant him a much smaller award than the £40,000 claim he submitted for the loss of his properties in America.

Incidentally, the Patriots who took over the country saw fit to restore much of Galloway's confiscated property to his daughter.

Jefferson Writhed

THE DOCUMENT CLEARED COMMITTEE WITH no changes. John Adams and Ben Franklin had already made their suggestions for changes in the draft.

Otherwise, the draft that Thomas Jefferson labored over was intact and still included his passionate antislavery clause when it went before the Continental Congress on June 28, 1776.

Nowadays, the attention is more on the signing and less on how it all came about. Little noted is how Jefferson, at thirty-three one of the youngest and most silent delegates to Congress, came to be on the Committee of Five; how he, instead of the better-known Adams or Franklin, came to be the author; how Congress, in two and a half days of often acrimonious debate, cut and added to the famous document, while Jefferson sat by "writhing" at what he later called "the depredations" and "mutilations" his fellow Patriots wrought.

Today, the Declaration of Independence stands as the nation's lofty covenant, as one of humankind's greatest statements, with Jefferson its renowned author. But the details of how this came to pass are less clear—the chain of events, the near chance that placed the pen in Jefferson's hand and the textual changes ordered by Congress. Less clear, too, are the discrepancies, ironies, and small mysteries that still cloud our knowledge of the document's adoption in the Pennsylvania colony's statehouse—known as Independence Hall—at Philadelphia in 1776.

Of course, the colonial delegates had gathered there in response to the revolutionary movement that culminated in armed battle between British troops and American colonists the year before. By 1776, the momentum of events was leading inexorably toward independence, but not without reluctance, and even opposition, by some of the Patriot leaders.

In quick order, Virginia in May of 1776 adopted and sent the Continental Congress a resolution of independence—a simple but drastic statement "dissolving" the colonial ties to England. Virginia's aristocratic Richard Henry Lee, widely considered second only to Patrick Henry as an impassioned orator, presented it to the Philadelphia gathering on June 7. After two days of debate, however, the leaders of the independence movement at Philadelphia postponed a vote on the measure. Support from some of the colonies still was too soft for a unanimous vote. The same Continental Congress, after all, only the year before had reaffirmed colonial allegiance to the British Crown.

However, Congress agreed to appoint three committees with tasks based on the premise that the proposed break with England would be adopted. One committee was assigned to draw up articles of confederation, the first step toward a U.S. Constitution. Another began consideration of foreign alliances and treaties. The third com-

mittee was charged with drafting a declaration explaining and justi-
fying the independence resolution.

That resolution did come before the entire Congress in time,
was debated hotly, and was adopted on July 2, a profound step that
initially led some of those present, notably John Adams, to consider
that date as America's Independence Day.

Yet, there also was the matter of the statement to the world, the
indictments to present against King George III, grave commitments
to be made toward a new course of government, to human equality
and liberty—the draft entrusted to the third committee earlier.

Enter Jefferson, who came to that committee by a combination
of what might be called destiny and chance. Here he was, fair, sandy-
haired, a product of the Virginia Colony's free-spirited frontier, yet a
member of the landed gentry, a gentleman and a scholar imbued
with the ideals and scientific logic of the Enlightenment. You could
also call him a New World Leonardo da Vinci, already engaged in his
lifelong project of building and rebuilding the home known as
Monticello at Charlottesville.

A slaveowner, paradoxically enough, he had been a member of
Virginia's rebellious House of Burgesses since 1769 and was associated with that body's most radical, liberty-loving group.

Unlike his Virginia colleagues Patrick Henry and Richard Henry
Lee, however, Jefferson never was a speaker. John Adams later said,
"During the whole time I sat with him in Congress, I never heard
him utter three sentences together."

But Adams also noted that Jefferson joined the colonial gatherings at Philadelphia in 1775 and 1776 with a reputation for a "pecu-
liar felicity of expression."

One reason for that reputation was Jefferson's *A Summary View
of the Rights of British America* of 1774, a 6,500-word treatise in
which he strongly asserted colonial America's right to self-govern-
ment and disputed Parliament's legislative authority over the
colonies but did not go so far as to challenge British sovereignty.

If, as most historians agree, the revolutionary leaders wanted a
Virginian at the forefront just now, Lee, after all, was the ranking
member of the Virginia delegation to the Congress. But he wasn't
entirely popular, and there was the possibility he would be returning to Virginia because of a family illness.

Here is what Adams recalled of Jefferson's selection: "Mr. Richard
Henry Lee was not beloved by the most of his colleagues from

Virginia, and Mr. Jefferson was set up to rival and supplant him. This could be done only by the pen, for Mr. Jefferson could stand no competition with him [Lee] or anyone else in elocution and public debate."

It also happened that the influential Adams liked Jefferson personally. To wit: "Though a silent member in Congress, he was so prompt, frank, explicit and decisive upon committees and in conversation, not even Sam Adams was more so, that he soon seized upon my heart, and upon this occasion I gave him my vote and did all in my power to procure the votes of others. I think he had one more vote than any other, and that placed him at the head of the committee. I had the next highest number and that placed me second."

Now, with the committee's membership established, came the question of drafting. In his own autobiography, Jefferson gives a simple account of his selection for that task. "The committee for drawing a Declaration of Independence desired me to do it. It was accordingly done, and being approved by them, I reported it to the House on Friday the 28th of June, when it was read, and ordered to lie on the table."

Adams, however, presents a more complex view in dialogue form. "Jefferson proposed to me to make the draught. I said I will not; you shall do it. Oh No! Why will you not? You ought to do it. I will not. Why? Reasons enough. What can be your reasons? Reason first. You are a Virginian and Virginia ought to appear at the head of this business. Reason second. I am obnoxious, suspected and unpopular. You are very much otherwise. Reason third. You can write ten times better than I can. 'Well,' said Jefferson, 'if you are decided I will do as well as I can.'"

By most accounts, Jefferson wrote in the evenings at his lodgings in the home of Philadelphia bricklayer Jacob Graff, a brick home reconstructed in recent years by the National Park Service as a historic site. He wrote his draft, or drafts, there—no one today is sure how many there were—in the second-floor parlor. He wrote on a portable writing desk of his own design.

In all, seventeen days passed from the start of his assignment to the draft's submission to Congress. Again, we don't know how long it took Jefferson to produce his first version, but Adams once said it was done in only two days.

Jefferson then apparently took it to Adams and Franklin for their suggestions. He recalled their "alterations" as two or three only, and "merely verbal." But historians examining the notes and papers of all three historic figures, as well as the rough draft now housed in the Library of Congress, say Adams made two changes and Franklin five.

At some point before Jefferson presented his text to the full committee, also including Roger Sherman of Connecticut and Robert Livingston of New York, his phrase "sacred & undeniable" in the second paragraph was improved to read "We hold these truths to be self-evident." The change on the rough draft appears to be in Franklin's handwriting. In any case, debate on the declaration awaited disposition of Virginia's resolution of independence. That proposal had been introduced on June 7, was debated June 8–10, then held over until the first days of July.

Jefferson explained: "It appearing in the course of these debates, that the colonies of New York, New Jersey, Pennsylvania, Delaware, Maryland and South Carolina were not yet matured for falling from the parent stem, but that they were fast advancing to that state, it was thought prudent to wait a while for them."

A united decision for independence had been shrouded in doubt from the outset.

"Majorities were constantly against it," Adams later wrote. But the momentum was building.

In one major development often cited by Adams, Joseph Hewes of North Carolina, an influential opponent of the proposed breach with England, suddenly and dramatically was converted to the cause by evidence of popular opinion among his own constituents. Adams tells the dramatic tale: "Mr. Hewes, who had hitherto constantly voted against it, started suddenly upright, and lifting up both hands to Heaven, as if he had been in a trance, cried out 'It is done! and I will abide by it.'"

In the end, twelve of the thirteen colonial delegations voted for Virginia's severance measure on July 2. The thirteenth, New York, abstained, because its delegation lacked recent instructions from home, but later did join in the action.

And now, finally, on the same day, the colonists took up Jefferson's declaration in a debate that would last two and a half days, until the evening of July 4. By his own admission, Jefferson "writhed" under the criticism and the debate over one change or another. But he sat quietly, and contented himself by taking notes.

During the same period, he bought his wife seven pairs of

gloves and, on July 4 itself, took the temperature of Philadelphia with a new thermometer. Carefully noted, his findings were: "A low 68 degrees at 6 A.M. to a high of 76 at 1 P.M.," a cool day for early July.

Meanwhile, blunt John Adams carried the defense for the 1,800-word original text on the floor—"fighting fearlessly for every word," as Jefferson gratefully acknowledged later.

While debate still raged, Ben Franklin allegedly told the suffering author a story about a hatmaker who asked his friends to edit a sign announcing his hattery. By the time they finished expunging one word after another as superfluous, only the hatter's name and the picture of a hat were left.

An amusing story, but probably of little comfort to Jefferson, whose text suffered some 80 changes and lost 460 words from his start to the finish by Congress. In the opinion of most scholars, however, Congress largely improved Jefferson's great document.

Still controversial in that respect, of course, is the most famous deletion of all, Jefferson's impassioned, somewhat wordy clause that accused George III of waging "cruel war against human nature itself" by sanctioning the slave trade. The problem was with the colonial role in the same trade and enslavement of human beings. Many of the delegates felt that such a hypocritical posture would undermine the remainder of the document. Others simply were unwilling to indict slavery itself.

As Jefferson said in his autobiography: "The clause . . . reprobating the enslaving [of] the inhabitants of Africa, was struck out in complaisance to South Carolina and Georgia, who had never attempted to restrain the importation of slaves, and who, on the contrary, still wished to continue it. Our Northern brethren also, I believe, felt a little tender under those censures; for though their people had very few slaves themselves, yet they had been pretty considerable carriers of them to others."

There were other changes, too. Congress added the text of its July 2 resolution of independence to Jefferson's prose. In deference to American Scotsmen, it struck a reference to Scottish mercenaries, and it toned down censures of the British people and Parliament.

Most of the revisions were matters of style or wording, however. The delegates hardly touched Jefferson's opening two paragraphs, the historic words that established the elevated tone of the entire document. They left the rhythmic drumbeat of his indictments against King George III largely intact. They apparently dared not alter his ringing close:"... we mutually pledge to each other our lives, our fortunes and our sacred honor."

Despite all the changes, said Jeffersonian scholar Merrill Peterson,"in no way had Congress diminished Jefferson's authorship of it."

So it was, late on July 4, 1776, that bells rang out—Congress had adopted a most startling and historic document, then styled, "a Declaration by the Representatives of the United States of America in general Congress assembled."

While Jefferson subsequently said a draft was signed by all present modern historians say his memory on that point was faulty. Later, the declaration, with its title somewhat amended, would be engrossed in official parchment form for the historic signatures we know today. The Declaration of Independence!

But first, on July 4, John Hancock, as president of Congress, placed his you-know-what on the adopted draft. And that very night, it went to the printer.

Time Out for Another War

South Carolina Gazette, July 1776: "We have certain accounts of the Cherokees having killed several white people, and taken some prisoners ..." So began another war within the war, this one against the Cherokee Nation and certain British instigators.

From the South Tyger River, at a spot near today's boundary between Spartanburg and Greenville Counties, came word, all too typical, of the Hampton family massacre—husband, wife, son, and infant grandson all killed on their farm, their house burned down, too. Away at the time was Revolutionary War hero Wade Hampton I, whose grandson by the same name would be a stellar Confederate general in another American war.

Wade I thus survived, but all up and down the backcountry of the Carolinas, even along the Georgia and Virginia frontierlands, the Cherokees were on the warpath the summer of 1776. Resentful of aggressive white settlement of the country they once roamed at will, the Indians were easily persuaded by the British to strike out at the "Up Country" settlers. While small bands might attack a single farm home, larger groups picked bigger targets. In one such case, two hundred war-painted warriors mounted an assault upon Patriot Fort Lyndley in today's Laurens County . . . and half or more of the "Indians" turned out to be white Loyalists posing as Cherokee braves.

In other areas, however, white Loyalists volunteered to serve with their Patriot brothers in a common war against the Indian predators. Settlers of all political persuasions had good reason to fear for their future safety—in South Carolina, reported Nat and Sam Hilborn in their book *Battleground of Freedom: South Carolina in the Revolution,* many abandoned their hard-won homesteads to take refuge in old stockade forts. "Plantations lie desolate, and hopeful crops are going to ruin," said one South Carolina settler. Further, ". . . unless we get some relief, famine will overspread our beautiful country."

Well, relief soon was on the way. By the end of July, South Carolina militia Major Andrew Williamson had gathered a force 1,200 strong to march against the Cherokees . . . but he then, with 350 men at his side, marched into an Indian ambush at Essenecca, or Old Seneca Town, close to the only fordable point on the Keowee River (now, at that location, the Seneca). His men scattered in confusion when the gunfire erupted in the dark. Williamson's horse went down and so did the major's compatriot alongside, Francis Salvador. Shot in the body and leg, Salvador fell among some bushes, out of sight from his fellow South Carolinians—but not from the Indians, who found and scalped him on the spot.

A friend had seen a human figure bending over the spot where Salvador disappeared in the dark and thought it was someone helping him. More likely, he later realized, it was an Indian scalping the wounded man.

Largely hidden behind a fence and in nearby houses, the large party of Indians had every advantage in the nighttime fight . . . until one officer, Lieutenant Colonel LeRoy Hammond, "saved the day by rallying a party of about twenty men who marched right up to the fence where the heaviest fire originated," reported the Hilborn book. "Shooting directly through the fence, Hammond's men then leaped over and charged the enemy. The Indians were so surprised at this unexpected attack that they immediately turned and fled through the darkness for the safety of the deep forests."

The ambush at Seneca Old Town (today the home of Clemson University) was only a temporary setback for the aroused colonists. First destroying that Indian town, Williamson and his militiamen in the next few weeks swept "relentlessly . . . through the mountain valleys, destroying all the Lower Towns of the Cherokee Nation that lay in their path." The settlers offered little mercy. "Their savagery matched that of the Indians as they burned, plundered, slaughtered, and destroyed."

By now, militiamen from Georgia, Virginia, and North Carolina also had joined the fight against the Cherokees. Returning from his first Cherokee foray, east of the Blue Ridge, Williamson soon amassed a force of two thousand for a late summer drive against Cherokee villages throughout the southern Appalachians, "butchering the animals and destroying the crops of the shattered Cherokee Nation." Finally, the Cherokees gave in and agreed to peace talks—which led in 1777 to a treaty by which the defeated Indians ceded immense chunks of their land and could "inhabit only a very small corner of the state."

Additional notes: Two and three years later, Patriot forces in the North turned to war against Indians after intolerable deprivations along the frontier, a result of British encouragement that could be traced across the Atlantic to Lord George Germain, Secretary of State for American affairs in London. Blame lay also with his Loyalist allies, as noted by Willard M. Wallace in his 1951 book *Appeal to Arms: A Military History of the American Revolution.* Said Wallace:

"Colonel John Butler; his spectacular and even bloodier-minded son, Walter; Sir John Johnson, and the great [Mohawk Leader Joseph] Brant kept western New York in a frenzy of terror. In July, 1778, Sir John Butler struck at the Wyoming Valley in Pennsylvania, which was largely settled by people from Connecticut. Hundreds perished in a dreadful massacre and the subsequent flight. Shrieking in anguish, men were burned at the stake and others roasted over live coals and kept pinned down by pitchforks while their horrified families looked helplessly on. Still others were arranged in a circle while a ghastly half-breed squaw, Queen Esther, chanting a wild hymn of triumph, chopped off their heads."

Another massacre of men, women, and children accompanied a strike by Brant and Walter Butler in New York's Cherry Valley on November 10. In response to such outrages, the settlers vowed total destruction of their Indian nemisis, with General John Sullivan appointed to command an expedition of nearly five thousand men in 1779 to do just that—destroy the Indian. He never did reach Fort Niagara, described by historian Wallace as "the springboard for these raids," but one column, under Sullivan himself, cleared out the Susquehanna River corridor upstream from Wyoming, while a second column, led by General James Clinton and moving up the Mohawk Valley, burned out fourteen Indian villages before linking up with Sullivan at Tioga Point. That was on August 22—a week later, the Sullivan forces decisively defeated some 1,500 Indians and Loyalists, including Brant, the two Butlers, and Johnson, at a site near today's Elmira, New York.

Overall during the punitive Sullivan campaign, "forty towns were destroyed, some of them consisting of more than one hundred houses." His men also destroyed Indian crops, granaries, and even fruit trees. As a result, "In the succeeding winter, one so severe that New York harbor froze over, hundreds of Indian families starved to death."

In the meantime, another expeditionary force—six hundred men led by Colonel Daniel Brodhead—had "devastated" Seneca Indian towns and crops in the Allegheny River Valley upstream from Pittsburgh. "This attack from the west diverted the attention of many Indians who would otherwise have joined against Sullivan."

Not that the Indian wars were all over—there still remained a good many more fights along the frontier, north and south, before the Revolutionary War was over, to say nothing of the continued friction as young America then pushed ever westward over the next century, into more and more Indian lands.

They Signed

WHEN THEY MUTUALLY PLEDGED TO each other their lives, their fortunes and their "sacred honor," they knew this was serious business. This was treason, and they had signed the document that would convict them before all of mankind. No doubt about it, lives, fortunes, and honor surely were at stake.

With the Revolution quashed and British law reinstituted, the supreme penalty for such traitors very well could be hanging. Long attributed to Benjamin Franklin is the possibly apocryphal statement, "Indeed, we must all hang together, otherwise we shall most assuredly hang separately."

Whether he actually made the remark is doubted today, since it didn't appear in print until fifty or so years after his death. But the signers, well aware of the risks they ran, undoubtedly engaged in some sort of wry gallows humor to relieve tensions. They knew there was reason for fear. Rhode Island's sixty-nine-year-old Stephen Hopkins supposedly signed the great document with the comment, "My hand trembles, but my heart does not."

As events turned out, none of the fifty-six actually would be hanged, but virtually all would be hunted by the British, fortunes indeed would be lost, family members would be hounded, incredible sacrifices would be made, various sudden deaths would thin the ranks before war's end . . . but not one of the fifty-six ever went back on his signature, on his pledge of sacred honor.

The first to sign the Declaration of Independence, as is well known, was wealthy John Hancock of Massachusetts, president of the Continental Congress when it adopted the Declaration on July 4, 1776. He affixed his large and bold signature then and there—and may or may not have said he did it in large enough letters for "John Bull" to read without recourse to spectacles.

The largest group of signers then added their signatures to the officially engrossed copy of the Declaration on August 2, 1776. Thus, not all who actually voted for independence on July 4 became signers, and not all who signed on August 2 (or even later) had been present for the vote of July 4. For one reason or another, changes in personnel had taken place.

The very last to sign apparently was Thomas McKean of the future state of Delaware. He did take part in the vote for independence, but just *when* he signed the document itself remains open to question. Living to the age of eighty-three, and at one point serving as governor of Pennsylvania, he later insisted he signed in 1776, but his signature was missing from the printed copy that Congress authenticated on January 17, 1777. That means he must have signed at a later date.

Like McKean, many of the signers were lawyers, but many of those doubled, in the South anyway, as planters. The group also included four physicians, a number of merchants, several farmers, a manufacturer or two ... and a college president who was the group's only clergyman—John Witherspoon, president of the College of New Jersey (the future Princeton University). The youngest signers were George Walton of Georgia and Edward Rutledge of South Carolina, both only twenty-six, and the oldest was Ben Franklin at seventy.

While there were men of simple rural lives and small means, the signers risking lives and fortunes also could count some of America's weathiest men in their ranks. In addition to Hancock, these would include Robert Morris of Pennsylvania, Philip Livingston of New York, Charles Carroll of Maryland, and Arthur Middleton of South Carolina.

Among the other signers were Pennsylvania's Dr. Benjamin Rush, famous in his day as an outstanding physician and lecturer in medicine, and New Jersey's Francis Hopkinson, the multitalented man often credited with designing the future American flag (rather than Betsy Ross).

The respective state delegations making up the Continental Congress voted under the unit rule—one vote to a delegation, no matter how many members. Thus, some states could claim many more signers than others. Pennsylvania, both for its large population and as the site where the Congress met, could boast the largest number of signers with nine, while more rural, less populated states such as North Carolina, New Hampshire, or Georgia, could claim only three each.

On a more individual basis, if no signer ever disavowed the Declaration, ever recanted his pledge to "sacred honor," what about lives and fortunes? Here, the news was not always so good.

The first of them to die was Pennsylvania's John Morton, only about fifty-three, a farmer from today's Chester County in Delaware. A member of the rebel Provincial Congress of Pennsylvania, then a delegate to the First and Second Continental Congresses, he was a swing vote within the Pennsylvania delegation for independence. At home, though, most of his neighbors and friends were avowed Tories who let him know of their disenchantment with his stand. On his deathbed in April of 1777, less than a year after signing the Declaration, he supposedly said: "Tell them that they will live to see the hour, when they shall acknowledge it to have been the most glorious service that I ever rendered my country."

Also in 1777, Georgia's Button Gwinnett died of wounds suffered in a duel with a political enemy back home.

Pure chance would add to the woes of the Patriot Lynch family from South Carolina. Only twenty-seven, rice planter Thomas Lynch Jr. had replaced his father, Thomas Senior, as a delegate to the Congress that summer of 1776 because the older Lynch had been incapacitated by a stroke. Thus, by accident, the younger Lynch became a signer. But he himself was in frail health, the result of a bilious fever contracted in 1775. He and his father left Philadelphia shortly after the August signing of the Declaration, and the elder Lynch died on the way home. Three years later, Thomas Junior's own health had worsened, due in part to his activity as a militia officer. Advised to take time out to save his own life, he and his wife, the former Elizabeth Shubrick, set sail for the West Indies as the first leg of a projected trip to southern France. Their ship disappeared at sea, never to be heard from again.

Many others who signed the document survived both the war and the vicissitudes of eighteenth-century life, but suffered a variety of woes. The wealthy merchant Robert Morris of Pennsylvania, often called "The Financier of the Revolution" for all his contributions to the cause, wound up in debtors prison before his death in obscurity three decades after he signed. George Wythe of Virginia, Thomas Jefferson's great friend and tutor in the law, was destined to become a murder victim—poisoned by an impatient heir, his own grand-nephew.

But those were outcomes unrelated to the revolutionary cause. The real story here is the fierce, unrelenting punishment the British imposed during the war upon a startling number of the signers. In

South Carolina, the state's three remaining signers, Edward Rutledge, Arthur Middleton, and Thomas Heyward, were actually captured by the British with the fall of Charleston in 1780 and imprisoned for months in St. Augustine, Florida.

Many others up and down the eastern seaboard were hunted with vengeance. In Virginia, outgoing governor Thomas Jefferson barely eluded a British raiding party led by "Bloody Ban" Banastre Tarleton in 1781. Even when the signers escaped capture, however, their families often suffered, and their homes and other properties were deliberately devastated. According to a detailed compilation by Rush H. Limbaugh Jr. (made famous by his son, the radio personality Rush Limbaugh), that was the fate of the extensive lands owned by the three South Carolina captives.

But there was worse. New Jersey's Judge Richard Stockton, hiding out at a friend's home with his family "was pulled from bed in the night and brutally beaten by the arresting soldiers."

Wrote the elder Limbaugh: "Thrown into a common jail, he was deliberately starved. Congress finally arranged for Stockton's parole, but his health was ruined. The judge was released as an invalid, when he could no longer harm the British cause. He returned home to fnd his estate looted and did not live to see the triumph of the Revolution. His family was forced to live off charity."

No better was the fate of his fellow signer from New Jersey, John Hart. Trying to visit his dying wife, he had to flee pursuing Hessian troops. "While his wife lay on her deathbed, the soldiers ruined his farm and wrecked his homestead. Hart, sixty-five, slept in caves and woods as he was hunted across the countryside. When at long last, emaciated by hardship, he was able to sneak home, he found his wife had already been buried, and his thirteen children taken away. He never saw them again. He died a broken man in 1779, without ever finding his family."

Perhaps the most tragic case the elder Limbaugh researched was that of still another New Jersey signer, Abraham Clark. Again in Limbaugh's words: "He gave two sons to the officer corps in the Revolutionary Army. They were captured and sent to that infamous British prison hulk afloat in New York harbor known as the hell ship *Jersey.* The younger Clarks were treated with a special brutality because of their father. One was put in solitary and given no food. With the end almost in sight, with the war almost won, no one could have blamed Abraham Clark for acceding to the British request when they offered him his sons' lives if he would recant and come out for the King and parliament."

But Abraham Clark answered their request with a heartbreaking no.

Another signer who had to make a sacrificial choice was Virginia's Thomas Nelson Jr. of Yorktown, who succeeded Thomas Jefferson as governor of Virginia in 1781 and doubled as commander of the state's militia. Present for the Siege of Yorktown, it is said, he told his compatriots to go ahead and fire upon his own handsome home of brick, which unfortunately had been taken over by Lord Cornwallis as his own quarters. The Americans did fire upon the Nelson house—cannonballs can still be seen today in one of its brick walls. The once healthy and wealthy shipper-planter Nelson died in near-poverty seven years later of asthma.

In some cases, spouses were subjected to the vengeance of the British. New York's Francis Lewis escaped harm himself, but his Long Island home was burned down by the British and his wife, Elizabeth, was made a prisoner. Her early death was blamed in large part on the deprivations she suffered as a prisoner. Her husband, his personal wealth undermined by the Revolution, lived to nearly ninety and is buried in an unmarked grave at Trinity Church at the top of Wall Street in Manhattan. (Incidentally, the last of all the signers to die was Maryland's Charles Carroll, one of the richest men in America . . . and the only Catholic signer. He passed away in 1832 at the age of ninety-five.)

Overall, four signers apparently died of Revolutionary War–related causes; another five were captured; nine endured British-inspired damage or destruction of their homes; and several lost their fortunes or family members . . . sometimes both.

Their future nation, their states, their own localities, though, would respond to their leadership in very tangible ways—two signers were elected president of the new nation (Jefferson and John Adams); three (Eldridge Gerry, Jefferson, and John Adams) would serve as vice president; at least seven became governors, and several were destined to serve as U.S. senators or congressmen under the Constitution that a handful of the signers themselves helped to frame at the Constitutional Convention of 1787.

More important, for all the pain and hardship visited upon them, the fifty-six signers gave the future nation an example of undeviating loyalty to the ideal at the very root of the entire revolutionary movement—freedom.

Additional notes: Connecticut's Roger Sherman served on the committee that produced the draft Declaration, was a delegate to the Constitutional Convention, then served in both the newly created House of Representatives and Senate. His Connecticut ally William Williams not only fought the British with his state's militia, but contributed his own funds to the Revolutionary cause. Also from Connecticut, Oliver Wolcott commanded fourteen militia regiments, took part in the victory at Saratoga, New York, and later served as governor of his state. So did Samuel Huntington, who first would serve a term as president of the Continental Congress itself.

Rhode Island's William Ellery, meanwhile, was another signer who saw the British destroy his home.

One of the four doctors affixing their signatures to the document was New Hampshire's Josiah Bartlett, later to be his state's first governor under the new U.S. Constitution. His New Hampshire ally William Whipple served their people as a militia brigadier general leading a brigade at Saratoga.

From Massachusetts came Eldridge Gerry, destined to become vice president under James Madison and to die in that office after serving as governor of his state, too. His is the name associated with voting districts deliberately distorted for political reasons—or *gerrymandered.* The Bay State also contributed both John Adams, first vice president and second U.S. president, and the longtime Revolutionary advocate Samuel Adams.

Meanwhile, New York's William Floyd, commander of the militia in Long Island's Suffolk County, had to stay away from his mansion and estate for seven years—while the British occupied them.

Maryland's Samuel Chase later would serve on the U.S. Supreme Court, while William Paca became governor of Maryland in 1782. Virginia's Richard Henry Lee, who introduced the resolution calling for independence, later served as Virginia's first U.S. senator under the new Constitution (which he had opposed, incidentally). Also from Virginia, future governor Benjamin Harrison would become famous as the father of one president (William Henry Harrison) and the great-grandfather of another (Benjamin Harrison).

North Carolina's Joseph Hewes in effect became the future nation's first secretary of the navy, since he chaired the naval committee in the Continental Congress. His Carolina colleague, John

Penn, led Patriot bands harassing Lord Cornwallis as he moved northward out of South Carolina from 1780 to 1781.

They Didn't Sign, But . . .

THEY DIDN'T SIGN THE DECLARATION of Independence, but these distinguished Patriots risked lives and fortunes anyway. Some, like the signers of the Declaration, would suffer greatly for their commitment. Most lived to see their cause triumph, and many became leaders of the new American nation themselves. Just a few of these early rebels or Founding Fathers . . .

- First and foremost was the revolutionary soldier and post-Revolution political and financial theorist who served as the new nation's first secretary of the Treasury and gave the country a sound financial system; who eased the ratification pains of the proposed Constitution by writing more of the Federalist Papers than anyone else (fifty of the eighty total); and who helped to create the two-party political system. Born on the island of Nevis in the British West Indies of an illegal marriage, left on his own at age eleven after his mother died, Alexander Hamilton came to the future United States at the age of sixteen, his travel expenses donated by family and a friendly Presbyterian minister. Never finishing college, he took command of a New York area artillery battery in 1776 at the age of nineteen—as youngest man in the group. He would soon become an aide to George Washington and later, returning to the field, would lead the Americans in storming the key Redoubt #10 at Yorktown, one of the last actions forcing Lord Cornwallis to surrender. Hamilton's postwar career included law studies and election to the Confederation Congress. He was a delegate to the Constitutional Convention of 1787 and later, after his Treasury service, the ranking major general in the U.S. Army. After George Washington's death in 1799, he became the army's most senior officer—and thus its commander in chief. He was discharged in 1800, and there is no telling what further achievements might have been his, but for the mortal wound he suffered in a duel with Aaron Burr in July of 1804. He died in New York the next day at the age of forty-seven.

- New Jersey's William Livingston, Yale graduate, attorney, columnist, essayist, and Continental Congress member, missed out on signing the Declaration because he had gone home to assume command of his state's militia. His brother Philip, delegate from New York, did sign it. Soon after, Brigadier General Livingston became the first governor of New Jersey. His home was fated to be destroyed by the British, but he moved around New Jersey often enough to elude British efforts to capture him in person. Little-known fact: In the 1770s, Livingston provided the schooling, including college classes, needed for a bright but penniless young man newly arrived from the British West Indies: Alexander Hamilton.

- When British General John Burgoyne marched on the Hudson Valley from Canada, New Hampshire was ready to send its militiamen into the fray along with their fellow New Englanders. But New Hampshire didn't have the funds available to pay their way to war. Never mind, said wealthy merchant John Langdon, Speaker of the New Hampshire House of Representatives, he would finance their deployment in the field. He did, and in fact, he joined them as a Continental Army officer serving in the Battles of Bennington and Saratoga. As early as 1774, he had shown he was a man of action—in December of that year he led hundreds of fellow colonists in a raid against a Royal fort in Portsmouth, seizing one hundred barrels of powder in the process. The future president and governor of New Hampshire, Continental Congress member, U.S. senator, and first president of the U.S. Senate also was a shipbuilder for the neophyte American navy—his *Ranger,* captained by John Paul Jones, was the first to sail under a boldly displayed American flag.

- This revolutionary figure didn't live long enough to see the fruits of his passionate advocacy, and he first was heard in South Carolina as a loud voice supporting the Crown. His uncle was Lieutenant Governor William Bull, acting royal governor. For all that, and a short but blazing rebel career, William

Henry Drayton is counted as one of South Carolina's early Patriot heroes. In less than two years' time, the Low-Country planter jumped from a seat on the royalist South Carolina Council to presidency of the rebel Provincial Congress. He became a pamphleteer and speaker, asserting that Parliament had no right to "exercise despotism over America." He directed raids against royal arsenals and, in November 1775, boldly sent the armed schooner *Defence* into a gunbattle with two British men-of-war in Charleston harbor (with himself on board). An early advocate of total American independence, he served as chief justice of South Carolina (despite lacking a law degree) and in 1778 joined the Continental Congress in Philadelphia. Always arguing against reconciliation with Great Britain, the tempestuous Drayton often was at odds with fellow Carolinian Henry Laurens, president of the Congress. They achieved a reconciliation, however, when Drayton, only thirty-six, contracted typhus in 1779 and lay on his deathbed. Members of Congress attended his burial in Philadelphia's Christ Church Cemetery.

- More than forty years in age, this Founding Father served as both a private and brigadier general in the militia, but his real contribution lay in the power of his pen. Not for nothing was John Dickinson of Delaware and Pennsylvania known as "The Penman of the Revolution." As early as 1765 he wielded his persuasive pen in the Stamp Act Congress' widely read *Declaration of Rights.* Even better known was his 1768 *Letters from a Farmer in Pennsylvania,* which condemned the punitive Townshend Acts. He followed up with the 1774 *Petition to the King,* adopted by the First Continental Congress, which stated colonial grievances but still pledged loyalty to the Crown. By 1775, matters had gone so far that his *Declaration on the Causes and Necessity of Taking up Arms*—also adopted by the Continental Congress—said the colonial resort to arms was absolutely necessary for the "preservation of our liberties." Still, as a member of the Congress, he opposed the final step of declaring independence, but once done, he rallied to the cause and even drafted the Articles of Confederation adopted in the late 1770s. He later served as President of both Delaware and Pennsylvania, and he was the founder of Dickinson College.

- Doubling as a New York revolutionary legislator and a member of the Continental Congress, the aristocratic attorney John Jay missed the crucial vote adopting the Declaration of Independence—and his chance to sign it—because he was at home attending sessions of the New York legislative body. Despite that omission, he still served the revolutionary cause and the new nation in a unique combination of roles over a twenty-five-year period, beginning with his membership in the First Continental Congress of 1774. In 1776, he took on the additional post of New York's chief justice, but became president of the Congress in 1778. Next he was U.S. minister to Spain; he helped frame the 1783 peace treaty with Great Britain in Paris; he became America's first secretary of state (of foreign affairs, at the time); and finally, he served as the first chief justice of the U.S. Supreme Court. Congressional historians will remember him as the member who, in 1774, solved brewing controversy over each state's voting strength by proposing that each and every delegation in Philadelphia would have one vote to cast, no matter how many members to a delegation . . . or people in its state.

- This Patriot wrote the preamble to the U.S. Constitution, those immortal words that are probably just as familiar as Thomas Jefferson's opening lines of the Declaration of Independence. In this case, the author, not nearly so famous as Jefferson, was Gouverneur Morris of Pennsylvania. His familiar lead into the body of the Constitution: *"We, the people of the United States, in order to form a more perfect union, establish justice, insure domestic tranquility, provide for the common defense, promote the general welfare, and secure the blessings of liberty to ourselves and our posterity, do ordain and establish this Constitution for the United States of America."* Serving in the Continental Congress in 1778 and 1779, he did his real work in the Constitutional Convention of 1787—James Madison, so-called "Father of the Constitution," once said Morris provided the wording of the final draft of the entire Constitution. Perhaps not as conservative and autocratic as some historians say, he certainly played a major role in creating the new American form of government. He consistently opposed slavery on moral grounds. And who could blame him for upsetting the guillotine-minded revolutionaries of France for his involvement—as U.S. minister to France in the 1790s—in the escapes of various nobles, the Marquis de Lafayette among them?

Battle of Long Island

WITH THE BATTLE OF LONG Island in late August 1776, reality came to the as yet untested American Revolution—and very nearly extinguished it. Here began a slide that lasted several months, one military defeat after another, that left even Washington so dismayed as to write (in mid-December): "I think the game is pretty near up."

The outlook for the still new commander in chief would brighten with his bold riposte at Trenton, New Jersey, after crossing the ice-floed Delaware River on Christmas night. Back in August, however, neither his reputation nor his young country's fortunes had appeared quite so ready for the test of war.

He had been wrong to occupy New York—the island of Manhattan was essentially a floating triangle that could be attacked at any point of the seaborne enemy's choosing. He had then compounded his error by splitting his forces and placing half of them across the East River at the butt end of another island—Long Island.

With total command of the seas, British leaders and their seasoned soldiers were in an excellent position to avenge the recent loss of Boston to Washington and his besieging Colonials. Recognizing a knockout opportunity when they saw one, the British gathered the greatest expeditionary force ever assembled in the British Isles for the assault upon New York.

In command would be General Sir William Howe, recently forced to evacuate Boston. His admiral brother, "Black Dick" Howe, brought in the fleet, fresh from England and carrying hired mercenaries—the Hessians! Hurrying up the coast from the fighting over Charleston were Generals Sir Henry Clinton and Lord Cornwallis with their troops. In all, including sailors from their huge fleet, the British had brought some forty-five thousand men to face

Washington's already once-divided twenty thousand. In the summer of 1776, the war might easily have ended then and there—it appeared the Colonials were caught in a trap of their own making.

Why should New York have been such a vital fulcrum? From British eyes, one may recall, the rebellious American territory was a thin coastal strip, much of it pure wilderness with no roads, from the St. Lawrence River in Canada to Florida, a distance of 1,200 miles north to south. The average "breadth," noted the twentieth-century British military historian J. F. C. Fuller, was only 150 miles. Thus, "it was strategically a good defensive country, and therefore difficult to subdue." To conquer north, south, and middle all at once was beyond British resources. The decision was made to subdue the politically important and heavily populated North, a task presumably to be made easier by having Canada as a base. With New York and New England under control, "even should the central and southern sectors continue to hold out, they would in time be subdued piecemeal," wrote Fuller. "The northern sector was, therefore, what Clausewitz, the renowned German military intellectual, would have called 'the strategical center of gravity of the war.'"

The gathering of the king's forces at New York was no great surprise to the Patriots, who had dug and erected defensive earthworks at key points in Manhattan and on the Brooklyn Heights, across the East River. And in Washington's defense, it should be noted that New York was a psychological and political symbol, as well as a strategic checkpoint at the mouth of the Hudson River. Its occupation was good for troop morale, and it was also a point of pride for the Continental Congress and the would-be nation.

But the Patriots of that day often tended to view events and possibilities through a fog of euphoria. Their expeditionary probe into Canada late in 1775 had been a debacle, but they had won the moral victory at Breed's Hill, forced the British evacuation of Boston, and had a victory at Sullivan's Island off Charleston to boast about, didn't they?

George Washington, however, was not so euphoric. He worried about short-term enlistments that allowed his troops to train and turn for home the moment training was done. Clearly, that was no way to run an army, but Washington's warnings and complaints to Congress went largely ignored until the British, in effect, declared that if it was war the Patriots wanted, that is what they would get— Long Island would be the terrifying opening blow.

With Washington's halved army east of the East River as the objective, General Howe's men, on the morning of August 22, streamed in a steady flow from Staten Island, occupied long before, onto barges towed by ships of the great four-hundred-vessel fleet. Soon on this clear, hot day, twenty thousand British troops, Hessians among them, would land on Long Island to face the American nine thousand posted at the Brooklyn Heights and in outlying woods or farmland.

To make matters worse for Washington, his split force on Long Island recently had undergone an eleventh-hour change in command. Originally, Rhode Islander Nathanael Greene had commanded Washington's eastern army. Greene would plan and supervise the erection of the Patriot defenses. But now he came down with fever and had to be removed. Replacing him as overall commander (and not nearly as familiar with the defensive scheme) was General John Sullivan, to be ably seconded by General William Alexander, also known as "Lord Stirling" for his claim to a vacant Scottish title.

The newly landed British and their Hessian allies enjoyed a quiet first night ashore after rushing about four and a half miles inland. The vanguard had landed near Gravesend, and only sporadic rifle fire from a few Pennyslvanians disturbed their march to Flatbush, a village three miles from the outer Patriot lines, for the night's encampment. On the Manhattan side of the East River, Washington did not dare send all available forces, since the Gravesend landing might only be a diversion, with the real British attack to come against his Manhattan perimeter. He did transfer some additional men to Brooklyn, but more important, a steady wind kept the enemy's sail-powered warships out of the East River for several fortuitous days.

The British, for the same reason, could not add to their Long Island landing force until August 25. More and more convinced that Long Island really was the British "grand push," Washington sent additional troops to his Brooklyn generals every day. The British spent their time consolidating a very smooth amphibious operation—and laying the groundwork for their next stroke. With the shift in the wind on August 25, more troops, more Hessians, began landing.

From where might the first blow come? On the American side, the reliable and sly General Israel Putnam held down the main defensive line on the Brooklyn Heights. Sullivan headed the Americans posted in the outer countryside to the center and left, and Stirling the men on the right. Three roads led in their direction from the beaches to the right and the British lodgment. One followed the beach into Brooklyn from the right flank; another led directly to the center of Brooklyn's frontal line; and the third snaked along Jamaica Pass, far into the left flank.

Of the American commanders on the scene, only Stirling was more than passingly concerned about the Jamaica Pass approach. By some accounts, he posted his own guards there and paid them out of his own pocket. (The far left, nominally under Sullivan, was in fact held by Pennsylvanians from Stirling's own brigade.) Since the pass was on the American left and Stirling was charged with holding down the right, there was little more that he could do.

On the night of August 26 Howe's subordinate, Henry Clinton, set off with ten thousand men behind him to launch the fateful British attack. Their favored pathway to victory would be the neglected Jamaica Pass, and at sunrise Clinton and his men bulled into the American left and simply rolled it up. At his signal, the British center and left erupted against the Americans, tying them down while Sullivan's wing was pushed, collapsing altogether, into the American center and even to the right.

Both Hessian and British taught any Americans still needing such a lesson that this revolution business was serious and deadly indeed. Sometimes not even firing a shot, the veteran Hessians worked with the bayonet. One of their own officers later said, "The greater part of the riflemen were pierced with the bayonet to the trees." To the American right, British cannon and mortars had engaged and kept American attention for four predawn hours, occasionally lopping off someone's head.

Everywhere up and down the hard-fought line, the Patriots discovered that their vaunted sharpshooting prowess was, in these close quarters, to their own detriment. As Washington's biographer Douglas Southall Freeman observed, "Everywhere the command seemed to be the same—to force the American volley and then close with the bayonet before the Continentals could reload."

Washington, hustling across to Brooklyn about eight o'clock that morning, faced the first real battle of his career as a commander. On the defensive from the outset, he and his revolving generals had determined to secure the Brooklyn Heights, which commanded the East River, with a line of parapets and occasional forts stretching from the salt marshes on Wallabout Bay to the north to the marshes at Gowanus Creek to the south. In front of the Heights by a mile and a half ran a row of hills, a welcome natural buffer.

Putnam had taken overall command practically on the eve of the British attack, leaving Sullivan in charge of the outer line along the hills. Assuming that his own troops would perform well and that the enemy would advance frontally, Freeman wrote, "Washington could hope his main strategical objective would be achieved to the extent that by holding the approaches to his position at Brooklyn, he could withdraw safely and in good order to that line after taking stiff toll of the enemy."

But the British had outwitted the Americans with the flanking march through Jamaica Pass. In the fighting that followed, the king's men sent the rebels streaming to the rear, with losses of 1,500 (200 actually killed) for the day, and Generals Sullivan and Stirling among those taken prisoner. Fierce rear-guard fighting (Stirling and his men on the right as standouts) did enable many of the Continentals to withdraw to the rear Brooklyn line, where for the next two and half days Washington and his men waited for the next British move. This time almost certainly an assault would require head-on confrontation. Instead, the British, led by the cautious Howe, began preparation for a siege. Fortunately for the Americans, the prevailing winds still prevented British warships from sailing up the East River to the American rear.

The weather, in fact, had been a steady ally of the Americans throughout these dramatic days. It would again be so on the night of August 29, when Washington began his famous retreat from Brooklyn to Manhattan, aided by a thick, early-morning fog. The British now had command of Long Island, but Washington's army eluded them for the moment.

The revolutionary path for Washington led almost all downhill for the next few months after Long Island/Brooklyn. Washington evacuated New York on September 12, but he fought off the British at Harlem Heights four days later. Late in October, Washington withdrew to White Plains but left a garrison holding Fort Washington at the upper end of Manhattan. Defeated at White Plains on October 28, Washington retired to North Castle.

The British then stormed and took Fort Washington on November 16. Next, they seized Fort Lee, New Jersey, on November 19. Washington now abandoned the New York area entirely, moving into New Jersey and steadily withdrawing under pressure from Lord

Cornwallis. Washington finally moved across the Delaware River on December 11 for refuge in Pennsylvania, while the Continental Congress abandoned its "home" in Philadelphia for Baltimore.

With his defeat at Long Island, Washington was on the run until he snapped back at his tormentors the night of December 25–26 at Trenton. All the while, though, he and his army were learning and hardening in both resolve and ability—and the British, for all their pressure and minor success, had not been able to bring about a final and decisive showdown with the rebels.

Fought Like a Wolf

HERE'S A QUICK TRIVIA QUESTION for the military history buff: Who was the British-style "lord" who fought on the Patriot side in the American Revolution? He was almost the *only* American hero of any stature in George Washington's folly at the Battle of Long Island. And it perhaps can also be said that in the early months of the Revolutionary War there was no greater *Patriot* hero than this same man with a claim to Scottish peerage.

This man was none other than William Alexander, native of New York City (circa 1726), resident of New Jersey, early brigadier general in the Continental Army, confidant and able lieutenant to George Washington, occasional scourge to His Majesty's forces in America . . . and (by his claim) sixth Earl of Stirling.

Certainly a colorful character of his day, a wealthy merchant and landowner, hard-drinking and thus typically described as "ruddy in complexion," he had laid claim to the "empty" earldom after the fifth earl died with no son to follow him. More than a few onlookers in England were consternated at having a Colonial stake out the title as a collateral descendant, especially when a Scottish jury went along with him.

The House of Lords finally put a stop to this nonsense in 1762, but William Alexander apparently was undismayed. He still went about calling himself "Lord Stirling"—and by that name he forevermore was known, even to his troops and Revolutionary officer colleagues, including Washington.

He did not emerge from the Revolutionary War a great strategist, a commander of historic campaigns, or even as the victor of a single major battle ... but few men around Washington would emerge with a greater collection of honorable battle stars or a greater list of little-known but important supporting roles.

He began his Patriot service by raising a company of grenadiers in New Jersey, and became colonel of New Jersey's First Militia Regiment. He was awarded his brigadier's rank after storming and seizing an armed British transport ship off Sandy Hook in January 1776.

Briefly serving as commander of New York City (before Washington came down from the Boston area), Stirling began the defensive work that produced Forts Lee and Washington on opposite sides of the Hudson, and Fort Stirling on the Brooklyn Heights.

He was involved in the Battle of Long Island that transpired the same summer of 1776, and would figure, largely in his various supportive capacities, at White Plains, Princeton, Trenton, Metuchen (his one well-remembered defeat), Brandywine, at Germantown, and Monmouth, where he distinguished himself for his command of the left wing.

He then presided at the court-martial of General Charles Lee, whose long-simmering disaffection with Washington had come to open confrontation between the two Virginia residents when they met Sir Henry Clinton's rear guard, under the command of Lord Cornwallis, at Monmouth, New Jersey, on June 28, 1778.

Soon after, it was Stirling who warned Washington of a malicious whispering campaign (the "Conway Cabal") undermining the latter's reputation and involving certain friends of potential rival Horatio Gates. Later, in 1779, Stirling would be most supportive of another Virginia Lee—Henry "Light-Horse Harry" Lee—in his attack on Paulus Hook.

By some accounts, Stirling might have saved the day—and early criticism of George Washington—at the Battle of Long Island, had his senior commanders paid greater heed to his advice. It seems that Stirling recognized the danger of a British flanking movement by way of Jamaica Pass and urged its stoppage with a heavy guard.

His advice was discarded and he acted as best he could ... apparently to order at least a skeletal guard of five to be posted there the morning the British force marched through the very same gateway leading to their victory.

Whatever the case, no commander could ask for a better historical epitaph than the accolade "Lord Stirling" would collect from his British adversaries in recognition of his brave stand with a forlorn rear guard later that very day.

Stirling was taken prisoner, but up until that one moment, said one British officer, he "fought like a wolf."

Escape from Brooklyn

THE ELEMENTS OF THE PROBLEM facing George Washington in August of 1776 were as clear and precise as those in a mathematical problem. Dispose of the factors one by one and a solution would be reached.

The problem was moving an army of nine thousand men across a mile-wide river in a single night without allowing the nearby, numerically superior enemy to take notice of the evacuation.

The factors needed to solve the problem were fairly obvious:

Find boats, lots of boats, and crewmen to guide them across the East River from Brooklyn to Manhattan.

Seek favorable winds and calm waters, making possible the use of sailing craft as well as oar-powered boats for the passage.

Keep the entire operation a secret until completion—no lights and no noise.

American Colonel Benjamin Talmadge ably summed up the endangered Continental Army's quandry when he wrote: "To move so large a body of troops, with all their necessary appendages, across a river a full mile wide, with a rapid current in the face of a victorious, well disciplined army, nearly three times as numerous . . . , and a fleet capable of stopping the navigation, so that not one boat could have passed over, seemed to present most formidable obstacles."

Keep in mind that August 29 was a mid-summer date, meaning one of the year's shortest nights.

Having decisively lost the Battle of Long Island to a British-Hessian host just days before, however, Washington couldn't wait for more favorable conditions. He had to withdraw his bruised, out-numbered army quickly, or possibly suffer an even more disastrous defeat with his back to the wide river and no room for retreat or maneuver. Fortunately, British General Sir William Howe once again was slow to follow up on his victory, a bad habit of his . . . but he could make his next move at any moment.

Out-generaled by Howe so far, Washington now began to turn tables on his foe. In fact, he was turning positively cagey. Having set-tled upon his desperate plan in his own mind, Washington found a clever way to prepare his men for the evacuation without revealing, even to them, that there would be an evacuation. He passed the word that he was bringing in reinforcements from New Jersey, and his men, entrenched on the Brooklyn Heights, had better pack up for a reshuffle of units on the front lines.

In the meantime, Washington had ordered two subordinates to round up every boat they could find, especially flat-bottomed craft that could carry heavy loads and horses. The commander in chief had previously been using ten barge-like vessels to ferry his troops back and forth, but now he needed an entire fleet of barges, boats, sailing craft—whatever could be found . . . without the British dis-covering what was afoot.

And a small fleet of boats was found, but today's historians don't really know where or how. According to George Athan Billias, biog-rapher of the Marblehead (Massachusetts) mariner John Glover, "At least one sloop was known to have been pressed into service, but little else is known about the other craft used in the evacuation" (*General John Glover and his Marblehead Mariners,* 1960).

We do know that Washington assigned two Massachusetts regi-ments to the job—Glover's Fourteenth and Israel Hutchinson's Twenty-seventh—and an outfit made up of mariners from Salem, Lynn, and Danvers. "These Massachusetts mariners were pitting their seamen's skills against three factors that might make a shambles of the operation—time, tide, and wind," said Billias.

On such a short night, it would be a race against the clock, a race that could be adversely affected by wind and tide. "If wind condi-tions were not just right, sailing vessels could not be used in the evacuation at all; and if boats had to be rowed against the tide, each trip would take longer."

As events turned out, the "boat-lift" began promptly at ten o'clock, with New York's General Alexander McDougall acting as a beachmaster, organizing the quiet shuffle into the boats. Despite the darkness, the small boats smoothly made their two-mile roundtrips until about midnight, but then an ebb tide and contrary winds knocked the sailing craft out of the game—"The evacuation seemed destined for disaster at this point; the number of rowboats on hand was not sufficient to carry off the rest of the men in a single night."

A more favorable wind soon returned but, as Billias noted, precious time had been lost. By the dawn, most of the nine thousand men had been delivered to the Manhattan shoreline, but not all. For those remaining on the Brooklyn side of the East River, the race against the clock seemed lost.

Or was it? Thanks to a thick fog blanketing the river banks, the boatlift was able to continue without interruption from the British. Said a British officer later: "In the Morning, to our Great Astonishment, [we] found they had evacuated all their Works . . . without a Shot being shot at them."

For the moment, Washington and his army were out of danger. In the Battle of Long Island, General Sir William Howe had fooled Washington, but now Washington had fooled Howe.

For the moment.

Pamphleteer, Soldier, Politician

GEORGE WASHINGTON CALLED HIM "A brave soldier and distinguished patriot." Indeed, he contributed to the birthing of a nation in countless ways.

Packing career after career into his fifty-four years, Scotsman Alexander McDougall was one of those early Patriots—key figures in the Revolution—who are hardly known today. In McDougall's particular case, though, we have to ask if many others gave so much, so repeatedly, so many different ways . . . before being largely forgotten.

A privateer out of New York in the French and Indian War, for the

British of course, he later became a controversial pro-liberty, anti-establishment pamphleteer.

As a result, he served time in jail. So many followers came to visit him, he had to draw up a visitor's schedule. The number forty-five, stemming from the title of a political tract, became so closely associated with McDougall that forty-five maidens visited him, as did forty-five men who joined him on his forty-fifth day of confinement in eating forty-five pounds of steak taken from a forty-five-month-old steer. All that was back in 1770, and somewhere in that crowd, quite obviously, there lurked an early public relations genius, perhaps McDougall himself. (Then, too, Scots-born Alexander McDougall certainaly was aware of "Bonnie Prince" Charlie's Rebellion of Forty-Five—1745.)

In previous years, after emigrating to New York with his parents from the Hebrides Islands of Scotland, he had been a milk delivery boy in the city. In his adult years, he had his hands full as a ship owner, merchant, planter's agent, venture capitalist, twice-married husband, and father. He was a wealthy entrepreneur by this time, and he didn't have to become a revolutionary. He didn't have to attack the policies of colonial New York and the British Parliament. He didn't have to lift a finger, or take the risks . . . except for his own belief in, and early commitment to, the cause of liberty.

Indeed, as a leader of the New York Sons of Liberty in the tumultuous 1770s, this burly, blunt-spoken entrepreneur soon saw his life going in new, often painful, directions.

In 1771, he was back in jail for his antiestablishment writings—called seditious writings by his accusers. In 1773, he was an organizer of a Boston-like "tea party" that dumped British tea into New York's East River.

He soon was at the forefront of those urging formation of a continental congress. In late 1774, fittingly, he was on hand in Philadelphia as an observer of the First Continental Congress. Before all the revolutionary shouting was over, in fact, he himself briefly would serve as a delegate to this historic body. But first, in 1775, he served in the New York Provincial Congress. That year also, he was a member of the Committee of 100, appointed to draft the blueprint for a New York state government. Still, in 1775 he became a colonel and regimental commander in the New York militia.

He lost a son in the ill-fated Quebec campaign of 1775–1776.

Newly appointed in 1776 as colonel of the New York First

Continentals, he (and his men) helped build the defenses of New York and then took part in the Battle of Long Island across the East River from Manhattan. With that battle lost, he provided crucial help in the secret, nighttime evacuation of Washington's army from Brooklyn. As the man in charge of loading the hastily assembled, makeshift fleet, he left on one of the very last boats to spirit the Americans to relative safety back in Manhattan.

Neither 1776 nor his military career was quite over yet, with the Revolutionary War now at hot pitch. Somewhere around this time, he successfully advised Washington to have his Continentals load their muskets with buckshot. Soon, McDougall and his brigade were in the Battle of White Plains . . . were credited, in fact, with holding the line against redcoats and Hessians at Chatterton's Hill until outflanked because of another unit's failure to hold.

Then following Washington's line of retreat through New Jersey to Pennsylvania, McDougall became ill and was inactive for a month. But he rebounded in early 1777 and was placed in charge of military stores in the Hudson Highlands, where, with only a relatively few men, he rebuffed a British raid and safeguarded the vital supplies. Over the next few years, McDougall often would be posted in the same area—with improved defenses at West Point one of his major goals and achievements.

In the meantime, though, there would be many interruptions for the ever-reliable Scotsman. Late in 1777, for instance, he and his brigade were called back to George Washington's side for the campaign against General Sir William Howe outside of Philadelphia— McDougall's brigade then became the spearhead for Nathanael Greene's flank attack in the Battle of Germantown and, when that failed, covered Greene's retreat.

Soon to win appointment by the Continental Congress as a major general, McDougall also provided valuable service in formal inquiries into the conduct of fellow general officers, notably that of "Mad" Anthony Wayne in the disaster of Paoli, Pennsylvania, that same fall. McDougall, now in command of a division, next joined Greene in fighting the Battle of Fort Mercer in nearby New Jersey, another loss for the Americans. As Washington took his army into winter quarters at Valley Forge, McDougall once again was laid low by illness—he spent the next two months recuperating in Morristown, New Jersey.

By the following spring, though, he was well enough to return to the Hudson Highlands for a short time, to spend the summer months with the Continentals in Connecticut, then return late in the year to his improvements at West Point. He would be in command of West Point itself over the next four years—always with a few more interruptions.

In 1780, McDougall spent seven weeks in Philadelphia lobbying the Continental Congress for an improved financial package for the army's general officers. Unsuccessful in the venture that year, he returned early in 1781, elected as a member of the Congress—from New York, of course. Now both an army general and a delegate, he lasted for thirty-seven days before his dwindling personal finances forced him to return to paid army service, however small the stipend to be earned. Indications are that Congress was relieved to be rid of a military man in its midst.

Another interruption soon came about—a court-martial stemming from feuding with a superior officer. As one result, Washington relieved McDougall from his command at West Point. The court-martial on seven counts produced a reprimand on only one of them; the rest were dismissed. For now, however, McDougall was on the outs with key figures among his fellow generals—"Lord Stirling," president of his court-martial; Henry Knox, McDougall's replacement as commander at West Point; and William Heath, the superior officer McDougall had feuded with in the first place.

Washington still thought enough of him to offer him a division command in the field, but McDougall's health forced him to decline. His financial health was failing as well—he and his wife now sold garden produce to help make ends meet. In late 1782 and early 1783, he reappeared before Congress as part of a three-man delegation again seeking pension relief for Continental Army officers. The Congress, as it had before, pleaded no funds. But later that year, pressured by officers meeting at Newburgh and New Windsor, New York, Congress found the means to give the officers a choice between half-pay for life or full pay for five years.

Meanwhile, joining hands with Knox, McDougall became a founder of the Society of Cincinnati as the Revolutionary War ended, and served as the first president of its New York chapter. On another gratifying note for this veteran revolutionary, he was able to march into New York with Washington when the British evacuated the city in November 1783.

Before his death just three years later at fifty-four, McDougall once again would see brief service as a delegate to the Continental Congress. He also served in the newly created state senate of New York and—at last returning to his beginnings as a New York businessman—as first president of the Bank of New York. Overall, through many difficult and tumultuous years, noted Washington at the time of McDougall's death in 1786, the transplanted Scotsman had been "a brave soldier and distinguished patriot." As Washington could have added, in twentieth-century terminology, few others could claim a revolutionary résumé quite so replete.

New York Lost

WAS THIS OUR UNFLAPPABLE GEORGE Washington that we see in all those stiff portraits of his day? The remarkable, seldom-discouraged commander in chief we read about in all the histories? On Manhattan Island one day, near today's busy intersection of Forty-second and Lexington, close to the future Grand Central Station, there he was, shouting, throwing his hat on the ground, lashing with his cane at men and officers streaming past him in frenzied retreat.

He shouted, Job-like, in pain and bewilderment: "Are these the men I am to defend America with?"

In his day, the nearby crossroads connected the Post Road and Bloomingdale Road. Boldly moving at noontime, in broad daylight, the British had landed four thousand men on the beaches of the East River, at a spot known as Kip's Bay. A heavy bombardment by the fleet offshore tore up the river embankment, created a thunderstorm of incessant noise, and succeeded in unnerving the Connecticut and New York militia stationed along the beach area, but did little physical damage.

Soon, nearly one hundred flatboats filled with troops left the big ships and headed for shore. The four divisions of British and Hessian soldiers landed roughly at the spot where today's East Thirty-fourth Street runs to the river. The militia by now had melted away, and the British drove inland with hardly any opposition.

Once again, disaster loomed for George Washington and his unseasoned army. The fact was, he again had made mistakes in his troop dispositions. Defending a thirteen-mile-long island against a numerically superior enemy in total control of the surrounding waters, he had divided his forces into three basic groups.

General William Heath and nine thousand men were to the north, at King's Bridge. This was the escape hatch for if and when Washington must quit Manhattan altogether. Below, at the southern end of Manhattan, were General Israel Putnam and five thousand men. Finally, stationed at the center of the island and able, in theory, to move either direction as circumstance might dictate, were General Nathanael Greene and another five thousand men.

The entire piecemeal arrangement invited British attack, but what else was the American commander to do? New York commanded the entrance to the Hudson River, strategically important as a veritable "highway" running far to the north; New York was a political and propaganda plum for whichever side held the city, and Congress had told Washington to hold the city as long as he could.

For the British, New York was a highly desirable objective for all the same reasons, plus the fact they needed a safe and reliable base of operations after being forced to abandon Boston. Now, in September of 1776, in the weeks after taking over Long Island and Brooklyn east of the East River, they could consider various options in planning their attack on Manhattan Island. They could (a) attack at King's Bridge and thus put a cork in Washington's only escape route out of Manhattan; (b) go ashore from the Hudson River in the vicinity of today's Harlem, high on the western side of the island; or (c) land a major contingent on the eastern banks of Manhattan, right in the middle.

What General Sir William Howe finally decided upon was the latter. Driving across the entire island, he would split the island like an apple, then deal with the separated American forces in detail.

He chose September 15 for his assault at Kip's Bay, just when Washington and his generals were beginning a withdrawal to the north from their doubtful-appearing New York positions. The big ships appeared in the East River that morning just two hundred yards from shore. The militia pulled back when the big guns opened up. Then came the attack by the British and Hessian troops, the Hessians once again putting the bayonet to deadly use. It was all too much for the green militiamen posted along the shoreline. Their initial withdrawal inland became an outright rout.

That's when an aggrieved—in fact, enraged—Washington tried to stem the stream of fleeing, panic-stricken militiamen. Having hastened to the scene after hearing the battle sounds from his headquarters, he now shouted commands to halt; to form defensive lines behind the nearest walls; even to "take the cornfield."

Apparently there was a pause in the tide of men, but the panic began again when a few redcoats came into view. Washington, ignoring the British fusillades aimed his way, stormed and raged at his terrified troops, but they paid little heed. The fugitives included members of two reinforcing brigades (2,500 men) who caught the panic fever and also turned tail, littering the ground with their discarded weapons.

His anger soon spent, an uncharacteristically listless Washington had to be led from the shameful scene by an aide before the advancing British could simply ride up and take him into custody.

To the north, John Glover's Marblehead mariners and troops under Colonel William Smallwood were instrumental in stopping the headlong flight from mid-Manhattan and halting further British advance up the eastern side of the island.

Fortunately for the revolutionary forces (and unknown to the British), Israel Putnam already was moving his men north from the New York City end of Manhattan along a route west of today's Central Park. By day's end, the previously dispersed American forces were consolidated in northern Manhattan, largely at the Harlem Heights.

Howe had not succeeded in cutting the apple in half. On the other hand, the Americans had conceded the city of New York in lower Manhattan—today's "Big Apple"—to the British. In the process, the Patriots had lost valuable military stores and more than fifty cannon.

They would fight a somewhat redeeming Battle of Harlem Heights the very next day, turning back a British reconnaissance in force and sending Howe in search of a more vulnerable flanking location. Washington, nursing his wounded pride, remained busy with the day-to-day perils of his small army, but he also was thinking ahead . . . thinking that he must buy time to train his Continentals and shape them into a professional army. The militia—bless them for what they could do—simply were too undisciplined, too unreliable for the job at hand.

Additional note: The Continental Army (also called the Patriot Army) was a creation of Congress, as opposed to the more loosely organized militia units and guerrilla bands from the various colonies. One reason the militia was woefully ineffective at times was because its members joined for a precise period of time, then were permitted to return home, regardless of the battle or campaign just ahead. This arrangement often allowed just enough time to train the men, only to have them disappear before they could be put to use. They often came back for subsequent enlistments and fought with great valor, making a major contribution to the success of the Revolution. But Washington and his commanders never knew when the militia would come through for them, especially in the first two years of the war.

It was Congress, incidentally, that coined the name for Washington's professional army—by acting in June 1775 to appropriate the grand sum of $6,000 to support a "Continental Army," with Washington named then and there as its first and only commander in chief. Through the next eight years of war, it is reliably estimated, he never had more than twenty-five thousand troops at his command at any single moment.

Stolen from History

JOHN GLOVER OF MARBLEHEAD, MASSACHUSETTS, is today a "forgotten hero of the war," complains his modern-day biographer, George Athan Billias. And true, Glover remains best known for his key role in Washington's remarkable evacuation of his troops from the shores of Brooklyn . . . but not much else.

The Massachusetts mariner certainly deserves wider recognition for his contributions as a consistent performer on the side of the Patriots. He was the one and only architect of an American stand against an overwhelming British force in the Battle of Pelham Bay, so forgotten these days that historian Lynn Montross has described it as "lost, strayed or stolen from the pages of history." It was October 1776, and the American army was in retreat from Harlem Heights to White Plains, New York, its men, horses, and equipment strung out over the eighteen-mile route. The withdrawal, conceding the British total control of Manhattan Island, would take four days. Glover and a brigade of 750 men had been posted to the east as one of several screening units deployed by Washington along the Long Island Sound against flank attack from the east. Glover's sentry post was Pell's Point on Pelham Bay, hard by a narrow road running into the American rear.

The morning of October 18, Glover mounted a hill overlooking the Sound, put a spyglass to his eye and was shocked to see a small fleet of British ships and boats out on the water. In fact, some of the British had already landed. Hurrying to send messages to his superiors and to deploy his brigade in a defensive posture, the militarily inexperienced Glover ran into a party of British skirmishers. Fortunately, he was able to slow them with a few men of his own, but he still faced a major problem in trying to keep the British from using nearby Split Rock Road to drive west, disrupting Washington's strung-out columns. But how could he and 750 men deal with a landing force of four thousand British troops? As he later wrote, "I would have given a thousand worlds to have had [General Charles] Lee, or some other experienced officer present, to direct, or at least to approve of what I had done."

And what had he done? It is suggested by the very name of the road he had been entrusted to guard—Split Rock.

Aptly named, it was a wandering lane flanked on either side by stone walls, with yet more stone walls in the fields alongside. "The stone fences running along this lane and located in the adjacent fields would, of necessity, force the enemy to advance down the narrow roadway," wrote biographer Billias in his book *General John Glover and his Marblehead Mariners.* "Glover skillfully hid his men behind these ready-made fortifications to take advantage of the cover and concealment."

While even the lowliest private of any army certainly would have thought to dive for cover behind the same stone barricades, the real genius of Glover's quick-sketch defensive plan lay in the deployment of three undermanned regiments staggered on alternate sides of the road while he held his fourth regiment in reserve.

"Glover instructed each regiment to hold the enemy in check as long as possible and then to fall back to a new position in the rear while the next unit in reserve took up the brunt of the fighting," explained Billias.

Glover's deployment of the three regiments meant that the advancing British first would face fire from the left, then the right, then the left, and so on interminably as one regiment took over from another. As each fresh regiment took up the shooting, the preceding unit would slip away into the fields and retreat to a new position along the stone walls to the rear.

With his men hastily thrown into position, Glover took the initiative by ordering his advance patrol to mount an aggressive attack against the British. After five rounds of fire were exchanged, the redcoats suffering from the American markmanship, the enemy began to reinforce the skirmishers. Soon, they pushed ahead, closer to Glover's men.

He ordered what appeared to be a retreat. Anticipating a rout, the redcoats "gave a shout" and rushed forward, into the mouth of Glover's deadly funnel. "Colonel [Joseph] Read's two hundred [the Thirteenth Continentals], who were crouched behind stone fences, sprang up and delivered a withering fire at murderously close range. Faced with a sheet of flame, the attackers broke ranks and retreated out of range of the American fire to await more reinforcements."

When they came on again ninety or so minutes later, British and Hessian, supported by six cannon, Read's men again delivered a devastating volley . . . again and again, seven rounds in all. The enemy fired back vigorously but still suffered the greater losses. Finally, Glover ordered his first blocking regiment to slip away to the rear while his second unit, Colonel William Shepard's Third Regiment, lay waiting on the opposite side of the road.

Once again suckered into thinking they had the Americans on the run, the British, with loud cheers, heedlessly raced forward. "But up leaped Shepard's men as if popping out of the earth and let loose a deadly hail of bullets which stopped the enemy."

This time, as the most heated fighting of the day, the Americans "pumped a total of seventeen rounds into hostile ranks."

Shepard's unit fell back, but up sprang yet another regiment, the Twenty-sixth Continentals, under the command of Colonel Loammi Baldwin, a fruit-grower for whom the Baldwin apple is named.

Glover's tactic probably could have continued for hours longer, but he learned around midday that more redcoats were circling around his left flank and could cut him off. Withdrawing for real this time, and in good order, he pulled his men back to the American side of Hutchinson's Creek. From there he exchanged artillery fire with the British until dark, then led his men to a nighttime bivouac three miles farther to the rear, "in the direction of Dobb's Ferry." As was General Sir William Howe's emerging pattern, the British once again did not hasten in pursuit.

Overall, the Americans had perhaps six killed and thirteen wounded, but the British must have lost hundreds in Glover's narrow funnel. As biographer Billias noted, "His men poured more than twenty-five volleys at close ranges of thirty to fifty yards into compact enemy columns along a narrow roadway."

Whatever the body counts, the key result was delay. "What Washington desperately needed on October 18 was time—time to extricate the Patriot army from the threat of Howe's encircling movement while American forces were in the process of withdrawing to White Plains," explained Billias.

After Glover's "spirited one-day stand," added Billias, "Howe's dilatory strategy did the rest." The British made no further threatening moves for another two days. Thus, Washington had the benefit of three days in all "to form a line of temporary redoubts behind the Bronx River to shield the retreating Americans from further attack by Howe's forces."

Deadly "Turtle" at Large

PEERING SEAWARD FROM THEIR FORT on Governor's Island, alert British lookouts spotted a strange-looking craft bobbing in the nearby waters of New York Bay. Inside his "American Turtle," Sergeant Ezra Lee saw *them*, too.

He could tell that he was the cause of considerable excitement. "When I was abreast of the island's fort," he wrote later, "300 to 400 men got upon the parapet to observe me."

The next development early that morning was a bit more ominous. "Then a number came to the shore, shoved off a 12-oar'd barge with five or six sitters and pulled for me."

But he had an ominous response of his own at the ready. "I eyed them, and when they got within 50 or 60 yards of me I let loose the magazine in hopes that if they took me they would likewise pick up the magazine, and we would all be blown up together."

The device he set loose began bobbing in its own fashion—and so alarmed the British seamen by its appearance that they turned about and, oars flashing, pulled for shore at the greatest speed possible.

Sergeant Lee floated on toward a more friendly reception committee awaiting him at the American-controlled South Ferry Landing at the bottom tip of Manhattan Island. They sent out a whaleboat to tow the "Turtle" and its exhausted crewman to shore. About the time he began telling his anxious colleagues about his night's adventure, a distant boom interrupted their excited conversation.

The mine had gone off.

The giant column of water and debris caused by the explosion did no harm, but a number of British ship captains were so alarmed they ordered their anchor lines cut, with their ships then floating down the bay in disarray.

Had they known the true potential of inventor David Bushnell's "American Turtle," they would have been even more shocked. A floating mine was one thing, but a hidden, submersible boat delivering explosive charges would be an even greater menace to the British fleet.

Fact was, the British onlookers that morning of September 7, 1776, had been treated to a historic glimpse of America's first submarine.

David Bushnell, a native of Saybrook, Connecticut, and a recent graduate of Yale, first demonstrated that gunpowder could be made to explode in an underwater container—as probably the world's first mine or torpedo. A Patriot determined to find some way to make up for the American scarcity of warships and cannon, he spent much of his time at Yale developing his mine: basically a watertight wooden keg holding a packed charge of gunpowder, a fuse, and a clock-timer device.

With the feasibility of such an anti-ship weapon proven, the next step would be to develop the means to deliver the device to its target, and that's where Bushnell's "American Turtle" entered the picture. He had conceived of a submersible boat while still a student at Yale. After graduation in 1775, he began building his revolutionary craft at home in Saybrook.

The result would be another watertight container, this one large enough to hold its operator, nine hundred pounds of lead ballast, a man-powered propulsion system, and a few basic controls—humankind's first operational submarine.

The strange craft was six feet in height, just over seven feet in length, and looked like a giant beached turtle when completed and displayed on Poverty Island . . . thus he named it the *American Turtle*.

Bushnell and his brother Ezra took the craft out on Long Island Sound one night, for its first operational test. "David squeezed in, then secured the entrance hatch, which he had designed so that it could be screwed tight (or unscrewed) by either the operator or someone outside," wrote Peggy Robbins in the October 1989 issue of *Military History* magazine.

"From his seat on the beam buttressing the sides, David looked by moonlight through the windows into the waters of the sound. Above his head, the two brass tubes admitted fresh air and behind him, the exhaust ventilator ejected stale air. Steering by compass and utilizing the craft's depth gauge, he successfully put his 'Turtle' through various practice operations," wrote Robbins.

With the air in his craft turning stale after thirty minutes or so, Bushnell surfaced. He was exultant—everything had worked as he hoped, even the length of time he could stay submerged.

His next task would be to perfect a method of delivering his mine to the target—a ship's bottom. But that, too, would be an entirely surmountable obstacle for the inventive Bushnell. All that was needed was a sliding tube running through an opening near the hatch of his submarine. Through the tube ran a detachable rod with a screw at its business end. Bushnell's idea was to float silently to the target ship's bottom, extend the tube and rod their full six inches, then bite into the wooden hull or keel with the screw, twisting it into firm place with a hand crank, then detach.

The screw, meanwhile, was connected to the mine at the "Turtle's" stern by a line attached to another screw holding the mine in place on the "Turtle's" outer skin. With that screw loosened and disengaged by the operator inside, the mine floated free of the undersea boat but remained tethered to the first screw, which was fastened to the target ship.

Bushnell also used the disengagement of the second screw as the trigger for a clock-like timing mechanism inside the mine that would detonate its explosive charge after the "Turtle" moved out of harm's way.

Would his step-by-step system actually work? Could just one man operating the underwater craft manage the hand-cranked propulsion system of two windmill-like oars, the rudder, the valves controlling ascent and descent—and fix the mine to a target ship, then safely move away—all in just thirty minutes or so?

For a final field test of all systems, the sometimes sickly David Bushnell gave way to his stronger brother Ezra as operator. "The 'attack,'" wrote Robbins, "was made on an old ship hulk that David had talked a Saybrook shipowner into donating to the cause. Much to everyone's delight, the hull was blown to pieces and Ezra returned quite safely. Surely, even the greatest ship in the Royal Navy could be destroyed the same way."

Now, in the late summer of 1776, with the blessings of George Washington, Israel Putnam, and a young liaison officer named Aaron Burr, the Bushnell brothers prepared to put their unprecedented weapons system to the ultimate test—an attack on the Royal Navy fleet off Manhattan Island.

Ezra Bushnell would have been the craft's pilot for the attack on Admiral Richard Howe's flagship, the sixty-four-gun *Eagle,* but Ezra unexpectedly was sidelined by a fever—someone else would have to do the job. After a hasty search, David Bushnell chose twenty-seven-year-old volunteer Ezra Lee of Lyme, Connecticut, for the high-risk mission in the untried craft.

George Washington himself once explained just how difficult and dangerous Lee's attempt would be. The underwater attack, said Washington, would require a pilot "hardy enough to successfully encounter the variety of dangers from the difficulty of conducting the machine and governing it underwater, on account of the current, and the consequent uncertainty of hitting the object devoted to destruction, without rising frequently above water for fresh observations, which, when near the vessel, would expose the adventurer to discovery and almost certain death."

After a brief training session—too brief, it turned out—"adventurer" Ezra Lee set out from the South Ferry Landing at the bottom of Manhattan Island shortly after midnight, September 7. Watching two whaleboats tow the experimental "Turtle" into the darkness beyond the wharf were David Bushnell and General Putnam.

The surface waters of New York Bay had looked perfectly calm, the ebb tide had been expected to be fairly weak, but after its release the "Turtle" was caught up in a strong current that swept it right past the target ship. Sergeant Lee exhausted himself battling back upstream with his hand-cranked paddles, but he managed to reach Howe's flagship, submerge, and slip beneath its keel undetected.

With only thirty minutes of "submerge time" at his disposal, he edged close enough to the ship's bottom to begin applying the screw that would hold the tethered mine in place while he floated out of range of the anticipated explosion's effects. But the screw refused to bite into the ship's keel, even though inventor Bushnell had promised it would penetrate copper sheathing as well as wood.

Try as he would, Sergeant Lee couldn't make the screw device work. Bushnell later surmised that Lee struck the iron fastenings of the big ship's rudder—"Had Sergeant Lee moved a few inches, which he could have done even without rowing, he would have found wood where he could have fixed the screw."

Lee may have tried to shift position, but he lost control of his craft at this point—like a cork, it bobbed to the water's surface. There, he saw that daylight was breaking. He could be seen by the ship's crew. That was when he turned for his launch point and was seen by the British on Governor's Island. The mine he released when their "barge" approached had been set to explode in sixty minutes. And it did.

As fate would have it, Bushnell's "American Turtle" never would succeed in blowing up an enemy ship. With the American evacuation of New York, it remained for a time at Fort Washington on the Hudson River side of upper Manhattan, and from there made two additional attacks on British ships, neither successful. America's first submarine then disappeared from historical record with the fall of Fort Washington to the British on November 16. Bushnell may have scuttled his craft to keep it from enemy hands.

His inventive mind now turned to the creation of history's first naval contact mine, and one of them did succeed in destroying a British schooner in the Connecticut River. His release of two dozen such mines in the Delaware River early in 1778 sank one of the enemy ships supporting the British occupation of Philadelphia, but ice in the river held up other mines and allowed British gunners to blow up many of them.

In the meantime, Bushnell's brother Ezra died, and David himself was captured by Connecticut Tories but soon was released. He joined the Continental Army's Corps of Miners and Sappers and reached the rank of captain after service at Morristown, Peekskill, Dobbs Ferry, and West Point.

"The Father of Submarine Warfare," as he is known today, dropped out of sight after the Revolution, only to turn up in 1795 in Georgia, where he practiced medicine under the assumed name "Dr. David Bush." He also taught school and remained in Georgia until his death in 1824.

While David Bushnell passed his post-Revolution life in obscurity, and while he may have thought his inventions had failed, he in fact fathered both the submarine and the naval mine as offensive weapons of war. A grateful twentieth-century U.S. Navy would remember his contributions by naming two submarine tenders for Bushnell, one in 1915 and the second in 1941.

"Strange Mode of Reasoning"

FOR THIS MAN OF EXTRAORDINARY ability and achievement, the black cloud dogging his life just wouldn't go away. After pulling and dragging his nearly starving men through the northern wilderness for a failed attack on Quebec at the end of 1775, he seemed at least to be recovering from a bullet wound in his left leg. But then his horse slipped on the ice, falling on the bad leg.

Painfully turning over his command to General David Wooster of Connecticut in the spring of 1776, he fell back to American-held Montreal, just in time for the visit of a three-man congressional delegation headed by Benjamin Franklin. With British reinforcements then arriving in Canada and the Franklin trio unable to line up Canadian support for the rebellion against Mother England, however, the Americans soon turned for home. First, though, the visiting congressmen authorized their host to take whatever supplies he would need from Montreal's merchants—"legal" plunder.

He, in the meantime, had won the praise of both Wooster and Washington for his Herculean efforts in the failed campaign against Quebec. Congress had given him brigadier general's rank without a single dissenting vote. He had freed a number of American prisoners in an attack against the British and their Indian allies thirty miles from Montreal.

Now, the tattered American column began the long withdrawal southward to Crown Point on Lake Champlain, its brigadier the last man to leave the Canadian shore.

Instead of the normal hero's welcome and fresh military assignment, though, he would be dogged by charges that he stole the Montreal supplies, most of them lost, ruined, or really stolen during the long march home. His chief accuser was Colonel Moses Hazen, a Canadian who had joined the American cause . . . but the brigadier accused Hazen himself of mishandling the Montreal supplies. The dispute went before a military court, and when its members refused to hear the brigadier's chief supporting witness, he completely lost his head, shouted at the judges, and challenged any one of them to a duel. They ordered his arrest.

Fortunately, this tempest in a teapot was bucked up the chain of command to General Horatio Gates, newly appointed as commander of America's northern army. Intent on assigning his fighting brigadier to more constructive battles, Gates wisely ignored the arrest order, dismissed the court, and forwarded the paperwork to Congress. "The United States must not be deprived of that excellent officer's service at this important moment," explained Gates. In the end, both Hazen and the brigadier would be exonerated of the charges against them.

The "important moment" had to do with the gathering of a British force in Canada for a thrust down the Lake Champlain corridor—by means of a small fleet the British were building at the north end of the huge lake. The troubled brigadier already had convinced Washington that the Americans should have their own squadron of warships patrolling Lake Champlain, and now, with added blessings from Gates, he was told to build, arm, and launch his flotilla as rapidly as possible.

A swarm of workers from all over New England descended

upon Skenesborough, New York, for the hasty construction of a six-teen-vessel American flotilla of oar-powered galleys and gondolas made out of mostly green lumber. Before setting off from nearby Fort Ticonderoga, they were armed with small cannon and swivel guns. They were under the command of the brigadier.

So it was that an American army general—Brigadier Benedict Arnold—set off in a small, lake-bound fleet to do possible battle with the Royal Navy.

Arnold sailed under specific orders from Gates to avoid battle with a superior enemy force. His surveillance of the British buildup in August through September of 1776 enabled him to report that the British indeed had assembled a larger fleet of heavier ships—twenty-nine in all. In fact, General Sir Guy Carleton was assembling a thirteen-thousand-man army for the thrust southward toward Albany, New York.

When Arnold suggested he could take a defensive stand between Valcour Island and the lake's western shoreline, Gates was ready to accede without a murmur of protest. In a letter dated October 12, he said he was happy to know that Arnold and his flotilla "ride in Valcour Bay, in defiance of our foes in Canada."

But the battle Arnold envisioned already had taken place . . . the day before. When Carleton's fleet moved southward, to be confronted by Arnold's brave little fleet in a hot, seven-hour naval battle, it was October 11. There was no doubt as to the victory laurels. Arnold lost his schooner *Royal Savage* and the gondola *Philadelphia* to the fire from the larger British ships, along with at least sixty men— some of them victims of galling musket fire from Indians infiltrating the woods on the island and lake shoreline. Fog and darkness ended the battle for the day, with the British pulling back slightly and beginning repairs on their ships. They would have plenty of time by the next day's light to finish off the impudent American flotilla. But Arnold, ever resourceful, fooled the enemy and managed to squeeze his surviving vessels past the line of British ships in the foggy night. The next day, some of his ships managed to reach Fort Ticonderoga, but others were so badly damaged they could only limp along. The British caught up with them at Split Rock on the thirteenth and finished them off.

Arnold stayed with his men to the last. "Lingering behind in his own row-galley, the *Congress,* to cover the retreat, Arnold fought a bloody rearguard action and ran his ship ashore rather than surrender," reported Willard M. Wallace in the book *George Washington's Generals and Opponents.* "After setting fire to the *Congress,* he and the bloodstained survivors of his crew slipped through an Indian ambush and soon arrived at Crown Point."

As one readily apparent outcome, Arnold had lost eleven of his sixteen ships, and his critics howled. Carleton, still on the move, soon seized Crown Point itself and drew close to Fort Ticonderoga . . . but, owing to the lateness of the season and the apparent ferocity of American defenders such as Arnold, he then retired to Canada for the winter. Thus, in the long run, Arnold's construction of a small fleet, together with his valiant defense at Valcour Island, had set back the British timetable and bought valuable time for the Revolutionary cause, just as it was undergoing a pounding at the hands of General Sir William Howe in the New York–New Jersey area.

As Arnold returned to New England, well deserving of both rest and thanks, his personal life was given no respite from the ever-present black clouds that seemed to attend his every move. The widower's proffer of marriage to a Boston woman (daughter of a Tory) was rejected, and his old enemies drummed up new charges against him. Canadian Colonel Hazen, for one, won a favorable court decision on the charge that he had been slandered by Arnold. General Gates ignored other charges, but by regulation was forced to forward the papers to Congress.

Then, in February 1777, Congress promoted five other brigadier generals to major general—all with less time in grade than Arnold. A perturbed and sympathetic George Washington, who had not been consulted in the decision, said the absence of Arnold's name on the promotions list showed "a strange mode of reasoning."

Resenting the "implied impeachment" of his character, Arnold made preparations to visit Congress and pursue the promotion issue in person. Before leaving his onetime home in New Haven, fortuitously enough, he heard about a British raid on Danbury, Connecticut, and galloped off to lead area militiamen in pursuit of the enemy. "He lost one horse, had another wounded, and was nearly captured and killed," added Wallace's account.

Arnold's renewed heroics evidently made their point. Congress in May of 1777 granted him a promotion to major general. At the same time, however, the legislative body failed to restore his seniority. The black cloud returned.

The Morning Charles Lee Dallied

IT WAS A FRIDAY THE 13th, an unlucky day indeed for the second in command of all American forces arrayed against the British in the former colonies. Before the day was half over, General Charles Lee found himself a prisoner, captured without a struggle, and by night's end, his horse had gotten drunk with the enemy. Yes—his horse!

Lee comes down through history as a prig of the first order. A bit of a fool, too, and an arrogant usurper of George Washington's authority.

Until December 13, 1776, the British-born Lee was a hero of the American Revolution, a rival in the minds and hearts of many Patriot partisans to his less experienced, less worldly superior, the Colonial-born General Washington.

Quite obviously, Lee was such a rival in his own heart. The very morning of his capture by the British he sneeringly wrote to his colleague General Horatio Gates: "Entre nous [between us], a certain great man is damnably deficient."

Prior to this day, Lee had fought at Ticonderoga, Niagara, and Montreal during the French and Indian War of the 1750s. He served the British in Portugal, winning accolades for his cavalry's rout of the Spanish at Villa Velha in 1762. He attended civil war in Poland and observed events of the Russo-Turkish War. His British army commanders had included luminaries such as John Burgoyne, James Abercrombie, and the ill-fated Edward Braddock.

In England, Lee had consorted with American sympathizers John Wilkes and Isaac Barre. He soon parted company with his homeland and king—and in the process, rightly or wrongly, blamed George III for unfulfilled hopes of promotion. Returning to America in October 1773, Lee promptly closeted himself with many of the brewing Revolution's strongest voices—Richard Henry Lee, Robert Morris, and Samuel and John Adams of Massachusetts. Soon, Charles Lee's own voice joined in the chorus of dissent.

Buying an estate in Virginia (now West Virginia), Lee became a neighbor to Horatio Gates and visited George Washington's Mount

Vernon. In 1775, the initial revolutionary blows struck, the Second Continental Congress acceded to Washington's urging and made Lee a major general—he at that time would be third in command of the Continental Army.

In the fighting outside Boston the same year, Lee ably commanded Washington's left wing and contributed to the logistics of a virgin army laying siege to a powerful enemy supplied by sea. Lee then helped organize the American forces in Rhode Island and the Patriot defenses of New York City.

His shining moment would come at Charleston, where he commanded as the British tried to take Sullivan's Island and failed. Hailed as a hero, Lee was awarded the thanks of Congress—along with thirty thousand Spanish dollars to offset his debts and the cost of his Virginia property. (Never mind that the real hero at Charleston harbor that June was William Moultrie.)

Moving to second in command with the retirement of the ailing Artemas Ward, Lee wisely urged Washington to leave New York after the lost Battle of Long Island. He also counseled against defending Forts Lee and Washington, which then fell to the British when Washington unwisely failed to heed Lee's advice.

As Washington moved through New Jersey and into Pennsylvania in the late fall of 1776, Lee was seen to drag his feet and even to disobey his commander's orders in order to pursue his own strategies. Washington wanted Lee with him in Pennsylvania, but Lee was set upon cutting into the British rear in New Jersey. He didn't think the British would attempt to cross the Delaware River in wintry December to attack Philadelphia (and he was right). He thought to relieve pressure on Washington by severing the British line of communication with New York. Others, doubtful of Washington's prowess as commander in chief, liked Lee's conception of things. The New York Council of Safety, for one, asked Gates to join Lee at this point, but Gates moved south instead to stand with George Washington in Pennsylvania.

After arriving at Morristown, New Jersey, on December 8 in pursuit of his own notions, Charles Lee was torn between continuing toward Washington's proposed rendezvous or attacking the British at nearby Brunswick or Princeton. Lee hesitated for three to four days before deciding to start his men on the march to Washington's side. They began their trek the night of December 11 under command of Lee's subordinate, General John Sullivan. Lee himself tarried. He chose to spend the next night at a tavern in tiny Basking Ridge, accompanied by only four officers and a guard of fifteen troops.

Earlier that day, Lord Cornwallis had dispatched elements of his Sixteenth Light Dragoons on a patrol intended to locate Lee's forces. Lieutenant Colonel William Harcourt and his men rode for eighteen miles and then billeted themselves in a house at Hillsborough, only to be routed from bed at 1 A.M. by a fire.

They rode on toward Morristown, and just a few miles short of Basking Ridge learned from a friendly Tory that Lee was staying at the Widow White's tavern there. Two American sentries captured farther down the road confirmed the tale.

Lee dallied again that morning, Friday the 13th. He was still at the tavern when the British closed in about 10 A.M. They quickly killed two of Lee's guard and wounded others outside the tavern. They then began firing into the lodging house itself.

At first Lee would not come out; the Americans fired back, but with no real result. Mrs. White, meanwhile, begged the British to spare her tavern, then begged Lee to surrender before the British burned it down. After about fifteen minutes, he did.

George Washington, naturally, was distraught to hear the "melancholy intelligence" of Lee's capture and told Congress he felt "much for the loss of my country in his captivity."

What Washington—and quite a few others—didn't yet realize was that Lee's capture would be a boon for none other than George Washington himself. With Lee held prisoner for the next sixteen months, Washington no longer had a second-guessing rival snapping at his heels. He forged on with no further advice from the worldly Englishman. He even garnered a few victories, starting with his own crossing of the Delaware and defeat of the Hessians at Trenton on December 26, 1776, just two weeks after Lee's removal from the playing field.

When Lee returned after a prisoner exchange, they had their famous contretemps at Monmouth, New Jersey. Lee again disobeyed orders, was halted in retreat from the enemy and, after remonstrating with Washington in insulting terms, was court-martialed and convicted. Insofar as the American Revolution was concerned, that was the end of Lee.

As for Lee's tipsy horse, it seems the dragoons who had seized Lee celebrated so earnestly that night that they insisted upon getting the great general's horse drunk with them.

The story doesn't end there. It also turns out, according to documents found nearly one hundred years later, that Lee, during his long captivity, submitted to the British a plan of his own *for subduing the rebellious colonies*! In his own handwriting no less, these documents were found, it seems, among the papers of a companion of General Sir William Howe, commander in chief of British forces.

Chosen with Purpose

FOR AN OAR-POWERED RIVER CRAFT, these were real monsters. Forty to sixty feet long, in use since 1750, the Delaware River's Durham boats could carry fifteen tons of iron ore, pig iron, or other cargo from Bucks County, Pennsylvania, downriver to Philadelphia. A crew of six, plus their captain, took the heavily loaded boats downstream, sped along by the current. The watermen steered and powered their craft as needed by great oars. The boats then returned, with cargoes up to three tons, with their crews pushing the way upstream with long poles.

The riverboats first appeared as a natural market outgrowth of the Durham Mine Furnance near tiny Riegelsville in Bucks County. Robert Durham built the shallow-draft boats with an eye toward carrying heavy loads while negotiating the river's rapids. Pointed at each end like canoes, they typically had an eight-foot beam and would float in five inches of water empty and thirty inches when fully loaded with heavy cargo such as pig iron.

An eventual fleet of three hundred Durhams manned by two thousand or so rivermen was destined to serve on the Delaware for more than a century, almost to the first days of the American Civil War. The boats plied their waterway from Easton to Philadelphia and back loaded with cargoes such as the traditional iron, produce, grain, soft goods, and even whiskey.

Their most dramatic moment, however, came on the wild, stormy Christmas night of 1776 at a point where the river is 1,000 feet wide. For here, at McKonkey's Ferry, George Washington was ready with 2,400 men to cross the Delaware—if it could be done—

and to attack the Hessians encamped at Trenton a short distance beyond the opposite shore.

No mere skiffs or rowboats, these were the commodious, heavy-duty craft that Washington and his men already had used in their first crossing of the Delaware early that December, just hours ahead of the pursuing British. And that choice had been no accident, that narrow escape no chance affair. Harassed and hounded by the British all the way south through New Jersey after his defeats in the New York area, the Virginian at the head of the tattered American army refused to panic and flee by any means that might present themselves. As he well knew, any means that might somehow pop into view also might not. The salvation of his army could not be left to mere chance.

The fact is that Washington had a plan: If he could reach and cross the Delaware, commandeer all its boats and destroy all its bridges for thirty miles or so in either direction, he would have a wide ditch between himself and the British.

He knew about the Durham boats that plied the Delaware. In fact, he wrote on December 1, "The boats all along the Delaware River should be secured, particularly the Durham Boats."

That is what he and his small army did when they accomplished Washington's "First Crossing of the Delaware" a week later, on December 8. Even with the leisurely pace adopted by the pursuing British under Lord Cornwallis, it was a close thing—very close. The redcoats reached Trenton and the river's eastern banks only hours after Washington and his men had pushed off for the opposite shore in their motley fleet of boats, Durhams included. The tall Virginian had stayed behind to the last, too. A Delaware captain, Enoch Anderson, later recalled those dismal days just east of the river: "We continued on our retreat—our regiment in the rear and I, with thirty men, in the rear of the regiment, and General Washington in my rear with pioneers—tearing up bridges and cutting down trees to impede the march of the enemy."

With the "ditch" now separating the opposing forces, Sir William Howe, overall commander of the British ground forces, was content to turn back for New York for a comfortable winter season spent in the city's warm, more civilized quarters, while leaving various garrisons in a line of posts through newly occupied New Jersey. One of those garrisons, of course, was the Hessian contingent left to guard the Delaware at Trenton.

As Howe, Cornwallis, and Company turned away, few on the British side thought the shattered rebel army would dare stir up any more trouble until the next spring, at which time the Americans could be defeated again. One of these days they would realize the futility of fighting the mighty, well-seasoned, -trained, -fed, -clothed, and -equipped British army. Wouldn't they?

Not if you asked George Washington, who even at this nadir of his country's fortunes was busy gathering his forces—his Durham boats in particular—for a second crossing of the Delaware, the one to be attempted at McKonkey's Ferry the night of December 25. As is well known, the weather was far from mild that wintry night. The wind howled as the men shuffled forward to take their places in the boats, many leaving bloodstains on the snow from their ill-shod feet. Snow already covered the ground. More was about to blow and swirl in their faces . . . sleet, too.

The water was high, the current was fierce, and ice floes filled the river—speeding floes that could smash into and capsize any small boat that might foolishly venture into the rushing water. "The floating ice in the river made the labor almost incredible," wrote Washington's artillery master, Henry Knox, later.

Even so, General John Glover and his saltwater sailors from Marblehead, Massachusetts, did their job that terrible night on a half-frozen, yet still-coursing freshwater river. Not a man or a gun was lost as they ferried Washington and his primary force of 2,400 men across the river for the surprise attack—and victory—at Trenton the next morning. They did their job, the troops did their job, Washington did his . . . and, last but far from least, the sturdy Durham boats, under the worst of conditions, did theirs.

V. 1777–1779: Settling Down to War

Civil War in the South

"I BEGAN TO GROW UP—times began to be troublesome, and people began to divide into parties." Friends of the past, now Whigs or Tories, "began to watch each other with jealous eyes."

That's the way it began and would continue in the Carolinas—a nasty civil war among friends and longtime neighbors of different ethnic backgrounds in some cases, and of different loyalties in all cases. The Whigs were the Patriots and the Tories the Loyalists. Except when the British or the Continental Army was on the march, the war in the Carolinas was a guerrilla war of unauthorized raids that could degenerate into atrocity and murder.

Gradually becoming involved in this maelstrom of violence, vendetta, and hatred was teenager James P. Collins. No longer an apprentice tailor who had one day amused himself by making a miniature suit for a cat (see "The Well-Suited Cat," p. 40), he now began his own guerrilla role for the Whigs as a local "collector of news" for a neighboring militia captain named Moffitt.

For a time, the "news" he brought back from his rovings on horseback within a thirty-mile radius of home was useful in frustrating Tory plans. He came to view Tories in three categories: those who truly believed in their cause "from principle"; those who were cowards and mere "tools" for others; and those who "believed it impossible for the cause of liberty to succeed and thought in the end, whatever they got, they would be enabled to hold, and so become rich. The latter resorted to murder and plunder, and every means to get hold of property."

Then there were, in his neighborhood, men "who pretended neutrality entirely on both sides; they pretended friendship to all." Young Collins obviously didn't think much of them—in fact, thanks to their nosiness and loose lips, the Tories learned of his spying activities and "swore revenge."

He gave up his intelligence forays for the time being, but the British capture of Charleston, South Carolina, in 1780 brought a new phase of the revolutionary struggle in the Carolinas. "[T]here was a proclamation for all to come forward, submit, and take protection; peace and pardon would be granted." Officers leading "guards or companies of men" were dispatched in all directions "to receive the submission of the people." "Vast numbers" of colonists stepped forward and submitted, whether through fear, outright willingness, or simply a hope for peace and quiet. But there were strings attached to the loyalty "submission" that the real Patriots could not accept.

Coming near Collins's home on a submission errand was "one Lord Hook, who came up and stationed himself at or near Fishing Creek at some distance below where we lived." Almost every man in the area went to hear what he had to say. "He got up, harangued the people in a very rough and insulting manner and submitted his propositions for their acceptance. Some bowed to his sceptre, but far the greater part returned home without submitting."

Their noncompliance provoked a deadly brawl typical of Carolina warfare. Lord Hook attacked a nearby iron foundry (Billy Hill's Ironworks), "killed several men, set the works on fire, and reduced them to ashes."

At that, Collins and his outraged father, Daniel, joined Moffitt's band of seventy Minutemen. "In a few days there was a meeting of several officers, and it was determined to attack Lord Hook, and take vengeance for the burning of the ironworks."

They approached the Briton's headquarters, making their way on foot through a peach orchard just after sunrise, "thinking the peach trees would be a good safeguard against the charge of the horseman [the British cavalry]." The headquarters sentries spotted the Americans, fired and ran off for help. Shortly, mounted British cavalrymen came into view—an imposing sight to the ragtag militiamen. "I had never seen a troop of British horse before, and thought they differed vastly in appearance from us—poor hunting-shirt fellows."

The trees did prove useful as hoped. "The leader drew his sword . . . and began to storm and rave, and advanced on us; but we kept close to the peach orchard."

The British drew closer, and their leader—apparently Lord Hook himself—shouted, "Disperse you damned rebels, or I will put every man of you to the sword."

At that, "Our rifle balls began to whistle among them, and in a few minutes my Lord Hook was shot off his horse and fell at full length; his sword flew out of his hand as he fell and lay at some distance. . . ."

At a loss, the stricken Lord Hook's men circled him uncertainly two or three times. "At length, one halted and pointed his sword downward, seemed to pause a moment, then raising his sword, wheeled off and all started at full gallop." In seconds, the troopers were gone and Lord Hook alone lay dead at the feet of Moffitt's men. In the nearby yard were two wounded cavalrymen who had been left behind as well.

After an argument between two of Moffitt's men over whose shots actually killed Hook, the entire group was ready to disband and go home. "We then bound up the wounds of the two [British] men, took three swords, three brace of pistols, some powder and lead, perhaps my Lord Hook's watch, and but little else, and departed, every man for his own place."

So it went in the Carolinas war, blow and counter-blow, reprisal for reprisal. This apparently had been the first combat for young James Collins, only sixteen. How would he recall that day? Read between the lines as he closes his account of the battle in his autobiography: "For my own part, I fired my old shotgun only twice in the action. I suppose I did no more harm than burning so much powder."

Additional note: Collins's tale of "Lord Hook" probably represents a skewed recollection of the fate dealt to a notorious Tory, Captain Christian Huck, operating in York County, South Carolina, in 1780. Huck, originally from Philadelphia, was known for his atrocities against Whigs in the Carolina backcountry—and for a special propensity for burning down Presbyterian churches. In his foray of July 1780 he destroyed William Hill's Iron Works in York County, then threatened militia colonel William Bratton's wife in an attempt to locate the officer. When Martha Bratton bravely refused to reveal her husband's whereabouts, a Huck aide had to stop him from doing her physical harm. That night, as Huck ("Hook?") and his men were encamped at nearby Williamson's plantation, Whig militiamen, led by Bratton and Colonel Edward Lacey of General Thomas Sumter's brigade, quietly surrounded them. In the attack that followed at dawn, Huck was killed. A stone tablet marking "Huck's Defeat" has stood near the site of the Bratton home for many years.

Rogue Warriors

ONE OF THE MOST NOTORIOUS partisan leaders, Tory or Whig, to emerge from the bitter infighting that afflicted the Carolina countryside during the American Revolution was David Fanning. Apparently abused as an orphaned youth, he was so badly disfigured by scalding water in a childhood accident that he preferred to eat by himself. Later in life, he always kept his scarred scalp hidden beneath a silk cap.

One of his enemies was the Whig militia officer Philip Alston, scion of an aristocratic family, and a desperado and murderer of the worst kind.

The terrain these two rogue warriors fought over in the name of Crown or Rebellion—or simply raided and plundered with their marauding bands—included the North Carolina sandhills best known today for the lovely resort and retirement towns of Pinehurst and Southern Pines.

Full résumés of these two are not available to us today, but in Fanning's case it's fairly clear that he was born at a place in Amelia County, Virginia, called Beech Swamp, probably in 1755. Orphaned as a child, then bound to a county justice in North Carolina and apprenticed to a loom mechanic, he wound up in western South Carolina just before the Revolutionary War broke out.

His first activity, as a Loyalist partisan, came in the same South Carolina backcountry—he fought the Patriots at Ninety-Six and Big Cane Brake in 1775. Twenty or twenty-one years of age by this time, he soon was leading Loyalist bands on raids and in skirmishes against area rebels. He was often captured by his enemies and, by his own account, just as often escaped their clutches.

Accepting parole at one point in 1779, he kept to the sidelines for a short time, but sprang back into action with the arrival of fresh British forces under Lord Cornwallis in 1780. He now shifted to a base on the Deep River in North Carolina, from which he operated as both a Loyalist militia leader and a scout for Cornwallis. He reported to superiors in the regular British army based at Wilmington, close to the coast.

No longer content with his minor actions of old, Fanning resolved to raid the Chatham County courthouse at Pittsboro to free Loyalist captives awaiting court-martial by their rebel foes. Taking the town by surprise in July of 1781, Fanning not only succeeded in freeing his compatriots, he also came away with a few dozen prisoners of his own, among them court officials, Patriot militia officers, and three members of the rebels' state legislature.

After a series of raids on rebel-owned plantations, he and 225 men triumphed in outright battle against twice as many Whig sympathizers—Patriots. Fanning and company killed 23, took 54 more prisoners and, as highly valued "booty," captured 250 horses.

Still ahead, though, was Fanning's most spectacular feat of all. With the ranks of his followers swelled to about nine hundred, he and fellow Loyalist Colonel Hector McNeil marched on Hillsborough, North Carolina, on September 12, 1781. Here, Fanning's raiders burst into town and cut a remarkable swath with no losses to his side. He released more Loyalist partisans being held captive, as well as a few British regulars in the same unhappy condition. He also took two hundred prisoners, including rebel Governor Thomas Burke, his Governor's Council, and a slew of state legislators.

After a bit of leisurely looting, the Loyalists withdrew, of course taking their prisoners with them. They had covered twenty-six miles by noon the next day, according to historian John S. Watterson III in *The North Carolina Historical Review.* McNeil was in the lead, and as fate would have it, he had failed to put out advance scouts.

It was an unfortunate omission for all in Fanning's band, in view of the inevitable pursuit that would follow their capture of Governor Burke. For now, at Lindley's Mill on Cane Creek, the Loyalists were themselves taken by surprise. McNeil was immediately shot and killed in the rebel ambush led by Whig General John Butler. Fanning managed to reorganize his men and circle around for a flank attack on his Whig tormentors. After four hours of gunfire, the pursuers finally backed off . . . but they might not have, had they known that Fanning had lost the services of his next in command, Colonel McNeil, along with twenty-seven Loyalists killed and another sixty wounded. Indeed, Fanning himself was wounded in the arm—badly enough, it seems, for him to go into hiding to nurse himself while his men pushed on by themselves.

Well, not entirely by themselves. They still had prisoners, who had been kept under guard in a nearby house for the duration of the

gunfight. By Watterson's account, the Loyalist survivors took Burke and his fellow prisoners on a 160-mile, 10-day trek through swamp, marsh, and all other manner of desolate terrain to Wilmington, where the governor was entrusted to eager British hands. As events evolved he spent weeks as a prisoner on Sullivan's Island at Charleston, South Carolina, before being granted parole to return to North Carolina. Fanning, in the meantime, escaped his pursuers and recovered from his wound.

As for his bloody rivalry with the Patriot partisan Philip Alston, they had clashed by the time Fanning raided the Chatham courthouse at Pittsboro. According to the account developed by Blackwell P. Robinson for his local history, *Moore County, North Carolina, 1747-1847,* their first notable encounter came after Fanning's band, along with a clot of prisoners, stayed overnight at Loyalist sympathizer Kenneth Black's home near today's golfing resort town of Pinehurst. They were returning to a Fanning hideout at Big Raft Swamp in Robeson County.

The next morning, Black guided the Loyalist band for a few miles, then changed horses with Fanning because his was injured. On his way home—alone and mounted on the lame horse—Black ran into a party of armed horsemen who were in pursuit of Fanning and led by Alston. Black turned his mount in an effort to flee, but it took the rebels no time to overtake and shoot him. With the Loyalist then at their mercy, wounded and lying face down in the muck of a swamp, "some of Alston's men smashed his head with the butt of his own gun as he was begging for his life," wrote Robinson.

Alston visited Black's widow the next day to express his regrets and blame the murder on his men.

When Fanning heard about his friend Kenneth Black's cruel fate, he wasn't about to forgive and forget. Accounts vary, but Fanning himself wrote in 1790 that he trapped Alston and twenty-five men in an unnamed house soon after the Chatham raid, "as I was determined to make examples of them, for behaving in the manner they had done to one of my pilots [guides], by name Kenneth Black."

After an exchange of gunfire lasting about three hours, with four of Alston's men killed and all but three allegedly wounded, the rebels offered to surrender, Fanning wrote. Alston's "lady" did the negotiating of terms—"begging their lives"—and Fanning, "on her solicitation," granted the desperate plea, even though he had lost two men in the gunfight and had seen four others wounded.

Another account, furnished by Patriot General Butler (who later would ambush Fanning's raiders after their Hillsborough strike), was much the same. But Butler noted that the "slabboards" house in question was Alston's own home on the Deep River, a historic structure still standing today and known as the "House in the Horseshoe." Butler numbered Alston's force as fifteen to twenty men instead of Fanning's estimate of twenty-five. Also, by Butler's count, Alston "had seven Men wounded and Fanning had one or two killed."

Far more colorful, but possibly a bit apocryphal too, is the version developed by the Reverend E. W. Caruthers for his eighteenth-century book, *Revolutionary Incidents: And Sketches of Character, Chiefly in the "Old North State."* Caruthers notes that the walls of the besieged Alston home were clapboard—meaning they were exceedingly flimsy. Thus, he goes on to write, the Loyalist shots just whistled on through. Inside, Temperance Alston had tucked her two children into the fireplace for safety's sake, then taken refuge in a bed. (Wouldn't under the bed have been better?) Thus, the bullets simply whistled overhead. So while some of the men in the Alston house fell, either wounded or killed, she and the children remained unharmed.

Outside on this Sunday morning in August of 1781, the Loyalists gathered themselves for a bold charge. That failed when the man leading it, a Lieutenant McKay or McCoy, was struck down in his tracks by a rifle ball in the heart. Fanning then ordered—or "bribed," says Robinson's summary—a free black man to slip behind the house and set it on fire. But he, too, was shot by the defenders . . . by Alston himself, it is alleged.

The defenders inside the house were suffering fewer casualties than their attackers. Nonetheless, there came a turning point when Alston saw Fanning bring up an ox cart filled with hay or straw—obviously intent on setting it ablaze and rolling it up against the wooden house. Alston and his men were forced to surrender, or be shot one by one as they emerged from the burning house.

And Mrs. Alston and her two children? What Fanning expected of their fate is unknown . . . thanks to the lady herself.

With her husband and his men afraid to venture forth, even under a flag of truce, she volunteered to take the risk herself and discuss surrender terms with Fanning. Alston, to his momentary credit, at first objected but then finally agreed that even Fanning's vengeful followers would balk at shooting down an unarmed woman. And so, Alston's wife was the first out the door.

Adds Caruthers: "As soon as Fanning saw her, he called to her to meet him half-way, which she did; and then, in a calm, dignified and womanly way, said to him: — 'we will surrender, sir, on condition that no one shall be injured; otherwise we will, make the best defence we can; and if need be, sell our lives as dearly as possible.' Fanning, who could sometimes respect true courage, whether in man or woman, promptly agreed to the proposal, and honorably kept his word. The men all then surrendered and were immediately paroled."

All well and good it might seem . . . except that Robinson cites another source saying that while the prisoners were allowed to go free, Fanning's men thoroughly looted and vandalized Alston's house, even cutting open the feather beds.

A family history of the Alstons, published in 1901, also suggests that Philip Alston was not so kindly treated after all. This account asserts that Fanning, in fact, sent Alston to the British base at Wilmington as a prisoner. The rebel partisan then was placed aboard a prison ship. After a time, half starved, he slipped overboard one night with a fellow prisoner and swam several miles to shore. They were so weak and hungry that they ate raw meat from the carcass of a dead sheep they found in a nearby swamp. From there they eventually completed their escape. While the Moore County Historical Society has branded this account as entirely fallacious, one has to wonder where its graphic detail came from.

Oddly enough, a nearly matching account turns up in John C. Dann's collection of pension applications by Revolutionary War soldiers, published in 1980 as *The Revolution Remembered: Eyewitness Accounts of the War for Independence.* In it, South Carolina native William Gibson is quoted as saying he and a Colonel Philip Alston of Moore County, North Carolina, squeezed through the portholes of a prison ship one night, dropped into the water below, and made their way to shore together in a joint escape from British captivity. It was several days before they reached friends and safety. They spent two days near Waxhaws, South Carolina, with a "Widow Jackson" who may have been future President Andrew Jackson's mother.

Gibson's account is faulty as to dates and in relating how they were captured to begin with, but other details bear an uncanny resemblance to those in the Alston family history.

Meanwhile, in the aftermath of Fanning's attack on Alston's home, outraged Patriot authorities sent a force of one hundred men after the Loyalist . . . to no avail. Fanning, in fact, was never brought to bay—he continued his harassment of North Carolina's rebels even after the Yorktown surrender of October 1781. In February of the following year, a militia major from the Deep River area wrote his superiors a bitter plea for help in dealing with Fanning's Tory band. "Their number is superior to mine at present," wrote Major Joseph Rosser, "but the cruelty they have used by cutting and plundering the inhabitants where they go I am resolved to lose my life in the attempt [to stop them], whether you reinforce me or not. . . ."

Warning that Fanning was expected to be "raising Men fast," Major Rosser also declared, "It would make you almost shed tears to see the barbarities of them wherever they go."

Naturally, accusations of "barbarities" coming from bitter enemies like Rosser could be dismissed as entirely predictable bias. And, true, both Fanning and Alston operated in a rough-and-ready environment in which neither side showed much constraint. All such considerations aside, though, there really is no doubting Fanning's tendency to go well beyond the limits of military necessity.

Consider the sequence of events set off the time that Randolph County resident Andrew Hunter had some unflattering things to say about the controversial Loyalist partisan. In response, according to Robinson's book, Fanning "characteristically resolved to murder him [Hunter]." And sure enough, Fanning and his band soon tracked down and surprised Hunter on an outing to "procure salt on the Pee Dee [River]." With their quarry seemingly well in hand, the Loyalists took the time to settle down and partake of the provisions they had seized from him—after telling Hunter he would be hanged in fifteen minutes.

Hunter had other ideas. He suddenly leaped into the saddle of Fanning's favorite mare, a horse named "Red Doe," and galloped off as his captors scrambled for their guns. They got off a volley of five shots but had to aim high for fear of wounding the leader's prized mount. One missile struck Hunter in the shoulder, but he simply kept riding and succeeded in avoiding recapture.

Fanning, being Fanning, would not let the matter rest there, especially since a favorite pair of pistols—presented by his British commander at Wilmington—had ridden off with the mare. In no time, Fanning and his men descended upon Hunter's home, looted it and—worst of all—abducted Hunter's wife, who was "far advanced in pregnancy," plus a number of Hunter's slaves. Fanning then held them all in an isolated wood on Bear Creek in today's Moore County, but sent word to Hunter offering to exchange the hostages for the horse and pistols.

After a mysterious lapse of five days, Hunter sent back word of his own. Too bad, he reported. He had gotten rid of the horse and could not now retrieve it.

Infuriated, Fanning gathered up his men, along with the slaves, and rode off. Hunter's pregnant wife was left to her own devices in the remote, wooded hideaway. Fortunately though, one of the Loyalist's men circled back and told her how to reach a nearby home. She followed his directions and in a short time was reunited with her husband, who not only recuperated from his wound but for many years "revelled in telling of this affair."

He and his wife subsequently lived on the Pee Dee River in South Carolina, above Mars Bluff, where Andrew Hunter was considered a man of "respectability and wealth." Thus, the hard times of the Revolutionary period ended happily for at least one couple.

Fanning, meanwhile, gradually faded from sight. As the hostilities ended, he moved back to South Carolina. Later, he took up residence in St. Augustine, Florida, followed by a final move to Nova Scotia, home in the end to many a disappointed Loyalist. He died there in 1825.

Begged Not to Fight

ON THE EVE OF THE American Revolution, Isaac Hayne of South Carolina's Low Country—devoted family man, planter, horse breeder, Royal Assembly member—seemingly was sitting pretty. He owned three plantations covering a total of 2,251 acres. He held valuable city lots in Beaufort and Charleston, along with additional acreage in South Carolina and nearby Georgia. And he was a partner in an iron foundry.

Born in 1745, he was twenty when he married a minister's daughter and only twenty-five when he was elected to the Royal Assembly in 1770. Clearly, the master of Hayne Hall in Collecton County was a widely respected young man with nothing but a bright future ahead of him. He was courageous and fully ready to stand up for his principles, too.

In the revolutionary turmoil that soon engulfed his state, however, there came a time when he repeatedly begged not to fight for either the Loyalist or the rebel side. Even so, by the end of 1781, Isaac Hayne was dead—hanged by the British.

What happened to make a martyr of this American Patriot?

His early military career is not well known, but it seems that he was an active rebel—a South Carolina militia colonel, in fact—when taken prisoner by the British soon after their seizure of Charleston in May 1780. No friend to the Crown on another score, he was also co-owner of the Aera Ironworks in York County, which supplied the Patriot cause with tools, cannon, and ammunition until destroyed in 1780 by a raiding Loyalist party led by Captain Christian Huck. By most accounts, Hayne accepted the standard, no-more-fighting parole status initially offered to him, rather than be a prisoner of war. However, in July 1780, the British recanted and demanded he swear allegiance to the Crown as well.

This meant a Hobson's choice between joining the enemy or accepting prisoner status. Adding to the tough circumstance for Hayne was the fact that his wife, Elizabeth, and some of their children had come down with smallpox. He was badly needed at home! Elizabeth, in fact, was so ill that she died the next month.

The agonized planter saw duty to his family as coming first and signed the dread oath after British officers promised he would not be asked to take up arms against his fellow Patriots. Even with that concession, however, his choice grated. "... [A]s they allow no other alternative than submission or confinement in the capital at a distance from my wife and family at a time when they are in the most pressing need of my presence & support," he wrote to fellow rebel David Ramsay, "I must for the present yield to the demands of the conquerors." At the same time, Hayne took pains to assure his compatriot that the decision to return home while freshly sworn to the British side was "contrary to my inclination" and, indeed, "I do not mean to desert the cause of America."

For the next year or so, Hayne abided by the terms of his new parole status, staying at home and staying out of trouble. Quite naturally, it was no easy task to refuse the entreaties of partisans from both sides to come out and fight—for their side, of course. Still, for that length of time, Hayne was able to reject all such "offers," even going so far on one occasion as to hide his horses from visiting Patriot militiamen so as not to appear to the British to be working with the Patriots behind the royal back.

Neither side was any too happy with Hayne's determination to keep to his parole. Both the Loyalists and the British themselves violated their own earnest promises that he wouldn't be asked to fight in their ranks.

On the American side, a fellow militia colonel, William Harden— the very man who didn't get to see those horses—was thoroughly annoyed by Hayne's stand. Writing to the famous South Carolina "Swamp Fox," Francis Marion, Colonel Harden said that Hayne was "staying on too much formality" in regard to the stringent British parole requirements. Harden also said he was "disappointed and impatient" with the reluctant Patriot.

In the end, though, Hayne at last came out and fought. It was in July 1781, a year after he had been forced to agonize over his parole-versus-prisoner choice. By now, British fortunes in South Carolina were at low ebb. The Crown's forces had been pushed into an enclave incorporating Charleston and environs. Still concerned with adopting a course of honor in the affair, Hayne decided that he no longer had to feel bound to a conquering enemy who had been forced to give up his occupied territory. Thus, Hayne hastened to Colonel Harden's side on the banks of the Ashepoo River—quite ready for action!

Days later, Colonel Hayne led his militiamen to the outskirts of British-held Charleston and, in spectacular style, surprised the alleged turncoat General Andrew Williamson in his bed and carried him off in the night, bedclothes and all, to answer the rebel accusation that he had turned traitor (a highly questionable charge, it so happens).

Unfortunately, a pursuing party of British dragoons caught up with the militiamen and recaptured Hayne. Now, it would be a British accusation lodged against him, with consequences equally as grave as those that Williamson might have faced. And it wasn't long before the British acted to make a drastic example of their newly re-captured prisoner. In one sense, he had broken parole. Worse than that, he had gone back on his oath of allegiance (never mind that it was forced upon him to begin with). Specifically, the ruling by a court of inquiry was that he had been found "under arms raising a regiment to oppose the British government, though he had become a subject and had accepted the protection of that government after the reduction of Charleston." The penalty prescribed would be death by hanging.

The outcry was instant, as rebels, average citizens, and even key Charleston Loyalists protested the severity of the sentence. Petitions were circulated and personal appeals taken to British headquarters, all to no avail. Not even an ailing William Bull, the colony's former royal governor, had any mitigating effect on the British military authorities when carried before them on a litter to add his plea for mercy in Hayne's case.

Despite all the public and private outcry, neither Colonel Francis Lord Rawdon, British field commander for South Carolina, nor his subordinate, Lieutenant Colonel Nisbet Balfour, commandant of British occupation troops in Charleston, would budge on the grim matter.

August 4, 1781: the appointed day of execution. Thousands lined the streets of Charleston, many openly weeping, as Colonel Hayne was marched past on his way to the gallows. A friend urged him to show the onlookers how bravely an American could die, and Hayne answered, "I will endeavor to do so." Minutes later, he stood on the cart beneath the noose. The hangman was fumbling with a cap, having trouble with it. What was he trying to do, Hayne quietly asked his executioner. Trying to pull it down over the eyes, the prisoner was told.

"I will save you that trouble," said Hayne, and he pulled the cap down over his face himself. Seconds later, it was all over.

Over, yes . . . except that the unfortunate Hayne never did strike his countrymen as a culprit deserving of hanging. Rather than sap or undermine Patriot resolution, his execution immediately strengthened it. Rather than an example, the British had created a memorable martyr to the American cause.

Deadly Duel in Georgia

IT WAS THAT KIND OF age, that kind of tension, and that kind of publicly declaimed insult. Button Gwinnett, delegate to the Continental Congress, signer of the Declaration of Independence, and president of Georgia, was, according to his political enemy Lachlan McIntosh, "a Scoundrell & Lying Rascal."

The Georgia general, a friend of George Washington, said it out loud on the floor of the Georgia Assembly on May 15, 1777, in front of everyone who counted, politically.

That very evening, a written challenge came flying back, demanding "satisfaction" the next morning, "before sunrise." The place: "Sir James Wright's pasture," property of the now-deposed royal governor, one mile from "downtown" Savannah.

The general replied that although the hour requested was an early one, he indeed would be there, "with a pair of pistols only."

In one way, their dispute echoed the long-standing tension between the two Whig factions of Revolutionary Georgia. One could well consider the two duelists as the icons of the moment for those two groups—the Savannah-oriented aristocrats of the colony versus the more plebian-minded coastal and backcountry residents. General McIntosh, Continental Army officer and socially prominent planter, was the very embodiment of the first group—the "Establishment." The English-born Gwinnett, on the other hand, a failed merchant and planter, was more the grassroots player of his day. Adept at politics, he arguably was the central figure in the formation of Georgia's Popular Party, which often was at odds with the more aristocratic faction (usually associated with Savannah's Christ Church Parish).

In another way, the dispute between the two was the outcome of more recent conflicts that were both political and personal in nature. Gwinnett, after taking over the presidency of the Georgia Council of Safety early in 1777, was under a double cloud: first, there was talk that his predecessor, Archibald Bulloch, had been poisoned; second, rightly or wrongly, he was blamed for a botched military venture against Loyalists based in northern Florida. One reason it didn't succeed was the prior tension between Gwinnett and McIntosh. For one, Gwinnett's Popular Party had accused Lachlan's older brother, William, a cavalry colonel in the state militia, of deserting his command area. He was later exonerated, only to be stung by a much more serious development—Lachlan's younger brother, George, was clapped into irons on a charge of outright treason!

While Gwinnett's dream of leading a punitive force against the Florida Loyalists was ill-considered from the outset, he had no choice in ordering the arrest of George McIntosh in March 1777. The damning evidence that now rocked Georgia's entire Whig establishment came from an impressive source—the redoubtable John Hancock, president of the Continental Congress.

A recently seized letter to British authorities from East Florida's royal governor, he reported, revealed that George McIntosh, a member of Revolutionary Georgia's governing Council of Safety, not only was trading with the enemy through a deceptive partnership but was considered secretly loyal to the Crown. Congress, rather than Gwinnett on his own, recommended the arrest that followed receipt of Hancock's documents.

While Lachlan McIntosh loudly defended his brother and fumed against Gwinnett—while the proposed military expedition still loomed in a limbo-like state—Georgia's Patriots were preparing for their first Assembly session under the new post-colonial constitution. Just then, George McIntosh was released on bail, with four fellow members of the Council among the guarantors of his bond. Charges of "Toryism" still filled the air when the newly created Assembly met in early May to organize Georgia's state government—and, not so incidentally, to elect the state's first governor.

Gwinnett, of course, would have been the leading candidate, but Georgia's political wars had stirred up so much rancor that a moderate coalition drawn from both Whig factions successfully nominated John Adam Treutlen instead. He was a member of the Popular Party, but no Gwinnett crony. The latter, in the meantime, could thank an Assembly investigation for declaring him innocent of any wrongdoing in the confused affair of the proposed military expedition.

What did that mean for General McIntosh, a potential commander of the strike force who had been both hot and cold to its for-

mation? If Gwinnett was blameless in the affair, did that mean General McIntosh was at fault instead?

Thus McIntosh took to the Assembly floor, assailing Button Gwinnett as both "Scoundrell & Lying Rascal."

They met, each with a second, the very next morning in former Royal Governor James Wright's pasture, as ordained by criss-crossing notes the night before. An eighteenth-century conception of honor—and considerable pent-up ill feeling—brought them there. And unfortunately, only one was destined to survive their brief duel by pistol.

The time was dawn; the date, Friday, May 16, 1777.

General McIntosh brought Colonel Joseph Habersham, fellow aristocrat, as his second; Gwinnett was represented by George Wells, friend and political ally from Augusta. Moving beyond the sight of some spectators, the four men halted to discuss the duel's deadly terms—most important, how far apart they should stand. McIntosh, clearly out for blood, gave the chilling reply, "Eight or ten feet should be sufficient." Gwinnett had already given the general that choice, but Habersham slightly altered the determination on distance when he suggested standing another foot or so apart.

Next, should they start back to back and pace off the steps between them? "By no means," declared the vengeful-minded McIntosh, "let us see what we are about." As a result, they stood facing each other, only a short distance apart. When all was ready, they could fire their single-ball pistols at will. And they did.

At the loud double report, Gwinnett fell to the ground. He had been struck above the knee, his leg broken by the vicious impact.

General McIntosh still stood, smoking pistol in hand, but he also had been wounded in the leg—a flesh wound in the thigh. He asked Gwinnett if he would like to go through a second exchange of shots, and Gwinnett gamely said yes, if he could be helped to his feet.

At this point, Wells and Habersham intervened, assuring the two duelists they had "behaved like gentlemen and men of honor." They now could go home, each with his sense of wounded pride assuaged, and they did . . . only Gwinnett went home and, on Monday morning, May 19, died of "mortification," known to us today as gangrene.

Prince's Heroine in America

ALREADY A WIDELY CELEBRATED HEROINE of one rebellion against the Crown, and later a highly visible participant in the American Revolution, Flora MacDonald MacDonald was a staunch Loyalist.

Oddly enough, long before she came to colonial America from Scotland in the mid-1770s, she had been branded an enemy of the British Crown . . . and had gone to prison as a result. Her offending action in that situation had been providing aid and comfort to Bonnie Prince Charlie, claimant to the English throne, three decades before the American Revolution. In a scenario that could have been dreamed up in Hollywood (and indeed has been re-created on film), she helped the heir to the House of Stuart to escape English fury after the Battle of Culloden in 1746.

Charles Edward Louis Stuart, born in Rome in 1720, was the grandson of King James II, who was deposed in favor of his daughter Mary and her husband, William of Orange, in 1688. In 1702, Anne Stuart, Mary's sister, ascended to the throne as the last of the Stuarts to rule England—under her reign, in fact, the combination of Scotland and England became Great Britain.

Four decades after her death in 1714, Prince Charlie, the young Stuart pretender, and the proud Highland clans of Scotland battled the English at Culloden Moor in a futile effort to restore Stuart rule . . . but lost both the battle and the Jacobite Rebellion to the Duke of Cumberland, himself a royal heir.

The duke's cavalry showed little mercy to their routed foes, whom they chased down and, in many cases, killed on the roads and in the fields surrounding the battle site. Bonnie Prince Charlie managed to slip out of the country and reach safe haven in France, thanks in large part to the young Scottish lass Flora MacDonald, then twenty-four and the daughter of a gentleman farmer of South Uist in the Hebrides islands.

For the Bonnie Prince's sake, she served time on a prison ship. Her crime: disguising the would-be king as her own maidservant, Betty Burke, and leading him to safety.

It was a famous act on her part—so famous that Dr. Samuel Johnson and his companion of journal-keeping fame, James Boswell, came calling upon her nearly twenty years after her release in 1747. By then, she had married one Allan MacDonald, produced several children, and moved to the island of Skye, also in the Hebrides. According to Boswell's journal, she was a small, mild-mannered woman of "genteel appearance, mighty soft and well bred."

But she and her husband were poor; they had lost all their livestock, and they very shortly decided to join the wave of Scottish Highlanders, hundreds from Skye itself, seeking better fortune in the American colonies. Spring of 1775—marked by the opening shots of the Revolution in Lexington and Concord—found Allan and Flora MacDonald putting down new roots in North Carolina. They first chose a spot in Cross Creek, at the site of today's Fayetteville. They then moved twenty miles to today's Cameron Hill as neighbors to Flora's half sister Annabella (Mrs. Alexander MacDonald), but their final move was to land adjoining Cheek's Creek in Anson County (today's Montgomery County).

Allan "had just begun to establish himself when the Revolution broke out," wrote Blackwell P. Robinson in *Moore County, North Carolina, 1747-1847*. He also noted that the MacDonald couple had sailed for Wilmington, North Carolina, aboard the wooden ship *Baliol* from Campbelltown, Kintyre, in August of 1774 with their sons, Alexander and James, and their daughter, Anne, and her husband, Alexander McLeod, and the McLeod children—a real family migration.

A migration from poverty, yes, but into a revolutionary storm— for here, once again, Flora MacDonald would find herself painfully caught up in political turmoil soon leading to battle among those supporting the Crown and those who violently opposed its continued rule over the colonies. And this time, Flora was clearly on the side of the monarchy, with husband Allan named a major and called upon by Royal Governor Josiah Martin to raise Loyalist troops to fight the rebels. Flora herself—still famous among her Scottish peers—was a popular speaker at meetings in support of the Loyalist cause.

Unfortunately, both Allan and son-in-law Alexander McLeod were among the Loyalist officers taken prisoner in early 1776 when the rebels won the Battle of Moore's Creek Bridge, sometimes called "the Lexington of the South." This time, it was the anti-royalist Whigs tracking down the shattered enemy. Soon the countryside was plagued by armed bands plundering Loyalist and Whig households alike, as a bloody, unorganized, and often senseless civil war took hold in the Carolinas.

By her own account, a not-so-young Flora MacDonald, suffering from fever, was "dayly oppressed with stragling partys of plunderers from their [the rebel] Army and night robbers who more than once threatened her life, wanting a confession where her husband's money was." Worse yet, the MacDonalds' friends and neighbors for some reason began to blame them for the depradations suffered at the hands of "inspectors" appointed to visit and protect the dependents of Loyalist "menfolk" carried off as prisoners.

Flora, in the meantime, fell off a horse and broke her arm. Then, in 1777, the rebels seized her land because she refused to take an oath of allegiance to their side.

With her husband still held prisoner in Pennsylvania, she was given refuge near the home of her daughter, Anne, by fellow Tory Kenneth Black—later murdered by Philip Alston's band of vengeful Whigs. Allan, meanwhile, appealed to the Continental Congress to free him in a prisoner exchange so he could help his wife, whom he described as "in a very sickly tender state of health, with a younger son, a Daughter & four Grand Children" to care for. In time, the Scotsman was freed.

Flora and her daughter caught up with their husbands in New York, then went along as the two men rejoined their regiment, the Royal Highland Emigrants, by then posted in Nova Scotia. In October of 1779, "at her husband's insistence," wrote Robinson in his Moore County history, Flora sailed for home aboard the *Lord Dunsmore*— not to North Carolina, but back to Skye.

"Thus passed from the Carolina scene the renowned Flora," adds the Robinson history, "no longer the comely lass who saved the life of the Stuart pretender, but a broken old woman who had sent her husband and sons to fight for the Hanoverians [the House of Hanover, which, in the person of George III, now held the British Crown] the usurpers of the throne that rightfully belonged, in her mind, to the Stuart line of Scotland."

It was bitter irony, and she later complained that she and her husband "both have suffered in our person, family and interest, as much as if not more than any two going under the name of Refugees or Loyalists, without the smallest recompence."

After her death in 1790, however, there were rewards of sorts. A final tribute to Flora MacDonald MacDonald was the epitaph contributed by the famed and learned Dr. Johnson that solemnly proclaimed: "Her name will be mentioned in history, and if courage and fidelity be virtues, mentioned with honour."

Still another, more dramatic, tribute came from the continual flow of admirers to her gravesite—admirers so fervent that they virtually destroyed her first two marble tombstones by knocking off chips to take home as venerated souvenirs. As a result of which, Dr. Johnson's fine words had to be inscribed on a third stone.

The Barley Did Prickle

THEIR OARS MUFFLED IN CLOTH, five American whaleboats stole through the summer night . . . on a mission of kidnapping. Aboard were thirty-six volunteers. Third in charge was Ensign Abel Potter of the Rhode Island militia. He would later write about the daring raid and chronicle that night's mission, soon to be known as "capture of the barefoot general."

The assignment in the summer of 1777 was to kidnap the unpopular British General Richard Prescott, commander of the five-thousand-man British force quartered in Rhode Island. Not only was Prescott heartily disliked, but the Americans also needed a prisoner of high rank to exchange for their own General Charles Lee, captured by the British in New Jersey half a year earlier.

Prescott would fill the bill nicely, but he wouldn't be an easy target. He was staying in a guarded private home five miles from his headquarters in Newport, a location that was protected to the south by the open sea, to the west by a Narragansett Bay filled with British ships, and to the north and east by his troop dispositions.

The house in which he slept was located a mile inland from the bay, which the Americans had chosen for their approach. In short order, they safely sidled past the warships in the dark after launching their boats from Warwick Neck, ten miles above their preferred landing spot. Leading the resolute party was Lieutenant Colonel William Barton, a hatmaker from Providence, with Ensign Potter's older brother James second in command. The raid had been Barton's idea from the start.

Upon the party's landing in a quiet cove, James "took the first two sentinels" the raiders encountered, wrote Ensign Potter. He himself took care of a third man, who was standing guard right at the door of the general's quarters. When that sentry issued a challenge and demanded a password, Abel Potter leaned forward as if to whisper the "countersign" in the other man's ear. As the sentry unthinkingly leaned forward to hear, Potter grabbed his weapon and warned that he would die if he spoke a word.

"The sentinel answered 'I won't' tremblingly," wrote Potter.

Passing inside, the intruders encountered either the man of the house or his widow—accounts differ. According to Ensign Potter's memory, however, it was the widow, a Mrs. Oberin.

She knew his brother the sea captain and cried out, "Captain Potter, what's the matter?"

He quickly reassured her. "You need not be scared, Mrs. Oberin. We are not agoing to hurt you. Where is the general?"

Upstairs, she said.

In a trice, the two Potters and their commander, Colonel Barton, burst into Prescott's bedroom. The startled British commander immediately heaved up in his bed. Clad in nightshirt and nightcap, he obviously had been prepared for a good night's sleep.

Any such hopes now dashed, he guessed the intent of his intruders right away.

"Gentlemen," he said, with considerable understatement, "your business requires haste, but do for God's sake let me get my clothes."

Replied Barton: "By God, it is no time for clothes."

And so, off they went, taking an aide-de-camp, the three sentries, and the general with them. He was "barelegged," wrote the younger Potter, and at one point they rushed through a field of barley, "which pricked him some."

In short order the Americans and their captives were back in the whaleboats and headed for home. Ensign Potter, wading in water up to his chest, was the last man to climb aboard the sturdy boats.

Back at the Oberin house, an overlooked British soldier gave the alarm ... but he had to ride first to the nearest British encampment.

Rockets then announced his news. Shots were fired, and they did come close to the escaping whaleboats, wrote Potter many years later. He and his fellows "saw the shot strike the water around [us]," he said, but "None was hurt."

So ended a highly successful raid that produced just as much embarrassment for the British as the American side had endured the year before with the humiliating capture of General Lee. As hoped, the acquisition of General Prescott enabled the Americans to exchange him in 1778 for Lee.

Congress later cited Barton for his bravery, awarded him a commemorative sword, and presented him with a confiscated Loyalist home in Newport. As time passed, he was promoted to brigadier general, but his fighting career was cut short by a wound suffered on patrol. Also grateful for his exploit, his fellow Rhode Islanders made him adjutant of the state militia and a state legislator. For all that, though, Barton died in debt, owing to unfortunate speculations in Vermont lands.

Young Potter, for his part, survived three tours of duty with the Rhode Island militia, moved to Vermont after the war, and one day sent a member of his family to school in Pownal, Vermont. The child's teacher was the sentry he had silenced so effectively, yet bloodlessly, at the door of General Prescott's quarters the night of July 9–10, 1777.

Murder Most Foul

SHE WAS YOUNG AND OH, so fair, with long, auburn hair, blue eyes, and a creamy white complexion. And she was in love with a young Loyalist serving, in 1777, with British General John Burgoyne's army coming down from Canada into upper New York.

It was a different time, so long ago, a time of war, but even then, human society was occasionally plagued by random, senseless, unplanned acts of violence.

Poor Jane McRae. How, even at a time of war, caught between

clashing armies, could she ever have anticipated the events yet to come? And wearing her wedding dress, too!

Before the Revolutionary War erupted, she had lived with her brother John McRae, a pioneer farmer who tilled the rich soil beside the Hudson River, south of Fort Edward. Nearby was the neighboring Jones family, and all of them recent émigrés from New Jersey where Jane McRae and the Jones boy, David, had been childhood friends. Now, some years later and all grown up, they no longer were mere friends—they were in love.

The war did intervene, to be sure. With revolution came a parting of the ways for the two families. John became a colonel in the rebel militia of their shared New York community. David, though, felt that his allegiance had to be with England. He soon was a lieutenant with Peter's Provincial Rangers, assigned to General Simon Fraser's corps, which in July 1777 was at the very spearhead of Burgoyne's army as it moved south, aiming, it appeared, right at Fort Edward itself.

Much larger Albany, of course, was a more important British objective. The overall plan was to split the northern colonies by seizing the entire Lake Champlain–Hudson River corridor, a vital transportation network.

David and Jane had made certain plans despite the uncontrollable tides buffeting their shared homeland. For the moment, it appeared they could benefit from one minor eddy gently carrying them into a small and quiet cove. They could marry! Quickly, quietly . . . even safely.

Accounts vary and the facts slip and slide. It may have been the sudden notice from David telling Jane that he was so close by. It may have been a plan of longer moment. They had been in correspondence, after all, ever since David went off to join the British in Canada. No one knows for sure. Only the principals themselves knew the details.

In any case, it seems safe to say that Jane, in response to notice from David, left her brother's farm to stay with a Mrs. McNeil, a widow who was related to David's superior officer, General Fraser. As the British force edged ever closer to Fort Edward, Jane was to await the most important message of all: that David soon would be close enough to send for her. She would then rush to his side, and they would marry!

And the message did arrive. Saturday, July 26, was to be the day.

Breathless with excitement, she donned her wedding dress. Looking back we surely don't know this young pioneer woman's reaction to the instructions sent by her would-be groom. He would be waiting for her in his army camp with a chaplain standing by, ready to marry them. All she had to do was walk the four miles through the woods into the camp, alone and unnoticed.

Well, not exactly alone. David had enlisted an escort for her—a band of Indians who would be creeping alongside her path, out of sight but ready to protect her. It was, after all, a time and place of war.

For Jane and David, both the moment and the place would prove unfortunate choices. Unknown to either young lover, a Patriot picket of several men was stationed in the wooded area near the widow McNeil's home. And a second band of Indians was prowling the same woods.

It is not known today exactly how they all met. Clearly, Jane had set out on her trek to the awaiting David's side, but after that . . . what? The second Indian band clashed with the rebel picket, killing some of the American militiamen, it seems fairly certain. The two Indian groups, both apparently allied with the British, then met near a stream or a spring in the woods, then fell to arguing over Jane, caught in the middle.

By one account, the maverick Indian band had murdered a near-by family of settlers, then seized both Jane and Mrs. McNeil. According to the widow herself, the American pickets had come in pursuit and killed Jane by mistake—with a badly aimed musket shot.

Another account is that of Samuel Standish, one of the American pickets and himself a prisoner of the maverick Indian band—he later said that the two Indian bands fell to arguing vehe-mently—apparently over possession of Jane—then used their muskets as clubs to hit one another. In the end, one Indian leader suddenly turned on the hapless Jane with his musket and shot her in the chest. She fell to the ground and he scalped her on the spot.

Most say her body was left in the woods, and all the Indians retreated to the British encampment where David Jones awaited his would-be bride. He saw the scalp. He recognized her hair. The story is, he never recovered from his shock and grief. By one account, he died young. Another says he deserted the British army the next day and fled to Canada.

Jane's brother John was also deeply affected by his young sister's senseless death.

Meanwhile, the previously unknown Jane McRae became a cause célèbre for the Patriots in death—a new symbol of the widespread rage over the British alliance with local Indians. American General Horatio Gates cited her murder in a letter of protest addressed to Burgoyne himself. In it, Gates complained that Indians had killed more than one hundred innocent settlers in the area, women and children included.

Burgoyne, for his part, denied an accompanying accusation of paying for scalps, but said his army did encourage its Indian allies to bring in prisoners—alive. He also explained Jane's death as a terrible accident.

In fact, it is said that Burgoyne himself went to the Indians in an effort to identify Jane's killer, but desisted when warned that pressing his demand would alienate his Native American allies, who were valuable scouts in unfamiliar American terrain. As events turned out, they soon left his army anyway.

Both the Indian-ally issue and the closely related murder of Jane McCrae only further enflamed the area's American militia and strengthened their determination to defeat the British invaders. Jane's name became a battle cry at Bennington, Vermont, shortly after her death. Her sad story soon became so widely known, it also is said, that the famous English parliamentarian and orator Edmund Burke cited it in one of his speeches. (He still is known for his stand against British use of Indians in the Revolutionary War.)

Burgoyne, in the meantime, was defeated in the Battle of Saratoga, New York, just weeks later in October of 1777. It was a signal victory for the Americans, not only because it ended the British threat of splitting the northern colonies but also because it helped to convince Europe—France, in particular—that the American revolutionaries were to be taken seriously . . . and just might win in their cause.

Hero's Path to Betrayal

NEVER MIND THAT HE HAD officially been cleared of any wrongdoing in the affair, calumnies in some corners still persisted.

"Money is this man's god, and to get enough of it he would sacrifice his country," said the scurrilous handbill circulated in early 1777 by Benedict Arnold's enemy John Brown, still agitated over the mysterious loss of supplies Arnold's withdrawing Continentals had taken from Montreal in the spring of 1776.

Arnold could shrug off such slander, but he still, in 1777, burned over the refusal of Congress to restore his seniority in rank. Never mind that his ally George Washington reported to Congress that Benedict Arnold "has always distinguished himself, as a judicious, brave officer, of great activity, enterprize [sic] and perserverance." Congress still balked, and Arnold resigned his commission in the Continental Army.

Aside from the personal slights, however, the war was moving on—with great things in store, both for Arnold and the still-abirthing nation. He could thank "Gentleman Johnny" Burgoyne of His Majesty's red-coated forces for a fresh lease on life, for it was General Burgoyne's advance southward into upper New York from Canada that set the stage for Arnold's next round of heroics, but also for yet another painful injury to his bad leg . . . and a round of fresh controversy.

First, though, learning of the events to the north and receiving orders to join General Philip Schuyler in upper New York, Arnold had to ask for a suspension of his letter of resignation. He then found himself, a New Englander, serving under a New York general at a time when New Englanders in general didn't get along with New Yorkers. But Arnold, quite used to controversies and embarrassments of various kinds by now, ignored all that and, in one of the most ingenious ruses of the war, proceeded to rescue an American fort besieged by a force of four hundred British redcoats, Germans, and Tories, plus a thousand Indians led by the notorious Joseph Brant (Indian name, Thayendanegea) . . . all without firing a shot.

The American stronghold was Fort Schuyler (sometimes also called Fort Stanwix), an obstacle on British Colonel Barry St. Leger's path from Oswego down the Mohawk Valley toward Albany, where St. Leger hoped to link up with Burgoyne's much larger force. A militia column under General Nicholas Herkimer, ambushed and cut to pieces at nearby Oriskany, already had failed to relieve the Americans holding out in the vital post on the portage between the Mohawk River and a creek leading into Lake Oneida. With the brave Herkimer stopped, and even bleeding to death from a leg wound, Arnold, backed by fewer than a thousand men, was the only officer—New Yorker or New Englander—volunteering to take over the rescue mission.

And then, in mid-August of 1777, came pure inspiration in the unlikely persona of a supposedly half-witted prisoner who, although related to General Schuyler, was a Tory and, in fact, was under a death sentence for having helped to plan a Tory uprising in nearby Tryon County. As Willard M. Wallace reported in his biography of Benedict Arnold contained in the book *George Washington's Generals and Opponents,* the Indians regarded Hon-Yost Schuyler (alternate name, John Joost Schuyler) with fear and superstition; they thought he was "under the protection of the Great Spirit."

It may be that Hon-Yost was a good deal shrewder than most people thought. Wouldn't he have been aware that his relatives begged Arnold to spare his life, that they "made a deal" whereby he would be spared if he played a difficult and dangerous role for Arnold? That his own brother would be held hostage to guarantee his faithful compliance with the American plan? That he, in essence, was being asked to betray his old allies in the War for American Independence?

Whatever Hon-Yost may have thought, he carried out his part of the plan with a display of consummate acting ability. He burst upon St. Leger's camp outside Fort Schuyler, his clothing thoughtfully shot full of holes at Arnold's order. He appeared out of the forest with breathless warning that he had just escaped his own hanging, that the Americans were approaching in absolutely overwhelming force, and there would be no standing up to them. In support of his story, and also by prearrangement, a friendly Oneida soon appeared to "warn" Joseph Brant's Indians of their pending "peril." And soon after him, still another carefully coached Indian emerged from the forest with the same dire tidings.

Already stung by their losses to General Herkimer's militiamen at nearby Oriskany, the Indians refused St. Leger's entreaties to stay and rebuffed his transparent attempt to ply them with liquor. They left in such disorder and anger, says Wallace, that they even scalped a few of their Tory allies who straggled behind in the general retreat. And general it was, even a rout, since St. Leger's more traditional soldiers saw no reason to remain behind, either. Indians and white men, all kept going until they reached the shores of Lake Oneida.

Benedict Arnold's relief column, in the meantime, marched into Fort Schuyler triumphant and totally unscathed.

But now there loomed what many consider the most crucial battle of the American Revolution. General John Burgoyne's main column of some six thousand men still remained in the upper reaches of the Hudson River Valley, even though his lieutenants had been turned aside at Fort Schuyler and, thanks to New Hampshire's John Stark, at Bennington, Vermont. These ominous events meant that Burgoyne must press on to Albany by himself. Then came word that General Sir William Howe in New York would not be moving up the Hudson to meet Burgoyne, as once planned, but would shift his forces to Philadelphia instead. Now "Gentleman Johnny" really would be left alone—in a hostile territory, with winter approaching, his foraging prospects limited by an American scorched-earth policy, and the settler population aroused by rumors of atrocities committed by his Indian allies.

He wouldn't be alone for long, since General Horatio Gates, taking over the Continental Army's Northern Department from Schuyler, was moving north from Albany with 7,000 men to confront Burgoyne and his 6,000. The British general, for his part, stubbornly clung to the plan he personally had presented to King George III in London the previous winter—rather than retreat back into Canada, Burgoyne moved south, toward Albany. The two generals collided on September 19 at Bemis Heights, ten miles south of Saratoga, New York, in what would be Round One of a two-round fight.

The issue in this round was settled when the British attacked the American left wing in the Battle of Freeman's Farm, only to run into troops commanded by Benedict Arnold and his subordinate, Virginia's General Daniel Morgan. While the Americans suffered 319 casualties, the British lost twice that, then stood off for more than two weeks.

During the fracas, Arnold had been nettled that Gates refused to reinforce him and ordered him to remain at headquarters in the rear, rather than lead further attacks beyond the American defensive breastworks. Later, Arnold would be absolutely furious to learn that his division was given no credit for the outcome at Freeman's Farm in Gates's battle report to Congress. Seething, he confronted Gates, his superior officer, so angrily that he was removed from command.

When Burgoyne again moved against the Americans on October 7, this time with a force of 1,600 men, Arnold was still in a military limbo, with no men under his command. Stuck pacing restlessly at a headquarters in the rear, he could hear the sounds of distant battle . . . but he could see nothing and do nothing. Finally unable to stand it any longer, he took to his horse and galloped off to the sound of guns.

There is no doubt that the Americans, 11,000 strong by now and fighting well, would have prevailed in this Round Two, but the sudden appearance of Arnold on his flying mare absolutely electrified his compatriots. "Regiment after regiment broke into cheers as the bay mare with its blue-coated rider dashed to the front," reported historian Wallace.

To the astonishment of all, Arnold took over the American left wing and led the troops in one attack after another. When the British stiffened in response, "Arnold now swung his horse to the left and spurred between the two armies under a hail of British lead," wrote Wallace. He rallied a Connecticut brigade and Daniel Morgan's riflemen for an assault on a German-defended redoubt to the British right, a key to uncovering Burgoyne's right flank. He pointed with his sword, his mount surged forward, and in short order the Americans had broken through the German line. Here was sweet victory . . . Burgoyne backed off a mile that night, and a few more miles the following night. On October 17, he surrendered—a thunderclap event to onlooking Europe.

Based in large part on the British defeat at Saratoga, France at last saw real prospect of an American victory and jumped into the fray as an ally in the war against Britain. In a short time, so did Holland and Spain. The Revolution suddenly had taken on the aspects of a world war.

Arnold, in the meantime, probably could take greater credit for the victory than any other single American . . . but he was left in no mood or condition to enjoy any such laurels. While storming the key

German-held redoubt, he had been severely wounded in his previously injured leg. This time he would end up a cripple, one leg shorter than the other.

As double reward for his latest, if unauthorized, heroics, however, Congress finally acted to grant his seniority in rank, and Washington would name him commandant of Philadelphia, which would be evacuated in the spring of 1778 by General Howe. Here, as his leg slowly healed, Arnold would meet and woo his future bride, Peggy Shippen, a young socialite who had spent a fair amount of time during the British occupation of the city on the arm of handsome British staff officer John André.

When she, eighteen, and Benedict Arnold, thirty-eight, were married in April 1779, his wounded leg was still not strong enough to allow him to stand for the ceremony without the support of a fellow soldier. Even so, for the sentimentalist, they made a romantic picture: the handsome, not-quite-so-old war hero still recovering from his wounds and the blushing, ever-so-young bride.

Rather than a rosy future, however, Philadelphia would present Arnold with his greatest dangers yet, and one of them was money, or the lack thereof. As Wallace reports, Arnold had to "live far beyond his means" to keep pace with the Shippens and their socially prominent ilk. "Hard-pressed, he developed a number of money-making schemes, most of them of a dubious character."

Speculating in real estate, he looked for property abandoned by the city's now-absent Tories. But the real trouble came from a pass he granted to a ship in which he had a financial interest, and from his personal use of government wagons. Facing charges on the last two items from the civilian Council of Pennsylvania, he asked for a court-martial, a strategy that resulted in an official reprimand in April 1780 from his old friend and ally, George Washington.

It was not long after these events that Arnold, vain, resentful of all his accumulated slights and still hurting financially, gladly assumed command of the American fortress overlooking the Hudson at West Point. He took over the command with his traitorous pact already made—for ten thousand pounds, he would surrender the fort to the British.

He, in fact, had been in touch with the British for a year, since the spring of 1779, about the time of his marriage to Peggy Shippen ... whose old friend and dancing partner, John André, was destined to be Arnold's chief intermediary among the British.

"Push Along, Old Man!"

IT WAS A FIGHT TO remember, all right. "A most infernal fire of cannon and musketry," recalled a British officer. "The musket balls ploughing up the ground; the trees cracking over one's head, the branches riven by the artillery; the leaves falling as in autumn by the grape shot."

Among those present, quite naturally, were George Washington and his British counterpart, Sir William Howe. But there were other major—or colorful—figures, too. Among the Americans were "Mad Anthony" Wayne, the "Fighting Quaker" Nathanael Greene, America's own "Lord Stirling" (also known as William Alexander), the Marquis de Lafayette (wounded, by the way), and the "Boy Hercules" of the Revolution, Peter Francisco.

All told, the engagement drew a combined turnout of an estimated 27,500 to 33,000 troops—17,000 British and 10,500 to 16,000 American, depending upon whose numbers we can accept today. Thus, it may have been the largest battle fought in North America until the American Civil War nearly a century later.

True, it does have close rivals for such grandiose claim. The Battle of Long Island (1776), with an estimated 27,000 troops in the field, is one. Another is the Battle of Monmouth, New Jersey (1778), with its estimated 26,400 men on hand.

In any case, this was one fought, and fought hard, but also one in which George Washington's forces were surprised by a British flank attack, just as they had been at Long Island the previous summer. It was a battle recorded for posterity as a defeat for the Americans . . . but an engagement that impressed the British—and an onlooking world—for the vigorous defense the outflanked Americans mounted. Some broke and ran as the overwhelming flood of redcoats advanced upon them . . . but not all.

Despite the battle's colorful historical figures, its size, and its drama, it is not one that readily leaps to mind in quick review of the major events of the American Revolution. By reputation, it is no Yorktown, Trenton, or Bunker Hill. Certainly no Lexington or Concord.

Nonetheless, it had its significance in the progression of Revolutionary events overall . . . and certainly in the chain of events that unfolded just west of Philadelphia in the autumn of 1777. The Battle of the Brandywine was a dramatic prelude to the series of events that ended with Washington entering winter quarters at Valley Forge. And that crucible of suffering, in the eyes of most historians, brought forth a changed, almost professional Continental Army that soon began to turn tables on the British foe.

Perhaps that process had really begun at Brandywine in September 1777.

For the men directly under Washington, it had been almost a year since they enjoyed real battlefield success at Trenton and Princeton—mere skirmishes in scope, compared to what was looming at Brandywine Creek west of Philadelphia.

Far to the north, Horatio Gates, Benedict Arnold, and company had inflicted stinging defeat upon Britain's "Gentleman Johnny" Burgoyne at Saratoga, New York, an impressive, eye-opening victory in itself . . . but still short of Brandywine's magnitude in sheer numbers. What set the stage for Brandywine was Sir William Howe's bold bid to seize the rebel capital of Philadelphia after landing his 17,000 troops on the shores of the upper Chesapeake Bay in late August. Washington hurried his 10,500 or so men over from southern New Jersey to block Howe's advance . . . on the wide and placid Brandywine Creek.

Still there and on view to visitors today (Brandywine Battlefield at Chadd's Ford, Pennsylvania) are the Quaker farmhouses where Washington and Lafayette quartered on the eve of the battle. The young Frenchman at this point, incidentally, was an unknown quantity to the Americans, a two-star visitor they didn't know what to do with. Somewhere nearby, too, was a giant teenager from Virginia who, for his size and fighting abilities, would become known as a young "Hercules"—Peter Francisco.

With his troops carefully disposed and his own grand strategy in mind, Washington waited for the British attack sure to come. And on the morning of September 11, it did—a 5,000-man frontal thrust against his center, right at Chadd's Ford. No cause for alarm . . . yet.

The trouble was, Sir William, thanks to his Loyalist allies in the area, had better intelligence than the rebels. He had learned of a ford on the creek they didn't know about, and he at that moment was marching his troops in a semicircle to cross the creek at that point in the rear and then attack the American right flank by surprise. It was exactly what he had done on Long Island the year before, only that time he had shocked the American left. The result on the Brandywine, after daylong fighting, was defeat for the Americans, although Generals John Sullivan, Adam Stephen, and "Lord" Stirling gamely fought the British outflanking their wing to the right. Anthony Wayne took over the fight at the center, to allow Nathanael Greene to rush his division to the aid of the overwhelmed right flank.

Imagine the chaos among the stunned American high command! Picture George Washington galloping from headquarters to the crisis point, jumping the neat Quaker farm fences, urging on his local guide, Joseph Brown, with the words, "Push along, old man, push along."

Nonetheless, many of the Americans held, backed off, then held again before final retreat from the tide of redcoats flooding the American rear. In many such pockets, it was only when the issue came down to the use of the bayonet that the Americans finally retreated—since, in most cases, they simply didn't have bayonets.

They retreated with considerable pride intact. Perhaps Captain Enoch Anderson of Delaware put his finger on the mood of Washington's army in the immediate aftermath. "Not a despairing look," did he see that evening, "nor did I hear a despairing word. We had our solacing words always ready for each other, 'Come boys, we shall do better another time,' sounded throughout our little army."

The untried newcomer, Lafayette, had proven his leadership ability in all the tumult, rallying and directing his new comrades despite a leg wound. The young giant Peter Francisco was wounded, but he would live to fight another day.

The same could be said for Washington's small army itself— wounded, but still able to rise and fight yet again. In just days, the same Continental Army would see Howe occupy Philadelphia, weather a stinging British raid on Wayne's troops at Paoli, mount a major attack of its own at Germantown (eventually repulsed), frighten off a Howe probe at Whitemarsh, and then head for winter quarters at Valley Forge—there to complete the wintertime metamorphosis producing a greatly toughened, professional army quite ready to take on the far more experienced British.

Still there to see, incidentally, are the very sites where these historic events took place—Brandywine Battlefield at Chadd's Ford, Cliveden House at Germantown (centerpoint of that battle), and the nearby Valley Forge National Historical Park.

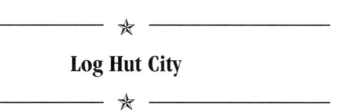

Log Hut City

"WE ARE ALL GOING INTO log huts," wrote the general to a brother, "a sweet life after a most fatiguing campaign."

As Nathanael informed his brother Jacob, it indeed had been a tough, wearing campaign against the British, but now, in the latter half of December, it was time to go into winter quarters. The order of the day was to build log huts. Hundreds of them—a virtual city of log huts, all by the commander's exact specifications. They were to build an eighteenth-century Levittown of neat, look-alike structures!

Also by the commander's order, the army was to be broken up into squads of twelve men each. Each squad would build a log hut 16 feet deep, 14 feet wide, and 6½ feet high, to hold its twelve members. There would be a front door, but no windows. A fireplace and chimney would be placed in the rear wall for heat. Gaps in the log walls would be chinked—filled in—with clay as mortar. The roofs would be made of crude shingles when possible, wood slabs, boards, even dirt supported by sticks, saplings . . . whatever could be found. The front door opening would be covered by primitive wooden slabs or boards, as well. Inside would be twelve bunks, six to a side wall, upper and lower. The bedding would be straw spread on wooden slats.

The army began trailing into its valley on December 19, and in one month's time, nearly one thousand log huts had been constructed. All told, about twelve thousand men were housed against the winter elements in their city of log cabins, after a historic explosion in log cabin construction for one place, at one time.

Historic, yes, but not for that reason alone. Much better known is another historical context entirely. Better known because it was Nathanael Greene who wrote his brother Jacob in January of 1778.

Because it was a commander named George Washington who issued the orders to build those huts and bed down in them. Because the valley chosen for his army's winter quarters in 1777–1778 was Valley Forge, Pennsylvania.

The men and officers wearily marching into Valley Forge were at a nadir in the fortunes of their rebellion against the British Crown. They were at the bottom of their hopes, and they could soon thank their lucky stars for those stout huts George Washington ordered them to start building right away.

They probably needed little urging, since the day chosen for the march to Valley Forge was dismal and bleak—cold, dark, windy, icy underfoot and, by evening, gritty with snow blowing into their faces. Just behind Washington's tattered army—at that moment only about eleven thousand strong—was a string of disappointing engagements with the British. Technical defeats, most of them, and yet examples of unexpected stubbornness shown by Washington's raggedy Continentals.

They came, historians say, shuffling along single file, some in bare feet. It took six hours for the whole column to pass any one spot on the trail. They came to a natural valley only eighteen miles northwest of Philadelphia, revolutionary America's capital city . . . newly occupied by the British.

Encompassing about two thousand acres, the triangle-shaped scoop in the Pennsylvania terrain was bounded on the north by the Schuylkill River, on the west by Valley Creek, on the southeast by a low ridge and, beyond that, on the east, by Trout Creek. This had been the home of an ironworks once known as the Mt. Joy Forge, but most recently called the "Valley Forge." As a supplier for the rebels, it had already attracted unwelcome British attention—in September of 1777 they raided the undefended valley and destroyed both the forge and a nearby sawmill, all belonging to Isaac Potts and his brother-in-law, William Dewees. With winter snows blowing now, though, the valley would be a safe refuge for Washington and his men. It was just far enough from the British to avoid surprise attack, yet close enough to harass their foragers and keep an eye on them—and it was defensible.

The British, too, had gone into winter quarters . . . but with the city of Philadelphia to pull down about their ears. Their commander, Sir William Howe, could be well satisfied with his achievements of recent weeks. He had sailed into the upper Chesapeake Bay, landed his men at Head of Elk, Maryland; skirted the Americans at Newport, Delaware; defeated them in the Battle of the Brandywine at Chadd's Ford, Pennsylvania; ambushed Anthony Wayne at Paoli (the Paoli "massacre"); raided Valley Forge; slipped between Washington and Philadelphia; and repulsed a subsequent American attack at Germantown. Now occupying Philadelphia, the British drove the rebels out of nearby Fort Mercer and Fort Mifflin south of the city and briefly engaged Washington again at Whitemarsh to the north.

None of the foregoing was a real knockout blow for the Continentals, but it certainly was a bedraggled lot now filing into the valley that Washington had chosen as a winter quarters. The sick were sent to Reading, Pennsylvania, just beforehand ... but with two thousand men marching shoeless and all the rest exhausted and now exposed to the elements, it wouldn't be long before many more would turn up ill.

They arrived at nightfall December 19, with only a light snow blowing. Christmas Day would bring heavy snow—four inches. Another four inches would fall December 28, and still more the next day. Obviously, from the very first moments at Valley Forge, shelter and food were needs that had to be met.

With Washington's log huts the shelters of choice, the men of his army fell to their mammoth construction project right away—"like a family of beavers," said the revolutionary pamphleteer Thomas Paine after a brief visit.

Even so, it would be more than a month before all were securely "hutted." Nor was it an easy task to build the huts. There were plenty of trees to chop down, but tools, even nails, were in short supply. So were draft animals—the men had to bend their own backs hauling the logs to their hut sites. The sites, by the way, were arranged on "streets" organized by military company, by enlisted men's quarters, and by officers' quarters. Which is not to say, as events turned out, that all the log huts were built exactly to Washington's prescription. The tired troops in many cases preferred to excavate a dirt flooring two feet below the ground to save a few logs in the walls above, even though that meant added dampness inside. In some cases also, the dimensions of the huts were a bit smaller than called for, or the fireplaces were placed in a different spot.

The most common variation may have been in the roofing materials, since wooden boards or shingles were not easily found. At least one squad used evergreen boughs, it appears, while others resorted to tent cloth as a temporary expedient. The roofing problem was so vexing that Washington offered $100, a goodly sum in those days, for the best suggested substitute for wooden boards.

By February 8, 1778, however, Washington was able to report "most of the men are now in tolerable good Hutts."

Obviously lacking in each case, of course, were toilet facilities—the so-called "necessaries" were located some distance away, and often, too often at that, the men used nearby ground rather than walk to the common toilet facilities. Sanitation problems and concomitant disease felled about two thousand of Washington's men that winter and spring, not strictly because of cold weather, but more likely due to the warm-weather interludes that allowed bacteria to grow. More men from the Valley Forge encampment, in fact, died in the month of May 1778 than in any other month.

The rest, however, survived . . . to form the nucleus of a toughened, more tightly disciplined, better-trained Continental Army that went on to secure victory in the Revolutionary War. The majority survived that winter in large part because their need for shelter had been met almost from the start in the form of their log huts.

With the advent of warm weather in spring of 1778, the men were ordered to punch windows into their often smoky, poorly ventilated log structures, and to remove the clay chinking between the logs. Once the men marched out—in pursuit of the British after they left Philadelphia—the weakened log huts didn't last long. Indeed, none survived the two-plus centuries since, but if you visit the Valley Forge National Historical Park today, you will see life-size replicas on view at the ridge-top site where Patriot General Peter Muhlenberg's brigade once was encamped.

Deliverance by a Prussian Gentleman

AT THE DREARY CAMPSITE OF General Washington and his bedraggled army the winter of 1778, there appeared an unlikely apparition of sorts fresh "off the boat." He rode into Valley Forge from Lancaster,

Pennsylvania, late one day in February. He was an unprepossessing fellow, nearly comical in his uniform of blue. Middle-aged, a bit stout, long-nosed and balding, he was given to expostulation, but never in English, since he could not speak a word of it.

But he was full of energy and enthusiasm for the Cause. And he carried credentials and he had recommendations (from no less than Ben Franklin in France, for one) that made him appear to be, if not exactly the right hand of Frederick the Great, at the very least a veteran lieutenant general who had served with the famous military leader and king of Prussia.

That the newcomer was not really a lieutenant general, but rather a mere captain—an unemployed, impoverished one at that—did not immediately come to light. Nor was it clear—for that matter, nor is it clear even today—exactly how *Baron* von Steuben came by his title.

What is clear is that the plump and jovial Prussian (with an Italian greyhound by his side) became, nearly by himself, the salvation of the ragtag army's morale and efficiency in the very winter of its composite soul. Beset, challenged, and questioned from all sides, saddened by the plight of his suffering men, facing another summer of battle with the well-stocked British, George Washington had found himself an angel of deliverance.

Previously stung by the smug posturing of earlier, self-appointed recruits, Washington did entertain some caution in greeting the latest volunteer. And it was a time of low ebb in American fortunes, perhaps even of disillusionment, with the Patriot constituency. While the British sat snugly in Philadelphia, both warm and well fed, or at least well enough fed, Washington's men huddled in their log huts, left bloody markings of their shoeless marches, and grew thin for lack of real food.

Around the destitute army, few of the citizenry seemed to rally. Counterfeiters, report George F. Scheer and Hugh Rankin in their 1957 book *Rebels & Redcoats,* were issuing better-quality thirty-dollar bills than was the American Congress. Farmers around Valley Forge sent their provisions to the British in Philadelphia for the reliable English pound, rather than feed their own suffering army at Valley Forge.

But now arrived Steuben with his glowing recommendations from Ben Franklin and Silas Deane in France—the sort of high praise Washington had heard before, only to be disillusioned with its subject. The Virginian was taken, though, by Steuben's own cover letter that had come in advance of the Prussian's arrival. In it, Steuben had proclaimed his greatest ambition was "to render your country all the services in my power and to deserve the title of a citizen of America by fighting for the cause of your liberty."

Washington didn't yet know that Steuben was no lieutenant general or that he had *not* served for twenty-two years under Frederick the Great, as claimed. But Washington saw some hope in the baron's simple request, and Steuben in fact had served in Frederick's army, knew his military lessons, and once had been among thirteen officers the great Frederick personally chose for his own instruction in general-staff work.

Baron von Steuben thus qualified for a tryout at drilling and training the wintering Americans while Washington kept close eye on the proceedings. That Steuben was successful with the first hundred men placed in his charge as a "test case," and later with thousands more, is history.

As history also records, Steuben wrought a cohesive magic for Washington's citizen army, which soon sallied forth from Valley Forge to sting the British at Monmouth Court House, New Jersey. He first became inspector general, then served well and faithfully throughout the Revolutionary War in various capacities—and, indeed, by the act of a grateful Pennsylvania legislature, did become an American citizen.

Lifted the Horse

A COLORFUL FIGURE OF THE American Revolution, teenage soldier Peter Francisco was a giant in stature and strength. Appearing in ten engagements with the British from New York to the Carolinas and five times wounded, the young Virginian became the subject of many a Bunyanesque tale told and retold at Patriot campfires.

By one such legend, he slew eleven redcoats at Guilford Court House, North Carolina, with his fearsome, extra-long broadsword. By another such tale, he carried away a 1,110-pound cannon on his back during the Patriot retreat at Camden, South Carolina. By his own later account, he did kill two of the enemy at each battle, and at Camden he also rescued his commander, a Colonel Mayo of Powhatan County, Virginia, from certain death.

His real exploits and feats of strength were remarkable enough. Not the least of his accomplishments as a mere private was his wide-ranging battle record. Serving first in the North, he took part in the Battles of Brandywine, Germantown, and Monmouth, and the capture of Stony Point. He also had a role in the Patriot raid of Paulus Point and fought at Fort Mifflin on Mud Island in the Delaware River. He suffered a musket wound in the right thigh at Monmouth and a serious bayonet injury at Stony Point. After recuperating and moving south, he survived Camden with no further harm, but encountered a British bayonet at Guilford Court House that laid open one leg from knee to hip. Left in a nearby log cabin with four others (who all died of their wounds), Francisco was found "by a good old man" who took him home and nursed him back to health.

In a petition to Congress for a pension, Francisco later gave his own, often graphic account of his various actions. At Camden, he saved Colonel Mayo's life "by killing an officer [British] who was in the act of taking his [Mayo's] life, when the battle had nearly subsided." And at Stony Point, he "was the second man who scaled the walls of that fort."

After recovering from the wound suffered at Guilford Court House, Francisco returned to Virginia (on foot) just in time for a run-in at Ward's Tavern in Amelia County with Tarleton's dragoons. The youngster was entirely on his own. Taken by surprise, he was accosted by nine of the British troopers. One of them demanded the young man's knee buckles and watch.

Francisco defiantly said the cavalryman would have to help himself, and when the unwary dragoon leaned over to do so, the unarmed Francisco seized the Englishman's own sword and killed him with a single blow to the head. He then turned to the rest of the company and killed two more, one of them a mounted trooper firing a musket at the young rebel.

At that point, a troop of four hundred more dragoons appeared, but Francisco confused his enemy by shouting for a totally fictitious force of his own to join him. He then made his escape with all but one of the horses belonging to the original nine. An enraged Tarleton sent one hundred of his men in pursuit, but to no avail. Francisco was clean away, his feat at Ward's Tavern soon memorialized in a famous engraving of the era.

Fittingly, the young soldier completed his Revolutionary War career at Yorktown in his "home state." He was not, however, a native of Virginia—nor even of the colonies. His origin, in fact, always has been a mystery, although it is now thought that he was of aristocratic Portuguese descent and perhaps was born in Azores.

He first came to light, historically, as a young boy, four to six years old, abandoned on the docks of City Point (today's Hopewell, Virginia), on the James River below Richmond. Judge Anthony Winston, a colonial legislator from today's Buckingham County, Virginia, heard of his plight, took him home, and raised him.

The youngster was exposed to the concepts of liberty and defiance espoused by Winston's nephew Patrick Henry and their mutual associates as the Revolution drew near. Francisco allegedly was present for Henry's "Liberty or Death" speech at St. John's Church in today's Richmond, Virginia. At about age sixteen, unusually large and physically developed for his age, Francisco eagerly joined the Revolutionary fray with the Tenth Virginia Regiment.

He did not attend school until after the Revolutionary War was won. From that experience, however, comes one testament to his truly extraordinary strength. His schoolmaster, Frank McGraw, is recorded as once saying that "Francisco would take me in his right hand and pass me over the room, playing my head against the ceiling as though I had been a doll."

In addition, a grandson claimed the adult Francisco once approached a cow and her calf stuck deep in mud and heaved them out by hand. Francisco's son, Dr. Benjamin Francisco, often recalled a funny story by which his father lifted a challenging brawler's horse over a fence (and thus avoided a fight with the thoroughly awed challenger).

Married three times (and twice widowed), Francisco tried his hand as a farmer, blacksmith, and operator of a tavern and country store before finally finding his niche as sergeant at arms for the Virginia House of Delegates late in life. A still-famous figure of the American Revolution, he died apparently of appendicitis at around age seventy. The states of Massachusetts and Rhode Island, both with significant Portuguese populations, for many years have marked

March 15 as Peter Francisco Day (in memory of Guilford Court House, March 15, 1781) and Virginia joined them in 1972 by officially recognizing the same date.

Personal Glimpse: Betsy Ross

QUITE POSSIBLY IN A HOUSE still standing on Arch Street in Philadelphia and open to the public today, Elizabeth Griscom Ross Ashburn Claypoole, well-known upholsterer in her day and a woman destined to be thrice widowed by the Revolutionary War, labored at what would make her an American legend for her very own contribution to the cause.

It was, legend says, the American flag! The Stars and Stripes.

No one knows for sure . . . yet no one can say for sure either that Betsy Ross did *not* create the American flag.

She did produce flags for the Pennsylvania navy, and her legend is specific in detail. William Canby, her grandson, presented a paper to the Pennsylvania Historical Society in 1870 in which he told how his grandmother, on her deathbed thirty-five years earlier, had told family members she sewed the first American flag at the behest of a secret committee of the Continental Congress, including George Washington, that visited her in May or June of 1776 in anticipation of the Declaration of Independence.

Allegedly, Washington sketched or showed her the basic flag scheme in the back room of her home and upholstery shop, but it was a design embellished with six-point stars. She showed him how a good seamstress could make more attractive five-point stars with a fold of the cloth and a cut of the scissors. The flag today indeed does sport five-point stars.

Good story, and the truth is that George Washington actually was in Philadelphia in the spring of 1776 for a visit with the Continental Congress. The "secret" committee supposedly was composed of himself, his good friend and congressional colleague Robert Morris, and George Ross, uncle of Betsy's late husband, John Ross.

As for her husband, therein lies the first of three sad stories to burden her life. A Quaker girl by family and upbringing, she had eloped to marry John Ross, son of an Episcopalian minister. As a result, she was read out of her family's Quaker Meeting. They married in November of 1773, and in January of 1776 Ross was mortally injured in the accidental explosion of a munitions storehouse he was guarding on the Delaware River. Betsy Ross, twenty-four and still childless, was a widow.

Meanwhile, Congress did not adopt the new national flag until June 14, 1777. Coincidentally, Betsy Ross married for the second time the next day, notes Paul J. Sanborn in an article written for Garland Publishing's two-volume encyclopedia *The American Revolution, 1775-1783.*

The official flag resolution called for "thirteen stripes alternate red and white" and "thirteen stars white in a blue field, representing a new constellation."

Betsy's second husband was Joseph Ashburn, an officer on the American brigantine *Patty.* They had two children, and she continued her upholstery business on Arch Street. Three years later, though, his ship failed to return from its latest voyage.

Two years or more after that, an old friend, John Claypoole, turned up at Betsy's door to report he had been in the Old Mill Prison in England with her husband, Joseph. His ship had been captured by the British, and sadly, Joseph had died in the prison.

Claypoole, himself, was a Revolutionary War veteran who had been wounded in the Battle of Germantown outside of Philadelphia and then somehow wound up at Old Mill in England. In a year's time, he became Betsy's third and last husband.

They had five daughters . . . but not an entirely happy life, since his health failed—perhaps because of his war wounds and the time spent in prison—and he spent the last seventeen years of his life bedridden, with wife Betsy taking care of him, their children, and her upholstery business.

After his death in 1817 (attributed, you could *certainly* argue, to Revolutionary War causes), she kept at her business until finally retiring in 1827 at the age of seventy-five—she had spent more than fifty years in her specialty by that time. She died in 1836 at age eighty-four.

Today, notes Sanborn, "historians generally agree that the Betsy Ross story is more legendary than historic." But he adds that there is another point of view. "Both sides come well prepared to argue their case. The debate still continues." Then, too, there is argument over the real location of the Betsy Ross house on Arch Street. Was it really 239 Arch? Some say yes, some no. "We only know she lived nearby, but in which house, no one is certain."

Whatever the facts, the Betsy Ross Memorial Association, started in the nineteenth century, "raised 1,040,270 dimes to help buy the house." When charges of graft muddied those waters, the city of Philadelphia stepped in, bought the property, and restored the house, now second only to the Liberty Bell as a tourist attraction in Philadelphia.

VI. Generally Speaking, Part 2

Indictment

To be sure, King George III reacted sternly to stiffening colonial resolve even before the convening of the Continental Congress. "The die is cast," he told his prime minister, Lord North, "the colonies either must submit or triumph; I do not wish to come to severer measures but we must not retreat."

True—the king and his ministers would not retreat, and the rest is history.

Part of the history was the Declaration of Independence adopted by the Second Continental Congress . . . and its very personal indictment of the king himself, even though, in some of those particulars, he was not really all that responsible. For Thomas Jefferson and his fellow delegates to the Congress, however, the British king served as a handy whipping boy and symbol of colonial grievances against the Mother Country in general. As a result, he took quite a rhetorical drubbing at Jefferson's hands. Herewith the indictment-like language stating the "case" against this symbolic but certainly not always guilty king:

"The history of the present King of Great Britain is a history of repeated injuries and usurpation, all having, in direct object, the establishment of an absolute tyranny over these states," wrote Jefferson in his preamble to the indictment portion of the Declaration. "To prove this let facts be submitted to a candid world:

> He has refused his assent to laws, the most wholesome and necessary for the public good.
>
> He has forbidden his governors to pass laws of immediate and pressing importance, unless suspended in their operation till his assent should be obtained; and when so suspended, he has utterly neglected to attend to them.
>
> He has refused to pass other laws for the accommodation of large districts of people, unless those people would relinquish the right of representation in the legislature, a right inestimable to them and formidable to tyrants only.
>
> He has called together legislative bodies at places unusual, uncomfortable, and distant from the depository of their

public records, for the sole purpose of fatiguing them into compliance with his measures.

He has dissolved representative houses repeatedly, for opposing with manly firmness his invasions on the rights of the people.

He has refused for a long time, after such dissolutions, to cause others to be elected; whereby the legislative powers, incapable of annihilation, have returned to the people at large for their exercise; the state remaining in the meantime exposed to all the dangers of invasion from without, and convulsions within.

He has endeavored to prevent the population of these states; for that purpose obstructing the laws for naturalization of foreigners; refusing to pass others to encourage their migration hither, and raising the conditions of new appropriations of lands.

He has obstructed the administration of justice, by refusing his assent to laws for establishing judiciary powers.

He has made judges dependent on his will alone, for the tenure of their offices, and the amount and payment of their salaries.

He has erected a multitude of new offices, and sent hither swarms of officers to harass our people, and eat out their substance.

He has kept among us, in times of peace, standing armies without the consent of our legislature.

He has affected to render the military independent of and superior to civil power.

He has combined with others to subject us to a jurisdiction foreign to our constitution, and unacknowledged by our laws; giving his assent to their acts of pretended legislation:

For quartering large bodies of armed troops among us:

For protecting them, by mock trial, from punishment for any murders which they should commit on the inhabitants of these states:

For cutting off our trade with all parts of the world:

For imposing taxes on us without our consent:

For depriving us in many cases, of the benefits of trial by jury:

For transporting us beyond seas to be tried for pretended offenses:

For abolishing the free system of English laws in a neighboring province, establishing therein an arbitrary government, and enlarging its boundaries so as to render it at once an example and fit instrument for introducing the same absolute rule in these colonies:

For taking away our charters, abolishing our most valuable laws, and altering fundamentally the forms of our governments:

For suspending our own legislatures, and declaring themselves invested with power to legislate for us in all cases whatsoever.

He has abdicated government here, by declaring us out of his protection and waging war against us.

He has plundered our seas, ravaged our coasts, burned our towns, and destroyed the lives of our people.

He is at this time transporting large armies of foreign mercenaries to complete the works of death, desolation and tyranny, already begun with circumstances of cruelty and perfidy scarcely paralleled in the most barbarous ages, and totally unworthy the head of a civilized nation.

He has constrained our fellow citizens taken captive on the high seas to bear arms against their country, to become the executioners of their friends and brethren, or to fall themselves by their hands.

He has excited domestic insurrections amongst us, and has endeavored to bring on the inhabitants of our frontiers, the merciless Indian savages, whose known rule of warfare, is undistinguished destruction of all ages, sexes and conditions."

In sum, added Jefferson, "In every stage of these oppressions we have petitioned for redress in the most humble terms: our repeated petitions have been answered only by repeated injury. A prince, whose character is thus marked by every act which may define a tyrant, is unfit to be the ruler of a free people."

Worst of All Winters

NOBODY HAD EVER SEEN A winter like this one—possibly nobody in the entire eighteenth century. And here, in December 1779, to the "military capital of the United States," came George Washington and his entourage of aides, servants, and Life Guards, plus an army of twelve thousand or more hungry, shivering men.

Awaiting them all behind New Jersey's Watchung Mountains, located at the base of five mountain-like hills, was the village of Morristown and its cluster of fewer than one hundred homes. The wintering Continental Army should be safe here from British attack. As an early warning system, a string of beacons stretched outward from Morristown to far-flung outposts. In the event of a British advance, fires flaring up on platforms at the top of a series of poles eighteen to twenty feet high would give the alarm. The fires closest to Morristown would be spotted by men stationed in Washington's "Fort Nonsense," a hilltop redoubt built 230 feet above the village.

Washington had brought his ragtag army here in January of 1777 for a much-needed winter's rest after the Battles of Trenton and Princeton. He and his army, ranging from three thousand to seven thousand in strength at various times, spent an uneventful and mild five months here in early 1777—uneventful, that is, except for Washington's orders to have his men inoculated against smallpox. Up to a thousand temporarily were laid low by the procedure before recovering.

The next wintering period was the tough one we always hear about, those harsh months spent at Valley Forge, Pennsylvania. But Valley Forge and its deprivations for the troops were as nothing compared to the winter spent at Morristown two years later, 1779-1780.

Once again, the soldiers shuffled onto the scene and ate up an estimated six hundred acres of timber in the process of building 1,000 to 1,200 log huts. They began to arrive in early December and again had to contend with snow. This time, though, they found two feet already on the ground, which itself was frozen. And in this extraordinary winter, a total of twenty-eight snowstorms would barrel into the area. It already had snowed four times in November. It would snow seven times in December, another six in January, four more in February, six more in March, and even once in April.

"The January 2-4 storm was notable in that it snowed four feet with high winds causing drifts of over six feet," said the account by Paul J. Sanborn in Garland Publishing's *The American Revolution, 1775-1783.*

It was so cold that rivers and harbors iced over. The British in New York City found they could transport men and supplies back and forth to Staten Island in New York Harbor on ice. The Americans, for their part, mounted a fruitless raid early in January in which General William Alexander (Lord Stirling) led three thousand men and artillery in five hundred sleighs across the ice to the British base on Staten Island. The assault proved fruitless because the British had learned of the foray in advance "and retreated into their defenses in plenty of time." The Americans had to return home with little accomplished.

The failed raid gave George Washington unneeded headaches because some of the "so-called Jersey militia were no more than plunderers and brigands who played the militia role to destroy, to rob, and to plunder the island." He now took steps to return identifiable looted items to the British on Staten Island, but it was too late. Stung by the episode, the British "struck back in retaliation by burning Newark Academy and Elizabethtown Meeting and Church."

Meanwhile, the wintry weather only continued. The ice and snow held up supplies that normally would have been transported by road, although the iced-over rivers sometimes served as substitute arteries of travel . . . by sled. Overall, however, the weather was a life-threatening nightmare for Washington and his twelve thousand-plus men. "Washington called upon Congress, then the states, and finally on New Jersey in a desperate attempt to feed his men," wrote Sanborn. "The men were reduced to eating birch bark, shoes and leather belts to survive."

Wrote Washington as early as December 16 (to Joseph Reed): "We have never experienced a like extremity at any period of the war."

Weeks later, on March 18, the commander in chief wrote to the Marquis de Lafayette, then visiting in France: "The oldest people now living in this country do not remember so hard a winter as the one we are now emerging from." In addition, Dr. James Thacher, traveling with Washington's entourage for much of the war period, wrote in his journal about the same time that it had been the "most severe and distressing" winter "we have ever experienced." Further, "an immense body of snow remains on the ground." And, worse yet: "Our soldiers are in a wretched condition for the want of clothes, blankets and shoes; and these calamitous circumstances are accompanied by a want of provisions."

Unsurprisingly, the truly harsh conditions contributed to a high number of desertions and even mutinous moments. More than a thousand men deserted the army that winter despite the threat of a death sentence if caught. Then, in a late-May incident, "two Connecticut regiments returning to Morristown from an extended tour of outpost duty found no pay and no food waiting for them," recalled the Sanborn encyclopedia account. Furious, the men talked about marching for home, "foraging for food on the way." An officer trying to reason with them was stabbed with a bayonet, but suffered only a superficial wound. A Pennsylvania officer then urged them to remember their cause and the fact that their leaders were suffering with them. "Pennsylvania troops were brought over if necessary to put down the revolt, but eventually everything settled down and the mutiny ended."

The shortages in pay and supplies continued, with many of the troops left resentful of their fledgling government's failure to support them. Fortunately, the worst winter of the century at last ended. It would remain a bitter memory for many, but the fact is that Washington's more professional army of 1779–1780 lost only eighty-six men to disease and exposure, compared to the thousand or more lost at Valley Forge two years earlier, in what was a much milder—but more famously remembered—wintering period for the Continental Army.

Sleeping Here and There

"GEORGE WASHINGTON SLEPT HERE," GOES the old refrain. And indeed, in the course of an eight-year Revolutionary War, the astute commander in chief slept in many places. He especially did his sleeping in New York, New Jersey, and Pennsylvania.

Why those three in particular? Simply because they were central. His war, for the most part, took place within a large clock face with the city of New York at center, upstate New York at twelve o'clock, and Valley Forge, Pennsylvania, at seven o'clock or so. His generals naturally operated a bit farther afield, and even for Washington, there were crucial events just beyond the edges of the clock face—at Boston in the beginning, just beyond two o'clock, and, toward the end, at Yorktown, Virginia, to the lower right, way beyond five o'clock.

Generally speaking, though, Washington spent most of his wartime days well within the circle of New York, New Jersey, and Pennsylvania. He certainly, even within that perimeter, was a man on the move, and constantly so. He indeed slept in many, many places.

When the British forced Washington to end a months-long stay in New York and environs late in 1776, he retreated across all of New Jersey and fetched up on the Pennsylvania side of the Delaware River, more or less opposite Trenton, New Jersey. He settled briefly into Philadelphian Thomas Barclay's 221-acre estate called Summer Seat. The same property later would be owned by Robert Morris, often called "The Financier of the Revolution." George Washington wasn't thinking of that just now, though. He was much more interested in military strategy, in striking a blow that would redeem America's sinking hopes of eventual victory against the professional British war machine. On December 14, Washington shifted base to one William Keith's farmhouse, a bit closer to the intended scene of action. Here Washington and his lieutenants laid their plans for the famous crossing of the Delaware on Christmas night of 1776.

After defeating George III's Hessian allies in the Battle of Trenton the next morning, Washington established a new headquarters in nearby Newtown, Pennsylvania, in the home of one John Harris. In three days, he removed to Trenton itself, to the home of a departed Loyalist, one John Barnes, on Queen Street, as recalled in John Tebbel's book, *George Washington's America*.

In another three days' time, Washington moved on to the True American Inn alongside Assunpike Creek, still in Trenton. Never heard of it? Hardly anyone even in those days had … until the British suddenly appeared on the scene. As Tebbel reports, "Down to this hitherto unimportant stream came Lord Cornwallis from Princeton, with what Washington shortly discovered was a much superior force."

But Washington, shown to be somewhat inept back in New York, had turned more wily by now—perhaps more determined, too, as shown at Trenton just days before. He left his campfires brightly burning to distract the enemy while he marched his army the ten miles to Princeton in the dark of night. He was then able to encircle the two regiments of British troops under Cornwallis, surprise . . . and rout them! Said the British commentator Horace Walpole afterward: "His march through our lines is allowed to have been a prodigy of generalship." Washington had broached his flanking plan in a council of war held in still another Trenton abode, that of one Alexander Douglass.

The Battle of Princeton took place on January 3, 1777, and Washington spent that night south of Princeton in the home of John van Doren. The next day he was off to Morristown, New Jersey, destined to be the first of his Continental Army's winter quarters. He stayed at Colonel Jacob Arnold's tavern—a "substantial frame building" on the northwest side of the town's public square that later became the United States Hotel.

Not only George, but Martha Washington as well slept here—she joined him in March 1777. "Martha, as usual, quickly established a social order, entertaining ladies of quality in the vicinity and the officers' wives who had come to the camp," noted Tebbel.

With winter past and spring bursting out all over, Washington moved about the New Jersey countryside while awaiting a decisive move by the British. They might remain in the New York area, they might go north, or they might go far south. Whatever they finally might do, one of Washington's stopping points during the summer of 1777 was the town of Pompton, just eighteen miles from Morristown. "Whenever Washington stopped at Pompton," wrote Tebbel, "he is presumed to have stayed at a place called the Yellow House, later the Old Yellow Cottage," and still later a tavern operated by a proprietor named Curtis. But there are those who dispute the entire story, Tebbel also noted.

Whatever the facts, the British at last surprised the awaiting Continentals by moving on Philadelphia, seat of the Continental Congress. They seized that key city, defeating Washington's pursuing forces at Brandywine Creek and at Germantown in the process. By then, it was time to move into winter quarters again—in this case, at Valley Forge, Pennsylvania.

When another June rolled around (1778), Washington again was in pursuit of a moving foe, for the British were now quit of Philadelphia and on the march northward, through hapless New Jersey and in the direction of New York. After another crossing of the Delaware—this time at today's Lambertville, New Jersey—Washington held a significant council of war on June 24 in nearby

Hopewell. He slept, it seems, in the Hunt house, located "about a mile from the Baptist Meeting House." Both structures survived into the twentieth century.

It was only four days later, on June 28, that Washington won the Battle of Monmouth Courthouse. The historical "headlines" have always seized upon the more sensational fact that Washington confronted and, in effect, sacked a truculent General Charles Lee in the midst of the fray at Monmouth. History tends to forget the cool generalship Washington displayed on the same auspicious occasion. As the Marquis de Lafayette later commented, "General Washington appeared to arrest fortune by one glance, and his presence of mind, valor, and decision of character, were never displayed to greater advantage."

Soon after, in mid-July of 1778, came a four-day stop at Paramus, New Jersey, marked by "the hospitality of lovely Theodosia Prevost, a widow who later achieved a more dubious fame by marrying Aaron Burr." Dubiously, too, it might be added, her late husband had been an officer in the army of His Majesty, George III.

Washington now moved on to White Plains, above the British stronghold of New York. He stayed there for several weeks, well into September, before shifting base to Patterson, a village close to the Connecticut boundary line. Then it was on to Fishkill in the Hudson River Valley, a frequent stopping point throughout the Revolutionary War. Here he stayed at the homes, alternately, of John and Derrick Brinckerhoff, uncle and nephew. Unexciting Fishkill, wrote Baron von Steuben, was "a center of dullness" and "the last place in the world for mirth."

Washington left Fishkill one day in October, traveled down the Hudson and briefly visited the home of his old friend—now a Loyalist—Colonel Beverley Robinson, originally from Virginia. Two years later, Benedict Arnold would be the home's occupant . . . and here Washington would discover Arnold's betrayal of the Patriot cause.

But this still was October of 1778, and by late November Washington and his army would be back in New Jersey, bedding down in new winter quarters at Middlebrook, now known as Bound Brook. Washington slept there in a home still standing and open to the public as a state historical site, the onetime John Wallace house. Located four miles out of town, the Wallace home was comfortable but small. Even so, Martha again appeared and entertained—but now, thankfully, she could count upon the wives of her husband's generals to do a bit of entertaining, too.

With the advent of another June, Washington, his generals, and his army were off again—this time to West Point on the Hudson, from which base they kept an eye on the British in New York, and spent a rather uneventful summer.

For his next wintering period, in probably the harshest winter weather of the entire century, Washington returned to Morristown. He (and Martha) stayed in the home of Colonel Jacob Ford's widow, Theodosia Ford—along with the four Ford children. The Washingtons took up residence on the second floor while the Fords squeezed into two downstairs rooms. Washington's aides and the Ford servants lived in two newly built wooden outbuildings. The general's Life Guards troop, always close by, was quartered in a barracks across the road.

Among other generals finding local quarters, Maryland's William Smallwood wound up sharing Peter Kemble's home with this known Tory, whose daughter was married to British General Thomas Gage, late of the Boston garrison.

Morristown was a small town of 250 persons living in sixty to eighty structures—the Continental Army's presence, more than twelve thousand strong that winter of 1779–1780, turned this tiny village into young America's sixth largest "city."

By the way, the Ford Mansion is currently located at 230 Morris Avenue, and is open to the public as a National Historic Site maintained by the National Park Service.

Two of the generals' wives joining Martha Washington here that harshest of all winters were Nathanael Greene's spouse, Kitty, and Henry Knox's wife, Lucy. The ladies organized two dances in February and March, as well as an April ball in honor of the visiting French minister, the Chevalier de la Luzerne. Benedict Arnold's court-martial for alleged improprieties as military governor of Philadelphia was under way here at Peter Dickerson's Tavern. Another "event" of this winter season was the illness and death of a Spanish diplomat, Juan de Miralles, visiting with the French minister's party. Stricken by bilious fever, he died in a second-floor room in the Ford Mansion, across the hall from Washington's own room. That was in late April of 1780. In May, the Marquis de Lafayette returned from a visit to France with the all-important news that France would soon be sending a second fleet to

American waters and an army of six thousand troops to help fight the British.

Arnold, in the meantime, had been convicted on two of the four charges against him, resulting in a slap-on-the-wrist reprimand from Washington. The firebrand from Connecticut should have been thankful for being able to keep his military career intact, but instead he was, as always, resentful of any such slight. Unbeknownst to anyone in the American camp, he had already opened negotiations with the British. And now he passed along Lafayette's momentous news.

It was late June when Washington and his army left Morristown to meet renewed British threat to New Jersey. He was soon settled into one of his favorite quartering places, the two-story brick home of Colonel Theunis Dey in the Preakness hills of New Jersey, close to Passaic Falls and today's Paterson. "There were vistas in every direction," reported Tebbel's book, "and the network of roads around it linked the place, from a military standpoint, to Newark, Elizabethtown, Springfield, Middletown and southern New Jersey; on the southeast to Totowa, Acquackanoc and Hackensack; and on the northeast to Paramus, Pompton, and Ringwood."

Here, in what was considered one of the finest homes in New Jersey, Washington established an "audience chamber" and private dining room on the first floor. He occupied four rooms in all and is said to have wallpapered the one that served as his office. He was in and out of the Dey House until late November. "The war that summer took him across the Hudson to Westchester County, and for a time to Teaneck, where his headquarters were at the Liberty Pole Tavern on Palisade Avenue in the present town of Englewood." He also briefly stayed at the Hopper house on the Morristown road, two miles from the New York state line.

The stop that really hurt in 1780 came in late September, after Washington's initial and historic visit with the newly arrived French commander, Comte de Rochambeau. On Washington's return from their summit in Hartford, Connecticut, he stopped at Colonel Beverley Robinson's home, the temporary residence of Benedict Arnold, and found Arnold mysteriously absent. The recently appointed commander of West Point had gone over to the enemy.

The evidence of his perfidy came from the arrest of British Major John André, in civilian mufti rather than military uniform.

Bearing incriminating papers, André obviously had been Arnold's contact with the British. Now, he would be executed as a spy.

It was in the parlor of the Johannes De Wint home in Tappan, New York, built in 1700, that George Washington signed André's death warrant and sat quietly ("almost alone among his papers," wrote Washington biographer Douglas Southall Freeman) as the hanging took place at midday, October 2, not half a mile away.

Not long after, Washington would bed down for the mild winter ahead in William Ellison's stone house overlooking the Hudson at New Windsor, New York. It was here, in the upper hall, that Washington and his young staff officer, Colonel Alexander Hamilton, exchanged a few heated words one February day in 1781. The commander in chief made an effort to reconcile, but Hamilton rebuffed the overture and left Washington's staff.

And so it went, one move after another, sometimes with historic significance or drama, sometimes not, as George Washington moved about through the months, then years, of ultimately successful revolution—moved in and out of a hundred or more borrowed heaquarters in all, by author Tebbel's calculations.

As yet unmentioned here is the Jonathan Hasbrouck house in Newburgh, New York, where Washington spent a total of fifteen months and eighteen days—"the longest period he lived in any of the houses he had occupied in seven states, from Massachusetts to Virginia." He arrived here at the end of March 1782, a somewhat more relaxing time in Washington's life, since he had spent some critical time the previous fall in his native Virginia—not merely for a visit to his beloved Mount Vernon, but, more significantly, to meet a familiar adversary from those early days in New Jersey . . . to meet Lord Cornwallis at Yorktown in October 1781.

Additional notes: At the very beginning of his career as commander in chief of the Continental Army, it should also be recalled, George Washington spent time at two major stopping points: Cambridge, Massachusetts, and New York.

Arriving in Cambridge, on the edge of British-occupied Boston, in July 1775, he briefly stayed in the home of Harvard President Samuel Langdon, but then moved into the stately Georgian mansion of departed Loyalist John Vassall. A short-term housemate here, oddly enough, was his future rival and rebellious subordinate, General Charles Lee. Fortunately, Lee soon found other quarters and left the large home to the commander in chief. "This fine old mansion, with its wide hall and spacious rooms, offered ample accommodation for Washington and his family," wrote Anne Hollingsworth Wharton in an 1897 biography of Martha Washington. "To the right of the front door was his office, with his staff room opening out of it, while beyond there was another room in which they probably dined. . . . On the left side of the hall were spacious reception rooms."

After a time, Martha Washington joined her husband in the John Vassall house, better known these days as the Craigie-Longfellow house—for future owners Andrew Craigie, apothecary-general of the Continental Army, and Henry Wadsworth Longfellow, the revered American poet. "The room to the right of the front door, in which Washington wrote his dispatches, was later the favorite study and reading room of the poet," added the Wharton account.

In April of the following year, after seeing the British evacuate Boston, the commander in chief shifted base to the city of New York, where he briefly stayed in the Broadway home of another decamped Loyalist, William Smith. When Martha again joined him, they took over the recently vacated country home of Abraham Mortier, the longtime British paymaster general, noted Tebbel in his book. "The Mortier house stood at the southeast corner of Varick and Charlton streets, now in the southwestern reaches of Greenwich Village, considered remote in those days because it was two and a half miles from the . . . Battery [at the foot of Manhattan Island]."

Despite well-founded expectations of British attempts to seize New York, the Washington couple furnished their temporary home with "feather bed, bolster, pillows, bed curtains, crockery and glass-ware." But Washington took advantage of New York's "more favorable prices" to purchase field equipment as well—"sleeping and dining tents, eighteen walnut camp stools and three camp tables of the same wood."

Briefly visiting Philadelphia in May for consultation with Congress, Washington insisted that Martha take the sometimes risky smallpox inoculation (risky, but usually better than contracting the deadly disease itself) and stay behind there to recuperate. On her successful recovery, she returned to New York around June 16, but

Washington wisely packed her off to Mount Vernon by month's end. It was only a matter of weeks before the British would fill New York Harbor with their troop-laden ships, take over Staten Island, defeat Washington in the Battle of Long Island, and occupy New York on the heels of several more defeats for the Continentals.

Such were the events that, by year's end, brought Washington to the Pennsylvania side of the Delaware River, where he finally turned and struck back at Trenton, at Princeton—to sleep onward, you might say, here, there, and everywhere, for another six and a half years of wartime maneuvering.

POWs in America

THE LAND LAY ON A pleasant plateau up a steep hill just four miles west of town, and well within view were the blue-shadowed mountains known as the Blue Ridge. The town itself wasn't much, just a courthouse, a tavern, and a handful of houses. The land belonged to Colonel John Harvie, a member of the Continental Congress. It could have stood a bit of clearing, as could so much of the untrammeled countryside in the 1770s.

Not far away, some miles to the southwest and high on another hill, this one actually overlooking the town, was Thomas Jefferson's grand home known as Monticello, or "little mountain" in Italian. This was the County of Albemarle, Virginia, and the small town was Charlottesville.

Before the winter of 1778–1779, a few Tory and Scots Highlander prisoners had been held here in this backwater of the Revolutionary War's fighting. So relaxed were the local citizens over these visitors that most of them were allowed to wander around town on parole, although four Tories once broke the gentleman's agreement implicit in parole and took off, escaped. Recaptured later, they then were held elsewhere. This was a minor episode in the life of Jefferson's community, really—but a major change was about to come. A result of the Battle of Saratoga, the stunning Patriot victory in today's upstate New York, it also had to do with prisoners. In this case, four thousand of them.

Quartered for a year in New England, they were marched south in late 1778, more than six hundred miles to the hilltop acreage volunteered by Harvie as a new home for the British and Hessian troops (and some dependents) captured at Saratoga in October of 1777. The climate in New England had been hard on them, and food had been scarce.

Ahead, by Jefferson's own description, they would find "the top and brow of a very high hill," with no fog to worry them and four springs at their disposal.

What the prisoners found, like George Washington's troops at Valley Forge a couple of years earlier, was . . . nothing! Like Washington's men, however, they built a sea of huts to house the enlisted men, while many of the officers found accommodations with local homeowners.

Less than three months later, in a letter to Governor Patrick Henry, Jefferson was defending the site as more than adequate for the sudden influx of prisoners. "Of 4,000 people," he wrote, "it would be expected according to ordinary calculations that one should die every day. Yet in the space of nearly 3 months there have been but 4 deaths among them. 2 infants under three weeks old, two others by apoplexy. The officers tell me, the troops were never so healthy since they were embodied." Jefferson was responding to suggestions that the prisoners should be relocated once more after encountering hardships in Virginia, reports historian John Hammond Moore in *Albemarle: Jefferson's County.* The Master of Monticello, unwilling to see his beloved Albemarle County lose out on the cultural and economic benefits of this European migration, "stressed the healthful atmosphere," as well as the plentiful availability of food, says Moore.

In fact, the prisoners had created a virtual town on their hill— the "Barracks."

"The soldiers, he [Jefferson] noted, had made their environs 'delightful,'" wrote Moore. "The Barracks was surrounded by hundreds of separate gardens and small pens filled with poultry. Baron [Friedrich Adolph] von Riedesel, the highest-ranking German officer, had spent some 200 for seed which he distributed to his troops."

Furthermore, noted Jefferson in his argument against moving the prisoners, they had built facilities of their own in excess of those provided by Congress. By Moore's account as well, the captive officers not only were "comfortably housed throughout the county," but "some had leased quarters which they were improving at considerable personal expense and they were stocking their new homes with grains and provisions of all kinds."

As for the officers, they at first were granted the freedom to live anywhere within fifty miles of the newly built Barracks, but that wide radius later was reduced. Naturally, they still were expected to supervise their enlisted personnel at the Barracks campsite. There, the Revolutionary War POWs were guarded by six hundred area volunteers, "young men apprehensive of being drafted into the Continental forces and eager to enlist for a year's duty close to home."

Jefferson's spirited defense of the Albemarle location had much in its favor, to be sure. Wrote Moore: "Although ... [his] appraisal may have been a bit too optimistic, it is true that Virginia could house and feed these troops in the midst of war more easily than any other state; and it is equally true that as the officers and men became accustomed to their surroundings, they discovered incarceration in the shadows of the Blue Ridge Mountains was not so wretched an existence as first supposed." Their Barracks campsite soon boasted "a commissary store, a coffeehouse and a theater." Further, "John Hawkins, an enterprising local citizen, built four houses of entertainment equipped with billiard tables, an undertaking inaugurated without permission from the authorities."

If, as Moore also reported, "the center of all this [POW-related] activity had taken on the appearance of a small town," a town "suddenly ranked as a major concentration of population within Virginia," why then the sharply declining population of said "town"? In barely a year, the four thousand POWs who had arrived in January of 1779 had dwindled to just three thousand, a loss of one-fourth.

They hadn't died; they hadn't been released. They escaped!

By the end of 1780, with British forces threatening to draw close, they were moved after all—by then, the POWs on hand numbered a mere two thousand, half the original roster. Moore suggests that perhaps the homegrown guard force was willing to wink at escapes "if the prisoners seemed intent upon settling in the New World and expressed no desire to fight again under the British flag."

Then, too, "Some of the British certainly joined up with (nearby) Cornwallis; but the Germans, for the most part, had little heart for this foreign expedition and by the hundreds fled westward across the mountains into surrounding counties of the Shenandoah Valley to be welcomed in their native tongue by their former compatriots [Valley settlers who migrated southward from Pennsylvania]. There they took wives, raised families, and became, through the vagaries of war, American citizens."

When all had left the Barracks, many with heavy heart, and a silence had settled upon their former campsite, the land's owner, John Harvie, notes historian Moore, stood to benefit from their recent presence. As he himself observed, "The prisoners by their own sweat and toil had cleared an area six miles in circumference around their little town."

Additional notes: Still more Hessian prisoners were held in Staunton, Virginia, then a town of about thirty homes and located right in the Shenandoah Valley about forty miles west of Charlottesville. According to a Hessian officer's letter to a relative, the enlisted men held there could enjoy a vegetable garden, church, wells, taverns, even a theater or "comedy house" that put on plays twice a week. Wrote the officer also: "Very good pieces are performed which, because of their satirical additions, do not always please the Americans, wherefore they are forbidden by their superiors to attend these comedies."

Back in the Charlottesville area, ranking German officer Riedesel and his wife "associated freely with Jefferson, his wife, and other local gentry," reported Moore. But the Germans "complained loudly of weather conditions which frightened them, especially extreme heat and high winds," Moore added. "The baron succumbed to sunstroke on one occasion, and the baroness expressed fear that Colle [the private home in which they were staying] might be wrecked during a storm."

Then, too, British officer Thomas Anburey, also a prisoner, later produced a popular, sometimes exaggerated account of his days in Albemarle. The owner of the plantation where he was housed, wrote the Englishman, began his day with a drink of rum and sugar, toured his fields for a few hours, then returned for a "breakfast" of cold meat, toast, hominy, and cider. Then came a noon drink, followed at

2 P.M. by dinner and a rest or nap for several hours. After that, more alcoholic beverages. Wrote Anburey: "During all this he is neither drunk nor sober, but in a state of stupefaction."

Be that as it may, the conditions under which the British and Hessian prisoners were held in Albemarle County were far better than the grim prison ships and other deplorable facilities where American prisoners were often held. So good was the situation in Albemarle, for that matter, that Anburey had to note the reluctance of many fellow prisoners to leave—especially since in their carefree days at the Barracks, they had spent personal funds improving their own living conditions.

No Panacea for Blacks

WHERE WERE THE BLACKS—WHO had only recently been brought to North America from Africa—during the American Revolution? Not only in stand-out individual cases, but also by the thousands they were very visible as allies for both sides, British and American. Their presence in America was very much on the white public's mind, especially in the Southern colonies.

In Virginia, for instance, Royal Governor Dunmore stirred up a boiling controversy and generated white resentment against his (and therefore, the Crown's) authority by his bald attempt in 1775 to free the colony's slaves—not from a sudden surge of altruism, but to recruit them as soldiers against the revolutionaries. If he sought to bend Virginia to his will, however, he didn't count on the fact that it was the slaveowners who held the reins of power, not the slaves themselves. To take advantage of Dunmore's offer, a slave would have to escape, make his way through potentially hostile countryside and reach British lines. Obviously, it was a situation fraught with all kinds of difficulties. If blessed with a family, would the slave go alone? But how could he take his family with him? And if alone, would he ever see his family again?

After Lexington and Concord, Dunmore had taken refuge with

his own family aboard the British ship *Fowey* in the York River. From there, he directed raids against Norfolk and environs. Still, his larger strategy was to raise an army of Indians, blacks, and Loyalist whites to fight alongside the few Royal Marines and other troops he had by his side. After scoring a painful victory over the rebels in early November, he issued his proclamation declaring "all indented Servants, Negroes, or others (appertaining to Rebels) free, that are able and willing to bear arms, they joining his Majesty's Troops, as soon as may be, for the more speedily reducing this Colony to a proper Sense of their Duty, to his Majesty's Crown and dignity."

As he apparently failed to see, he immediately touched upon long-held white fears of slave insurrection—indeed, he seemed to be encouraging that very spectre to take form. As the radical Virginian Archibald Cary once said, the white colonists were all the more united against Dunmore because they "resent the pointing of a dagger to their throats, through the hands of their slaves." To the relief of white Americans, few slaves took up the royal governor's call to arms. By Dunmore's own statement, no more than three hundred blacks responded to his call. Defeated in battle at the end of 1775 at Great Bridge, Virginia, Dunmore soon was gone from the scene.

Even so, white fears of possible slave revolts still lingered on. Thomas Jefferson's Declaration of Independence, adopted in mid-1776, at one point charged that the king "excited domestic insurrections amongst us." Three years later, Patrick Henry asserted that if the British returned to Virginia, they would offer "an asylum for our slaves." Worse: "[The slaves] will flock to their standards, and form the flower of their army. They will rival the Hessian or Highlander, if possible, in cruelty and desolation."

The fact is, thousands of blacks, perhaps 100,000 by some estimates, did flee from outright slavery or from Patriot strongholds to go behind British lines and even to serve the British, North and South, before the Revolutionary War ended—but in supportive, often menial jobs rather than as combatants. Thus, they were employed as wagoners, laborers, cooks, even as musicians. A few served as spies, passing back and forth between the lines. Or they could be scouts and guides in territory unfamiliar to the British.

The British themselves sometimes appeared to be leery of converting former slaves into real soldiers, Lord Dunmore's strategy notwithstanding. Lord Cornwallis, for instance, could have used considerable added manpower in his Southern campaign leading up to the debacle (for him) at Yorktown in 1781. Yet, in February of that very year, he issued orders forbidding blacks attached to his army to carry firearms. He subsequently decided they should carry identification tickets or be arrested. In other cases, all-black regiments fought for the British or the Patriots, just as individuals did. The British had their Black Pioneers, a company within the Guides and Pioneers, and their King of England's Soldiers in Georgia. The American side saw a regiment of blacks from Rhode Island take to the field in an abortive attack against the British at Newport in 1778. Then, too, French Admiral Charles d'Estaing carried an all-black regiment from Haiti with him for his abortive attack on the British at Savannah, Georgia, in 1779.

By some estimates, for that matter, by 1779, fifteen out of every one hundred Continental Army members were black. Not only were free blacks allowed to enlist, but whites drafted for army duty by their states could send slaves in their place, often with a promise of future freedom for doing so. In the South, though, many thousands of slaves "joined" the British, but not always of their own volition since many actually were seized from their American owners. Thousands were more like refugees or camp followers than trained soldiers. They wound up as orderlies, cooks, other kinds of servants, even mistresses to white soldiers.

Still others dug and erected fortifications, as at Yorktown. And there, said onlooking German officer Jonathan Ewald: "All our black friends, who had been freed and dragged away to prevent them from working in the fields, and who had served very well in making entrenchments, were chased toward the enemy. They trembled at having to go back to their former owners."

Among the Americans, of course, it was a contradiction in terms to see many leaders in the fight for freedom, independence, and personal liberties continue to own slaves. Thomas Jefferson owned slaves until the day of his death. George Washington, who went to war with his mulatto manservant Billy Lee at his side, freed his slaves in his will . . . but not until his wife, Martha, passed away as well.

Black Hessians

THE "BLACK HESSIANS" WERE ENGAGED in the fighting on behalf of the Crown, in ranks of the British. No, make that the ranks of the Germans . . . the Hessians. In fact, the Hessians in America welcomed blacks as recruits, allowed many of them to take up arms as fellow soldiers, and apparently accepted them more or less as equals, without racial stigma.

The numbers were not great, only 115 by one informed estimate. And it must be said that paid soldierly service with the Hessians was no panacea even for a former slave. Many of the "black Hessians" died from smallpox and other maladies, while roughly 20 percent found it desirable to desert, according to David L. Valuska in *The American Revolution, 1775–1783.* Deserters who returned on their own volition normally were not severely punished, but woe to the man who failed to return and later was caught! One Jacob, reports the encyclopedia account, deserted some time after enlisting in a Hessian military unit at the age of thirteen. Caught two years after disappearing, he was "sentenced to run a gauntlet of 200 men for two successive days."

Most of the black recruits taken in by the Hessians entered service as drummers, then became a musketeer or grenadier when they grew bigger. Perhaps Jacob was one of that younger crowd, perhaps not. In any case, not every black approaching the Hessian units could count on becoming a fighting man. According to records available in the Hessian military archives in Marburg, Germany, some of the black recruits were listed as servants, orderlies, wagoners . . . even "lackeys."

Whatever their assignment, says the Valuska account, "African-Americans were willingly recruited into the Hessian service. The motivations for black enlistments were quite simply freedom and security." In some cases, the black Hessians went back to Germany with their comrades-in-arms after the war was over. "There are records of black soldiers in Hesse being baptized or married," writes Valuska. Further, "Old manuscripts and paintings provided documentation of blacks serving in the guard battalions of Hesse-Kassel. Church diaries of the garrison congregations contain entries of the births and deaths of black soldiers and their dependents."

By 1830, though, the records in Hesse-Kassel contain no more mention of the American blacks or their descendants—in less than one hundred years, it appeared, they had been completely assimilated by the surrounding German community.

Long before, ironically enough, the body of a black Hessian who died in Germany was the subject of an anatomical dissection at the Collegium Carolinium in Kassel—"reportedly the first autopsy in Europe of a black cadaver," says Valuska. Great was the surprise of the German scientists when they found his internal organs were "exactly like those of the white[s]."

Additional notes: Disappointment often was the ultimate outcome for many other former slaves who temporarily found freedom and employment with the British during the Revolution. About three thousand who had found sanctuary in British-held New York were allowed to migrate to Nova Scotia with other Loyalists. All of them, white or black, expected to receive outright grants of land as reward for their loyalty. With a total of thirty thousand or so Loyalists descending upon officials in Nova Scotia, however, the land grant bureaucracy was simply overwhelmed. Only about half the blacks entitled to grants actually received them, and even then, the land parcels were ten to fifty acres in size, instead of the one hundred promised earlier.

Years later, two thousand or so blacks from Nova Scotia and adjoining New Brunswick joined in a migration of London-based free blacks to Sierre Leone, Africa. Here, too, however, the promises of land grants rarely became a reality, thanks in large part to infighting among the inexperienced organizers. Even more heartbreaking, disease and other hardships took such a toll that only about one thousand of them were left alive after their first rainy season in Sierre Leone. Thirty years later, not one of the surviving Loyalist settlers was a full-time farmer, as originally envisioned. Instead, just about all were traders or craftsmen.

Back in post-Revolutionary America, meanwhile, the practice of slavery persisted, largely in the South, and would continue until the

Civil War came along nearly a century later. South Carolina's Patriot leader Henry Laurens had seen to it that the peace treaty of 1783 between Great Britain and the newly formed United States would forbid the British from taking away blacks who were the "property" of slave-owning Americans. Some blacks, of course, retained their freedom anyway, some were sold to a bleak life of slavery in the West Indies, and others became slaves in America again.

Lord Cornwallis, defeated at Yorktown in 1781, left four thousand former slaves milling around on their own in Virginia. More fortunate were the three thousand or so former slaves who found their way into British-held New York. They owed their subsequent safe conduct to Nova Scotia (and its often harsh uncertainties, true) to British General Sir Guy Carleton, who decided on his own that the new peace treaty could not apply to blacks who had been in his British-held territory for more than a year. After such a long period, they simply weren't anybody's property, he decided.

Two thousand, or two-thirds, of the blacks granted his certificates of freedom came from the four Southern states of Virginia, South Carolina, Georgia, and North Carolina.

Incidental Intelligence

WHEN "GENTLEMAN JOHNNY" BURGOYNE SET sail for his invasion of upper New York from Canada in June of 1777, he graced the waters of Lake Champlain with a flotilla of boats and barges a mile long. Rarely one to do without the luxuries befitting a favorite of the king, he carried with him many comforts of home, along with an artillery and baggage train that would require 1,500 horses to haul once he and his 8,000-plus men reached land and began their tedious overland journey toward Albany and the vital Hudson Valley corridor. It would require thirty carts to lug Burgoyne's personal baggage upon that same rough terrain that lay ahead.

Nor was Burgoyne singular in looking to personal comfort. His second in command, the German Baron Friedrich Adolph von

Riedesel, thoughtfully brought along his wife, their three young daughters, and two maids.

Seizing carelessly garrisoned Fort Ticonderoga with ease, Burgoyne continued his ponderous way as far as Skenesborough without major incident or trouble. "Here in the yellow fieldstone house of Tory Philip Skene," reported George F. Scheer and Hugh F. Rankin in their book *Rebels & Redcoats,* "Gentleman Johnny Burgoyne lived up to his name, dining choicely, grumbling genially over the paucity of good madeira and port, and radiating charm for his new mistress, the wife of one of his commissaries."

Just twenty-three miles away, beckoning as his next stop, was Fort Edward on the Hudson. As events turned out, Fort Edward might as well have been many leagues away, so long did it take Burgoyne's army to complete that short leg of his Hudson Valley campaign. He could have returned to Ticonderoga for a shorter, easier overland route, but he chose instead to follow Wood Creek for seven or so miles, then to slog through swamps, bogs, forests, broken-down bridges, and the like marking an unusually primitive wagon trail to Fort Edward.

Burgoyne was forced to rebuild the wilderness road for his huge supply train, a Herculean task made more difficult by American General Philip Schuyler's axmen, a thousand of them, busily felling trees and destroying bridges ahead of the redcoat column. Reported Scheer and Rankin: ". . . Schuyler's men felled giant pines, so that the branches intertwined and made abatis that could not be dragged away but had to be hewn apart. In Wood Creek they made crude dams of trees and mountainous boulders around which the rain-fattened waters spread, filling existing swamps and creating vast new bogs."

Burgoyne had his own squads of axmen and other laborers toiling those hot summer days amid swarms of mosquitoes in an effort to clear a path through the wilderness and repair the damages wrought by the Americans. As he wearily reported, his wagon road not only had to forge past the felled trees, but his men had to build more than forty bridges and repair others, "one of which was of logwork over a morass two miles in extent."

In sum, it took Burgoyne nearly twenty days to move twenty miles, a fitting omen for the remaining days of his ill-fated campaign, which would end in October with his surrender of an entire British army.

"Tricks of the trade" some might call these tactics tried by the Patriots of South Carolina. Soon after the British abandoned their position at Camden in 1781, the Americans and British fought a minor battle over possession of Fort Watson at a key road intersection in the Santee country. The Americans surrounded the British outpost, built on top of an Indian mound, but lacked the artillery to make life uncomfortable for the redcoats inside the stockade walls. No big problem, suggested militia Colonel Hezekiah Maham, simply build a tower of logs with a protected platform for sharpshooters.

General Francis Marion, the Carolina "Swamp Fox," was quick to see the tower's potential and ordered its immediate construction. Working under cover of night, the Patriots quietly assembled their sixty-foot "Maham Tower" close to the stockade walls.

The next morning, American riflemen could look down from their tower and shoot at anyone moving within the interior of the fort. After two American assaults, backed by the lethal fire from above, the British surrendered.

Not long after, General Nathanael Greene, commander of the Continental Army's Southern Department, was stymied in his siege of the Loyalist garrison at Ninety-Six, the British outpost on the state's western frontier. Greene also tried to cover the interior of the enemy strongpoint with rifle fire from a "Maham Tower," but was frustrated when the Loyalists behind a star-pattern earthen redoubt simply raised the height of their parapets with rows of sandbags.

Greene also tried setting afire houses within the "Star Fort" by shooting burning arrows onto the roofs, but the Loyalists foiled this plan, as well—they stripped all the wooden shingles from the houses. They also found and stopped a tunnel being dug in their direction by Greene's Polish-born engineer, Thaddeus Kosciuko.

After Virginia's Colonel Light-Horse Harry Lee arrived from freshly vanquished Augusta, Georgia, with reinforcements, he was assigned the next trick of the trade in siege operations—cut off the enemy's water supply. He was only partially successful, but enough so that the Loyalists tried digging an emergency well. When that effort failed utterly, the Loyalists came up with a trick of their own— they sent out naked black men at night to fetch water from a nearby stream, on the theory that they would blend in with the nighttime darkness.

In the end, with two thousand fresh redcoats on the march to the relief of Ninety-Six, Greene lifted his month-long siege after a single, all-out, and costly assault on June 18 that failed to crack the Loyalist defensive ring. Nonetheless, soon after withdrawing, Greene had the pleasure of seeing the British abandon the Ninety-Six strongpoint, their last fortress in the South Carolina backcountry.

James McElwee was a brave man indeed—an American captured when Savannah fell to the resurgent British in December 1778 and then held aboard a British prison ship for eight months.

Then came the day when he and other prisoners were offered a good dinner, a drink of rum, and clean clothes if they would join in a birthday toast to King George—that is, to simply say, "God save the King!"

That wouldn't do for McElwee. He yanked off his own shirt, waved it like a flag, and shouted, "God save George Washington and the American colonies." In the stunned silence that followed, he said it again: "God save George Washington!" Tossing aside the truly offensive shirt, he then turned to the outraged commander of the prison ship and said, "Now, sir, I and the lice will die together." According to Nat and Sam Hilborn in their book *Battleground of Freedom: South Carolina in the Revolution,* he fortunately survived, was exchanged months later, "and lived many years afterward."

Emily Geiger was quite a remarkable young woman! She was all of eighteen years old when the Patriots needed her services to carry a letter of instruction from one American general to another through Tory country in the South Carolina Midlands in the summer of 1781. General Nathanael Greene wished to inform partisan leader Thomas Sumter, the Carolina "Gamecock," about details of British Lord Rawdon's withdrawal into the Low Country from the newly abandoned British stronghold of Ninety-Six on the state's western frontier. With no one on Greene's staff willing to risk the long ride through hostile territory, Emily volunteered. She agreed not only to carry Greene's letter, but also to memorize its contents as a safeguard against loss of the document itself, which she stuffed into her bodice for safekeeping.

Sure enough, she was caught by the British on the second day of her mission. According to the legend told and retold many times since, Emily's highly suspicious male captors took her to a nearby headquarters for interrogation, but didn't have the effrontery to search her person. For that delicate purpose, they sent for a Tory woman and left Emily locked in a room in the interim. That was their mistake. Alone, she took out the incriminating piece of paper, tore it into small bits and ate them, one by one. When she was searched, there was nothing left to find.

Released in due course, she continued on her journey, found Sumter, and relayed Greene's message verbally. Fortunately, her memory served her—and Sumter—quite well, despite the harrowing hours she spent as a captive of the enemy.

At Large in England

THE PRISONERS, IT SEEMS, WERE sometimes a bit unruly. Uncowed by the threat of solitary confinement in the "black hole," they treated guards and other staff with obvious contempt. They staged organized demonstrations to celebrate their country's victories. They petitioned high enemy officials with their grievances. They even heckled one of their wardens "so vociferously . . . that he was forced to seek refuge in his office."

And escape! They were always planning escapes, making escapes, coming back from unsuccessful escapes—and even making good on still more escape attempts.

"Their often well-planned escape methods included climbing the walls, jumping the pickets, laboriously digging tunnels, bribing guards or staff, stealing keys, picking locks, feigning illness to use the less secure prison hospitals, and assuming an assortment of disguises," wrote Sheldon S. Cohen in his 1995 book, *Yankee Sailors in British Gaols: Prisoners of War at Forton and Mill, 1777-1783.*

Indeed, one of the Yankee mariners held prisoner in England's two large prisons assigned to the American rebels went so far as to replace a real body in a casket. Alexander Tindall's ruse did not go unnoticed, but no great matter—after another failed attempt a month later, he succeeded in a third and final escape attempt less than six months after the casket caper.

Nor was he alone in achieving such a farewell to incarceration in England. At Forton, near Portsmouth, England, about sixty prisoners popped out of a tunnel that unexpectedly came up short— "breaking up in a cellar of an old woman," according to American privateer officer Luke Matthewman. She shouted for help after recovering from her shock, but the escaping prisoners hastily gagged the poor old woman and went about their business. Fate was not on their side in this particular case, it turns out. Fifty-eight men were recaptured in short order, although Matthewman and his privateer skipper, John Smith, did reach safety in continental Europe.

Europe, with its helpful American agents such as Benjamin Franklin, was usually the goal. Before reaching the English Channel, though, American escapees often could count on a sort of "underground railway" of English sympathizers to help hide, feed, and clothe them—sometimes for weeks at a time.

In all, about three thousand men, both early American navymen and privateer crewmen, passed through the gates of the two land prisons in England established to house captured American mariners. "As a group," wrote Cohen, "they ranged in age from boys of nine to aging men of about 60. They were mostly white, though a small, indeterminate number of black seamen could be found in their ranks (and two American Indians)."

Gustavus Conyngham, for instance, born an Irishman, had captured or sunk sixty British ships as skipper of Continental Navy cutters or privateers such as the *Revenge* until his first capture in 1779. Eventually confined at the Mill Prison, he escaped its confines not once, but twice. In the first instance, he and four companions made their way to the London home of Thomas Digges, born in Maryland but now a mercantile agent in England—and a known escape-helper. The five men reached his Villars Street address about a week after their breakout. Digges gave them money and made arrangements for them to slip onto a Dutch ship sailing for Rotterdam—and freedom—two days later.

"Mr. Digges did everything in his power to save me and all my countrymen that chance to fall his way," wrote Conyngham afterward. And further: "Happy we have such a man Among that set of tyrants the[y] have in that Country."

Conyngham's first escape, consummated with the help of Digges, was in November of 1770. The Irishman's next flight, in 1781, apparently was accomplished by bribing guards at the Mill Prison.

Other methods of escape noted at Mill Prison included the time twelve prisoners stuck a long wooden beam out a window, then climbed down a rope made of hammocks tied together, one after the other. Escapees were known to volunteer a trip to the nearby bay with prison laundry tubs, then leap into the water and swim off. Some made their way through sewage flues into the bay. Bribery, though, remained the easiest, safest means of escape . . . unless the *bribee* betrayed the *briber.*

Money, four guineas it is said, did change hands in the spectacular double-barreled exploit of Baltimore-born Joshua Barney, a Continental Navy officer sent to the Mill Prison in December 1781. Developing a friendship with a sympathetic guard, then feigning a sprained ankle and, finally, donning an English officer's uniform, he chose the staff lunch hour to make his bid at escape.

He climbed the shoulders of a tall fellow prisoner to clear the inner wall and gate, then walked past his friend the guard (while passing him four guineas), and, unnoticed in his British uniform, simply glided beyond another unsuspecting guard at the outer gate. Barney found refuge with English sympathizers who provided a safe house and a boat to take him and a fellow American across the Channel. They were picked up, however, by a British privateer near the Channel Islands, but Barney "was able to slip off the vessel [as it neared English soil], seize her dingy, and flee to the Devon village of Causen," wrote Cohen. Then, it was back to the safe house, followed by a six-week stay under wraps in London, and finally a packet boat to Belgium—and freedom.

Not all hands were able to escape, and some—a relative few— did defect to the enemy and join *his* navy, noted Cohen. Conditions in the two land prisons were not the best, but they were nothing like the rotting hulks in New York Harbor and elsewhere. Any Americans confined to the "detention vessels" were lucky to survive—Cohen cited one historian's estimate that twelve thousand prisoners simply didn't.

Personal Glimpse: Lafayette

GEORGE WASHINGTON HAD JUST MET the young French officer, who had arrived in the American camp in August 1777 with high recommendation from America's agents in France. Congress had granted the untried nineteen-year-old temporary rank as a major general, but Washington and his staff had heard it all before. Not all of these foreign volunteers were of any great or lasting use to the American cause. For the time being, Washington decided to keep the newly arrived Marie-Joseph-Paul-Yves-Roch-Gilbert du Motier, the Marquis de Lafayette, close at hand to evaluate his potential.

As was often the case for Washington and his Continental Army, it was a critical moment. The British, after leaving New York and sailing up the Chesapeake Bay, were moving on Philadelphia. Maneuvering repeatedly for advantage, to deny Sir William Howe easy access either to the American capital or to American supply bases to the west, Washington tried to engage the British in set-piece battle on Brandywine Creek . . . on his terms.

As at Long Island the summer before, Washington was outflanked, but this time on the American right. Galloping to the scene with the commander in chief was his new staff aide, Lafayette. Leaping from his horse and trying to rally the men streaming in retreat was, again, Lafayette. Wounded in the leg but disappearing in the confusion of battle for a time, was Lafayette. Found by Washington later, twelve miles away, weak from loss of blood but trying to rally soldiers in a defensive formation at a bridge over Chester Creek was, yet again, Lafayette.

At this point, Washington had seen quite enough. Summoning his own personal physician, Dr. James Craik, Washington ordered: "Take care of him as if he were my son." So began the very historic and very personal relationship between the usually austere, reserved American commander and the ebullient, eternally optimistic young nobleman from France.

Interestingly, the middle-aged Washington never had children of his own, although he had two stepchildren whom he loved and adopted. Lafayette, on the other hand, never had known his father, who had been killed in the Battle of Minden before his son reached the age of two. The French youth had been raised in the country by a grandmother and two aunts rather than with his mother in Paris. He moved to Paris at age eleven, however, to further his schooling. Both his mother and a wealthy grandfather died two years later. As a result, he came into a large inheritance. At age sixteen, he married into an aristocratic family close to the French court.

Still a teenager, he joined the Black Musketeers, an elite arm of the royal household troops. He also, like Washington, became a Mason. And as a lover of liberty, he became enthralled by the American Revolutionary cause, which happened to challenge the interests of Great Britain, that old enemy of Lafayette's own country.

Immensely wealthy, he bought himself a ship, *La Victoire,* and in early 1777, at nineteen, set sail for America, arriving in South Carolina. He traveled north to Philadelphia to offer his services to the Continental Congress, which, while wary, went along with the recommendations of America's agents in France (Silas Deane and Benjamin Franklin) who had endorsed the young nobleman. Given temporary rank of major general, Lafayette met Washington on August 1 of that year.

It was both a glad and dreary time to make such an acquaintance. On the one hand, Lafayette was present as witness to Washington's defeats that fall in the Battles of Brandywine and Germantown, to Howe's occupation of Philadelphia, to the massacre of Anthony Wayne's none-too-alert troops at nearby Paoli and, finally, to the miserable winter the Continental Army spent at Valley Forge. To make matters worse, Lafayette soon was recuperating from the leg wound suffered at Brandywine.

Even so, the Frenchman not only shared the poor rations and other hardships of the men under his command at Valley Forge, he also reached into his own pocket to provide them clothing.

Lafayette again rose to the occasion when Irish-born volunteer General Thomas Conway, himself a product of French military training, made contact with Lafayette to enlist him in the anti-Washington rumble known as the Conway Cabal. Lafayette promptly warned Washington of the sub-rosa effort to vault Horatio Gates into Washington's post as commander in chief. A sharp letter from George to Horatio put a sudden stop to the whole affair.

As for truly glad tidings, the fall of 1777 was notable for its electrifying news of British General Burgoyne's surrender of his entire army at Saratoga, New York, ostensibly as a result of Gates's generalship, but actually due in large part to the front-line heroics of one Benedict Arnold. Thanks to the pivotal Saratoga victory came another bolt from the blue—the word received the following spring that France had agreed to a formal alliance with the American revolutionaries.

That did not mean Washington would acquiesce to Lafayette's dream of leading a new expedition into Canada, but it did mean the arrival of a French fleet under Count Charles d'Estaing in July of 1778. Oddly, the presence of Lafayette's own countrymen was to prove an unexpected, often forgotten test of the young nobleman's mettle, especially his diplomatic prowess.

D'Estaing, Lafayette's distant cousin, at first approached New York but decided against confrontation with the British fleet harbored there. Washington had been hoping for action against New York, but had to settle for the alternative of a joint operation against British-held Newport, Rhode Island. The plan that quickly took shape anticipated a landing by General John Sullivan on Aquidneck Island at Newport with four thousand Continentals and a number of New England militia. D'Estaing would contribute four thousand French marines and the considerable fire support of his ships. Lafayette would command one of the two American divisions under Sullivan, act as liaison with the French, and generally coordinate the entire operation.

What looked good on paper, however, was not to prove viable in reality. Sullivan, for one, balked at abiding by young Lafayette's suggestions. The latter's French "cousins," on the other hand, made no secret of the fact that they viewed both the American Continentals and the militia as something akin to mere rabble. Lafayette's delicate and difficult job was to keep everybody happy.

Meanwhile, Sullivan crossed over from the mainland with his troops on August 8. Unfortunately, the very next day, d'Estaing learned the British fleet he had avoided at New York was approaching Newport. With a confrontation now unavoidable, he hastily turned his ships seaward to find room to maneuver.

The French and English briefly exchanged fire, but a gale stopped their naval battle and damaged ships on both sides. D'Estaing then informed his allies at Newport that he must sail to

Boston to refit his damaged ships, leaving a furious Sullivan alone at the north end of Aquidneck Island and vulnerable to attack by the British in Newport. His militia quickly melting away, Sullivan turned his fury on "middleman" Lafayette, who himself was so angry he almost challenged the American general to a duel.

In the end, on the night of August 30, under expectant attack by the British, Sullivan was able to ferry his harried Continentals back to the mainland . . . and just in the nick of time, since Sir Henry Clinton appeared the very next day with another five thousand red-coats fresh from the British base of New York. In Boston, meanwhile, Admiral d'Estaing's men faced insults from Americans encountered on the street.

It had not been an auspicious start to the Franco-American alliance. Nor were matters greatly rectified when d'Estaing rejected Lafayette's plea to attack Nova Scotia and sailed off in his refitted fleet for the British West Indies.

To generate a more substantial contribution to the American cause, Lafayette returned to France in early 1779. He was greeted with excitement, wide acclaim—and a slap on the wrist by King Louis XVI for failure to obtain permission to join the American army. At the same time, he was allowed to purchase and command the king's dragoons . . . but he wouldn't be returning to America for more than a year, not until April 27, 1780.

His wife, in the meantime, had produced an infant son, prompt-ly named George Washington; France had prepared to invade England and then backed off from that plan, and the king, finally, agreed to send a substantial body of troops and a second fleet across the Atlantic to help the Americans win the Revolution.

D'Estaing, in the meantime, had not been entirely idle. After seiz-ing the islands of Grenada and Dominic in the sunny Caribbean, he sailed northward once more and thought he saw easy pickings in the form of Savannah, capital of Georgia. He was wrong, and he and his American ally, Major General Benjamin Lincoln, were repulsed, losing one thousand men in the process. It was a defeat that paved the way, materially and psychologically, for a British sweep through all of Georgia and up into South Carolina, a drive capped by Sir Henry Clinton's arrival from New York and the siege that led to the capitulation of Charleston in the spring of 1780.

Thus, Lafayette reappeared in America at a second critical point in the Revolution. And once again, Newport was front and center of events—but this time as a base for the French rather than the British, who had moved out their Newport forces for their siege of Charleston. Washington soon conferred with the latest French commander on the scene, fifty-five-year-old Compte de Jean Baptiste de Rochambeau. Eager to make use of the count's army of ten thousand, Washington once again brought up his dream of ousting the British from New York. But Rochambeau doubted that even together the allies could overcome such a stronghold. He remained in Newport, stalled, and generally did little the rest of the year . . . except send his own son back home to France with an urgent request for more men, more ships, and more support.

The winter and spring of 1781 only brought more bad news for the American cause. The "central government" that went under the name of Congress basically had been broke for months, its paper money close to worthless. One result was that food and pay were not reaching the men of the Continental Army. The separate states had been unable, or unwilling, to take up the slack.

Another result was outright mutiny. In January 1781, Pennsylvania troops wintering at Morristown, New Jersey, rebelled, killed two officers, and began marching to Philadelphia to confront Congress. Stopped by Major General Anthony Wayne and New Jersey's Continentals, then promised better treatment, they eventually calmed down. But weeks later, New Jersey's own troops mutinied, too. Washington had four of their leaders arrested and executed two of them. In his diary, he dejectedly wrote: " . . . [I]nstead of having the prospect of a glorious offensive campaign before us, we have a gloomy and bewildered prospect of a defensive one. . . ."

As another bit of bad news, the traitor Benedict Arnold had invaded Virginia with two thousand men, cruised up the James River with impunity and seized Richmond, the state's capital. Not far south, in the Carolinas, the armies of Lord Cornwallis and America's Nathanael Greene were in a deadly dance with an uncertain outcome. Few onlookers would have guessed that the British surrender at Yorktown was only months away.

Lafayette, it so happened, was destined to play an important role in the events leading up to that denouement of British fortunes. Delegated to march south into Virginia at the head of a relief force, Lafayette missed any confrontation with Arnold but found plenty of other British forces to keep him busy. Recapturing and then holding Richmond in late April, Lafayette could thumb his nose at his opposing commander, General William Phillips, the very man whose artillery battery had killed Lafayette's father at Minden in 1759. (Phillips fell ill and died in May of 1781, the very next month.)

As events also turned out, Lafayette arrived in Virginia almost at the same moment that Lord Cornwallis bulled his way across the border from North Carolina. American General Wayne had joined Lafayette by June, and their small force of two thousand or so nipped at the heels of the Cornwallis army of four thousand as it moved down the James to Williamsburg, then to Portsmouth and, finally, in early August, to Yorktown and Gloucester, Virginia, at the mouth of the York River.

In the north, Washington still had been trying to talk Rochambeau into a joint assault on New York. But any such thoughts were abandoned when they received word on August 14 that French Admiral Francois Joseph de Grasse was setting sail from Haiti in the Caribbean for Virginia's Chesapeake Bay with thirty warships and three thousand fresh troops. That news signalled the final course of the war. Washington and Rochambeau marched south to Virginia, de Grasse was able to plug up the watery approaches to Yorktown—Cornwallis was trapped, and in October he surrendered. In the meantime, Lafayette had commanded the successful assault on one of two key redoubts taken from the British in the final fighting of the siege.

Two months later, the now widely lionized (and still very young) Lafayette returned to France for an entirely new military and political career as "hero of two worlds." It was a career of many ups and downs that carried the liberal idealist through the French Revolution and the years of Napoleon's rule. He would return to his beloved America for a famous year-long tour in 1824, accompanied by his son, George Washington de Lafayette.

Lafayette's old mentor, the original George Washington, long since had gone to his grave (in 1799), but not before the French nobleman sent him the key to the Bastille with the message that he offered this treasured symbol of the French Revolution as "a tribute which I owe as a son to my adoptive father, as an aide-de-camp to my general, as a missionary of liberty to its patriarch."

Many Moments of Truth

While they didn't enlist in the Continental Army expecting to fight as soldiers, a number of women emerged from the Revolution as real battlefield heroines anyway. Some of them were legendary—"Molly Pitcher," for instance—and some not. Elizabeth Zane of Fort Henry, Virginia, probably falls into the latter category.

Her terrifying moment of truth came one late-summer day in 1782 with Indians and redcoats surrounding the small frontier fort. The odds were about 350 besiegers outside the fort versus about 60 men, women, and children inside. The Americans inside had been told to surrender or face a massacre.

Of the 60 inside the fort, mind you, only 18 were fully grown, able-bodied men.

Several assaults had been made against the small fortress, but the defenders so far had been able to beat them back with spirited, well-aimed gunfire. Still, the gunpowder was running low. Soon, there would be no defense . . . and then what?

Not far away—a mere sixty or so yards, all the defenders knew—was a cabin belonging to "Betty" Zane's oldest brother, Colonel Ebenezer Zane. And inside the empty cabin, as yet undiscovered by the enemy, was a store of gunpowder.

But . . . how to retrieve it? The eighteen men vied with one another for the privilege of making the dangerous dash to the cabin and back.

Betty Zane became the volunteer instead. She was granted permission to try the desperate, suicidal errand after arguing, with irrefutable logic, that the defenders couldn't risk losing a single man. Further, the frontier-toughened lass asserted, she could run as fast as any man there.

But run she did not . . . at first. She meandered out the gate. She merely walked, almost in promenade, while the British and their Indian allies gawked—and held back from rushing forward, since she was under the guns of her allies inside the fort. Before the besiegers knew it—or divined her intentions—she was inside the cabin.

There she wasted no time. She grabbed a cloth, broke open a keg of gunpowder, and poured the contents onto the middle of the cloth, then jerked it up by the four corners to create a makeshift bag.

So far she had been extraordinarily lucky, but she knew she couldn't simply walk back to the fort with her prize. This time, she would have to run . . . run as fast as she could. Casting all thoughts of eighteenth-century modesty aside, she pulled off her long skirt, then stepped out of her petticoats as well.

In seconds, her freed legs pounding, she was out the door and racing for the fort.

The woods all around erupted in gunfire, immediately answered by her comrades inside the fort. They still had a small store of gunpowder, but they would need every bit more that Betty Zane carried in the "bag" slung over her shoulder.

She ran like the wind, untouched so far; but then, partway home, she tripped and fell.

Before the enemy could take advantage, however, she scrambled to her feet and flew on.

Seconds later, she dashed through the hastily opened gate. And that was that. Gunpowder safely delivered, the Americans were able to hold out until their assailants gave up the siege a day and a half later and withdrew.

After the surrender of Fort Washington on Manhattan Island, New York, to the British in November of 1776, a horribly wounded American captured just outside the fallen bastion was given parole, then ferried across the Hudson River to the relative safety of New Jersey. Next, the battle victim was placed in a wagon that would bump and grind its way to Philadelphia on the primitive roads of the era. The suffering victim's jaw, upper chest, and left arm all had been shredded by grapeshot. She would be lucky to survive, much less keep her mangled arm.

Apparently the first American woman to become a battlefield casualty of the Revolution, Margaret Cochran Corbin had stepped forward to take her artilleryman husband John Corbin's place at his small-bore cannon after he was killed in the midst of the British and

Hessian assault on Fort Washington. He himself, earlier in the action, had stepped forward to take the chief gunner's place when he was struck down.

All three had begun the day in a two-piece battery belonging to the Pennsylvania Artillery's First Company. Margaret Corbin, twenty-five, was present at the redoubt guarding nearby Fort Washington as one of those wives allowed to accompany Continental Army troops as a cook, laundress, seamstress, and nurse all wrapped in one.

Hardship was no stranger to the redhead, a native of Franklin County, Pennsylvania, who had been orphaned at age five when raiding Indians killed her father and abducted her mother. Raised by relatives, Margaret never saw her mother again.

She found brief happiness when she married Virginia-born John Corbin in 1772. They were living in Pennsylvania when the Revolutionary War erupted. Husband John joined his artillery company in 1775, and Margaret then followed him into the teeth of war.

When not tied down by her encampment chores among his fellow troops, she liked to watch husband John's artillery drills. Thus, she saw and learned how to load and fire his battery's guns.

As the British bombarded Fort Washington both from land and from their ships in the Hudson River in late 1776, she bravely stood by her husband's gun position. British cannon shot rained down on rudimentary Fort Washington. Redcoats and Hessians overran one American position after another.

Toward the end, the Pennsylvania artillerymen, accompanied by Virginia militiamen, still held out against the Hessians swarming toward their redoubt on Laurel Hill, a ridge just north of Fort Washington's perimeter. Then came the fateful salvos that killed Margaret's husband.

That's when she stepped forward to load and fire John Corbin's gun again and again ... until she, herself, was struck down by British grapeshot, her left arm nearly torn off. The triumphant Hessians found her among the American wounded and, after giving her basic medical care, granted her parole rather than hold her as a prisoner.

The hardy young woman survived her wounds, but her arm was crippled for life. In response to Margaret Corbin's heroics, the Pennsylvania Executive Council later gave her nominal financial relief (thirty dollars!), while the Continental Congress allowed her to wear a soldier's uniform and granted her half a soldier's pay for life. For the remainder of the Revolutionary War, she served as a guard in the Corps of Invalids at West Point, New York, as the only woman member of the unit. She in fact married for a second time to an older Corps member, recalled Joe Lieberman in the February 1999 issue of *Military History* magazine.

Officially separated from the Continental Army in 1783, she spent the rest of her life at Highland Falls near West Point. Living until 1800 (she was only forty-nine when she died that year), she unfortunately became known as a gruff, hard-drinking local character with a penchant for wearing a petticoat and a uniform jacket. People called her "Captain Molly," a nickname often applied to the women who had followed their Continental Army husbands into camp . . . sometimes, like Margaret Corbin, even into battle.

A monument in the cemetery at the U.S. Military Academy at West Point today marks her final resting place, while a second monument at Fort Tryon Park in upper Manhattan reminds visitors of her heroics that day in 1776 that her husband and so many of his comrades-in-arms fell victim to the British-Hessian assault on Fort Washington. Fort Tryon, which the temporarily triumphant British renamed for Royal Governor William Tryon, previously was known as Laurel Hill, the very spot where Margaret Corbin stepped forward to take her fallen husband's place.

Another battle and another heroine stepping forth to fire her fallen husband's cannon in the midst of hot combat were elements in the story of Mary Ludwig Hays McCauley.

By her real name most Americans today would not know her or her feats. By her nickname of Molly Pitcher, however, who doesn't know the basic story?

While no less deserving of recognition, her actions in June of 1778 in fact were almost a carbon copy of Margaret Corbin's nearly two years earlier.

Apparently born in Mercer County, New Jersey, Mary Ludwig eventually became a household servant in Carlisle, Pennsylvania, where she married a local barber, one John Casper Hays, in 1769. With Revolution breaking out, he became a Pennsylvania artilleryman. He then re-enlisted as an infantryman in the Seventh Pennsylvania; his wife, Mary, soon followed him into camp and was on hand for the Battle of Monmouth, New Jersey, on the hot day of June 28, 1778.

Because of the heat, she was kept unusually busy carrying pitchers of water to the thirsty troops on the front lines. She also helped tend the wounded and in one case allegedly carried a man to the rear on her back.

But then her husband, assigned to the infantry's attached artillery battery, was laid low by enemy fire. The remaining soldiers attending the artillery piece were about to take it off the line, says the legend, when Mary Hays dramatically said no, she could take over her husband's duties of swabbing, loading, and firing the cannon. She then, like Margaret Corbin, kept his cannon in action until the battle was over—an American victory in this case.

With Mary now called "Molly Pitcher," "Sergeant Molly," and even, again like Corbin, "Captain Molly," both she and her husband survived the war and returned to the Carlisle area, where he died shortly before 1790. She later remarried, to Revolutionary War veteran John McCauley.

Given a forty-dollar annuity by the Pennsylvania legislature in 1822 for her Revolutionary War services, Mary Ludwig Hays McCauley lived another ten years. Sources suggest her birth date could have been as early as 1744 or as late as 1754. Either way, she would have been an old woman—and already a legend—by the time of her death in 1832.

Other women met their moment of truth in more muted but no less heroic circumstances. Their husbands off fighting the British elsewhere, South Carolina sisters-in-law Grace and Rachel Martin learned that an enemy courier would be passing their way near the British Fort Ninety-Six. He would be carrying important dispatches, the two young wives were told.

They decided to intercept the courier that night.

Carrying rifles and dressed in their husbands' clothing, they waited behind a rail fence and some bushes. Sure enough, along came the courier—and two armed escorts.

Brandishing their own rifles and trying to use deep, male-sounding voices, the brave pair stepped out of hiding and ordered the trio to halt. Totally surprised, the British soldiers not only surrendered, but gave up the courier's dispatches with hardly a murmur. In seconds, the two exultant wives faded from sight, the redcoats relieved to be allowed to go their own way unharmed.

They, in fact, turned back toward their base at Fort Ninety-six but decided to stop for the night at a house they had passed earlier. The owner, a middle-aged woman named Mrs. Martin, agreed to their request . . . and even heard their complaint of being stopped on the road by the two local rebels.

The three redcoats ate a hearty breakfast before setting out again the next morning. They briefly met the older Mrs. Martin's two daughters-in-law, Grace and Rachel. Apparently the three soldiers never quite realized. . . .

Still more women contributed to the final outcome in briefly told, yet not-so-small ways. In South Carolina again, Rebecca Motte told her fellow Patriots to go ahead and burn down her plantation home overlooking the Congaree River, literally to smoke out a British garrison that had turned it into a fortified outpost. Flaming arrows set fire to the roof, forcing out the redcoats—who then joined with the besieging Patriots in fighting the fire and saving what they could of Rebecca Motte's magnificent home.

In New York, fall of 1776, Mary Lindley Murray entertained British General Sir William Howe and his officers with a fine, slow-moving dinner at her Murray Hill estate in mid-Manhattan . . . while American General Israel Putnam was moving out his troops on the west side of the island. Howe was glad to join Mrs. Murray because her husband, Robert, was a well-known Loyalist. Not so Mrs. Murray, however. She delayed Howe's departure in every conceivable fashion ("More wine, Sir William?"), well aware that Putnam's withdrawal from lower Manhattan was under way.

Nor should we overlook the impact of little-known Hannah White Arnett of Elizabethtown, New Jersey, one night in late 1776 when the prospect of an American triumph over the British appeared very dim indeed. With the redcoats in hot pursuit, George

Washington's crumbling army was headed for the hills and beyond, to Pennsylvania eventually.

Gathered at the home of Hannah Arnett and husband, Isaac, was a dispirited clot of would-be rebels. They were debating whether to accept British offers of a pardon for previously unruly Americans now willing to declare their allegiance to the Crown by a certain deadline. After hours of argument pro and con, they had to admit the great cause of Revolution appeared destined to failure—the wise course for them, however reluctant they might feel, would be to go ahead and accept the British "peace offering."

Entering the discussion at this point—literally stepping into the doorway—was Isaac's wife, Hannah, furious and scathing. Were they men or traitors, she wanted to know. Without waiting for an answer, she reminded them that the American colonists were in the right, not England. "We are poor, weak and few, but God is fighting for us!" she declared. "We entered into this struggle with pure hearts and prayerful lips. We had counted the cost and were willing to pay the price, were it in our heart's blood."

But now look! "And now, now because for a time the day is going against us, you would give up all and sneak back like cravens to kiss the feet that have trampled upon us. And you call yourselves men!"

She reminded her stunned listeners that they were the "sons of those who gave up home and fortune and fatherland to make for themselves and for dear liberty a resting place in the wilderness!"

For shame, she exclaimed. "Oh, shame upon you, cowards!"

Hannah didn't finish until she had threatened to forsake home, hearth, and even husband Isaac if the men didn't recant their decision to accept the British offer of amnesty.

She had offered strong medicine as cure for their low spirits, to be sure, but it worked. However bitter the taste of her railing, the men meeting at Isaac Arnett's house that night reversed themelves and pledged to continue their support of the Revolutionary cause. A woman arguing with passion had swayed them all.

VII. 1780–1781:
On to Yorktown

"Bloody Ban" Tarleton

FOR SPORADICALLY EMBATTLED SOUTH CAROLINA, the war just wouldn't go away. Even after the British gave up on cracking the Patriot defenses at Sullivan's Island, and after the Cherokee Nation was subdued in 1776, there always seemed to be a fresh storm cloud on the horizon. In 1779, the Carolinians watched in dismay as the British and their Loyalist friends regained command of Savannah—and virtually all of Georgia—with relative ease. Next on the Crown's agenda, quite obviously, would be the key port city of Charleston.

In time, South Carolina would come up with a new set of heroes. In the affair of Sullivan's Island, it had been William Moultrie, militia colonel. In the case of the Cherokee uprising, it was militia colonel Andrew Williamson. Next on the horizon would be militia colonel Andrew Pickens, Francis Marion, the "Swamp Fox," and Thomas Sumter, the "Gamecock." First, though, the British would produce Banastre Tarleton as ranking villain of the piece. Only twenty-five, son of a slave trader in Liverpool, "Bloody Ban" had purchased his commission in the British army, as permitted by custom of the day. Lieutenant Colonel Tarleton commanded the hard-riding, green-jacketed British Legion.

As the British, under General Sir Henry Clinton, tightened a nearly inescapable noose of siege works and naval and land forces around Charleston in the spring of 1780, Tarleton and his men were sent riding in the middle of an April night toward a place called Monck's Corner. There, thirty-two miles from Charleston, American General Isaac Huger guarded the last open corridor of escape from the besieged city. But Tarleton and his men burst upon their loosely guarded camp at three in the morning, killing dozens of Americans, scattering others far and wide. General Huger and his subordinate Colonel William Washington had to plunge into the nearby swamps to escape Tarleton's wrath.

With the American escape hatch closed, General Benjamin Lincoln, in a matter of days, was forced to surrender his army defending the old port city. This proved to be the worst American defeat of the Revolutionary War by the numbers. The British scooped up nearly 5,500 armed prisoners (seven generals among them), nearly 400 artillery pieces, 376 barrels of powder, more than 8,000 cannonballs, nearly 6,000 muskets, and 33,0000 rounds for small arms. Even worse, the Continental Army no longer could claim a presence in the South.

No presence, that is, except for the Third Virginia Regiment, all of 350 to 400 strong. Previously on their way to help man the defenses at Charleston, these Continentals now turned back for safer territory to the north. Accompanying Colonel Abraham Buford and his men were South Carolina's Governor John Rutledge and fellow Patriot officials, all in flight from British-occupied Charleston. They soon found out, however, that they were under hot pursuit by Tarleton, who would like nothing better than to snare a rebel governor and entourage. Covering a startling 150 miles in a twenty-four-hour period, the young Englishman's cavalry and mounted infantry just missed taking the Rutledge party, but caught up with Colonel Buford's Virginians at the Waxhaws settlement near the North Carolina border.

Even though Tarleton claimed to have 700 men with him, rather than his actual 270, Buford refused a demand to surrender. Before he could catch his breath, Tarleton attacked. The Americans waited until too late before firing their first volley. Before the Patriots could reload, the dragoons were among them, cutting and slashing them with bayonet and saber.

The numbers tell the story—5 dragoons killed and 14 wounded to the staggering Patriot totals of 113 killed and 150 wounded. It had been a massacre; it would be known far and wide as the Waxhaws or Buford Massacre. From this battle, too, came the expression "Tarleton's quarter," which meant no quarter, no mercy, since Tarleton's dragoons showed no mercy to their fallen enemy, repeatedly attacking them with the bayonet. "The demand for quarter, seldom refused to a vanquished foe, was at once found to be in vain," reported onlooking army surgeon Robert Brownfield.

It may be, in the heat and confusion of battle, that some Americans continued to fire on Tarleton's force after the white flag of surrender appeared. Be that as it may, such desultory resistance still doesn't explain the bloodbath that followed—for fifteen minutes "after every man was prostrate," said Dr. Brownfield later, the dragoons moved around the battlesite, "plunging their bayonets into everyone that exhibited any sign of life." In some cases, they used their bayonets to push aside bodies on top of bodies to "come at those beneath." Tarleton's lame excuse: His Loyalists erroneously thought their commanding officer had been killed.

In one case symbolic of the entire bloody affair, a Patriot officer, Captain John Stokes, suffered a total of twenty-three wounds. He started out parrying the blows of one dragoon with a small sword, but then a second dragoon assailed Stokes and "by one stroke, cut off his right hand through the metacarpal bones," reported Dr, Brownfield. Still trying to parry blows aimed at his head, Stokes next lost the forefinger of his left hand and his left arm was "hacked in eight or ten places from the wrist to the shoulder." He finally went down with his head "laid open almost the whole length of the crown to the eye brows." He then was subjected to "several" cuts on the face and shoulders. Incredibly, the worst was yet to come. When a dragoon asked if he expected mercy, the still-conscious American said, "I have not, nor do I mean to ask quarters. Finish me as soon as possible." The dragoon complied all too readily, twice plunging his bayonet into the American's body. But still he lived. "Another asked the same question," related Dr. Brownfield, "and received the same answer, and he also thrust his bayonet twice through his body."

Despite his ordeal at the Waxhaws, this remarkable man lived ... to serve his new country after the Revolution as a federal judge in North Carolina. Think of him when driving through his namesake, Stokes County.

Banastre Tarleton, meanwhile, in the single stroke of the bloody Waxhaws affair, became the most feared—and hated—minor officer among the British based in the South. He would continue his fierce, hard-riding style for the next two years, most notably to lose the Battle of Cowpens and to command the raiding party that almost snared Virginia's outgoing governor Thomas Jefferson at Charlottesville in 1781.

Unfortunately for the British hoping for the support of the Carolinas, Tarleton's no-quarter reputation simply hardened the attitude of many Americans. A second factor that pushed many neutral onlookers into active rebellion was a foolish and arrogant edict issued by Clinton before he left freshly subdued Charleston for unfinished business in the North. Not content with the parole rendering captured Patriots inactive neutrals, Clinton issued a proclamation restoring both the rights and duties of Carolina citizens who had accepted the neutralizing parole status—this meant that failure to defend the Crown against their own, still-rebellious countrymen would result in their being branded rebels themselves. Forced to take sides, many took to the field against the Crown rather than for it. South Carolina, far from being subdued, now would be freshly aflame with rebellion.

Andrew's Rage

THE YOUTH BEFORE THE BRITISH officer was tall and skinny. His unruly hair was brush thick, his eyes a deep blue. He came from a poor and fatherless home, and he frequently was an angry, angry young man. Even a bully at times. But he and his brother Robert, only slightly older, were in a tight spot now. Rebel partisans without a doubt, they were prisoners of the officer of dragoons. They wouldn't be treated kindly.

Focusing upon Andrew, fourteen, the officer ordered the young American to clean his boots.

We can imagine those unforgettable wild eyes flashing in defiance—they always did when his temper flared, even years later as seventh president of the United States.

"Sir," he allegedly exclaimed, "I am a prisoner of war and claim to be treated as such."

But the officer of dragoons could flare up, too. Enraged at such impertinence, he swung his sword at the youngster, who ducked and at the same time attempted to parry the blow with his left hand. The results were an ugly laceration of his head and a gash across his fingers—he would carry the scars of the partially deflected blow for life. More immediately, however, he and Robert must do their best to survive their plight as prisoners of British soldiers sick and tired of the unending resistance offered by Patriot partisans—even youngsters like these two teenage brothers—in the Carolina backcountry. For now, the furious officer was done with them. Surrounded by their captors, they were consigned to a prison camp forty to forty-five miles away in Camden, South Carolina, and they would travel there on horseback.

In their condition, that would be no easy journey. The destination, though, was worse. It was a country jail surrounded by a stockade that contained 250 prisoners and no bedding, no medicines, little food other than twists of bread, and no medical attention, though many others were also wounded.

Fortunately, they wouldn't freeze to death, since warmer temperatures had arrived in that spring of 1781. Still, other dangers stalked the two brothers. Separated and robbed after their arrival, they soon came down with the dreaded smallpox.

Said the future president years later: "They kept me in jail at Camden about two months, starved me nearly to death and gave me the smallpox. . . . When it left me I was a skeleton—not quite six feet long and a little over six inches thick!" Fortunately, it was at this point that a real angel of mercy arrived on their behalf—their mother, Elizabeth.

This brave but distraught woman was absolutely tireless in her efforts to rescue and care for her two sons. For years, she had refused to be beaten down by various blows sustained since immigrating from Ireland to a tough homesteading life on the poor red soil of the Waxhaws area. She had lost her husband to natural causes and been forced to move in with relatives. And she had buried an older son who died in the Revolution.

According to twentieth-century biographer Gerald W. Johnson, Andrew's mother, Elizabeth, at this point had arranged with other partisans to exchange thirteen captured British soldiers for her two sons and five comrades incarcerated at the enemy's pestilent jail in Camden. More recent biographer Robert V. Remini's account offers a slightly different version, saying that the boys' mother arrived "just as an exchange of prisoners was being arranged between the American and British commanders." As a result, "she persuaded the British to include her sons in the exchange, along with five Waxhaw neighbors."

Whatever the exact detail, she succeeded in freeing both her boys, but all three now faced the long trek home with only two horses to carry them. Robert was still so sick he could not stand or even sit upright without support. Andrew was also weak and feverish. Undismayed, Elizabeth lashed her older son into place on one horse, then mounted the remaining one, and the trio set off—with

Andrew stumbling along as best he could on bare feet. Their newly freed neighbors traveled with them as well, also on foot.

Close to journey's end, a merciless rainstorm drenched them all. In their weakened condition, the cold soaking was the last thing the two boys needed. Just forty-eight hours later, Robert was dead and Andrew was delirious from his fever. Somehow, though, the teenager rallied. His exhausted mother managed to bring him—and herself—through the ordeal. It would be months before Andrew was back to normal . . . only to face yet another cruel blow from the gods of war.

Imagine his astonishment—fear and anger, too, we can guess—when his mother announced she would be leaving home to help care for the truly wrteched American prisoners held in British prison ships at Charleston, 160 miles away. She had seen the conditions at Camden, and so she had an idea of the deplorable environment on board the prison ships. There were Waxhaw men held there, too, among them two nephews.

Leaving young Andrew, now fifteen, with the relatives who had opened their doors to her and her children previously, Elizabeth Hutchinson Jackson was gone only a short while before she contracted cholera while nursing the men aboard the prison ships. She was buried just outside the city, her personal belongings sent to her son at the Waxhaws in a small bundle.

Somehow, this same teenager managed to overcome the loss of his immediate family. Somehow, young Andrew Jackson outgrew and overcame the deprivations—but never all the anger—of his formative years, to become a territorial governor, a U.S. congressman, a U.S. senator, seventh U.S. president and, along the way, hero of the Battle of New Orleans, which of course he fought against the hated British.

Shooting Uphill

THE WEATHER THAT MORNING, ACCORDING to a man—a teenager, really—who was there: "The sky was overcast with clouds, and at times a light mist of rain falling." With hundreds upon hundreds of the enemy already gathered on top of a steep, skyward-soaring hill—King's Mountain, South Carolina—the pursuing militia and frontiersmen from Carolina and eastern Tennessee soon would face a moment of truth. They had indeed sought it out; they had been in pursuit of Major Patrick Ferguson's sharpshooting Loyalists and a host of fellow Tories for days, but now, like a wild beast at bay, the hunted had turned to deal with the hunter. As it often was in the Carolinas, the mood was grim and ugly.

Sixteen-year-old James Collins, soldiering today with his father but at his callow age already a veteran Carolina partisan, understood the challenge very well. "Our provisions were scanty, and hungry men are likely to be fractious," he later wrote; ". . . each one felt his situation; the last stake was up and the severity of the game must be played; everything was at stake—life, liberty, property, and even the fate of wife, children and friends, seemed to depend on the issue; death or victory was the only way to escape suffering."

Death or victory! As in any battle, it indeed would come down to that before day's end . . . but for whom? And why?

As related by James Collins, and confirmed by many others, he and his fellow militiamen "came in sight of the enemy" about two o'clock on Saturday afternoon. The British-led Loyalists were at considerable advantage right from the outset. For one thing, they had halted their march northeastward and about-faced at a moment and a place of their own chosing.

There whould be no surprising them, quite obviously. They could wait, prepared for battle and fully assured of their foe's appearance.

Ominously, too, Major Patrick Ferguson's well-trained troops, about 1,100 strong, held the high ground. "The enemy," said Collins later, "was posted on a high, steep and rugged ridge, or spur of the mountain, very difficult of access."

This "mountain," a chip chiseled off the Blue Ridge to the west, abruptly rose six or more stories high from a flat slab of land on South Carolina's border with its northern namesake. The Americans quickly surrounded its base, then made ready to assault the enemy above. By the account of the young Mr. Collins, the Americans would climb alongside a stream on the right, with another stream to the left. He described the slope to be conquered as a veritable cliff. At least, that was the slope he and his regiment faced, looking up.

It was no encouraging prospect, he admitted in his autobiography written many years later. As the Americans prepared their multifaceted attack, he wrote: "Each leader made a short speech in his own way to his men, desiring every coward to be off immediately; here I confess I would willingly have been excused, for my feelings were not the most pleasant—this may be attributed to my youth, not being quite seventeen years of age—but I could not well swallow the appellation of coward."

Young Collins looked about him and saw that others, many of them older than himself, were obviously thinking the same thing. "Every man's countenance seemed to change," he wrote. "Well, thought I, fate is fate, every man's fate is before him and he has to run it out, which I am inclined to think yet." And so began the assault up the northeastern end of the mountain. Militia Colonels Isaac Shelby, John Sevier, and William Campbell were in command of the three American columns now streaming up the mountainside. They numbered 1,200 to 1,500 or more by various accounts.

The men advancing with young Collins carried "four or five" musket balls in their mouths—"to prevent thirst, also to be in readiness to reload quick." His regiment, incidentally, was commanded by Major William Chronicle.

Above, Major Patrick Ferguson had ordered his men to ready their bayonets—those not so equipped were told to cut down the shaft of their hunting knives and jam them into the business end of their rifles. Ironically enough, the Scottish-born Ferguson, a marksman and firearms expert, previously had invented a rapid-fire rifle far advanced for its day . . . but the British high command in the American colonies failed to take advantage of the possibilities it offered. Incidentally, Ferguson was the able British officer who decided against shooting a mounted American officer in the back near Brandywine Creek in Pennsylvania in the fall of 1777 . . . quite possibly, Ferguson later surmised, sparing the life of a reconnoiter-ing General George Washington.

Now, three years later, he was operating in the backcountry of South Carolina as commander of the left wing of a three-pronged attempt by Lord Cornwallis to move into North Carolina and Virginia from his base at Charleston. While operating against the backcountry rebels, Ferguson had gathered a force of a thousand or more Loyalists. He recently penetrated into North Carolina territory, but he received intelligence that militiamen from west of the Blue Ridge—"over-the-mountain" men, many of them Scottish Highlander settlers or descendants—were gathering in significant numbers to oppose his drive north. Aware that he had stirred up a hornets' nest, he began to shift eastward, thinking to link up with Cornwallis in or near Charlotte, North Carolina. He issued a call for the Loyalists of North Carolina to "run to camp" with him and thus escape the "back water men," whom he unfortunately called "a set of mongrels."

He sent word to Cornwallis asking for a reinforcement of three hundred to four hundred "good soldiers, part dragoons" to "finish the business." Now pursuing him through several days of heavy rains were the ragged over-the-mountain men he had so unfairly dispar-aged. It all came to a head at King's Mountain the afternoon of October 7, 1780.

The Loyalists awaiting the day's action atop the heavily wooded promontory were startled by the appearance of the Americans after all. "So rapid was their attack," wrote a Loyalist officer from South Carolina, "that I was in the act of dismounting to report that all was quiet and the pickets [were] on the alert when we heard their [the Americans'] firing about half a mile off."

Loyalist Captain Alexander Chesney had just returned from a reconnaissance that revealed no approaching Americans. Now, how-ever, they were very much in evidence . . . and Ferguson's choice of a standoff site perhaps was not fated to be a favorable one. Explained Chesney later: "King's Mountain, from its height, would have enabled us to oppose a superior force with advantage, had it not been covered with wood, which sheltered the Americans and enabled them to fight in the favorite manner."

And what was the "favorite manner"? After driving back the Loyalist pickets and reaching the crest, the Americans "opened an irregular but destructive fire from behind trees and other cover."

Ah yes, trees! Indeed, another teenage American warrior, Private

Thomas Young, barefoot and all of sixteen also, later recalled, "Ben Hollingsworth and myself took right up the side of the mountain and fought from tree to tree. . . ."

From the perspective of young Collins, meanwhile, reaching the crest had not at all been such an easily accomplished goal. Hardly had he and his companions begun their climb, he later wrote, when, "The shot of the enemy soon began to pass over us like hail." Cool as the day apparently was, he quickly was in a sweat. And there was no fast advance in his sector of the assault. Said he: "My lot happened to be in the center where the severest part of the battle was fought. We soon attempted to climb the hill, but were fiercely charged upon and forced to fall back to our original position. We tried a second time, but met the same fate. The fight then seemed to become more furious."

About this time, Major Ferguson "came in full view within rifle shot, as if to encourage his men, who . . . were falling very fast." Ferguson, it seems by many accounts, was a highly visible figure wheeling about on his horse, dressed in a checkered hunting shirt over his uniform, brandishing his dress sword, blowing commands with a silver whistle held between his teeth. He was unfortunately too visible for his own good, as events turned out. "He soon disappeared," wrote Collins. "We took to the hill a third time. The enemy gave way. When we had gotten near the top, some of our leaders roared out, 'Hurrah, my brave fellows! Advance! They are crying for quarter!'"

And so it ended, about an hour after the first shots were fired. The Americans had won a great victory, one that would set back Cornwallis's advance north into Virginia by a full year. The over-the-mountain men, the ragtag militia, had killed 157 of the Loyalist force, wounded 163, and taken 698 prisoner.

Among the enemy dead was Patrick Ferguson, his body riddled by shot. When young Collins walked over to look at the British officer's body at the top of King's Mountain, he saw a sight he could still describe nearly six decades later with clarity and convincing detail. Ferguson had been the target of many rifles at practically the same moment, it appeared. "Seven rifle balls had passed through his body, both of his arms were broken, and his hat and clothing were literally shot to pieces."

Therein lay the secret of the American victory that day, added Collins. Rather than prove advantageous, holding the high ground had been the undoing of the British force. "Their great elevation above us had proved their ruin," wrote Collins in 1836 at age seventy-four. "They overshot us altogether, scarce touching a man, except those on horseback, while every rifle from below, seemed to have the desired effect."

Add to that the heavy woods denying the Loyalist defenders a clear view while affording the attacking Americans good cover, and there stand two persuasive reasons why the casualties of the comparatively ill-trained, unprofessional Americans amounted to only twenty-eight killed, with another sixty-two wounded, in defeating the British-led Loyalists at King's Mountain in the fall of 1780.

Food for Wolves

EVERY EXUBERANT SATURDAY HAS ITS Sunday to follow . . . and every triumphant battle its aftermath of sorrow, even remorse. So, too, at King's Mountain, South Carolina, in the wake of the American victory over those loyal to the Crown of England.

"Next morning, which was Sunday, the scene really became distressing," wrote James Collins many years later as an old man. He and his fellow survivors of the fighting on Saturday afternoon had seen a full quota of bodies and grievously wounded men. He personally had gazed upon the distinctly mortal remains of the British commander, Major Patrick Ferguson, a now-lifeless body riddled by rifle shot.

But now, on the Sunday morning following, the scene had only grown worse. "The wives and children of the poor Tories came in, in great numbers." And what they saw! Better, perhaps, in later times, for loved ones to learn of maiming wound or death from afar, by wire or messenger, without the grim firsthand view. In this case, they were on the scene—they rushed to it. "Their husbands, fathers and brothers lay dead in heaps, while others lay wounded or dying."

Worse and worse. "We proceeded to bury the dead, but it was badly done." Meaning? "They were thrown into convenient piles and covered with old logs, the bark of old trees and rocks." This hasty arrangement, it soon came about, was no protection against the "beasts of the forest, or the vultures of the air." Indeed, in those days, wolves prowled the wilder Carolina countryside . . . "and the wolves became so plenty, that it was dangerous for anyone to be out at night, for several miles around." Pigs, too. "Also, the hogs in the neighborhood, gathered in to the place, to devour the flesh of men." In fact, many area settlers "chose to live on little meat rather than eat their hogs, though they were fat."

And worse still . . . "half the dogs in the country were said to be mad, and were put to death."

Collins later had occasion to pass the grim site. "I saw, myself, in passing the place a few weeks later, all parts of the human frame, lying scattered in every direction."

As he said, the American losses had been few by comparison. Still, "some of our bravest men" had gone down. "These we buried in the flat ground under the hill, near where the battle commenced. . . ."

But there still was more to the battle's aftermath. "Of the troop, or company, to which I belonged, we had two badly wounded; one, a lieutenant, by the name of Watson, the other, a private, named Caldwell; we carried them to their own homes, in the evening, where they both died, in a few days. Poor fellows! they were raised together, fought together, died nearly at the same time in the same house, and lie buried together."

On a small scale, the participants that very evening shared in what Collins frankly called "plunder." The militiamen were told they could disband for the moment and go home. Collins and his father first "drew two fine horses, two guns, and some articles of clothing, with a share of powder and lead."

That night "every man repaired to his tent, or home." They were well aware that the battle had been a watershed event. "It seemed like a calm after a heavy storm had passed over, and for a short time, every man could visit his home, or his neighbor, without being afraid."

Significantly, too, once the great American victory at King's Mountain became known, ". . . [W]e seemed to gather strength, for many that before lay neutral, through fear or some other cause, shouldered their guns, and fell in the ranks; some of them making good soldiers."

Man in Red Shoe

SOMEONE WAS WATCHING WHEN BENEDICT Arnold made his sudden break for British lines. Someone . . . a young American soldier assigned to Arnold's security detail, his one-hundred-man "life guards." A young man at first puzzled by the strange events unfolding before him, then realizing what they portended. He was Alpheus Parkhurst, twenty, a Massachusetts native drawn from a Patriot company based at West Point to serve in Arnold's life guards, and he didn't really mean or plan to watch a historic moment that early morning. He was just there, as he was supposed to be.

For years afterward, he remembered America's most notorious traitor as "a lame man, having been wounded in his ankle, and on that foot he wore a large red shoe." Aside from that oddity, stemming from his wounding in the Battle of Saratoga, "He was a smart-looking man about middling size."

As Parkhurst reported years later in his petition for a service-related pension, Arnold at the time (summer of 1780) was living in the Beverley Robinson house across the Hudson River from West Point, while the "guard" lived in "tents and barracks" around the house. "Their business was to stand guard and sentry around the house and to go on errands to different places and was all the time under arms." The middle-aged Arnold had just recently married his twenty-year-old wife and been appointed commander of the key American fortress on the Hudson.

Then came the most dramatic morning of young Parkhurst's duty with the Arnold security detail. The young man guessed something was up when an aide-de-camp "rode up in great haste and the general came to the door and the aide-de-camp ordered the general's horse to be brought as quick as it could be done." A bay horse soon appeared. "The general and his aide started off together for the river, and the aide soon returned and brought back the general's horse."

In the meantime, Parkhurst had seen "the general dismount, step into a barge that lay there, and draw his sword, and the barge started off in great speed." He saw the barge make its way for about a mile downriver, with Arnold "sitting down."

Downstream was the location of His Majesty's ship *Vulture* and other British vessels . . . but it was to the *Vulture* that Benedict Arnold made his way that morning.

Back at the Robinson house, meanwhile, the excitement was not yet over. No more than forty or fifty minutes after Arnold's strange departure, the young soldier "heard a great rumbling and trampling of horses and, looking round, saw a great smoke of dust, the weather being dry, and in a few moments General Washington with 160 horse rode up." In the confusion that followed, Parkhurst could not quite hear what was said, but the soldier knew something indeed was amiss when, after only fifteen minutes there, George Washington turned for West Point.

A remarkably fortunate witness to history in the making, Parkhurst soon found himself across the river at the American fortress of West Point—the Arnold guard force was marched off just an hour or so after Washington left the Robinson house. Parkhurst thus arrived at West Point in time for a glimpse of the third actor in the drama, Major John André, chief British intelligence officer in New York . . . and the traitor Arnold's contact man. It, of course, was his capture two days before, with incriminating papers tucked in his boot, that had set off the chain of events witnessed by young Parkhurst.

At West Point, Parkhurst later said, he "saw General Washington and Major André with him, and he [André] was then dressed in blue citizen's clothes." The British officer obviously was a prisoner. "Andre's arms were pinioned back, but he rode on horseback."

Parkhurst's story ends there.

It ends, except that he had somehow managed to witness one other "inside" event that day. It came earlier, as Arnold himself was responding to the alarming news that André had been captured. What Parkhurst witnessed at this point had to do with Arnold's wife, the former Peggy Shippen, widely known as a close André friend and suspected Loyalist. Parkhurst recalled that "as Arnold stepped to the door, when his aide rode up, he turned to his wife and said, as near as . . . [I] can recollect, 'Something has come to light and I must bid you goodbye forever,' and then mounted his steed and galloped away."

According to Parkhurst, too, Arnold's wife "had fits and appeared to be in great distress of mind," which is exactly as she appeared later in the day to a nonplused and aggrieved George Washington.

Hysterical Wife

For George Washington, Alexander Hamilton, the Marquis de Lafayette, and sundry other of Washington's many aides, the scene in the rambling old house on the Hudson was singularly unnerving ... nothing at all like their battlefield experiences of the past few years.

They were gathered in the home of Washington's old-time (but pro-British) friend, Colonel Beverley Robinson, in Westchester County, New York, across the river from West Point. In an upstairs bedroom a young wife and mother was screaming and yelling. Not yet twenty, she wore a nearly sheer nightgown as she shrilled that her husband had left her, that only Washington could remove a hot iron burning into her head and that, no, the concerned Washington who had come to visit and comfort her was not really he, but rather a stranger intent upon murdering her infant son!

Among the stunned onlookers was Washington's faithful aide from Maryland, Tench Tilghman, a first cousin to the hysterical young lady—the former Margaret (Peggy) Shippen of Philadelphia.

The fact is, she had good reason to be upset—nor is there any doubt that Washington and his entire party also were upset.

George Washington had arrived that morning, two days after his first meeting (in Hartford, Connecticut) with the Comte de Rochambeau, commander of the French forces newly landed in America as allies in the Patriot cause. Washington appeared this morning of September 25, 1780, expecting a hearty breakfast. He also anticipated greetings from Benedict Arnold, the temporary occupant of the Robinson house and commander of the garrison at nearby West Point, just two miles away as the crow flies. The lady of the house was the commander's new wife, and her infant, his child.

Naturally, Washington, Hamilton, Lafayette, Tilghman, and company were surprised to be told that their comrade-in-arms, himself a major general, had suddenly left the house at breakfast time. But they presumed he would be awaiting them at West Point, across the river. Still, it all seemed a bit odd.

The visitors hurried off to cross the wide Hudson by rowboat and visit the fort above. For the commander in chief, it was an anxiously awaited opportunity to inspect the key bastion. Unaccountably, though, the trusted commander was not there. Unhappily, too, Washington saw that the fort's defenses were poorly designed and carelessly maintained—they never would suffice in the face of a determined British attack, an attack expected at any moment.

The unpleasant truth dawned with a messenger's news of a stranger's capture two days before with incriminating documents found tucked into the bottoms of his stockings. A thoroughly shocked George Washington glanced through the papers: a pass signed by Arnold, plans of the defenses at West Point, minutes from a recent council of war and other prime intelligence. The captured stranger, it soon became clear, was British Army Major John André, adjutant general and aide to Sir Henry Clinton, commander of the Crown's land forces in America.

Now every added hour brought to light new pieces of the puzzle. André was an admiring acquaintance of Peggy Shippen from the days, just a couple of years earlier, when the British had occupied her hometown of Philadelphia. Further, at breakfast that very morning, Arnold had received a mysterious message. Clearly agitated, he had left the house minutes later. Obviously, he had been warned of his contact André's capture.

And now, late in the day, there came to the Robinson house a letter to Washington from Arnold himself. He had penned it from sanctuary aboard the British man-of-war *Vulture* in the nearby Hudson. (Colonel Robinson, in fact, was on board the *Vulture,* too!) Acknowledging "the world" might "censure" his behavior "as wrong," Arnold wrote that he had but one favor to ask—"I am induced to ask your protection for Mrs. Arnold from every insult and injury that a mistaken vengeance of my country may expose her to."

While Washington did treat the young woman with gentlemanly kid gloves, his more immediate reaction was to beef up the defenses and manpower at West Point that very night. Soon after, a board of fourteen general officers named by the commander in chief condemned André as a spy and ordered his execution. Washington, in full agreement, refused all appeals to relent, and André went to the gallows at Tappan, New York, on October 2.

As for Peggy Shippen, later shown to be a Loyalist through and through, the hysterics passed and she left the Robinson house on

September 27 for sanctuary of her own in familiar Philadelphia. The storm of public outrage over her husband's perfidy did erupt, and it later became quite evident that she herself had played a conscious role in his treasonable activities.

History still has to wonder. Did she fake her hysterics to gull Washington and his aides into letting her escape a compromising situation (which they did)? Or, as one previously known to fall into hysterics on various occasions, was she simply frustrated by discovery of the plot to deliver West Point to the enemy?

Two Brave Men Hanged

IN PHILADELPHIA THE WINTER OF 1777–1778, he stayed at Benjamin Franklin's house as an aide-de-camp to British General Charles Grey. He then became a staff officer to General Sir Henry Clinton in New York and adjutant general of the British army. Taking over Clinton's correspondence, playing handball with his boss, and generally proving indispensable, the younger officer, twenty-nine, also took charge of British intelligence functions.

In May of 1779, he was in touch with a secret informer, code-named "Monk."

Just a month before, "Monk" had married the very young Peggy Shippen, one of the girls the young British officer had socialized with during the British occupation of Philadelphia in 1777–1778. "Monk" had major secrets to pass along. For instance, he could help the British seize the American fortress of West Point on the Hudson Heights near Newburgh, New York.

In the summer of 1780, plans were being made for the two to meet for the first time.

It was September 22 before they finally met in the early-morning darkness at the foot of Long Clove Mountain, on the west bank of the Hudson, just below Haverstraw. The British major had traveled upriver for the meeting aboard the armed sloop *Vulture*. Leaving the safety of the ship, he covered his uniform with a blue greatcoat and used the name John Anderson in place of his French Huguenot name, John André.

The meeting lasted until after dawn. In the bright light of day, André could not return to the *Vulture* undetected. His companion, American Major General Benedict Arnold, commander of the West Point fortress, suggested they repair to the nearby home of intermediary Joshua Hett Smith, an abode called "The White House."

When they did, they breakfasted together and continued their discussion. But they also saw American artillery based at Fort Lafayette across the river begin to hurl cannonballs in the direction of the *Vulture,* which was forced to slip anchor and ease downstream.

Arnold discreetly left, but not before handing André documents showing the plan of defense for West Point. Now André had to find some way to return to British lines while bearing those highly incriminating papers. Smith talked the British officer into wearing civilian clothes under his heavy coat.

Later that day, the two crossed over to the east side of the Hudson at King's Ferry, then proceeded south to White Plains, New York. They stayed that night in the home of a friendly Westchester County Tory.

The next day, September 23, they parted company and André continued on his way alone. He first headed south again, toward New York, but then veered westerly, toward the Hudson. As Paul J. Sanborn wrote in *The American Revolution, 1775-1783,* André had no desire to encounter the Tory "Cowboys" or rebel "Skinners" who preyed upon the unwary in the "no man's land" lying between the Croton River and the British lines.

Unfortunately for him, it was three American militiamen who stopped André outside of Tarrytown, searched his person, and found the incriminating papers in his boots.

Forewarned of André's arrest, Arnold made his way to the *Vulture* early the morning of September 25 to complete his betrayal of America.

Events now moved very rapidly. André was moved to Washington's headquarters at Tappan, New York. On September 29, he went before an American military court of inquiry headed by General Nathanael Greene and including Generals Lafayette, Von Steuben, Lord Stirling, Henry Knox, John Stark, and John Glover among its fourteen members.

André testified that he indeed had come behind American lines but as a British officer on a mission for his chief, Sir Henry Clinton. In effect, he admitted the circumstances but clung to his concept of a mission rather than acknowledge outright spying. The court unanimously found him guilty as a spy. Washington, on September 30, agreed. André was sentenced to be executed in short order, on October 1.

Officially informed of the inquiry results by the Americans, Clinton sent an envoy to plead for André's life. Meeting with General Greene, Clinton's spokesman, General James Robertson, said the British would exchange any prisoner they held for André.

But Washington's position was unequivocal. He would exchange André for only one man—Benedict Arnold.

That, Clinton would not do. Delayed for a day by the fruitless conference, André's execution was set in motion at noon on October 2. He asked to die before a firing squad, but was denied. His fate was to be hanging.

He approached his death calmly . . . and in uniform, including the red regimental coat with green facings of his Fifty-fourth Regiment. Placing the rope about his neck himself, he said, "I pray you to bear me witness that I meet my fate like a brave man."

And he did. Buried on a Tappan hill, his body was removed in 1821 to Westminster Abbey in London, where he could join a long roster of Englishmen who bravely served their country . . . and often died in the act.

In André's case, hardly anyone familiar with the details could have found pleasure or satisfactory vindication in the outcome. As Sanborn's account recalled, even Washington once said, "He was more unfortunate than criminal." According to some, too, Washington's hand had trembled when he signed André's death warrant.

When the word reached the Connecticut Rangers that Washington needed a volunteer to infiltrate British lines on Long Island and gather intelligence, no one stepped forward . . . at first.

These were men chosen, for their bravery and aggressiveness, to serve as scouts ranging in advance of the main Continental Army. But none wished to go behind British lines and act as a spy. Lieutenant

James Sprague, for one, told his commander that fighting the British was one thing, but he had "no wish to go among them, be taken and hung like a dog."

At last, a young captain, a recent Yale graduate and schoolteacher, said he would go. Friends tried to talk him out of it, but his mind was made up. "I wish to be useful and every kind of service, necessary to the public good, becomes honorable by being necessary," he supposedly said. As Sanborn noted, the volunteer was "an extremely poor choice" for his undercover mission. "His face had been scarred by exploding powder. He was literally a marked man." Further, although proven as a soldier (and so marked, too), the young officer had no training in intelligence work. He had to come up with his own "cover story" and other tricks of the spy trade.

Wasting no time, he set off on his intelligence mission in mid-September 1776, not long after Washington's defeat in the Battle of Long Island and retreat onto Manhattan Island.

The untried agent was "inserted," as spy parlance goes, by an American sloop that carried him to Huntington on Long Island's north shore. Dressed in civilian clothes and carrying his Yale diploma, he posed as a Dutch schoolmaster looking for a teaching job. In this guise he hastened to catch up with the British forces, which by now had made the jump onto Manhattan as well. This made the mission on Long Island "obsolete," said Sanborn, but the unschooled American spy "somehow crossed over into New York City, following the British there sometime after September 15."

There, he gathered valuable intelligence and sketched British troop dispositions and fortifications. But now he had to find some way of carrying his information back to General Washington. The famous fire of New York City that destroyed a quarter or more of the town on September 20 forced him to leave "probably before he could complete his plans to escape back to his own lines." Unfortunately, that is when he was captured, his incriminating notes and sketches found hidden in his shoes.

He was taken to General Sir William Howe's headquarters at the Beekman mansion on the East River side of Manhattan, close to today's intersection of Fifty-first Street and First Avenue. Infuriated by the fire, and suspecting American complicity in the conflagration, Howe issued the order to hang the prisoner the very next day, without benefit of trial.

The next morning, September 22, he was carried to a gallows set up on an estate near today's juncture of Market Street and East Broadway. A mulatto named Richmond hooded the condemned man and placed the noose around his neck.

Blind, the young Patriot stumbled climbing the ladder before him—the "gallows" being the branch of a stout apple tree.

There would be no appeal, no delay, no other outcome . . . and every schoolchild in America for nearly two hundred years has been told of his shining last words, given from under the hangman's hood while standing on a rung of a ladder leaning against an apple tree. Those last words of Nathan Hale: "I only regret that I have but one life to lose for my country."

His famous utterance, incidentally, is based upon a line in Joseph Addison's popular eighteenth-century play *Cato.* Oddly, Hale's valiant end went unknown for many years. A British officer impressed and even touched by Hale's gallantry had relayed the story to Americans in a meeting on exchanging prisoners. But Hale's friends, thinking the fate of a spy was nothing to be proud of, didn't pass along the story of his brave death for another fifty years.

Cruelties of War Contemplated

Swirling around central North Carolina, each more or less chasing the other's tail, were the army of Lord Cornwallis, the southern branch of the Continental Army led by Nathanael Greene, British Colonel Banastre Tarleton's dragoons, American Colonel Henry ("Light-Horse Harry") Lee's light cavalry, and various homegrown guerrilla outfits that were either Tory or Patriot. The internecine war in the Carolinas was at a bitter pitch, and the Haw River on February 23, 1781, was a dangerous place to be, as members of an errant Tory troop found to their very deep regret.

According to the story later told by Moses Hall, a native of Rowan County, North Carolina, his militia company fell in with Lee's light horse troop shortly before encountering a group of Tories commanded by Colonel John Pyle. "Our troops and this body of Tories and Colonel Tarleton all being in the same neighborhood, our troops on the march met said body of Tories at a place called the Race Paths," recalled Hall years later.

The Patriots, by plan or by accident, were in two columns, apparently riding abreast but some distance apart. Lee was in charge of one and Militia Major or Colonel Joseph Dixon in command of the other.

"[T]he Tories passed into this interval between our lines," said Hall. Or perhaps the Tories had been halted, and the two Patriot columns then passed on either side of the Tory outfit. He wasn't sure many years after the fact. In any case, the Tories thought the newcomers were allies . . . friends!

"They frequently uttered salutations of a friendly kind, believing us to be British." A fatal mistake, it turned out. The Patriots realized the situation and pretended to be the friends the Tories thought them to be. Just about all the officers "kept up the deception." All, that is, except Hall's own company commander, a Captain Hugh Hall, who recognized the strangers as Tories, but thought that Lee, himself a stranger in these parts, would assume them to be fellow Patriots rather than the enemy. "Colonel Lee," shouted Captain Hall, right across the Tory column in the center of things, "they are every blood of them Tories!" Why that warning failed to alarm every single Tory is unclear, but Captain Hall at least desisted when Lee gave him "a sign to proceed on with the execution of the command, which was to march on until a different command was given."

The Tories, meanwhile, docile as before, still remained at center, between the two Patriot elements. "In a few minutes or less time, and at the instant they, the Tories, were completely covered by our lines upon both flanks, or front and rear as the case may have been, the bugle sounded to attack, and the slaughter began." No, no, cried the completely fooled Tories, "Your own men, your own men, as good subjects of His Majesty as in America."

According to Moses Hall, two hundred Tories were killed on the spot. Unfortunately, too, a reflection of the brutality sometimes exercised by both sides in the civil war of the Carolinas, the Patriot band later that day killed six prisoners as an act of revenge for some earlier Tory brutality. Wrote Hall as an old man in 1835: "I was invited by some of my comrades to go and see some of the prisoners. We went to where six were standing together. Some discussion taking place, I heard some of our men cry out, 'Remember Buford,' and the prisoners were immediately hewed to pieces with broadswords."

Hall, then a young man of twenty-one, already was a veteran of several short enlistments in the bloody regional strife, but clearly he had never seen anything like this. "At first I bore the scene without any emotion," he said, "but upon a moment's reflection, I felt such horror as I never did before nor have since." He returned to his quarters and threw himself down on his blanket, his emotions now in turmoil as he "contemplated the cruelties of war."

The next day he still was "gripped by a distressing gloom," but it was about to be relieved, oddly enough, by sight of yet another horror. His company the next day made its way to British dragoon Banastre Tarleton's abandoned campsite. On the side of the road, Hall wrote, "I discovered lying upon the ground something with appearance of a man." The "something" proved to be a boy, about sixteen, who had "come out to view the British through curiosity." But they thought he might provide the Americans in the area information about them. So, "they had run him through with a bayonet and left him for dead."

Although the teenager was able to speak, it was obvious he would die from his bayonet wound. Moses Hall now was furious. "The sight of this unoffending boy, butchered rather than be encumbered [sic] . . . on the march, I assume, relieved me of my distressful feelings for the slaughter of the Tories," wrote Hall.

In this kind of war, one brutality brought on another, which brought on reprisal, which also brought on reprisal, and so on. Relieved of his distress over the Tories the day before, Hall frankly wrote that he now "desired nothing so much as the opportunity of participating in their destruction."

His group pursued Tarleton's troop of dragoons, but the Briton picked up reinforcements, then turned on his pursuers. After a brief clash driving back the Americans, they became the pursued . . . until darkness halted the chase for that day.

Personal Glimpse: Nathanael Greene

"WE FIGHT, GET BEAT, RISE and fight again," he once said. And quite so. In capsule form, that was the limping Quaker Nathanael Greene's strategy that won the South for George Washington and the American Revolution.

When he arrived in Charlotte, North Carolina, in December of 1780, to replace Horatio Gates as the head of the Southern branch of the Continental Army, Greene inherited a fighting force of 2,300 in theory . . . but only 1,500 healthy effectives in fact. His British antagonists, on the other hand, could count on 8,000 men, based largely in Georgia and South Carolina. Worse, the dispirited Americans recently had given up an army of 5,000 with the loss of Charleston, South Carolina, and another army in their defeat at Camden, South Carolina, all in less than a year's time.

After somehow putting together another army, it would be the thirty-eight-year-old General Greene's job to stop British Lord Cornwallis from sweeping north and adding North Carolina and Virginia to the territory under British control.

Ironically, the man asked to perform such a Herculean task had entered the Revolutionary War as a militia private with no military experience; he came from a Quaker background and was an asthmatic with a permanent limp from a childhood knee injury.

In the days before hostilities broke out, Greene operated a family iron foundry in Coventry, Rhode Island. He often visited Boston— in particular, the bookstore belonging to Henry Knox. As war clearly loomed, future American Generals Greene and Knox shared a growing interest in books on military science. Back home, Greene helped to organize a militia unit, the Kentish Guards, but his bad knee kept him from becoming an officer. Meanwhile, in July of 1774, his plunge into military affairs resulted in expulsion from his anti-war Quaker congregation.

That same summer, on a happier note, he married the vivacious (non-Quaker) Catherine ("Kitty") Littlefield of Block Island, thirteen years his junior. While they in time had five children, the cascading events of revolution and war would shatter any hopes they held of a lifetime to be spent in quiet tranquility.

The very next year, 1775, Greene was active after Lexington-Concord (and Menotomy) organizing Rhode Island's contribution to the American troops besieging Boston—more than that, the future state's Patriot legislature appointed him a brigadier general, rather than private. Greene then, in June of 1775, led Rhode Island's three regiments to Washington's side at Cambridge, Massachusetts, outside Boston.

There, the Continental Army's new commander in chief was favorably impressed as he looked over the thirty-three-year-old neophyte before him. Within a year's time, added historian Theodore Thayer in the book, *George Washington's Generals and Opponents: Their Exploits and Leadership,* the commander in chief would become "convinced" that his own best replacement at the head of the army would be Rhode Island's Nathanael Greene.

After guarding the western sector of the American siege lines for months, Greene was Washington's choice to take charge of Boston once the British left town in the spring of 1776. As yet another measure of Washington's growing esteem for the inexperienced officer, Greene in the summer of 1776 was given the job of preparing the defense of Long Island across the East River from Manhattan Island, New York.

No one will ever know how Greene would have fared as Washington's chief subordinate in facing the massive British invasion of Long Island and Sir William Howe's surprise flank attack on the American defenders, which resulted in a sharp defeat. Greene missed the dismal show because he fell ill with a violent fever.

Recovering as Washington and company tried to regroup from one pasting after another in the struggle for control of New York, Major General Greene next took over the Continental Army's fast-response reserve force known as the "flying camp." But this was unfortunately the moment of the greatest mistake of his military career. Based at Fort Lee on the New Jersey side of the Hudson River, he advised an all-out effort to hold Fort Washington across the Hudson on the northern end of Manhattan Island, by then overrun by the British. When General Howe mounted a major attack on the American bastion in November 1776, it fell, with nearly three thousand men and valuable supplies lost to the Continentals. Washington, about to be rowed across the river from the doomed fort, refused to let his young general stay behind. Afterward, an obviously hurting Greene wrote to old friend Henry Knox, "I feel mad, vexed, sick, and sorry; Never did I need the consoling voice of a friend more than now."

Although the ultimate decision to defend Fort Washington had been the commander in chief's, Greene took much of the blame, but the fast pace of war allowed little time for deep reflection. Washington's tattered army now was busy simply surviving as it abandoned Fort Lee and retreated across New Jersey to the Delaware River opposite Trenton.

It wasn't long before Greene had redeemed himself with his coordination of men and supplies during the difficult withdrawal, and his command of an American wing in Washington's surprise attack on the Hessians at Trenton the morning of December 26. At this point, Washington might have been wise to follow Greene's urging to follow up with an attack on a presumably shaken Hessian garrison at nearby Burlington, but Washington this time rejected his subordinate's advice—and later acknowledged that perhaps he did miss "a golden opportunity."

In any case, Greene was a good right arm in the Battle of Princeton that followed the stunning American success at Trenton. And that winter, Greene was in such good favor that Washington sent him to Philadelphia to consult with the Virginian's ultimate "boss"—the Continental Congress.

Returning from his attempt to acquaint the politicians with the army's pressing needs, Greene sounded a theme heard in many variations ever since. The "talking gentlemen" of the Congress, he said, "tire themselves and everybody else with their long labored speeching that is calculated more to display their own talents than to promote the public interest."

Later in 1777, Greene was highly visible in Washington's Pennsylvania campaign outside Philadelphia against the once-more invading General Howe. At Brandywine Creek that September, with Washington again surprised by an end-around, Greene rushed his men to the collapsing right flank, covering four miles in barely fifty minutes, and held long enough to allow the rest of the Continentals an orderly withdrawal. At Germantown, he led the army's main column against the British encampment but was delayed in taking up position by a fog so heavy that even General Howe's dog lost its way and was recovered by the Americans—who later returned the pet under a flag of truce, notes Thayer's account.

Although the Americans were rebuffed at Germantown, many considered it a moral victory in which the Continentals showed they were made of stern stuff indeed. They had to be, since their next trial was the miserable winter spent at nearby Valley Forge. But here, again, Greene displayed impressive skills after Washington ordered him to take over the vital, if dull-sounding, chores of quartermaster general, a job he held for two years . . . and hated. His accomplishments in this primarily administrative post were "little less than miraculous," writes historian Thayer. "Laboring long hours, he managed to keep the army going from season to season despite shortages of funds, supplies, and means of transportation." The Continentals emerged from Valley Forge in the spring of 1778 better fed and clothed than when they built their wintering log huts the previous December and January. Washington was more than willing to credit Greene, who, the commander in chief said, "enabled us, with great facility, to make a sudden move with the whole Army and baggage from Valley Forge in pursuit of the Enemy."

Greene briefly held a battlefield command again at Monmouth Courthouse, New Jersey, that same summer, but only to relieve General Charles Lee at the head of the American right wing after Lee was dismissed by a furious Washington. Otherwise, Greene was stuck with his commissary duties until summer of 1780, except for a momentary "sojourn" in his homestate of Rhode Island at the side of John Sullivan for the Battle of Newport in the fall of 1778. That the Franco-American affair ended badly was no fault of Greene's, nor of Sullivan's.

Finally emerging from his despised purgatory as a supply officer, rankled by occasional charges that he had personally profited from the quartermaster post (stoutly denied), Greene in 1780 was handed his greatest challenge yet. In August of 1780, news came from South Carolina that Horatio Gates had squandered his army in the Battle of Camden. The redcoat tide soon would engulf North Carolina and even Virginia, the bottom half of the rebelling colonies, unless someone erected a buffer stopping the flow northward. With Congress leaving the choice of a new Southern commander up to him, Washington picked Greene for the seemingly impossible task. "My dear Angel," Greene wrote to his wife, Kitty, "What I have been dreading has come to pass. His Excellency General Washington by order of Congress has appointed me to the command of the Southern Army." Greene headed south so hastily that he didn't get to say goodbye to

Kitty in person. He gathered key officers and units as quickly as possible, too. He made stops to recruit "Light-Horse Harry" Lee and his dragoons; Colonel William R. Davie as commissary officer; and Polish-born Thaddeus Kosciuszko as engineer officer for the campaign ahead. Once on station, Greene also planned to make full use of the fighting prowess of Virginia's Brigadier General Daniel Morgan and Lieutenant Colonel William Washington's cavalry.

Greene didn't really expect to find much of an army awaiting him in Charlotte, but what he did find was shocking to see. "All that was left after the Camden battle were two thousand ragged and famished creatures who resembled scarecrows more than soldiers," notes Thayer.

An encouraging note, though, was the recent Battle of King's Mountain, in which American "over-the-mountain men" from the Appalachians and beyond had defeated a significant Loyalist and British force. The victory was to be more crucial than anyone at first realized. Explains Thayer: "[Lord] Cornwallis [commander of British troops in the South] still had an army that was far superior in numbers to any force that Greene could put in the field, but the British soldiers were scattered throughout South Carolina and Georgia in numerous small forts and garrisons. After the British defeat at King's Mountain, these occupied states grew restless, and Cornwallis did not dare to enlarge his main force at the expense of the garrisons." So, Cornwallis would hunker down at Winnsboro, South Carolina, and await reinforcements before forcing the new American commander's hand.

Greene, too, needed time to prepare—to build—an army for the tough campaign ahead. Risking all, he divided his already-small command, sending Morgan, a few cavalry, and seven hundred light troops circling north of Winnsboro in position to harass Cornwallis—"and discourage any Loyalists who might think of enlisting under Cornwallis." Greene then retired with his main force to Cheraw Hill, South Carolina, seventy-five miles east of Cornwallis, to train his troops, to "rebuild his army unmolested." In the meantime, his subordinates harassed the British and conducted raids—with the help of militia and officers such as South Carolina's Francis ("Swamp Fox") Marion engaging in guerrilla tactics.

Cornwallis, reinforced by an added 2,500 or so men in January 1781, was finally ready to leave his lair. As his first move, he sent the usually reliable Banastre Tarleton after the pesky Morgan, cavalryman William Washington, and their combined force of Continentals and untried militia. Tarleton, of "no quarter" notoriety, caught up with them at little-known Cowpens, South Carolina. But this time, for once, it was Tarleton who emerged from battle with a badly bloodied nose.

The news set Cornwallis off in pursuit of Morgan, but high water in the Catawba River intervened and gave Morgan and Greene a moment's respite to hold a council of war. Although the veteran Morgan worried over Greene's bold strategy of a fighting retreat to Virginia, he stuck by his far younger superior. Together they outraced the needled Cornwallis to the Dan River on the Virginia–North Carolina border.

This part of the campaign was no easy task. "Greene's little army trudged along clay roads that turned into slippery mud as the rains began to fall," wrote Thayer. "His men suffered terribly. Hundreds of soldiers were without shoes and left bloodstains behind to mark the army's route."

At this point, winter of 1781, Cornwallis was not quite ready to contemplate going after Greene and company beyond the Virginia border. He halted, "hoping to replenish his supplies and to enlist more Loyalists." He didn't find much of either commodity—and Greene didn't give him the leisure to deal with such problems in any case.

Instead, an aggressive Greene plunged back into North Carolina before Cornwallis could regroup from their difficult race north. They now met in battle, real battle, at Guilford Courthouse, today's Greensboro, North Carolina, in March of 1781. The outcome, by the numbers, was a defeat for the Americans, but more important, it was a Pyrrhic victory costing Cornwallis irreplaceable losses in personnel and materiel. Furthermore, as he now saw growing problems facing him, there was only one solution other than retreat to the south. "Convinced that British control could not be sustained in the Carolinas as long as Virginia remained an American supply base, Cornwallis made a fateful decision. He would march into Virginia and join the British forces already there. Greene, he was quite sure, would follow him, and the combined sections of the British army would make short work of destroying the Southern army."

One half of Cornwallis's plan actually came about—he did march into Virginia, and at first quite successfully so. Greene, however, made no attempt to follow. Instead, Greene dashed southward to take on and gradually defeat, piecemeal, all the various forts and garrisons that Cornwallis had left uncovered. That took a while, and Cornwallis, in the fall of 1781, wound up at Yorktown . . . many thanks to American General Nathanael Greene and his brilliant campaign in the South.

Death by His Own Sword

"THE BRITISH COMMANDER TOOK THE sword and thrust it through Colonel Ledyard. This I heard and saw."

And what Connecticut militiaman Joseph Wood heard before seeing his commander, Lieutenant Colonel William Ledyard, slain by sword was Ledyard's proffer to surrender Fort Griswold to the attacking British.

"When Colonel Ledyard found that he was not able to withstand the attack upon the fort, he opened the gate to surrender," wrote Wood years later in his plea for a service pension. The British officer confronting Ledyard asked, "Who commands this fort?"

According to Wood, Ledyard replied, "I did, but you do now." And: "He presented to the British commander his sword." That's when the officer turned the same sword against Ledyard and ran him through, an infamous incident of the Revolutionary War. But . . . was it intentional, or even true?

While the British capture of Fort Griswold on the Thames River at New London, Connecticut, on September 6, 1781, was a notoriously bloody affair, some historians have questioned the literal truth in reports that the defenseless American commander was murdered in the act of surrender. That he and 156 of his 157-man complement were killed, wounded, or captured, however, has been accepted as the terrible price the militiamen paid for opposing a British raiding party of 800 or so. It may be that the Americans paid more than the usual penalty because they had killed two British troop commanders in the heat of battle that day, just a month or so before Yorktown.

By many accounts, only one defender escaped British wrath as the fort fell to the redcoats—seventeen-year-old Nathanial Avery fled through a sally port in the fort's south wall, ran down a hill beyond and eluded British capture. On the other hand, John C. Dann's collection of pension petitions by Revolutionary War veterans *(The Revolution Remembered)* presents Wood's detailed, eyewitness account of Ledyard's death at the hands of an unnamed British officer. "The only firsthand description of the murder . . . ," says Dann in his editorial introduction to the Wood account.

Nor was that the end of the scene witnessed by Wood before he, too, escaped (linking up with young Avery outside the fort), he also said. According to Wood's account, militia captain Allen immediately reacted to Colonel Ledyard's brutal slaying. "Upon that, Captain Allen, who was standing nearby in the act of presenting his sword to surrender, drew it back and thrust it through the British officer who had thus killed Colonel Ledyard. Captain Allen was then immediately killed by the British. This I also saw. I then leaped the walls and made my escape." Outside the fort, Wood encountered Avery, and together the two found a boat a mile or so up the river and rowed across to safety.

For the Americans, the grim day had begun with a British ruse allowing the attackers to surprise would-be defenders of New London, a port and sanctuary for American privateers harassing the British at sea. Led by the turncoat Benedict Arnold, himself once a Connecticut militia officer, a British and Loyalist force of more than 1,700 men descended upon the river entrance in twenty-four vessels. They arrived at 2 A.M. and began landing troops five hours later. Half the expeditionary force, under Arnold himself, would attack incomplete Fort Trumbull on the right-hand (New London) side of the river; the other half would assault Fort Griswold and its twenty-two cannon on the Groton Heights opposite. While Fort Griswold boasted casemates, stone-faced walls, and outer barriers of pointed pickets, a ditch and a ring of nasty tree limbs (an abatis), much of the fort was in disrepair. There were gaps in the abatis line and ditch, and some gun platforms were rotted through. Worse, only relatively few charges for the cannon were ready for use that morning.

The American in charge was the unfortunate Lieutenant Colonel Ledyard, a militia artillery officer with roughly 140 men at his disposal as daybreak revealed the presence of the British landing force. Normally, Ledyard could have counted on hasty militia reinforcements from the surrounding countryside. Two quick shots from a Griswold artillery piece was the signal for help.

And his men fired off the two-shot alarm signal as instructed. But the British were well aware that a signal of *three* quick shots meant that all was well; that, typically, an American privateer or prize ship was returning to harbor . . . take no alarm. As soon as the British heard the two-shot alarm sounded at Fort Griswold, they fired off a third cannon.

The ruse was completely successful. The distant militiamen who heard the three cannon shots stayed home. The only reinforcements Ledyard would receive that day were men fleeing across the river from Benedict Arnold's attack on weak Fort Trumbull. Even so, the fighting for control of Griswold was fierce and bloody. Leading his troops forward, the overall British commander, Lieutenant Colonel Edmund Eyre, was mortally wounded. Next, a Major Montgomery, leading a second attack across the ditch, past the sharpened stakes, and through a cannon embrasure, was felled as well.

It was soon after, with the maddened British swarming over his south and northeast walls, that Colonel Ledyard decided to surrender and ordered his men to desist. While some of them continued fighting, he made his way to the north gate . . . where he would die by his own sword.

The British, reported a Sergeant Hempstead, one of the few surviving Americans, "wantonly went to shoting [sic] and bayoneting of us, the quarters [mercy] was continuously cryed for from everyone but to no purpose." The sad result was the Fort Griswold "massacre," another nail in the coffin of Arnold's reputation, even though he wasn't present in person.

Meanwhile, Avery and militiaman Joseph Wood fell in with "large numbers of the militia on their way to New London," said Wood in his pension request many years later. "It was near night when we got to New London. It was before dark. When we got there, Arnold had burned the town and left with his forces."

German Ally at Yorktown

IF THE BRITISH HAD THE widely hated, bayonet-wielding Hessians as allies in the Revolution, then the Americans also could claim a German force as their ally. Granted, this ally was not even a brigade in size; America's German ally was but a single regiment.

Even so, the tiny Zweibruecken Regiment was able to play a key role in the Patriot triumph at Yorktown, with its wounded commander, Count William Deux-Ponts, hailed by George Washington's French allies as "the hero of Yorktown," wrote David T. Zabecki in *The American Revolution, 1775–1783.*

Indeed, Count Deux-Ponts was entrusted with the enviable task of returning to France and officially presenting King Louis XVI with the surrender terms, along with captured British flags. No surprise, then, that Deux-Ponts "was received at Versailles as a conquering hero." The French king was so moved, he awarded the young commander of the Zweibruecken Regiment the Order of Saint Louis, an honor still eluding many more senior—more French!—officers of that era.

Note: Both the name of the regiment and that of its commander translate the same—"two bridges." The fact is, the commander and his men were German—they hailed from the Duchy of Zweibruecken in the region today known as the Rhineland-Palatinate. They spoke German, even thought German, but they were fighting with America's French ally. Indeed, their 1,200-man contingent was one of only seven regiments comprising the entire expeditionary corps that France had dispatched to help the American revolutionaries. So, it appears the Zweibrueckens were German, and yet . . . you could say they were a tiny bit French, too.

As Zabecki explains, their home territory had "passed back and forth between France and Germany for centuries and was even owned by Sweden for a brief time in the early eighteenth century." Then, in 1731, "it passed back into German hands under the rule of the Birkenfeld-Bischweiler line of the ruling house of Bavaria."

The duchy's ruler of that era, Duke Christian IV of Zweibrueken, arranged with French King Louis XV to have the duchy's "tiny, one-regiment army" serve as part of the French army. And so it had, ever since 1757. By the 1770s, the regiment was so well thought of that Count Jean Baptiste Rochambeau, commander of the French land forces sent to the rebellious American colonies, specifically asked to have the Zweibrueckens at his side.

The request was in response to more than the regiment's apparently excellent reputation. Thought also was given to the many thousands of Hessians hired out by the German state of Hesse as mercenaries for the British side. The idea was that the German-Zweibruecken presence might induce many an unhappy Hessian soldier to "come over" from the other side ... and many Hessians did desert, but most simply disappeared into the vast American frontier and agricultural lands. Only a relative handful joined the Zweibrueckens.

Nor were they the only Germans "employed" by the French for the American Revolution. "Even Rochambeau's French regiments had a high proportion of German-speaking troops from Alsace and Lorraine," noted Zabecki. Rochambeau's cavalrymen were Germans, Poles, and Irishmen; their regiment was "considered a 'German Regiment.'" But it had been raised in France "as the 'Voluntaires Etrangeres de la Marine.'"

Aside from all that, however, the Zweibrueckens comprised the only Rochambeau regiment "raised on German soil." And they wore a different uniform from their comrades-in-arms—"deep celestial blue coats," as opposed to the "standard white uniform of the French infantry."

Like the rest of Rochambeau's army, Count Deux-Ponts and his men marched down the East Coast and into Virginia in the fall of 1781 to take up the Siege of Yorktown alongside the Americans. As the Allies' parallel entrenchments advanced toward the British-held town, it became obvious that the besiegers must seize two key redoubts in order to continue progress and move up their cannon to more advantageous position. The decision was to storm the redoubts the night of October 14 with two four-hundred-man columns, one American and one French. Alexander Hamilton would lead the Americans against Redoubt No. 10, also known as the Rock Redoubt, while Count Deux-Ponts would command his own Zweibrueckens as the lead element in the French attack on Redoubt No. 9.

And so it was done, albeit with inevitable losses and some difficulties. At the base of Redoubt No. 9, Deux-Ponts and his men were
halted by the defensive abatis that still stood in the way, despite
advance "softening" by Allied artillery. With the eager Zweibrueckens
slowed and withering under enemy fire from above, the regiment's
axmen fought furiously to chop a path through the barrier.

Later, in relating the events, Deux-Ponts said, "We threw ourselves into the ditch . . . and each one sought to break through the
fraises and to mount the parapet."

And mount the parapet the Germans finally did. The enemy
charged the intruders, but were repelled by a volley of musket fire.
Now, the attacking Zweibrueckens were at the top of the redoubt
and firing down into their opponents huddled below. Deux-Ponts
was just ordering a bayonet charge when the troops below put
down their muskets and surrendered. "Vive le Roi," shouted the triumphant Germans—in French.

It all happened very fast. After clearing the impediments in front
of the redoubt, it had taken Deux-Ponts and his men only seven minutes to capture the redoubt. Nearby, Alexander Hamilton and his
Americans had seized their objective as well. Now the Patriot cannon could move up and rake the British forward lines at will. For
Lord Cornwallis, his back against the York River, the siege was a lost
cause. In just five days, on October 19, 1781, he would surrender.

In the Battle of Redoubt No. 9 the Zweibrueckens lost a few
good men, to be sure—fifteen killed, apparently, and seventy-seven
wounded. It was only after the smoke of battle had cleared, however, that they were deprived of their veteran commander, Count
Deux-Ponts.

When a newly placed sentry cried out warning of an enemy
patrol nearby, Deux-Ponts peered over the parapet to see what he
could see. Just then a ricocheting cannonball struck close by and
painfully peppered his face with shrapnel-like gravel. He had to be
evacuated immediately, but he would soon recover sufficiently to
carry the surrender terms to the king of France.

Drums Covered in Black

SHE WAS IN THE CONTINENTAL Army as a wife, cook, and washerwoman married to a commissary sergeant, and while she never made general, she was a familiar figure at West Point. She was in the trenches at Yorktown, she traveled with generals, she had a glimpse of the defeated Cornwallis, and she took home memories of a conversation with Commander-in-Chief George Washington. Few men and almost no women witnessed such great events or rubbed elbows so frequently with the historic figures of the Revolutionary War.

Married to Aaron Osborn as a twenty-four-year-old servant, Sarah Osborn for a time did washing and sewing for American soldiers at West Point. She and her husband were there at the time of Benedict Arnold's defection to the British and the capture of his contact man, British Major John André.

She, herself, saw two of the bargemen who, at his order, took Arnold to a waiting British ship in the Hudson River. She herself heard them say that after General Arnold "jumped aboard," they and their fellow bargemen were invited to join him in defection. They all went aboard the British vessel, "[a]nd some chose to stay and some to go, and did accordingly."

Sarah Osborn was also with the American force that hurried south in the summer of 1781 with Washington's French allies, in the effort to trap Lord Cornwallis on the Virginia peninsula between the York and James Rivers. She later recalled riding on horseback through the streets of Philadelphia (where she had to bake bread for the troops). Her only female company consisted of two white women and a black woman named Letta.

On the way to Philadelphia, all were "under the command of Generals Washington and [James] Clinton." Her husband's immediate boss all this time was Captain James Gregg, who delighted in showing off "the bare spot on his head where he had been scalped by the Indians." He occasionally "had turns of being shattered in his mind," it seems. Perhaps this was a result of the scalping, which had come about while he and two companions were pigeon hunting one day in upstate New York. The other two had been killed in the same incident.

From Philadelphia, meanwhile, the march continued southward to Baltimore, where the Osborns accompanied General Clinton's entourage aboard a ship sailing down the Chesapeake and ultimately up the James River toward Williamsburg, Virginia. The tide carried their vessel only twelve miles upstream from the river mouth, but the voyagers were happy enough with that—the tide now out, they had "a fine time catching sea lobsters."

Next, of course, it was on to nearby Yorktown, in those days often called "Little York." Here, Cornwallis occupied the town, with his back firmly pressed against the York River. Trapped, he was under siege with the American entrenchments creeping closer and closer, and the artillery booming incessantly.

Sarah Osborn took it all in upon arrival—still with her husband's commissary contingent—at an encampment about a mile from the town itself. What she couldn't at first comprehend, though, was the number of dead black people, "lying round . . . [the] encampment." She was told that the British either had forced them out of supply-short Yorktown to starve or they had already starved and were then "thrown out."

Sarah set to work at her duties outside Yorktown—"washing, mending and cooking for the soldiers," with help from the other three women in her party. The "roar of the artillery" went on for days. At some point before the siege ended, she herself went into the American entrenchments, where she "cooked and carried in beef, and bread, and coffee to the soldiers in the entrenchment." That's when (and where) she met Washington. He asked if she wasn't "afraid of the cannonballs."

"No," she quipped, "the bullets would not cheat the gallows," and, more seriously, "It would not do for the men to fight and starve, too."

Washington's forces, meanwhile, "dug entrenchments nearer and nearer to Yorktown every night or two till the last."

The British, too, had been firing artillery, but the next morning, about nine o'clock, a silence fell. Then came the enemy's drums, beating "excessively." Not only that, the American officers around her "all at once hurrahed and swung their hats." The British had surrendered!

Sarah soon would witness even more history in the making. Mounted British officers filed out of the town and ceremoniously proffered their swords to their American counterparts. Next came the British army, "who marched out beating and playing a melancholy tune, their drums covered with black handkerchiefs and their fifes with black ribbons tied around them, into an old field and there grounded their arms and then returned into town again to await their destiny."

She saw Washington, Clinton, and the Marquis de Lafayette among the victorious American officers, some on foot, some on horseback. She saw Cornwallis and decided that he looked small, "diminutive," and cross-eyed. She saw the "large, portly" British General Charles O'Hara, Cornwallis's second in command, surrender on behalf of the British army. She didn't mention that he tried to slight the Americans by offering his sword to the French commander on the scene, but was refused and directed to the American second in command, Major General Benjamin Lincoln. She did mention that as O'Hara passed by her vantage point, she saw him "full face, and the tears rolled down his cheeks."

From Slavery to Freedom

APPEARING IN THE REVOLUTIONARY HISTORY just before Yorktown, was "Jim," valet, groom, and spy for the Marquis de Lafayette. A slave, he was "lent" to the young Frenchman when he was campaigning in Virginia against invading British forces in 1781. Weeks before the siege of Yorktown, Jim volunteered to present himself to the British as a runaway slave and gather information for the Frenchman. Seeing the potential value of such a plan, the marquis went along with Jim's proposal.

At this moment, the British had seized and then vacated Richmond, leaving a smoking, partially burned-out town behind. They were now moving east along the north bank of the James River toward Williamsburg. Lafayette, strengthened by the arrival of Anthony Wayne and nearly a thousand Pennsylvania troops south of Fredericksburg, Virginia, had turned from retreat before the British and now, with two thousand Continentals and a few thousand Virginia militia, was in pursuit. He caught up with the enemy near Jamestown in early July, with a brief but fierce firefight resulting on July 6. The next day, intent on reaching British-held Portsmouth, Lord Cornwallis crossed over to the south bank of the James.

In response to a plea for reinforcements from Sir Henry Clinton in New York, Cornwallis agreed, but warned that he was wary of seeing his army backed up against the waters and swamps of Tidewater Virginia—and thus "liable to become a prey to a foreign Enemy, with temporary superiority at Sea." Mere weeks later, with French Admiral Francois de Grasse blocking British access to the York River north of the James, and Cornwallis by then under siege at Yorktown, that is exactly what happened.

For now, though, Lafayette was content to take up a watch-and-wait position at Malvern Hill, still on the north bank of the James and located between Williamsburg and Richmond. By now, his black servant Jim was in position, too—as a new servant on the staff of Lord Cornwallis himself! Jim had appeared out of nowhere during the British crossing of the river, and they apparently had accepted his word that he was a runaway slave. He now worked in his Lordship's own tent.

"But though he reported faithfully on every move of the army as it moved eastward to Portsmouth," said Burke Davis in his book *The Campaign that Won America: The Story of Yorktown,* "he could learn nothing of future British plans. As Lafayette complained, 'his Lordship is so shy of his papers that my honest friend says he cannot get at them.'"

He may not have stayed all the time with the Cornwallis entourage, though, and he repeatedly was at risk of being caught. According to Virginius Dabney's *Virginia: The New Dominion, A History from 1607 to the Present,* "He made a number of trips to Portsmouth, then held by the British, delivered letters to other American spies and kept his eyes open for useful information."

Close to month's end, Jim had momentous but tantalizing news. The British soon would be leaving Portsmouth, but where they would go he didn't know.

On August 1, Lafayette found out—they were landing at Yorktown and, just across the mouth of the York River, at Gloucester Point. The Marquis sent this electrifying news straight to George Washington to the north. And now, dreamed Lafayette, if only the

French-American allies could place a blocking fleet in Hampton Roads. But he soon received word that a fleet of warships indeed had entered the Chesapeake Bay and was moving toward Hampton Roads. But whose fleet—British or French?

Of course, as the Marquis found out a few hours later, it was his countryman Admiral de Grasse. By his presence, with twenty-eight warships and three regiments of troops, Cornwallis was doomed, caught on a peninsula with his back to waters controlled by the enemy. It was only a matter of time before Washington's Continentals and Rochambeau's French land forces joined Lafayette in placing a tight, inescapable ring around Yorktown.

After the surrender, the defeated Cornwallis was invited to visit Lafayette's headquarters. He did . . . and was stunned to find the slave Jim at Lafayette's side. As events turned out, Cornwallis also had sought to turn Jim into a spy—against the Americans— but Jim, turning double agent, had fooled the British in that regard also.

With the war over, the Virginia General Assembly agreed to Lafayette's request to grant Jim his freedom. The legislature did the same for Saul Matthews, another slave-spy active in the Tidewater Virginia area, and gave Jim an annual pension of forty dollars.

He, in turn, adopted the last name of his French "spymaster" and lifelong friend . . . to become a freed black, James Lafayette by name.

Inventing a Navy

IN THE BEGINNING, THE ENTIRE fleet was the sloop *Hannah,* a charter. Later, but in the beginning also, the first commander in chief, Commodore Esek Hopkins, was ordered to protect the Chesapeake and Narragansett Bays, whereupon he instead sailed to the Bahamas and seized two poorly defended forts. But he also seized enough British weaponry—cannon, mortars, and their ammunition—to require two weeks to load aboard his half dozen newly commissioned warships.

Hopkins then really did sail northward to Narragansett Bay, but just before he could reach land that early April of 1776, he and his flotilla were forced to do battle with the twenty-gun British warship *Glascow.* Since they approached her one by one, *Glascow* was able to pummel each American vessel, then proceed on into the bay while the Americans staggered into harbor at New London, Connecticut.

Five months later, Hopkins was censured by a court-martial board and still later his commission was revoked.

Hannah, for her part, had not fared so well, either. Chartered from the Marblehead (Massachusetts) Regiment's John Glover, the sloop's first attempt at naval action had resulted in capture of a ship belonging to a New England Patriot. *Hannah* next ran aground in flight from the British.

It wasn't long after these false starts, however, that the original elements of today's U.S. Navy found more noble beginnings. Significantly, *Providence* was one Hopkins ship that escaped the encounter with the British *Glascow,* and in May of 1776 the *Providence* acquired a new skipper. Born in Scotland, but thoroughly committed to the American cause, he was Lieutenant John Paul Jones.

Ordered to interdict British shipping in Nova Scotia waters, Jones, in two months' time, seized sixteen prizes. He next was ordered to raid British fisheries on the Grand Banks—this time commanding two ships, *Providence* and *Alfred.* After *Providence* returned with weather damages, Jones pressed on aboard *Alfred* and seized seven prize ships in a raid at Canso, Nova Scotia. By the time he returned in triumph to Boston, the navy's first thirteen frigates authorized by Congress were nearly ready for duty—unfortunately, five never made it to sea and none of the thirteen would survive beyond 1781, thanks to British actions.

In the meantime, three 74-gun ships of the line and seven more frigates were under way as Congress proceeded with plans to build a real Continental Navy.

The future naval hero John Paul Jones was not alone in his depredations against the British. In May 1778, Captain Lambert Wickes led the *Reprisal, Dolphin,* and *Lexington* in taking well over a dozen prizes in the Irish Sea. *Lexington* and *Reprisal,* unfortunately, were lost on the way home.

The next American raider to be heard from was Irish-born

Gustavus Conyngham, who in 1777 obtained first one cutter (seized in a French port) and then another, which he named the USS *Revenge*. With *Revenge*, he blazed a fiery trail through the North Sea and on to the Irish Sea, grabbing off twenty prizes. Seemingly unstoppable, he then operated out of Spain, preying on British vessels sailing the Bay of Biscay and the South Atlantic. By the time he returned to America in late 1778 to take up a new career as a privateer, he had accounted for more than sixty enemy prizes taken over an eighteen-month period.

Along America's Atlantic coastline, meanwhile, the fledgling Continental Navy had not fared so well. Lost in, or as a result of, British action in 1777 and 1778 were the frigates *Congress, Montgomery, Effingham,* and *Washington,* all burned by their crews to avoid capture by the British. In addition, *Delaware* was seized by the enemy. *Virginia* and *Raleigh* not only were seized when they ran aground, but they were turned against the Americans as Royal Navy ships by the same name. Meanwhile, off Barbados, the American frigate *Randolph* blew up while engaged with the British sixty-four-gun *Yarmouth.*

The naval war was an up-and-down business, as events proved time and time again. In 1779, Captain Abraham Whipple's three-ship squadron garnered more than $1 million in prize money by seizing eleven merchant ships cut out of a sixty-ship convoy bound for England from Jamaica. Whipple found the richly laden train of ships passing through the Grand Banks in a thick fog. He grabbed off his prizes one by one without notice by their neighbors.

Offsetting that momentary triumph was the debacle of Penobscot Bay in future Maine—a failure for the largest ship assembly the Americans sent in harm's way during the entire war. Under Captain Dudley Saltonstall aboard the frigate *Warren,* three Massachusetts State Navy ships, sixteen specially commissioned privateers, two more Continental Navy ships, and twenty vessels carrying militiamen nosed into the bay 150 miles northeast of Boston July 25, 1779, in an operation intended to eject the British from a newly established base.

The British had only three sloops and four troop ships to defend their Penobscot interests, but the incoming American fleet failed to close and engage for ten or more days. Overly cautious Saltonstall and company then awoke one morning to find seven heavily gunned Royal Navy warships bearing down on them from the sea.

The American units fled, some running aground, others (like the *Warren*) blown up by their own men. The outcome was fourteen ships destroyed, twenty-eight captured, five hundred Americans killed or captured . . . and Saltonstall later court-martialed and cashiered from the navy.

Taking on the most powerful navy in the world, of course, meant the neophyte American navy would suffer more than an occasional bloody nose. It meant, too, that the revolutionaries could not possibly expect naval dominance at home or abroad. But they could, and did, let their presence be known, often in searing fashion. And often, too, the instigator was the colorful, if somewhat self-aggrandizing, John Paul Jones.

By mid-1778, the public on both sides of the Atlantic had heard of his spectacular sounding deeds: his capture of the twenty-gun British sloop HMS *Drake* in the Irish Sea, his raid on shipping at Whitehaven, England, and his raid on an earl's estate in Jones's own hometown of Kirkcudbright, Scotland. His successes as temporary skipper of the frigate *Ranger* caught the public's eyes and ears, but had no great military effect.

With Jones, however, there almost always would be more to come. After waiting a year or so in France for the right ship to become available, he talked Benjamin Franklin into wheedling French permission for the purchase of the merchantman *Duc de Buras,* docked at Nantes. Refitting the former East Indiaman into a fighting ship, Jones named her the USS *Bonhomme Richard* in tribute to Franklin, creator of *Poor Richard's Almanac.* Also, Jones was given command of a naval squadron including the new frigate *Alliance,* the French frigate *Pallas,* and the brig *Vengeance.* However, Jones would be the squadron's only American skipper.

About five weeks after the squadron set off on a round of commerce-raiding in the waters of the British Isles, Jones and company came across a forty-one-ship British convoy escorted only by the forty-four-gun *Serapis* and the twenty-gun *Countess of Scarborough.* For reasons of their own, the French skippers of *Alliance* and *Vengeance* stood off as *Pallas* made for the *Countess* and Jones was left to deal with the frigate *Serapis* himself.

They closed at sunset and fought to a bloody standstill over the next two hours, their hulls grappled cannon-port to cannon-port for most of the time. Jones had lost the use of his eighteen-pounders at the outset when two of the heavy guns blew up in the face of their crews. He didn't dare use them again. Instead, when the *Serapis* tried to cross his bow, Jones rammed into the British frigate. He saw that grappling and boarding the enemy ship was his only hope of surviving the battle at sea.

The British ship's Captain Richard Pearson didn't understand at first. "Has your ship struck?" he yelled, meaning struck her colors in surrender.

This is when John Paul Jones spoke his immortal words: "I have not yet begun to fight."

As the two ships swung together, hull kissing hull and cannon still firing at point blank range, neither adversary was able to storm the other with a boarding party. Jones's crew kept the fight going with fierce musket fire that cleared the main decks of the *Serapis,* but her lower guns kept on firing straight through the hull of the *Bonhomme Richard.* During this period, Pierre Landais, French captain of the *Alliance,* fired upon his American ally's ship, too.

Finally, as crowds watched the dramatic sea battle from England's nearby Flamborough Head, a topman from the *Richard* was able to crawl across the entangled yardarms and drop grenades onto the decks of the enemy ship below. One of the missiles careened through a hatch and exploded in the gunpowder stored on the gun deck. Most of the British guns still in service were knocked out of action by the blast that ensued. With half or more of his crew made casualties—but the convoy safely over the horizon— Pearson surrendered to Jones. His own crew sorely diminished and *his* ship actually sinking, Jones transferred to the *Serapis* and sailed to safety in neutral Holland—and to a permanent place in the lore of naval warfare, too. No surprise that he eventually returned home to accolades as the young navy's best-known hero (and Landais to a court-martial and sacking).

The *Bonhomme Richard-Serapis* engagement of September 1779 could be called the high-water mark of the Continental Navy's war against the British. From this point, occasional flare-ups excepted, the French in effect took over the heavier naval duties of the conflict, with their blockade of waters below Yorktown the naval episode that hurt the British the most . . . that, you could argue, lost them the war.

Additional notes: Many other seafaring men would be heroes of the naval war fought by Americans against the British, whether as sailors in the fledgling Continental Navy and the various state navies or as privateers. Virginian James Barron, for instance, who began his campaign to protect Virginia ports and the Chesapeake Bay in 1775, never stopped fighting until after contributing to the victory at Yorktown in 1781

Barron, born in 1740, had been at sea since the age of ten. As an adult, he sailed ships to the Caribbean and England as their master. Late in 1774, however, he resigned his captaincy of a merchantman bound for London, saying he must throw in his lot with the colonies and his native Virginia. He and brother Richard Barron then began organizing a militia unit among friends and fellow watermen.

In 1775, Royal Governor Dunmore fled to the British warship *Fowey,* while a number of Loyalists also found sanctuary aboard British ships off the Virginia shores. When they sent foraging parties ashore in search of provisions, Barron responded by taking over British merchant ships.

His first real brush with the Crown came as British warships approached Hampton, Virginia, in October of 1775, threatening to reduce the port town to ashes. Once the British dropped anchor in the harbor, however, the militia led by Barron joined with other men in fusillades of musket fire from the shore that drove off the enemy before he could do any harm.

From that start, one thing led to another for James Barron and brother Richard. They were accustomed to the water, and the gigantic Chesapeake was their sea. Sailing the two armed schooners *Liberty* and *Patriot,* they formed the nucleus of the Virginia State Navy—destined in time to become the largest of the state navies. As they began seizing unwary British shipping, a real prize was the British *Oxford,* carrying two hundred Highlander soldiers.

Barron next would have commanded a full-size, twenty-six-gun frigate being built for the Virginia navy at Portsmouth, but a sudden British strike in 1779 destroyed dozens of Chesapeake vessels and the shipyard at Portsmouth just before his frigate was to be launched.

A year later, Governor Thomas Jefferson officially named James Barron commander of the state navy. Barron responded by raiding

Tangier Island in the bay, destroying Loyalist materials and making off with five prize vessels. That October, however, discretion was the word when a British fleet of fifty-four ships carrying 5,000 troops briefly came to rest in the Hampton Roads area. The Virginia navy went into hiding. Barron's own flagship *Liberty* was stripped of her masts and sails and sunk out of sight in the Nansemond River.

When the British armada left, *Liberty* was refloated and refitted for duty. In December, however, the British were back in the area with thirty-one ships and 1,800 troops under Benedict Arnold. Most of the Virginia navy's vessels were caught and bottled up in the James River, although *Liberty* and *Nicholson* were relatively free to sail in and out of the York River as carriers of dispatches and supplies. Joined by another 2,000 troops under General William Phillips in March 1781, Arnold's force ranged up and down the James as far as the state capital of Richmond, destroying boats, ships, and ship-yard facilities in the process. It now appeared the Virginia navy was out of business.

But stubborn James Barron still had the *Liberty* and *Nicholson* at his disposal as the Siege of Yorktown began in the fall of 1781. The French fleet effectively barred the Royal Navy from coming to the rescue of Lord Cornwallis—but the tiny Virginia navy did its part in achieving final victory as well. With sixteen thousand American and French troops ringing the British in Yorktown for days on end, a steady supply of foodstuffs was a critical need. Coordinating with the Continental Army's commissary officials, Barron rounded up a fleet of small boats, barges, and craft as small as canoes from up and down Tidewater Virginia's waterways to collect and deliver the tons of provisions needed to feed the French and American armies.

After the British surrender at Yorktown, Barron's remaining navy of four vessels continued to patrol the waters of the Cheasapeake to keep them clear of enemy ships—and even pirates—until the official end of hostilities in 1783.

Which was the real American navy? It could be argued that young America's 1,100 or more privateers were as much a navy on war footing as the official but fledgling Continental Navy. After all, they are credited with seizing more than six hundred British ships carrying an estimated $18 million in goods during the eight-year war. Their masters, though, were a notoriously unruly lot who, by definition as privateers, planned their own missions without much regard for any grand, coordinated strategy. And their ships, manned by equally adventuresome, resourceful crews, quite naturally took those same men away from the manpower resources available to the official navy.

Killed in "Paltry Skirmish"

FATHER AND SON—POLITICIAN-DIPLOMAT and heroic soldier, respectively—Henry and John Laurens of South Carolina were destined to be captured by the British in the year 1780 . . . but quite separately. One would survive the revolutionary period, and one would not.

Aristocrats of the Patriot leadership in the 1770s and 1780s, they played dramatic and historically important roles in the Revolutionary cause—Henry as onetime president of the Continental Congress, his son John as a staff aide to George Washington. Henry at one point would languish as a prisoner in the Tower of London for more than a year. His son would be present for the surrender of Lord Cornwallis at Yorktown—he would be instrumental in dictating the British surrender terms, with his father that very moment still held in the Tower. Ironically, Constable of the Tower by title, although some distance removed, was none other than Lord Cornwallis. Himself now a prisoner, Cornwallis later would be exchanged for a ranking American prisoner—Henry Laurens.

Henry Laurens was born in Charleston, South Carolina, in 1724, with son John following suit just thirty years later. Their wealth came from a profitable import-export business and extensive landholdings. The elder Laurens served in his colony's House of Assembly for eleven years and was a militia officer in an early Cherokee War. With the revolutionary storm looming, he became president of the South Carolina Provincial Congress in the 1770s, then headed the Council of Safety. With the departure of Royal Governor William Campbell,

Henry Laurens became the former colony's executive. Joining the Continental Congress in 1777 as a delegate, he was elected president of the body just three months later, succeeding John Hancock in the post.

His would be a tumultuous stewardship, since Congress had to vacate its Philadelphia seat for safer quarters in York, Pennsylvania, as the British advanced on Philadelphia in the fall of 1777. It was at this makeshift capital, with Laurens as presiding officer, that the Congress made further history by adopting the Articles of Confederation, which served the onetime colonies as a governmental framework until the ratification of the U.S. Constitution in 1788. The same Laurens-led Congress approved a treaty with France recognizing American independence and promising military aid in the war against Great Britain.

Son John, in the meantime, returned to North America from law studies in London in 1775 to join the revolutionary cause as an officer. He saw combat at Brandywine and Germantown in late 1777, and at Valley Forge became an aide to General Washington.

He also fought at Monmouth, New Jersey, in 1778, and later in Rhode Island and at Savannah. His capture came about with the British seizure of his own Charleston in 1780, but he soon was exchanged. He turned up in Paris as a special envoy at the side of Benjamin Franklin, employing his fluent French in helping Franklin obtain a $2 million loan.

The younger Laurens, brave to the point of recklessness in battle, had proposed creation of a small slave army to fight the British. He would have financed one such regiment of blacks himself and eventually granted them their freedom, it seems, but none of the states went along with his idea of sending slaves into battle. As for his courage, he was so zealous in battle, it is said, some cavalry officers refused to ride with him.

He and his father possibly might have enjoyed a brief reunion in Europe in 1780, since Henry Laurens, no longer congressional president, was on his way to Holland in the late summer to seek a treaty with the Dutch and a $10 million loan for the American war effort. Just off Newfoundland, however, a British patrol craft captured his ship—and Laurens himself.

To make matters worse, the British recovered the papers Laurens heaved overboard in a weighted sack—among them a draft of the proposed treaty with the Dutch. As a result, England declared war on Holland, and Laurens wound up in the Tower of London "on suspicion of high treason," there to languish for fifteen months.

His son John, meanwhile, reached the rank of colonel and rode with Washington and his entourage through one campaign after another, up to and including Yorktown. There, he joined Lafayette, Colonel Alexander Hamilton, and others in taking the Rock Redoubt in a key night of action just before the British surrender. Colonel Laurens then had the pleasure of joining the surrender "commissioners" dictating terms to the vanquished British—making sure they met the same conditions imposed upon American General Benjamin Lincoln in the seizure of Charleston the year before.

This was not the end of the war for young Laurens, especially with the British still holding New York, Savannah, and Charleston. He soon was back in South Carolina with the Patriot forces harassing the British at Charleston. By August of 1782, the enemy had been forced to give up Savannah. To the north, in South Carolina, the British were hemmed in on Charleston Neck by the forces of General Nathanael Greene, but they still had bite. Leading his men against a British foraging party along the Combahee River that August, Laurens ran into an ambush near Tar Bluff. As the British rose from hiding places in the tall grass and fired, he went down in the first volley—killed, finally, in what Greene would call "a paltry little skirmish."

Released from the Tower of London earlier that year, Henry Laurens had joined Benjamin Franklin, John Adams, and John Jay in the Paris peace treaty negotiations destined to bring the Revolutionary War to an official close in 1783. The elder Laurens was one of those who signed the preliminary peace terms in November 1782—the same terms as those in the officially ratified treaty of September 3, 1783.

The elder Laurens, returning home to a war-wracked plantation, his health also affected by his many trials, would live until 1792.

Perils of George (Cont.)

BEFORE THE REVOLUTION, YOUNG GEORGE Washington had survived a bout with smallpox, frontier fights with the French and their Indian allies, and a plunge into an icy wilderness river. Now, he and his country were at war with probably the world's most powerful nation. Still, as commander in chief of the American forces, he had many protective buffers between himself and the various perils of war, did he not?

Not exactly. As the general in charge of forces in outright rebellion, he could be hanged if captured. But Washington was no desk-bound general; throughout the Revolutionary War, he faced one peril after another.

In early summer 1776, for instance, about the time Congress was adopting the Declaration of Independence at Philadelphia, he was in New York City awaiting a widely expected British blow. Indeed, British warships already filled the waters off lower Manhattan Island. The city was tense; rumors of desertions, betrayals, infiltration by Tories were rife. So was talk of an assassination plot against Washington, allegedly by poisoning. Whether that detail was true, a ring of traitors was rounded up—their apparent leader, a deserter named Thomas Hickey, was court-martialed, convicted of "mutiny, sedition and treachery" . . . and was hanged on June 28 before twenty thousand onlookers.

The British, meanwhile, began landing thousands of men on Staten Island on July 3. They assaulted Long Island and defeated Washington's forces in front of the Brooklyn Heights by means of an unexpected flank attack. In the nighttime withdrawal of all his men—a transfer by boat across the East River to Manhattan—General Washington was perhaps the very last to climb into one of the departing boats.

The British, of course, followed. The day the redcoats landed on Manhattan Island, at Kips Bay on the East River, Washington rushed to the scene of action, screamed and yelled in frustration as his amateurish militia fled the British regulars, and then had to be led away by an aide before the redcoats could reach him.

For the commander in chief of the Patriot forces, there naturally was peril attending almost his every move ... for the duration. Battle is battle, after all, and Washington never was one to stay behind in the "war room" while his men went forth to fight. Some situations, though, were more dangerous than others. And so it was that famous Christmas night of 1776, when Washington crossed the Delaware River in harsh wintry conditions together with his men—battling ice floes in open boats—to mount their audacious attack against the Hessians at Trenton the next morning.

There would be many times when the revolutionary fortunes were low—Valley Forge, remember?—with ultimate and final defeat a real risk ... but the resolute Virginian in command always managed to rebound and overcome all such perils of war, always ready to join his men at the crisis point. In the Battle of Brandywine Creek, (September 1777), when the British once again turned his flank, General Washington immediately took to his horse and galloped to the point of unexpected attack, jumping farm fences and urging on his local guide, "Push along, old man, push along!"

Even on the verge of victory, George Washington was willing to take risk after risk. In the Siege of Yorktown, September–October 1781, he did not shrink from those areas under steady, often deadly bombardment. One time, a cannonball struck so close by that it covered a companion's hat with sand. Washington merely advised his companion, a chaplain, to take the spent ball home "and show it to your wife and children."

One night during the siege, a group of American sappers and miners working in the dark far in advance of the Patriot lines was visted by a tall man clothed in something like a cape. After looking around, he left—but first he warned that if they were captured, "be sure the enemy doesn't find out that you're sappers and miners." Under the rules of warfare then existing, he was reminding them, they could have been executed as terrorists instead of soldiers simply doing their duty. Their nighttime visitor, himself risking capture, had of course been General George Washington.

On another night during the siege, he, General Benjamin Lincoln, General Henry Knox, and several other officers stood in the open close to the fighting for control of two key redoubts in the British line. Colonel David Cobb, a staff officer, warned: "Sir, you're much too exposed here. Hadn't you better step back a little?"

Washington replied (none too graciously, at that): "Colonel

Cobb, if you are afraid, you have the liberty to step back." A short while later, he told his officers he was pleased with the capture of the redoubts and told an aide, "Hand me my horse." He then returned to his paperwork at headquarters.

The next day, interestingly, Alexander Hamilton was at newly captured Rock Redoubt with Knox, pooh-poohing Washington's new order for his soldiers to yell a warning if they heard an artillery shell approaching. Knox was defending the idea as a way to save lives. Just then, two shells fell near them. Both men dove for cover, the diminutive Hamilton crouching behind the portly Knox. But Knox rolled over and left Hamilton closest to the as-yet-unexploded shells. When the shells exploded, neither officer was harmed, but Knox said, "Now what do you think Mr. Hamilton, about crying 'Shell'? But let me tell you not to make a breastwork of me again!"

The artillery fire sweeping the Revolutionary War battlefields was no joke, and that was true for the men and officers of either side at Yorktown. Days before, Lord Cornwallis had stood on a British parapet next to a fellow officer, Major Charles Cochrane, as the hapless major literally lost his head to an Allied cannonball.

This story may be apocryphal, but if true, Washington's greatest single moment of peril during the war came in connection with the Battle of the Brandywine in Pennsylvania, on the morning of September 11, 1777 . . . the moment that he perhaps unwittingly rode his horse within shooting distance of an armed British officer, Major Patrick Ferguson, who stepped out of his hiding place in the bushes, hailed the American before him, and tried to detain him.

The American calmly turned his back and rode on . . . after stopping for a moment to look Ferguson up and down. The British officer easily could have shot the American—"But it was not pleasant to fire at the back of an unoffending individual, who was acquitting himself very coolly of his duty, so I let him alone."

Not so incidentally, Ferguson was an accomplished gun-handler and marksman who had invented a rapid-fire rifle quite advanced for its day. As he said, he "could have lodged half a dozen balls in or about him before he was out of my reach."

And why do historians think it was George Washington who had been in Ferguson's sights that morning at Brandywine?

Well, himself wounded at Brandywine, Ferguson wrote to a relative that a British doctor treating American wounded repeated their information that General Washington had been with his light troops that morning, accompanied by a French officer in hussar uniform (Lafayette?). Ferguson had seen his man accompanied by an officer in hussar uniform, too. And his potential quarry had been dressed and mounted just as described by the wounded Americans, Ferguson asserted. Sadly, Ferguson was killed three years later in the American victory at King's Mountain, South Carolina (October 7, 1780).

VIII. Final Throes

Battles Sometimes Overlooked

GEORGE WASHINGTON'S FOUR COLUMNS WERE supposed to reach jump-off position by 2 A.M., move out at 4 A.M., and hit the British hard and simultaneously at daybreak. But the Americans should have reckoned upon variables such as the thick, early-morning fog that killed visibility, forced uncertain guides to feel their way along and contributed to delays for all four columns. They should have realized that straying soldiers were likely to be gathered up by the enemy and then to reveal the plan of the day, thus thwarting any hope of surprise. They might also have guessed that communication among the four columns by horse-mounted messengers could fall prey to various kinds of interruption . . . such as the fog.

What no one could have guessed, however, was that a single stone house would prove the major obstacle for Washington in his attack against Sir William Howe at Germantown, just outside of Philadelphia, that Saturday, October 4, 1777. And at first it certainly didn't appear that way.

Roaring down the Georgetown Pike, with the British Light Infantry in precipitate retreat before them, the men of American John Sullivan's column streamed right past the sturdy Cliveden summer mansion belonging to the Philadelphia Chews. Rather than be overrun, elements of the British Fortieth Regiment under Lieutenant Colonel Thomas Musgrave took refuge inside the stone house . . . unnoticed. It wasn't long, however, before the British inside the house were firing upon the Americans passing outside. It was no major threat to the overall scheme of attack by four columns, but the light fire was galling enough to force Washington and his officers into a council of war in a neighboring house. The commander in chief had to chose between moving on and leaving a mere regiment to cover the Cliveden House—or following the warning of Henry Knox against leaving any enemy element in the rear.

Washington chose the advice of his artillery chief.

Unfortunately, when his Lieutenant Colonel William Small advanced on the house with a white flag to offer the redcoats inside a chance to surrender, he was shot—fatally. Minutes later, an American cannonball barreled through the front door, streaked down the hallway inside, and burst out the back. And that was only the beginning of the intense fire the Americans lavished upon the Cliveden house and its frontal wall of stone two feet thick, without ever managing to dislodge the redcoats holding out inside.

Elsewhere in this major battle, the Americans were far more successful in driving the British back, despite the ropey fog that clung on and on, aided and abetted by clouds of smoke from the cannon and musket fire. Americans and British alike suffered here and there from the confusion of battle and limited visibility, but overall the Americans fought ferociously—they might have prevailed but for still more of those omnipresent variables of war: For one, a drunken General Adam Stephen mistakenly led his men into the rear of Anthony Wayne's flank and gave his officers contradictory orders; for another, the Americans pressing the British up front ran short of ammunition.

By 10 A.M., with the Cliveden house still unyielding and more than fifty American dead strewn about its front lawn, Washington and his men were pulling back. Among their other losses by now had been the son of Dr. John Witherspoon, president of the College of New Jersey (the future Princeton) and a signer of the Declaration of Independence. Fatally wounded by the same cannonball had been General Francis Nash, his name destined to live on when some of his soldiers founded the city of Nashville, Tennessee, just two years later.

Although Washington basically had been repulsed at Germantown, his men once again had shown they could and would fight. Another American army in just two weeks would show the same resolve under General Horatio Gates at Saratoga, New York—a clear-cut victory.

The Cliveden house remains on site and is open to the public today as a historic landmark.

A double or even triple first was the Skirmish of Cooches Bridge, Pennsylvania, on September 3, 1777. Here, the Continental Army's first light infantry corps fought its first engagement of the

Revolutionary War, this one against Sir William Howe's advance elements as the British moved on Philadelphia. The American light infantry consisted of a hundred or more officers and men serving under an Irish-born British army veteran, Brigadier General William Maxwell. More important, the minor clash earned its place in history as possibly the first time the Stars and Stripes was raised in battle.

With the most punishing winter in memory just past and the Continental Army riddled by dissent and desertions—even suffering ripples of mutiny—wouldn't this be a good time to attack . . . perhaps even to end the war on a victorious note? So figured Wilhelm von Knyphausen, commander of the German troops fighting the American rebels on behalf of the British.

Down in the south, the dust was still settling from Sir Henry Clinton's victorious siege of Charleston that June of 1780, while not far from von Knyphausen's seat in New York, Washington and his ragged, winter-struck Continentals still lingered at Morristown, New Jersey, in part for a lack of horses.

Backed by seven thousand men, the German marched first for the passes in the Watchung Mountains screening Morristown from just such an attack from the east. With the passes secured, he figured, he could descend upon Washington's base at Morristown and clean it out.

It didn't work out that way at all. First, the German's advance elements ran into an ambush by an American patrol that slowed the attempted night march until the next morning. Next, the New Jersey militia "turned out in surprising strength," wrote Thomas Fleming in his book, *Liberty! The American Revolution.* Further, ". . . the New Jersey Continental brigade, stationed east of the mountains, made a fighting retreat that gave Washington time to get his men into the vital passes and onto the high ground beyond the village of Springfield." The end result was a defeat for the German and his men, who only added to local enmity by burning down most of Springfield and nearby Connecticut Farms, the future city of Union, New Jersey.

Oddly enough, the Americans didn't see their resilient response as anything to crow about. Would you believe, wrote Alexander Hamilton later, that a German baron and a few thousand men, in the month of June, "insulted and defied the main American army with the commander in chief at their head with impunity and made them tremble for the safety of their magazines forty miles in the country?"

Militiaman Ashbel Green touched on another aspect of war altogether when he looked about the scene of battle a day later. He registered his impressions of "gloomy horror—a dead horse, a broken carriage of a fieldpiece, a town laid in ashes, the former inhabitants standing over the ruins of their dwellings and the unburied dead, covered with blood and with the flies that were devouring it." Green felt compelled to ask: "Is the contest worth all this?"

"The Truly Unfortunate Day," is what one of the junior British admirals called it, and he was *truly* right. Pure ineptitude on the part of the British had made it so. *Truly Unfortunate Day* was the Battle of the Virginia Capes, which easily could have gone over to the British and spared them the embarrassment of surrender at Yorktown, but didn't.

British Admiral Sir Thomas Graves lost the seabattle to the French, thus raising the question of who really was to blame for the British debacle at Yorktown. Most historians, of course, blame Lord Cornwallis for sitting at Yorktown and waiting for the British fleet to arrive and pick him up, like some kind of bus service.

The fact is, Admiral Graves was the "bus driver" who somehow went astray and allowed himself to be hijacked by the French.

He did try, and for that reason, he did appear off the mouth of the Chesapeake Bay on September 5, 1781, with nineteen ships of the line, his orders to proceed across the lower bay and enter the York River and right there, at Yorktown, to pick up his passenger, Cornwallis. British intelligence was such that he wasn't completely startled to find a fleet of French warships blocking his way in Lynnhaven Bay behind Virginia's Cape Henry, although he might not have known the precise number of French ships was twenty-four, including the world's largest warship, the 104-gun *Ville de Paris*.

Immediately upon spotting the approaching British, the French cut their anchor lines and stood to sea, to find maneuvering room for the battle sure to come. Graves bulled on into the bay before the strung-out French could form up for battle, but he didn't attack. By early afternoon, the fleets were passing one another on parallel lines and ducking in and out of thundersqualls. "Graves dithered while [French Admiral Francoise] de Grasse waited for the center and rear divisions of his fleet to catch up," reported Joseph N. Valliant Jr. in the October 1995 issue of *Military History* magazine.

What Admiral Graves was thinking aboard his ninety-gun flagship the *London* is not clear. After a time, his ships "running up on Middle Ground Shoal," he ordered them to turn and reverse course. "The turnabout placed the slowest and leakiest of the British ships opposite the strongest and fastest Frenchmen," added Valliant. "Then, to the astonishment of French and British alike Graves ordered his ships to slow to a drift."

Naturally, the French now could close all gaps and tidy up their formation—even button their shirt collars if they so chose. But Admiral Graves was going by the admiralty "book" and its "Fighting Instructions" issued to captains like himself. And those told the British sea fighters always to fight the enemy in neat, line-to-line engagement.

In this particular case, however, Graves could have laid waste to the French in piecemeal fashion by attacking their separate lead division right away, "but he evidently never thought to violate the Admiralty's sacrosanct canon of combat."

And there still was worse to come . . . from the British point of view. About three hours after the French first emerged from Lynnhaven Bay, Graves decided the enemy's first two divisions were properly lined up for battle, even if the French rear was still lagging behind. He signalled his fleet: "Bear down and engage." But his *London* already was flying, and *still was flying* the signal: "Line ahead." This was a flagrant contradiction in terms.

Neither instruction, in fact, was the apt one for the situation facing the British fleet. "The 'line ahead' signal," added the Valliant article, "was understood to mean that the British fleet would edge toward the enemy, keeping its rigid line intact. The 'bear down and engage' signal ordered each ship to run downwind and approach the enemy at a sharp angle. Both approaches put the British force at a disadvantage."

Confusion reigned aboard the British ships as *London* "turned toward the French." Leading the lead English division, Rear Admiral

Sir Francis Drake went with "bear down and engage." But Sir Samuel Hood, leading the British rear, went with "line ahead."

As a gap opened between the British divisions, they lost their advantage of proper formation and momentary numerical superiority to the French ships in line opposite the British ships. Soon, *London* found herself between the French and some of the British ships. Ships trying to follow "began crowding together." The guns on both sides began to speak . . . the frantic signals from Graves were lost in the clouds of gunsmoke that now billowed.

"The diagonal approach of the British ships was a gift to the French," noted Valliant. "They hit the British lead division before all its guns could bear on them."

Three of the lead British ships took an immediate pounding—*Shrewsbury*, 74 guns; *Intrepid*, 64 guns; and *Ajax*, 74 guns. All were crippled.

Four French ships were also staggered: *Marseilles, Bourgogne, Diademe*, and *Pluton*, all 74 guns. Two slightly smaller French ships also were badly hurt.

With significant damage done to both sides, Graves at last pulled down his "line ahead" flags, "giving Hood clear orders at last." His ships began to close with their French opposite numbers, but without much effect on either side. Thirty-five minutes later, Graves signalled: Desist. The firing stopped for the night as the sun set.

As the sun rose in the morning, the two fleets again were on parallel courses but holding off from further action. Graves and his senior subordinate Hood "were barely speaking" that day. Graves felt that Hood should have attacked the enemy's rear division more quickly, while Subordinate Admiral Hood "was furious because Graves had not thrown his whole fleet against the leading French division while it was isolated."

Sitting down to compile a memorandum called "Sentiments upon the Truly Unfortunate Day," Hood was convinced that Graves simply drifted for ninety minutes and that gave the French all the opportunity needed to close the gap in their line, and thus withstand the British attack.

For another night and day now, the two fleets eyed each other while surviving crewmen busied themselves at making repairs. Meanwhile, the fleets had been easing out to sea. "By sunset on September 7, two days after the battle, they were 100 miles out to sea, off Cape Hatteras, N.C."

Forgotten, overlooked, and ignored by Graves, meanwhile, was the real issue at stake—getting to Cornwallis at the mouth of the York River. Perhaps he was, as Valliant suggests, "preoccupied" with his crippled ships. In any case, Graves made no effort that night or the next day to place his ships across the entrance to the Chesapeake, a distance of only ten miles, and thus keep the French out. Now, September 8 passed by, the ocean waters rough, with neither fleet making the effort to sail back to Virginia.

At last, though, one fleet did make its move. The night of September 9 saw that fleet turn back for the Chesapeake. It raised Cape Henry on September 11, only to discover that a French squadron of eight ships of the line, "plus frigates and transports carrying men, siege guns and supplies," had just arrived from Newport, Rhode Island.

The admiral returning to the scene of battle had no fears at finding the French ships awaiting him, since Admiral de Grasse was French, too. And now, he had a total of thirty-six ships of the line, and Graves only had eighteen left in anything near fighting condition. The issue was settled. Cornwallis's fate was sealed. His "bus" would not be coming.

Graves did sail back to the scene, coming close enough on September 13 to make a count of the French ships lined up against him, shake his head, and sail on . . . back to the British base at New York. There he refitted and repaired, and on October 19 set sail again for the bay and Yorktown with a refurbished relief force. Too late, of course, since that was the very day that Cornwallis formally surrendered Yorktown.

Spies in from the Cold

FOR SEVERAL OF GEORGE WASHINGTON'S men—spies, actually—rejoining their own people at or near war's end was not always a simple task. His eighteenth-century "moles" had been so successful at infiltrating the enemy, they needed a ranking superior's good word to redeem their reputations among neighbors or former comrades-in-arms.

One such "mole" was Sergeant John Champe of Virginia, who pretty much had been minding his own business as a member of Henry ("Light-Horse Harry") Lee's cavalry troop in New Jersey . . . that is, until the American camp discovered in September 1780 that General Benedict Arnold had gone over to the British.

As everyone could have guessed, Washington felt personally outraged at such betrayal by an officer he had gone out of his way to befriend and even to protect. Washington was expectantly furious at such an act of treason in any case.

But that wasn't all—the commander in chief also was determined to bring the traitor back by any means possible.

He meant abduction, kidnapping . . . by whatever means, go get Benedict Arnold!

He entrusted Lee with the tricky assignment, and Champe volunteered. And what a task it would be! A real Mission: Impossible.

First of all, pretending to be a fleeing deserter, Champe was to "break away" from Patriot lines on the west banks of the Hudson River, leap into the water, swim out to a British frigate, and convince its crew that he really was a deserter. This much Champe did . . . while almost being shot and captured by American soldiers unacquainted with the abduction plot.

Next, he was to establish himself in Manhattan, where Arnold was known to be residing—preparing to become a brigadier general in the British army. Champe was to find out where Arnold was staying and then join the still-forming Arnold's Legion. All the while he was to make contact with Washington's spies in the city, all of which the tall, very capable Virginian did.

Finally, with the help of his fellow secret agents, Sergeant Champe was to intercept Arnold in one of his nocturnal strolls at the rear of his garden at No. 3 Broadway, overpower and kidnap the turncoat, then carry him back across the Hudson to American lines by boat. This much Champe never did do . . . but through no fault of his own. Unfortunately, Arnold and his Legion were shipped out before Champe could act. As a "new recruit" in the Legion, Champe was shipped out with them, all the way south to Virginia, far out of touch with his former commanding officer Light-Horse Harry Lee. Yet, only Lee knew the true status and mission of supposed turncoat Champe.

As Arnold and his men ranged up and down the James River,

largely in Tidewater, Virginia, Champe lived in fear of capture by his fellow Patriots and execution at their hands as a deserter. Pretty soon he deserted the British and began hunting for Lee, the only man who could verify his story.

Happily, Champe finally did track Lee down in South Carolina, where he had been deployed after Yorktown to campaign with Nathanael Greene during the war's final months.

Lee gave his fellow Virginian an honorable discharge, and that was that . . . except that Champe never received a pension for his wartime service, nor any recognition for his unusual role. Two decades after his death in 1818, his family went to Congress and extracted his posthumous "promotion" to ensign, lowest officer's rank in the army of the day, plus pay for the period when he was listed as a deserter, but of course was far from deserving such a label.

Another of Washington's agents who later "came in from the cold" of operations in the field, the *enemy* field, was Irish-born John Honeyman, a former grenadier in the British army's Forty-eighth Regiment of Foot. In that capacity, he took part in the campaigns against Louisbourg on Cape Breton Island in 1758 and against Quebec in 1759, both actions led by General James Wolfe.

Favored by Wolfe for catching him in a fall down a ship's companionway, the brawny Irishman rowed in Wolfe's own boat in the assault on Quebec, then was one of the three men who carried the fatally wounded Wolfe from the battlefield.

Honeyman subsequently settled in the American colonies, became a weaver and married. He chose Griggstown, New Jersey, as home for himself and his wife, Mary, also an immigrant from Ireland. When the Revolutionary War broke out, he not only joined the American cause but volunteered his services to George Washington in person. Honeyman was able to show Washington a letter of recommendation from the late General Wolfe.

After a series of meetings in 1775 and a final one in November of 1776, it was decided the onetime British soldier would travel about in British-occupied territory posing as a butcher and Loyalist. His war record presumably would win the confidence of the British at that moment in hot pursuit of Washington's tattered army as it retreated across New Jersey to the Delaware River and the Pennsylvania line.

As a result, Honeyman supplied the Hessians at Trenton with their beef as the Christmas holidays of 1776 approached. Seeing the relaxed, festive mood of the Germans and scouting the dirt "highways" and byways of the vicinity, "butcher" Honeyman was quite ready to report when Washington's outlying troops captured him (at the commander in chief's orders) and hauled him into headquarters at Newtown, Pennsylvania. The notorious "Loyalist" was closeted for a time with Washington himself—and perhaps with staff aide Tench Tilghman, as well. He imparted all the information he had on the Hessian defenses and troop dispositions at Trenton. Emerging from that vital conference, Honeyman was remanded to the custody of a stout stockade, its guards told he would be court-martialed and then hanged as a spy the next day.

That night, not-so-oddly enough, a nearby fire distracted the stockade guards, a door was left open, and Honeyman was able to dash for the river in a shower of musketfire that fortunately missed him altogether. At the river, he found a conveniently abandoned boat, which provided him a vehicle for crossing the river and reaching "safe haven" among the Hessians.

He related his tale of narrow escape and regaled the holiday-minded Hessians with stories of the pitiful condition of the rebels in their encampments on the Pennsylvania side of the river. Bidding the Hessians farewell that Christmas Eve, Honeyman disappeared into the New Jersey countryside. Two days later, at dawn on December 26, the "pitiful rebels" surprised the Hessians at Trenton in one of the greatest American victories of the entire Revolutionary War. They again struck hard at the enemy—this time at the British themselves—a few days later at Princeton. It is thought that additional intelligence-gathering by Honeyman contributed to that victory as well.

The former British soldier continued his spying for much of the war, albeit somewhat less spectacularly. He was so deeply entrenched as a "mole," he was again arrested by American troops. An emissary sent by George Washington arranged bail that won his temporary release from jail, then he disappeared again.

Just as potentially serious, an angry Pariot crowd gathered at his New Jersey home one night, frightening his wife and seven children and threatening to burn their home to the ground. Her fellow townspeople desisted only when she produced a piece of paper ostensibly signed by George Washington, saying that the wife of "notorious spy" John Honeyman of Griggstown should be "protected from all harm and annoyance from every quarter until further orders."

When Honeyman returned home from his wartime travails in 1780, his friends and neighbors treated him with open hostility, still thinking he was a committed Loyalist. Only a personal appearance by George Washington himself dissuaded them—and overnight transformed their hated neighbor into the town's best-known hero.

Additional notes: George Washington's extensive spy networks for most of the wartime period were "run" both by himself and his intelligence chief, Colonel Benjamin Tallmadge. With focus upon British headquarters in New York, their spies, or "moles," included Samuel Rivington, editor of the strictly Loyalist *Royal Gazette* in New York, and one of his writers, local merchant Robert Townsend. The latter wrote his Loyalist-appearing pieces as a cover while actually supplying information to one Samuel Woodhull, a farmer on the north shore of Long Island. Woodhull in turn signalled his frequent receipt of Townsend's latest tidbits by hanging garments a certain way on his clothesline. Americans in Connecticut across the Long Island Sound spotted the signals with their spyglasses, then sent a boat across the water to pick up the latest Townsend message, usually written in invisible ink . . . and then usually rushed to Washington himself.

These two, Townsend and Woodhull, went by the code names of Culper Junior and Senior.

According to Thomas Fleming in *Liberty! The American Revolution,* the "Culper" pair could take credit for aborting British plans for a potentially crippling attack on the French when they landed at Newport, Rhode Island, in 1780. An early exponent of disinformation, Washington reacted to the "Culper" information by spreading word that he planned to attack New York about the same time. The British, as a result, kept their forces "at home" rather than weaken the New York garrison.

Another key spy for Washington, Fleming notes, was American-

Irish tailor Hercules Mulligan, who provided "invaluable" information, also from inside the British bastion of New York City. Staff aide
Alexander Hamilton was Mulligan's "handler," said Fleming.

At war's end, Washington took the necessary steps to rehabili-
tate his dug-in "moles" in the eyes of their Patriot neighbors and
friends. In Mulligan's case, he did this by publicly having breakfast
with the tailor one day. He also openly visited with editor Rivington.
The roles of Townsend and Woodhull became known as well.

Frontier Standoff

OUT IN THE UNTAMED WILDS of Kentucky, with their American fort under
attack by Indians and British together, women and young boys
would be the heroes of the day. It was the women and girls who
actually ventured beyond the stout log walls of Bryan's Station to
fetch water from a spring sixty yards away, close to bushes and trees
potentially hiding the enemy.

"While we were dipping up the water I chanced to see under
the bushes the feet of one Indian and the hand of another grasping
a tomahawk," said fifteen-year-old Hetty Tomlinson later. "They were
not twenty steps from me, and I trembled so I could barely stand."

The settlers crowded inside the log fort and its twenty cabins
knew the Indians were out there—they just didn't want the Indians
to know that they knew.

August 16, 1782, had started with an odd "display" by several
Wyandot Indians to the rear of Bryan's Station. They were shooting
off their muskets and jumping around with no effort to conceal
their presence. Old Indian hands among the fort's settlers, forty-four
of them armed militiamen, suspected a trap—correctly so.

Rather than a mere handful of oddly behaving Indians, the
wilderness beyond the fort's confines held a hidden force of more
than three hundred Indians from various tribes, plus fifty British and
Tory members of Butler's Rangers led by Captains William Caldwell
and Alexander McKee. Also on hand was the notorious Simon Girty.

The mixed force, in fact, had crept forward during the previous night to surround the fort. Caldwell's plan and hope was that the American defenders would rush forth in pursuit of the small Wyandot group and thus leave the fort itself vulnerable to attack by the entire 350-man raiding party.

But this was the "Year of Blood" out on the frontier; a year of repeated attacks on frontier forts and settlements by the British and their Indian allies; a year of atrocities and horror stories, too. The Americans inside the log walls of Bryan's Station were understandably jittery. And suspicious.

They were also prepared for a fight. Learning that Hoy's Station in nearby Madison County had been attacked, the men at Bryan's had spent the night before cleaning their weapons and molding bullets in preparation for a march to the aid of Hoy's Station. They expected to run into Indians . . . albeit not quite so soon as outside their own fort the very next morning.

At that point, their captain, Elijah Craig, warned of a possible ambush by a larger, well-hidden force and refused to send anyone to confront the Wyandots. He did dispatch two messengers—bursting out of the fort gates on horses at full gallop—to nearby Lexington with an urgent plea for help. Now, those left behind the stockade walls must prepare to hold out until help came. The longer they could pretend to be unaware of the hidden Indians, meanwhile, the longer they might delay the inevitable attack by the entire force. Let the enemy wait and to see if the fort's fighting men could be drawn out by the demonstrating Wyandots. That was the reasoning inside the log walls.

Unfortunately, the trapped settlers had not yet gone for their daily water supply. The spring was outside the fort, just sixty yards away . . . a long, unprotected sixty yards. They would need drinking water if the fort came under siege for any length of time. Just as vital, they also would need water to put out fires if the Indians attacked with flaming torches, a known and proven tactic on the frontier. Then, too, it would be "normal" to send the women out for water as was customary. Anything to lull the watching enemy into holding back his full-scale attack.

So it was that a cluster of incredibly brave women and girls left the relative safety of the fort and walked to the spring with their containers, ambling as casually as they could, chattering among one another as usual . . . their hearts in their mouths all the while. When it came to killing and scalping, they well knew, Indians did not balk at making women their victims along with the menfolk.

As Hetty Tomlinson later reported, the Indians were certainly close by as the women filled their containers. They then strolled back to the fort, restraining every natural impulse to run as fast as they could. In minutes, the gate was shut behind them. For the moment, they were safe. And the fort's occupants had a supply of precious water.

Later in the morning, the Wyandots again appeared to the rear of the fort and again demonstrated. This time, the settlers pretended to be fooled and sent out a party of men, who drew close to the small Indian band, but, by plan, fled when the Indians fired on them. Inside, the rest of the men had been on guard against the anticipated full attack against the front of the fort.

And now at last it came. Girty reacted to the noisy but bogus clash at the rear by signalling the expected, all-out assault. Brandishing flaming torches, his Indians erupted from the woods and raced forward, fully intent on reducing the entire fort to smoldering ashes. Holding their fire until the last second, the defenders finally let loose a crashing volley that halted the charge, cutting down at least thirty of Girty's warriors. The Indians retreated, but not before starting fires in a few empty cabins outside the stockade. Fortunately, a favorable wind kept the fires from reaching the fort itself.

But the enemy was not through with Bryan's Station. With sniper fire forcing the defenders to keep their heads down (and killing two of them), the Indians fired off flaming arrows that repeatedly found their mark in the log walls and among the shingles on the inward-sloping cabin rooftops.

Now came the contribution of the fort's second set of unusual heroes—agile young boys who ignored the occasional flying bullets or descending arrows to scramble about the rooftops putting out the small fires before they could take hold.

No one on the scene knew it yet, but help was on the way. Militia Colonel Levi Todd and Captain William Ellis were on the march with forty-seven men, about a third of them mounted. They came upon the scene in early afternoon, the shooting long since stopped, the woods surrounding the fort silent . . . still.

Determined to avoid an ambush, Colonel Todd decided to lead his men on foot in a flanking movement that would bring them to the fort's gate from the side, rather than the front. In the meantime, Captain Ellis would lead more of their men on horseback in a sudden gallop up the buffalo road leading directly to the fort's front gate. Todd's caution proved well founded, for the enemy had not left the scene. As Ellis and his troop raced up the buffalo path before the fort, they stirred up a cloud of dust—and a burst of musket fire from the woods alongside. The men of Todd's flanking force, just then picking their way through a corn field on one side of the fort, heard the gunfire, turned toward it, but soon realized they had encountered an overwhelming enemy force. Fortunate for them, they rushed up before most of the Indians could reload their weapons after firing on the fast-moving horsemen. Even so, Colonel Todd's flankers had to back off after seeing two of their number killed and two more wounded.

By then, Ellis and his companions had reached the sanctuary of the fort. Now, they joined the defenders in well-aimed fire upon any attackers carelessly exposing themselves in the foliage surrounding the wilderness bastion. If they could just hold out, more help soon would be on the way. Colonel Todd, retreating the few miles to Lexington, would see to that.

Girty and his British allies were well aware of these facts. Their time on the scene would be limited.

The Indian leader now shouted to the Americans in the fort that they had better surrender, or face the threat of British reinforcements armed with artillery due to arrive that very evening. He allegedly warned the defenders they would be tomahawked and scalped if they kept on fighting. All that Girty could accomplish, however, was to exchange shouted insults with loud-voiced American leader Aaron Reynolds inside the fort.

In the end, the Indians and the British-led Rangers retreated on August 17—but not before destroying the settlers' corn crop, slaughtering their livestock (hogs, cattle, and sheep), and eating what they could of it. The next day, a posse-like force of 180-odd frontiersmen and militia set off in pursuit . . . with disaster awaiting them at Blue Licks by the Licking River.

Fears of Cowardice

DANIEL BOONE WARNED THE OTHERS that an ambush probably lay ahead. He knew the Kentucky's lower Blue Licks by heart. He had hunted and fished on the Licking River. He had "made" salt here. He had even been captured by the Shawnee here. And if he knew one thing about Indians, he knew they did not often show themselves without some purpose.

"You see the Indians have shown themselves on the hill beyond the river, loitering, as if to invite pursuit," he told his fellow frontiersmen that day in August of 1782. What's more, he also warned, "There are two ravines there, filled with brush and timber for their protection; it is not wise to heedlessly run into the trap set for us."

But his caution would be brushed aside as other leaders of his two-hundred-man party argued over strategy—and worried about looking like cowards. Even Boone, when it was hinted that he was a coward, is said to have reacted defensively. "If you are determined to go and meet the enemy at this great disadvantage, go on," he bristled. "I can go as far into an Indian fight as any man."

Militia Colonel Daniel Boone and his fellow Kentucky frontiersmen of course hoped to run into Indians—Indians and their British or Tory leaders who just days before had attacked Bryan's Station, forty miles to the southwest, near present-day Lexington. The Kentuckians were in hot pursuit of more than three hundred warriors and their white allies, but even so, it would be best to avoid an ambush. Indeed, it appeared that Tory Captain William Caldwell's party, including the notorious Simon Girty, deliberately was leaving a well-marked trail for the pursuers to follow.

The leaders of Boone's group included militia Majors Hugh McGary and Silas Harlan, along with Lieutenant Colonels John Todd and Stephen Trigg, but Major Levi Todd of Fayette County was in overall command as ranking local militia officer. Reinforcements were expected to show up any day, under Benjamin Logan from St. Asaph's Station. For that reason, Boone had argued that it would be wise to await Logan and his added manpower. But McGary, upset at insinuations that he was a coward, was adamant in urging immediate pursuit. Others went along, arguing that if they waited, the Indians and their leaders could escape.

So it was that the pursuing party set out on August 18, reportedly nearly two hundred militiamen on horses following the well-marked trail of the enemy ahead. When they reached Caldwell's campsite from the night before, Boone examined the area and said the enemy column could number as many as five hundred. He warned against an ambush, but once again, others were adamant . . . and again there was that fear of being branded a coward.

As a council of war was held to debate the next step, reported one of the onlooking officers later, "The principal officers appeared to be confused in their councils—each afraid to speak candidly for fear of being suspected for timidity." In the end, the pursuers rushed on, only hours behind their quarry on a buffalo trace leading to the lower Blue Licks.

Soon after dawn on Monday, August 19, they reached a ridge across from the Blue Licks. This was when they saw, on another ridgetop north of the river, Indians briefly "showing themselves," as Boone termed it.

The famous woodsman was unable to convince his compatriots to wait for Logan and his reinforcements before proceeding any farther. That failing, he pleaded, at the very least, that they send a flanking party around behind the likely Indian ambush site just ahead.

Still arguing over their best strategy, the pursuers moved down from their ridge to a ford on the southern side of the Licking River. It was now that Major McGary insinuated that Boone himself was less than a paragon of bravery. After Boone's retort that he could fight the Indians as well as any man, Major Harlan declared, "We have force enough to whip all the Indians we will find."

As the argument continued, McGary finally lost all patience, according to one of the onlookers. In a "passion," he "cursed them for a set of cowards, and swore that as they had come so far for a fight they should have it, and that they should fight or he would disgrace them; that now it should be shown who had courage and who were damn cowards."

With all that said, McGary "dashed into the river and called upon all who were not cowards to follow him." Boone then appealed to Levi Todd as overall commander to stop McGary, but the militia officer allegedly replied, "Let them go and we will remain in the rear;

and if they are surprised the blame will be on McGary."

Basically, that is what transpired within the hour. All the frontiersmen soon had crossed the river. McGary's group of about twenty-five moved on in advance of the main party, which followed in three single-file columns proceeding abreast, one of them led by Boone and including his son Israel, then twenty-one. They hadn't gone quite a mile when, in a ravine, shots and Indian whoops broke the heavy silence.

All but two of the men with McGary went down with the first volley. The Kentuckians behind fired back, but in minutes Trigg and the men in his column were killed, and Todd's column fell to pieces as well. Only Boone and some of his seventy men were unscathed. Miraculously, McGary survived as well.

The survivors, apparently on foot for the most part, turned and ran for the river ford behind, with the Indians in hot pursuit. Some of the Indians joining in the chase grabbed and mounted horses belonging to the Kentuckians. Said Todd later: "Several attempts were made to rally, but all in vain."

In all, seventy-seven of the Kentuckians were killed in the wilderness fracas, often called the last battle of the Revolutionary War—the last Indian battle in the Kentucky of today, as well. At least twenty were captured, most of them to be tortured to death or burned at the stake. One of that group who escaped said the odor of a burning human being was "the awfullest smell" he had ever experienced. In all, a sad day for the Kentuckians . . . a sad day on a very personal level for Daniel Boone, too.

While fleeing the Indians on foot, he stopped to seize a loose horse for his son's possible escape, but Israel wouldn't leave his father behind. The younger Boone was then struck by a musket ball and fell into Daniel's arms, mortally wounded.

With three Indians closely pursuing, Boone tried to run while carrying his son, an impossible task. The unimpeded braves gaining on him by the millisecond, Boone stopped suddenly, turned and shot the closest Indian, then plunged into the nearest thickets before the other two Indians could react. By now, Boone realized that all he could do for Israel was to hide him, which he did. The elder Boone then made his way back to the river, swam across, and rejoined his fellow frontiersmen as they regrouped.

Bolstered by Logan and his force, the Americans returned to the scene a few days later. According to Boone's own account, it was a grisly scene. "Being reinforced, we returned to bury the dead, and found their bodies strewed every where, cut and mangled in a dreadful manner." Worse yet, some had been "torn and eaten by wild beasts; those in the river eaten by fishes, all in such a putrefied condition that none could be distinguished from another."

Nonetheless, Boone was able to recover his son's body, which he carried back for proper burial at Boone's Station.

Along the Kentucky frontier, recriminations flew back and forth as various survivors and officials sought to place blame for the debacle. Among the militiamen who survived, meanwhile, many thought they at least had made their enemy pay dearly for his success in the fifteen-minute Battle of Blue Licks—Levi Todd, for one, later said, "The enemy must have suffered considerably."

As for those themes of courage versus cowardice, on view at the battle site today is a historical marker bearing a few final words from Daniel Boone: "So valiantly did our small party fight, that, to the memory of those who unfortunately fell in the battle, enough of honor cannot be paid."

Personal Glimpse: Simon Girty

WHEN HE WAS TEN, HIS father was killed in a duel. When he was fifteen, his family was captured by Delaware and Shawnee Indians allied with the French. His new stepfather was tortured and burned at the stake. The teenager was then sent to live with Seneca Indians in northern New York.

He was with the Senecas for the next eight years, and he became widely reputed as a hunter swift of foot in summer or winter.

Returned to white society with the end of the French and Indian War, he was reunited with two brothers also raised by Indians. All three became interpreters for traders and the British Indian Department at Pittsburgh.

Of the Girty brothers, though, it was the adopted Seneca Simon who became best known for good relations with their Indian contacts and even influence among the western tribes. "At home" in Pittsburgh, however, he was ostracized by fellow whites. In short order, he was allied with the Virginia interests in a long-smoldering dispute with Pennsylvanians over claims to virgin lands in the Ohio country. Then, on the eve of the Revolution, came Lord Dunmore's War against the Indians. Simon Girty became a distinguished "frontier scout, spy, soldier, and peace negotiator," wrote Phillip Hoffman in *The American Revolution, 1775-1783.*

As the tide of rebellion against British policies turned into armed conflict, Girty started out "an enthusiastic American Patriot." He served the cause as a messenger, emissary, and spy, repeatedly sent out among the tribes in the lonely wilderness.

Still, raids by Indians aligned with the British rocked the frontier—in some circles, distrust and suspicion were attached to anyone thought to be "soft" on Indians. "Returning from another solo mission to the Senecas—his own adopted tribe—and narrowly escaping after they had taken him prisoner for an American spy," said Hoffman, "Girty reached Fort Pitt, only to find he had been fired."

Resigning his commission in the Continental Army, he joined the Pittsburgh militia as a lieutenant. With the arrival of a new commander for the war on the frontier, however, he was arrested, his old associations with suspected Loyalists (and the Indians) an obvious reason. The charges against him soon dropped, Girty was with the Pittsburgh militia when the new frontier commander, General Edward Hand, mounted a drive against hostile Indians in early 1778, apparently failed to find any, then allowed his frustrated men to turn their wrath on a "few innocent old men, some women and a child, all of whom were at peace with America."

It was only a few weeks later that Girty, trader Matthew Elliott, and Alexander McKee, former assistant deputy for Indian Affairs, went over to the enemy at Detroit. Quickly granted a colonel's rank, McKee was placed in charge of Indian operations for the British, while the well-known Girty "was hired by the Indian Department to incite, arm, provision and join the Indians at war." Soon his two brothers, James and George, joined him.

But it was Simon who rose to the fore—this time becoming known among his former countrymen as the worst kind of monster, villain, traitor, and murderer imaginable. He was hated, notes Hoffman, "both as a traitor to his country and to his race." He accordingly "was blamed for every attack and accused of the most outrageous and barbaric crimes." The new state of Pennsylvania convicted him of treason in absentia and put a price on his head.

In the years of often horrifying frontier warfare that followed, Simon Girty undoubtedly fought alongside the Indians, saw atrocities committed and, fairly or unfairly, was associated with them. According to Hoffman's account, Girty at first sought out military targets, had asked his superiors in Detroit to urge restraint upon the Indians, and had rescued various prisoners from death at the hands of their Indian captors. "No less than 21 American captives, both men and women, claimed Simon saved them from torture or gave them aid."

Even so, he became known as "a sadistic, bloodthirsty 'White Savage'" throughout the frontier. Indeed, for the two centuries following his death in Canada in 1818, "Simon was cast as the villain of American books, articles, folk songs, plays and films."

One major reason, said Hoffman, was an unfortunate incident on the frontier in June 1782 that followed the capture of American Colonel William Crawford by Indians of various tribes. Infuriated by an earlier American-staged massacre of neutral Christian Indians in the vicinity, Crawford's captors condemned him to death at the stake, Hoffman relates.

"The colonel asked for Girty, whom he had known for years, and begged his help. Simon promised he would do his best. Unfortunately, Crawford was a captive of Delawares, with whom Girty had little influence. Simon argued strongly for Crawford's life but was finally rebuked and threatened with death himself."

Girty tried to talk Crawford into a secret escape plan, but the colonel turned down that offer. The next morning, "Crawford was stripped, tortured for hours, and then slowly burned to death."

Here the grim story becomes complicated by two conflicting eyewitness reports. One witness, said Hoffman, "later stated that Girty departed the village before the execution to avoid watching his friend's agony." But Dr. John Knight, an onlooker who escaped later, said that Girty "had done nothing to save Crawford and had even laughed cruelly when the colonel begged him to shoot him through the heart to end his misery."

Although Knight's version of events "differed completely from a number of other reports by witnesses," his was the story that was told and retold throughout America. Already badly besmirched, Girty's name was absolutely blackened from then on.

According to historian Hoffman, however, "Exhaustive research into Girty's life, involving years of reviewing unpublished holographic materials, many of which were either omitted on purpose or simply missed by earlier biographers, leads one to the conclusion that Girty is not deserving of the reputation that has plagued him all these years."

His real problem, suggested Hoffman, was early American "racism." His real sin, trying to achieve a balance between his two worlds of Indian and white. Whatever the true underlying facts, Girty emerged from the frontier wars of the Revolution a fighter . . . with his Indian allies, with the British, and sometimes both. Thus he led the Wyandots in the mixed force that defeated Governor Arthur St. Clair of the American Northwest Territory in 1791. He was with the tribes in their own defeat by Anthony Wayne at Fallen Timbers in 1795. Disillusioned, turning to drink, and failing in health, he removed to his farm in Canada when the British gave up their Detroit base to the Americans in 1796.

Taking up quarters with friendly Mohawks on the Grand River after hearing of an assassination threat during the War of 1812, he later returned to his farm in 1815, blind by this time. Dying there three years later, he left a wife who, like himself, had been a white captive raised by Indians from age fourteen to seventeen . . . at which point, in 1784, she had been found and rescued by Simon Girty himself.

Odds and Ends

ODD MOMENTS SEEN, HEARD, OR experienced on the road to Revolution:

It may be apocryphal, but two of George Washington's companions in his campaign travels through New Jersey the summer of 1778 later said he did stop one day to visit an unfortunate hydrocephalic near Passaic Falls. Known far and wide as a sort of freak, the unhappy Peter Van Winkle "had a head so enormous that it needed a framework on the back of his chair to support it," said an openly skeptical John Tebbel in his book *George Washington's America.* Further, this unfortunate "could not be moved without help." Washington supposedly asked the man about his politics. Was he Whig or Tory?

"Well, it do not take an active part on either side," he replied, "it" apparently a reference to his huge head.

Peter's nephew Peter G. Van Winkle later would become a U.S. senator from West Virginia after growing up "in a stone house at the foot of Bank Street, in Paterson, New Jersey, a house that was later the Passaic Hotel."

That awful winter of 1779–1780 the Continental Army spent in Morristown, New Jersey, supposedly the worst of the century, had its odd or light moments. But how to classify the story of Miss Temperance Wick's outing on her handsome horse one day?

While she was certainly an object of more than passing interest among some men of the army, it was her horse that others really coveted. In the Revolutionary period, a good horse in that neighborhood was known to have commanded a price of $20,000 in devalued Continental dollars. Still, there was no excusing the conduct of those Continentals who interrupted her ride on Jockey Hollow Road one day.

"She was pursued and surrounded by several soldiers who claimed her horse for use of the army," wrote Anne Hollingsworth Wharton in her 1897 biography, *Martha Washington.*

But for this "fearless rider," no real problem. She simply whirled her steed about and set off at hot speed for home, a farm at the end of Jockey Hollow Road. She "so outdistanced her pursuers" that she had time to reach her home, dismount, and carefully lead her horse out of sight. That meant taking the mount through the kitchen and parlor to a bedroom in the rear of the house.

The pursuing soldiers rode up moments later, but search as they would, they couldn't find Miss Wick's fine horse—"no indiscreet neigh or whinny revealing his presence in 'my lady's chamber,' where he remained undisturbed until the troops had left the neighborhood."

A kind gesture . . . or psychological Trojan horse?

That was the issue George Washington dealt with after the widow of a British officer attempted to use a flag of truce to send an ailing Mrs. Washington a box of "Necessary Articles for her recovery." It was a Martha to Martha gift at that. But would there be invisible strings attached?

Background: Martha Washington, while staying at her husband's quarters at New Windsor, New York, in May of 1778, came down with a gallbladder attack. She suffered abdominal pain, biliousness, and jaundice. She was laid low for a solid month.

General Washington mentioned her illness in a letter dispatched May 31 with three others, including a note from Martha herself. They were intercepted by the British.

The next thing the Americans knew, Martha received a note from Martha Mortier, widow of the former British army paymaster in whose New York home the Washingtons had stayed the spring of 1776. Mrs. Mortier made no bones about being informed of Mrs. Washington's illness by way of "some Intercepted Letters." Unasked, she also sent Martha Washington a considerable amount of "Necessary Articles." To wit: a keg of medicinal tamarind seeds; two pounds of tea; four boxes of sweetmeats; a box of oranges and a box of lemons; two dozen pineapples; and two hundred limes, among other items.

General Washington reacted quickly and decisively the moment he learned of Mrs. Mortier's gift, sent up the Hudson to New Windsor by boat. No, he told his subordinates, do not allow a single item to be landed, they all must be sent back. He also wrote Mrs. Mortier a short note thanking her and saying that Mrs. Washington was "so perfectly recovered as to set out for Virginia in a day or two." That being the case, he added, "General Washington hopes Mrs. Mortier will excuse his returning the several articles which she in so kind a manner sent up by the Flag [of truce], assuring her at the same time that he shall ever entertain a grateful sense of this mark of her benevolence."

Thus, noted Joseph E. Fields in his book *"Worthy Partner," The Papers of Martha Washington,* "Old Fox" George Washington had forestalled possibly embarrassing charges, whether by Tories or Patriots, of accepting favors from the enemy.

It was the kind of party that would have been a major media event in the twentieth century—the guests carried downriver to the mansion on gaily decorated barges, bands playing all the while, and even a salute by warships in the harbor. And then at the party site, ceremonial jousts between the "Knights of the Blended Rose" and the "Knights of the Burning Mountain," replete with broken lances, swordplay, and pistols. And next, the appearance of the young ladies represented by their knights—leading socialites dressed in fancy satins and silks, topped with turbans, feathers, and tassels.

The ill-fated Captain John André was a chief organizer of the grand affair, called the *Meschianza,* based upon Italian phraseology for happy mingling. His lady fair for the evening was Peggy Chew, daughter of a prominent Philadelphia family. André later would be hanged for his role as Benedict Arnold's contact man in their plot to betray the American fortress at West Point, and Peggy Chew would later marry an outstanding rebel officer, John Edgar Howard, a hero of the Battle of Cowpens, South Carolina, future governor of Maryland and U.S. senator from Maryland.

After the outdoor entertainments of the afternoon at the Wharton family's riverside Walnut Grove estate, the five hundred or so guests moved inside for dancing, refreshments, or gambling at a faro table. Around midnight came fireworks, followed by a sumptuous banquet served in 1,030 dishes by twenty-four housemen, while 108 musicians played 108 oboes, and lighting was supplied by 1,200 top-quality candles.

The toasts were plentiful—to King George III, to General Sir William Howe (the guest of honor), and to Howe's brother, Admiral Richard Howe of the nearby British fleet. And therein lay the reason for the party spectacular outside Philadelphia on May 18, 1778— General Howe was returning to England after resigning as commander of His Majesty's forces in America. André and his fellow officers were determined to give the popular Howe an appropriate and memorable sendoff—a real blowout.

And that it was; the dancing and gambling went on until sunrise the next day.

To be sure, there were a few discordant notes to be recorded, as well as all the gaiety. For instance, the Whartons, owners of the estate, were being held prisoner that very evening in Winchester,

Virginia, by Patriot forces. Then, too, more than fifty rebels held captive in Philadelphia by the British chose that night to escape by tunnel. In addition, the rebels attacked British outposts but with no real effect on the party.

Meanwhile, another young Philadelphia socialite, teenager Peggy Shippen, had thrown fits that day because her father would not allow her to dress in the same finery as the other young ladies championed by the jousting "knights." Peggy, of course, just a year later would marry American General Benedict Arnold.

Document on the Move

IF THE BRITISH HELD HIGH hopes of seizing the esteemed author of the Declaration of Independence during the American Revolution (and they did), wouldn't they have pined for that ever-so subversive document itself? In case they did, the American revolutionaries were careful to keep the precious piece of paper out of enemy hands.

Through the thick and thin not only of *that* war, but others still to come, the Declaration survived one peril after another.

Incidentally, the handwritten document approved by the Continental Congress the evening of July 4, 1776, is *not* the same piece of paper hermetically sealed behind bullet-proof glass at the National Archives these days.

The original sheet, sent to printer John Dunlap the very evening of its approval and then run off with minor typographical errors, has long since disappeared. Thomas Jefferson's own, hand-marked rough draft does still survive—but that, too, is not the official Declaration of Independence.

The one and only document that counts is the engrossed (hand-copied) yellowed parchment prepared after July 4, 1776, and placed before the signers on August 2 of that year. John Hancock, as president of the Congress, signed first, followed by all those others who pledged lives, fortunes, and sacred honor.

If some of those so pledging faced real perils as a result, so did their famous document. In its lifetime of two centuries, the document has been moved twenty times. It has traveled by horse-drawn wagon, by ship, by train, by truck, and even by tank-like armored vehicle. It "fled" from three wars, including one in the twentieth century. Its repositories ranged from a gristmill outside of Washington to sturdy Fort Knox, Kentucky.

The first war to be eluded, of course, was the Revolutionary War. If, as historians assume, the document stayed with the Continental Congress during that period, it would have accompanied the legislative body at sittings in Philadelphia, Baltimore, Lancaster, and York, Pennsylvania; Princeton, New Jersey; and Annapolis, Maryland.

It "came home" to Washington, the new capital city, in 1800 after further sojourns in Trenton, New Jersey; New York; and Philadelphia once again.

The journey to Washington was by ship, via the Delaware River, the Atlantic Ocean, the Chesapeake Bay, and the Potomac River.

During the War of 1812, State Department clerk Stephen Pleasonton hid the document in a gristmill at the Virginia end of the Chain Bridge crossing of the Potomac, then moved it to a minister's empty home in Leesburg, Virginia. The British at the moment were sacking public buildings in Washington, thirty-five miles away.

Later, and now endangered by its own keepers, the document hung on a wall opposite a sunlit window in the old Patent Office Building (today, the National Portrait Gallery) for thirty-five unhelpful years. Still later, it resided for another seventeen years in a State Department cabinet in a library accessible to smokers and containing an open, smoking fireplace. After added years locked away in a safe, the Declaration and the U.S. Constitution were transferred, in 1921, to the Library of Congress. Three years later, both documents went on public display in suitable casings.

Just three weeks after Pearl Harbor, however, they were on their way to the U.S. gold depository at Fort Knox for safekeeping. They traveled in a Pullman railroad car guarded by armed secret service agents. By 1944, with the war danger receding, they were back on public display in Washington.

Their final move, together, was to the National Archives in Washington in 1952. Joined by the Bill of Rights, they normally reside there today, sealed from outside air in a thermopane glass unit filled with humidified helium for preservation and shielded from ultraviolet light rays by special filters of laminated glass—except when briefly removed for repairs and improvements under way at the vault, as was the case at this writing.

All three documents are fully visible by day, but at night they sink from sight into a twenty-foot vault below the display cases, with interlocking leaves of metal and concrete closing over them.

As for the armored vehicle, that's how they traveled the short distance from the Library of Congress to the Archives Building—courtesy of the U.S. Marine Corps.

No Retirement for This Rogue

THE END OF THE REVOLUTIONARY War in 1783 meant retirement of one sort or another for most of the adversaries. But not for the Whig partisan fighter Philip Alston of Moore County, North Carolina. This murderer in Patriot's clothing was not yet done with his scheming or violent ways.

The Patriot cause at last triumphant, Alston briefly became a regional kingpin . . . despite his many enemies among the rebels themselves. In that vein, fellow militia officer Robert Rowan once said of Alston, "a greater tyrant is not upon the face of the earth according to his power."

Controversial or not, Alston wore many hats. A former representative in the North Carolina General Assembly, he now moved up the ladder to the more exclusive state senate. He also became a justice of the peace in newly formed Moore County, and remained the county's leading aristocrat.

It should be mentioned also that Alston briefly found time to serve as the new county's clerk of court, in addition to all his other activities—and herein lies a grim tale of intrigue and murder.

The time came, in the immediate post-Revolution years, when Alston desired to resign as clerk of court, but at the same time to "save" the post for his son James to take over when the young man was mature enough. The elder Alston made a deal—he thought—with Dr. George Glascock, himself a Revolutionary War veteran, to take over the post on a caretaker basis. That is, Glascock would serve as clerk for now, but on some future day he would step aside for Alston's son.

The reason Philip Alston wanted to resign was to take his newly acquired seat in the state senate on behalf of Moore County. No sooner had he done so, however, than he was accused of murder—the victim, a man named Thomas Taylor, had been a Tory during the recent hostilities, an active enemy. Alston was leading his militiamen against the Tories at the time. An Assembly committee investigating the murder charge not only recommended no prosecution but also proposed that Governor Richard Caswell officially pardon Alston.

Unmollified, many leading citizens still felt that Alston could have taken Taylor into custody as a prisoner instead of killing him. Governor Caswell did issue the pardon, but later bowed to public protest and called for another Assembly investigation, which went nowhere. "Apparently the Assembly let the case drop, as there is no further record on the matter," wrote Moore County historian Blackwell P. Robinson.

Whatever the outcome, Alston had stirred up other troubles as well. Sitting on the bench at home as a county justice, he treated the new court clerk, George Glascock, "in a very abusive manner," the court's own minutes assert.

After Alston was reelected to the state senate, Glascock joined with the county solicitor and a member of the state's House of Commons in challenging Alston's right to take his seat. "As a result of their depositions," wrote Robinson, "the Senate Committee on Privileges and Elections found that Alston stood indicted at the Superior Court of the district of Wilmington for murder."

In the end, Alston's troubles simply piled up too high for him to overcome. He was ruled ineligible to take his senate seat. And at home, a citizens' group protested his fitness to continue as a county justice, resulting in the state senate's stripping him of that post as well.

Not long after, Alston's latest enemy, County Clerk George Glascock, was found dead—murdered. Could the perpetrator have been Alston, the most obvious suspect? By county "tradition," said historian Robinson, Alston had established a pretty solid alibi—he gave a dance at his home the night of Glascock's murder, inviting "the countryside" and remaining very much in view of his guests throughout the evening.

How did he do it, then? He sent his slave Dave, it seems, and Dave was subsequently charged with the deed, then released on bail of £250—furnished by Alston of course. Dave then disappeared; he never appeared for trial, and Alston forfeited the bail money as a result.

Which is not to say that Alston got off easy. None of this is an easy trail to follow, but historian Robinson cited records showing that Alston also had to post bond to release himself from jail in Wilmington, but later was remanded back to the same lockup. Then a newspaper account enters the picture . . . and focuses it. It was the *Fayetteville Gazette*'s issue of December 1, 1790, that carried a most significant tidbit of regional news—"Broke gaol [jail] on the 5th inst., Philip Alston, late of Moore County, committed as accessory to the murder of George Glascock."

No one really knows the final outcome. Alston had sold his home and plantation on the Deep River earlier in 1790. At the end of that year, he owed the state a judgment of more than £142. Almost a year later his son James was accepted as administrator of the estate left by the now-deceased Philip Alston.

Deceased? Apparently so. "Tradition has it," wrote Robinson, "that he fled the state, and was finally murdered by the same Dave." More recent research, offered by the Moore County Historical Society, suggests that Alston was murdered in his bed in October 1791 after fleeing to Washington County, Georgia, on the heels of his jailbreak. This account makes no mention of the slave Dave or of his ultimate fate. And so ended the post-Revolution "career" of the man Robinson described as Moore County's "most notorious citizen."

They Also Fought

LEST WE FORGET, HERE ARE a few others who fought the good fight, the memorable fight . . . the sometimes ruthless fight:

Washington, Jefferson, George Mason, Patrick Henry—all six feet or more in height, were just a few of the Virginians noted for their imposing stature . . . but to that list add one more outstanding and tall Virginia revolutionary leader, George Rogers Clark.

Often forgotten today, this native of Jefferson's own Albemarle County achieved Herculean tasks on behalf of his future nation. A surveyor and frontiersman in future Kentucky when the Revolutionary War erupted, he had served as an officer in Lord (Royal Governor) Dunmore's war against Indians resisting the white man's incursions west of the Appalachians. Now, in 1776, he briefly returned to Virginia to obtain a load of gunpowder needed to help defend his largely uncharted territory—and to persuade Virginia authorities to create a "Kentucky County."

The tall, red-headed Virginian and his fellow frontiersmen spent the next year in the far-flung wilderness fighting off British-incited Indian attacks, but the dangers were only increasing rather than diminishing. The time soon came to mount an offensive, in Clark's view. He returned to Virginia again in late 1777 to obtain Governor Patrick Henry's approval for a strike against the British fort at Kaskaskia in future Illinois by an expeditionary force of 350 men.

Keeping the formation of his minuscule army as secret as possible, newly appointed Lieutenant Colonel Clark of the Virginia State Line led a mere 175 men on a six-day march from the future site of Louisville through dangerous Indian territory to Kaskaskia, arriving on July 4, 1778. The fort quickly fell to Clark and his semi-starved men. In just weeks, Clark also took control of nearby Cahokia and Vincennes.

In Williamsburg, the Assembly designated the vast Illinois territory another new county of Virginia.

But the fight for control of the territory, then called the Northwest, was not yet over. Leaving his base in Detroit, British Lieutenant Governor Henry Hamilton struck back with a mixed force of British regulars, Indian allies, and suborned French settlers. In December of 1778, he recaptured weakly garrisoned Vincennes with hardly a fight.

"At this point," wrote Virginius Dabney in his 1971 history, *Virginia: The New Dominion,* "Clark performed one of the most memorable feats in the annals of war. It was midwinter, the rivers were high and much of the country was flooded. In the face of these apparently insuperable obstacles, Clark set out to recapture Vincennes 180 miles away." That meant slogging through ice-cold waters, sometimes shoulder high, and going for days at times without substantial food since game animals had fled the flooded terrain. "As they neared Vincennes, many [of Clark's men] became exhausted and had to be rescued by their companions from drowning." All the while, the remarkable Clark was "in the van, encouraging and exhorting."

The one factor in Clark's favor was surprise—the recent conquerers of Vincennes never dreamed the Americans could pose a threat in the prevailing wintry conditions of that late February of 1779. As history records, "The sudden emergence from this waterlogged wildernesss of Clark's muddy, buckskin-clad warriors, with their flintlock rifles and tomahawks, took the Vincennes garrison so completely by surprise that the fort fell, after a brief struggle."

Thus were the Illinois and Kentucky Territories saved for young America; thus in the peace treaty of 1783 was America ceded its huge territory between the Appalachians and the Mississippi River. Clark, in the meantime, managed in 1780 to stop a British drive on St. Louis.

In a visit to Virginia's new capital of Richmond in 1781, Clark, with 240 "borrowed" militiamen, briefly took part in the fighting against Benedict Arnold's invading force by ambushing the Queen's Rangers, but Clark's next objective was the western British base at Detroit. While plans for a Detroit expedition were laid, they never became a reality for lack of men, funding, and the necessary coordination among the various Continental Army and state militia units needed.

By now a Virginia brigadier general, Clark continued to fight the British and their Indian allies west of the Appalachians from his base at Louisville until the peace treaty of 1783 at last ended the Revolutionary War. He at one point led a major expedition against Shawnee Indian villages in the Ohio country in retaliation for the massacre of Kentucky frontiersmen at Blue Licks in August of 1782.

George Rogers Clark, incidentally, was the much older brother of William Clark, who with Meriwether Lewis, also a native of Albemarle County, Virginia, formed and led the famous exploratory Lewis and Clark Expedition west in 1804 and 1805 from St. Louis to the mouth of the Columbia River on the Pacific Ocean.

After Spain joined France as an American ally in 1779, Bernardo de Galvez, the thirty-two-year-old governor of Spanish Louisiana, took up the revolutionary crusade with American agent Oliver Pollock at his side. After subduing the British garrisons at Baton Rouge and Natchez, they turned on British-held Mobile and Pensacola and captured them, too.

The enthusiastic governor's army was a mix of Spanish regulars, French Creoles, free blacks, American settlers, and Indians. It may never have numbered more than two thousand or so men all told, yet it kept an equal or greater number of British troops busy protecting the Crown's sparsely populated and highly vulnerable Florida flank, which at the time encompassed a huge territory today consisting of the state of Florida and big chunks of Alabama, Mississippi, and Louisiana. Until Galvez came along, Pensacola had been capital of British West Florida, while St. Augustine was the center of activity in British East Florida.

Often forgotten today is the fact that even before Spain officially jumped into the American Revolutionary War, Galvez had been coordinating with Pollock to ship military supplies up the Mississippi River in barge-like boats flying the Spanish flag. He also funneled major loans of money through the same Irish-American, who was based in New Orleans.

Which other future president—other than General George Washington, of course—fought in the Revolution as an American officer? Not John Adams, busy in the Continental Congress. Not Thomas Jefferson, busy serving as governor of Virginia, although very nearly captured by Banastre Tarleton at Charlottesville, true.

And, no, not James Madison, fourth U.S. president, busy at first helping to develop a Virginia constitution and later another Continental Congress member.

Andrew Jackson, future hero of the Battle of New Orleans in the War of 1812 and a future president, was briefly a prisoner of the British, but only an angry teenager at the time, not an officer during the Revolution itself.

All of which leaves James Monroe, fifth U.S. president, 1817 to 1825, but first, during the revolutionary period, a young officer who took part in the Battles of Trenton, Brandywine, Germantown, and Monmouth. Monroe, in fact, nearly died at Trenton when struck in the shoulder by a musket ball that severed an artery. Fortunately, a doctor on the scene was able to stop the bleeding in time to save his life. Earlier in the same battle, he had crossed the Delaware with George Washington's troops, then, with Captain William Washington, led a charge against Hessian soldiers trying to set up a pair of cannon for use against the attacking Americans.

Later in the war, he served as an aide-de-camp and then adjutant to brigade commander "Lord Stirling" (William Alexander). His scouting reports before the Battle of Monmouth contributed to the effective deployment of the American troops before the British attacked.

Although Monroe later (and unsuccessfully) tried to raise commands at home in Virginia, he also was busy studying law under Jefferson, then serving in the Virginia legislature and, eventually, the Confederation Congress. He took time out to travel southward in 1780 to set up communication links between Virginia authorities and military units to the south. The idea was to provide warning if and when it appeared the British would be advancing toward Virginia borders ... which a year later they did.

They called this man "Sure Shot Tim," and perhaps he really did shoot John Burgoyne's key front-line general at Saratoga . . . and Burgoyne's aide-de-camp as well.

It may really be that his own General Daniel Morgan briefed a group of sharpshooters and told them to look for British General Simon Fraser in the pending battle. It may also be that Morgan told his marksmen, Timothy Murphy among them: "That gallant officer is General Fraser. I admire and honor him, but it is necessary he should die—victory for the enemy depends upon him."

It may be that Murphy's third shot from two hundred yards away did pull down General Simon Fraser, who was fatally wounded in the two-step Battle of Saratoga, New York, in October of 1777. On the same day as Fraser's fatal wounding, October 7, Sir Francis Carr Clerke, aide-de-camp to the overall British commander, General ("Gentleman Johnny") John Burgoyne, also went down with a gunshot wound. Clerke died that night and Fraser the next morning.

Who was this Murphy—half man, half legend?

Born in 1751 in the Delaware Gap section of New Jersey, then raised in Pennsylvania's Wyoming Valley, he came to the Revolutionary War untutored in letters but wise in the ways of frontier life. He served with the Americans besieging Boston in 1775, and was present for the subsequent Battles of Long Island, Trenton, and Princeton, plus George Washington's campaign of 1777, until joining Virginia's Daniel Morgan and his newly formed Rifle Corps at Saratoga.

There, in addition to his alleged shootings of two key Burgoyne officers, Murphy is said to have captured another British officer right in his own tent. He returned to Pennsylvania in time to spend the winter of 1777–1778 with Washington and his troops at Valley Forge. The next June, after the Battle of Monmouth, Murphy and three companions captured a British general's coach nearby.

Next came the frontier-raised soldier's turbulent career as a famous but often merciless Indian fighter in the western reaches of New York and Pennsylvania. In 1778, he and a companion assassinated a Tory who had helped Loyalist raiding parties. That same year, he also helped burn down an Indian town in reprisal for an earlier Indian attack. He barely escaped capture or death several times over the next two years.

After serving in General John Sullivan's punitive Indian expedition of 1779, Murphy was with a party of twenty-four that was ambushed while scouting an Indian town. Only Murphy and one other man escaped. The lieutenant leading the scouting party and a sergeant were captured, tortured, and beheaded. Another time, in 1780, Murphy and another companion were actually captured by eleven Iroquois and tied up together. But the two prisoners managed to slip their bonds during the night and quietly kill all but one of the Indians. And he fled.

Later that year, Murphy was at the Middle Fort in the Schoharie Valley of upstate New York when it came under siege by the Tory Sir John Johnson and a mixed force of nearly two thousand British redcoats, Loyalists, Indians, and even a few Hessians. Inside the stockade of logs and dirt embankments were about four hundred soldiers and militiamen under Major Melanchthon Woolsey.

When his light artillery failed to breach the fort's walls, Johnson sent forward an officer under a white flag of truce with a surrender demand. Murphy and constant companion David Elerson immediately fired upon the flag-bearer, stopping him in his tracks. Woolsey then ordered Murphy's arrest, but not a man moved toward the frontiersman.

In a second and a third attempt to make contact with the fort, Johnson's emissaries were still thwarted by Murphy's fire. Finally threatened with death by his own commander, Woolsey, Murphy told him, "Sooner than see that flag enter this fort, I'll send a bullet through your heart."

Not only Murphy, but the militiamen siding with him well knew that he, and perhaps the entire garrison, could expect unusually brutal treatment from the Indians if the fort did surrender. As events turned out, Woolsey stepped down from command, and the Johnson raiders moved on after a desultory, failed attack on a nearby fort.

Later, in 1781, Murphy was in Virginia for the Marquis de Lafayette's clash with Lord Cornwallis near Jamestown on July 6 and for the siege of Yorktown in October of that year. He then went back to Indian fighting on the New York frontier until the official end of the Revolutionary War in 1783.

IX. Last Glimpses

Final Orders

THE FINAL BRITISH LEAVE-TAKING of New York, the final British bastion in the former American colonies, would not take place until November 1783, but as early as April 15, 1783, Sir Guy Carleton, commander of all British forces remaining in North America, issued this order:

> It is the Commander in Chief's *orders,* that the following Extract, from the Seventh Article of the *Provisional Treaty,* between Great Britain and the *United States of America,* be STRICTLY, attended to and COMPLIED with, by all Persons whatsoever, under his Command, And his Britannic Majesty shall, with all convenient Speed, and without causing any *Destruction* or carrying away any *Negroes,* or other *Property,* of the American Inhabitants, withdraw all his Armies, Garrisons, and Fleets from the said UNITED STATES. [Italics and capitalization his.]

Flagpole Greased

THE BRITISH EVACUATION OF NEW York (Manhattan Island, actually) on November 25, 1783, ended seven years of occupation by *the enemy.* The time set for the official relinquishment of British power in the city was high noon, and, at first, all seemed to be going well . . . and more or less on schedule.

At a key barrier, American General Henry Knox, the former bookstore-keeper from Boston, was on hand at 8 A.M., but then had to wait, exchanging pleasantries with British officers also awaiting the turnover.

Finally, at 1 P.M., the British withdrew their troops from their last posts. The Americans marched in, with General Knox in the lead. The new and only temporary occupation force included the Second Massachusetts Regiment, a single troop of dragoons, two artillery companies, and a battalion of light infantry.

George Washington, of course, was very much in evidence that day as well.

As the Americans took over, a parade formed, the new thirteen-stripe flag was unfurled, a thirteen-gun salute was prepared, bells rang, and pride and excitement reigned city-wide. Throngs greeted the incoming troops—and Washington—with shouts and tears of joy.

One woman later recalled the terribly moving scene: "We had been accustomed for a long time to military display in all the finish and finery of garrison life; the troops just leaving us were as if equipped for show, and with their scarlet uniforms and burnished arms, made a brilliant display; the troops that marched in, on the contrary, were ill-clad and weatherbeaten, and made a forlorn appearance; but then they were *our* troops, and as I looked at them and thought upon all they had done and suffered for us, my heart and my eyes were full, and I admired and gloried in them the more, because they were weatherbeaten and forlorn."

Despite all the excitement, there would be one small hitch. Down at the Battery was freshly evacuated Fort George, and in its parade ground, a tall flagpole—still bravely flying the British flag!

Not only that, the halyards had been stripped away from the flagpole. The cleats had been removed. Further, the pole itself had been smeared over with grease. An American sailor tried to shinny up the pole three different times and simply couldn't make it.

With a ceremonial thirteen-gun salute scheduled to be fired from the fort, this would never do. The impasse was finally resolved with the application of tools allowing the Americans to cut themselves footholds in the pole, climb it, and remove the offending flag.

The British did not entirely leave the area that very day, incidentally. It would be the first week of December before they vacated Governor's Island and Staten Island; it would be December 4 before their troop ships sailed off; and not until December 5 did their last commander on American soil, Sir Guy Carleton, say his final farewells to New York.

Farewell to "His Grieving Children"

ON NOVEMBER 25, 1783, AS the British began to depart New York City, George Washington and his entourage passed by Kip's Bay, the spot on Manhattan Island where he had shouted in despair and rage at his retreating men back in 1776. That had been a low point, a rare moment of visible emotion for the commander in chief.

Now, in the last days of 1783, came a high point—at noon on December 4—a moment of high emotion, outright weeping, for the same George Washington.

The clock was still striking its twelve beats when he stepped into the longroom at Fraunces' Tavern to address four of his generals and a crowd of lesser-ranks. Emotions were running high. The grave, immovable George Washington they all knew so well started to speak, could not, turned away, reached for a morsel of food . . . and could not swallow.

He reached for a glass of wine. So, too, stiff and silent, did his audience.

That might have helped, but few actually sipped.

Washington's hand shook ever so slightly, his face was angled downward, and his expression was hard to see. His voice, when at last it issued forth, was not his normal voice. "Queer and choked" is the way twentieth-century author John Tebbel has imagined it to be. "Odd, tight," is the description chosen by twentieth-century historian Bruce Lancaster. Both seem so right.

The men in attendance that day were gathered in a famous tavern room boasting two fireplaces and five windows on the street side. The windows had been polished, the floors waxed and the tables set with linen cloth. They held decanters of wine, along with platters and dishes heaped with food for the buffet lunch about to be served. Once the De Lancey mansion, the building at the corner of Pearl and Broad Streets now was Fraunces' Tavern; its proprietor was West Indies–born "Black Sam" Fraunces. He had hosted the Americans, George Washington among them, before the British occupied New York in 1776, and he then, until late 1783, had served the British in the same longroom. Chances are that he also listened and spied for the Americans during the long British occupation.

As Washington stepped into the longroom on this December day, however, Samuel Fraunces quietly withdrew. No secrets were to be imparted, but still it was to be a very private affair, very personal . . . it was to be George Washington's farewell to his officers.

As the commander in chief finally regained his composure, he began: "With a heart full of love and gratitude, I now take leave of you. I most devoutly wish that your later days may be as prosperous and happy as your former ones have been glorious and honorable."

He stopped and raised his glass. His officers raised theirs, sipped, shuffled, murmured, stammered . . . all paralyzed by the emotion of the moment. An odd silence took over for some moments.

Finally, Washington managed to add a few words, the tears on his face fully visible. By all accounts, he stopped and stammered as he said, "I cannot . . . I cannot come to each of you but shall be obliged if each of you will come and take me by the hand."

First to step forward was General Henry Knox, who had been with Washington ever since 1775 outside Boston when the outcome of the rash American rebellion was totally uncertain. Now bulky Henry Knox, all of 280 pounds, moved forward extending his hand. "Washington started to take it," wrote historian Lancaster, "but memories of the old years together swept over him and he threw his arms about his Chief of Artillery. . . ."

Added Tebbel's account of the same moment: "Frankly weeping, he [Washington] embraced his Chief of Artillery and kissed him on the cheek."

Then, without a word spoken, according to Washington's spymaster Benjamin Talmadge, each of the officers in the room—Baron von Steuben and Alexander McDougall among them—stepped forward to receive the same warm embrace.

"Such a scene of sorrow and weeping I had never before witnessed, and hope I may never be called upon to witness again," wrote Talmadge later. As he also wrote, the explanation was a very human one. "The simple thought that we were then to part from the man who had conducted us through a long and bloody war, and under whose conduct the glory and independence of our country had been achieved, and that we should see his face no more in this world, seemed to be utterly unsupportable."

Talmadge, of course, was entirely wrong in one respect—they soon *would* see George Washington back in New York, in residence at the temporary federal capital as the new nation's first president. Tavernkeeper Samuel Fraunces, for that matter, would reappear as President Washington's steward.

But none of those embracing General Washington at Fraunces' Tavern that emotional day could see into the future. All they knew was that this was farewell to their leader before he left the city for home, rest, and respite, at his beloved Mount Vernon in Virginia.

Nor did the moment last beyond endurance. "But the time for separation had come," wrote the onlooking Talmadge, "and waving his hand to his grieving children around him, he left the room. . . ."

Even now, though, the "separation" for that one day was not quite done. Outside the tavern, a guard of honor and crowds awaited Washington as he made his way to Whitehall Ferry and an awaiting barge that would carry him across the Hudson to Paulus Hook as the first stage of his long trip home.

"People along the way remembered as long as they lived his tense, set face, the convulsive throbbing of his jaw muscles . . . ," wrote Lancaster.

Following him from the tavern were his officers, unwilling as yet to turn for their own paths homeward. They followed, wrote Talmadge, "in mournful silence."

At the wharf, "a prodigious crowd had assembled to witness the departure of the man who, under God, had been the great agent in establishing the glory and independence of these United States."

The climax of the day came quickly. Washington took his seat on the awaiting barge. Recalled Talmadge also, "and when out in the stream, our great and beloved General waved his hat and bid us a silent adieu."

Soldier and Observer

Leaving New York with the British on November 25, 1783, was Johann von Ewald, one of the seventeen thousand Hessians—and thirty thousand German troops in all—who fought the American rebels on behalf of the British during the Revolutionary War. Serving in the Hessian Field–Jaeger Corps from October 1776 on, Captain Ewald distinguished himself in a number of ways; his was the lead unit in the British flanking movement against George Washington at Brandywine Creek; and he led the British occupiers into Philadelphia in the same fall of 1777. Usually fighting on horseback, he also appeared at Monmouth in 1778, at Charleston in 1780, with Benedict Arnold in Virginia, also in 1780, and with Cornwallis at Yorktown in 1781.

Paroled after the Yorktown surrender, he recovered from a nearly terminal illness and was allowed to tour West Point with General Henry Knox as his host.

All well and good, but Ewald's real fame came only after he returned to his native Kassel, Germany, in 1783. He was soon widely recognized as an expert on light infantry tactics. He gained fame also from his 1785 *Essay on Partisan Warfare.*

A commoner by birth, he was destined to end life as a "noble," thanks not to his Hessian compatriots, but to Denmark. Apparently unhappy at his lack of promotion at Kassel, he resigned and joined the Danish army, where he vaulted from his onetime Hessian captaincy to the rank of lieutenant general by the time of his retirement in 1813. In the interim, he helped Denmark to remain neutral in the Napoleonic Wars and fought with bravery and distinction once events forced the Danes into Napoleon's camp. The Danes were so pleased with Ewald, they granted him nobility in 1790.

He died of dropsy at his estate near Kiel in June of 1813, still a national hero to the Danes. His name, though, would achieve enduring new fame in the twentieth century, thanks to the publication of his Revolutionary War diary in 1948 . . . thanks, in turn, to the efforts of translator-historian Joseph P. Tustin, who located all four volumes of the eighteenth-century, first-person account after World War II.

That war, incidentallly, was not so kind to the onetime Jaeger captain's earthly remains—blown up when Allied bombs fell upon the Kiel Cemetery in the last months of the war.

The Word Did Spread

SIR HENRY CLINTON, COMMANDER OF His Majesty's forces in America, first heard the grim news of Yorktown on the deck of a wooden ship not all that far away from the recent action. Likewise for Admiral Thomas Graves, in command of the fleet carrying Clinton's relief force and approaching the entrance to the Chesapeake Bay just days after the Yorktown debacle. Loyalists coming out to meet the fleet in small boats conveyed the bad news.

By the time the fleet turned and sailed back to New York, Cornwallis had dispatched a written communiqué to his superior Clinton informing him of the surrender. The Cornwallis dispatch was waiting for Clinton when he reached New York.

France would learn the news before England, incidentally. Apparently a visitor from Paris first brought the news to London on November 25, weeks after the surrender of October 19, 1781. A captured American privateer, now the HMS *Rattlesnake,* arrived in London later the same day with the official word from Admiral Graves. He had written his dispatches for London aboard ship just off the entrance to the Chesapeake.

Even in 1781, the prime minister's office was at the 10 Downing Street address so well known today. Lord George Germain, secretary for American Affairs, now hurried there to inform Lord North of the stunning setback. And the prime minister was stunned. "Oh God," he said. "Oh God, it is all over, it is all over!"

King George III at first refused to acknowledge the disaster. Addressing Parliament the next day, he never mentioned Yorktown. He then wrote Lord North a note saying that with the proper measures taken, "a good end may yet be made to this war."

That, of course, never happened. In several months' time, Germain, chief proponent of the government's ill-fated American policies, was gone . . . dumped. Lord North insisted on resigning against the king's wishes . . . after persuading George III not to abdicate the throne in his own distress over the American failures. Thus, it was a new government that would begin to negotiate a peace treaty with the victorious Americans in 1782.

Casualties

IT DID NOT GO EASY. Of the estimated 200,000 American men under arms during the eight-year Revolutionary War, both militia and Continental Army, 25,324 were lost forever . . . but not all of them in the war's 1,331 land battles and seafights. Of those who died of war-related causes, 6,284 were killed outright in battle, while another 10,000 (at least) died of diseases, with smallpox and dysentery leading the list. Another 8,500 men, more unnecessarily, died as prisoners.

Among the figures also reported by Thomas Fleming in his book *Liberty! The American Revolution* were percentages—12.5 percent of the American men under arms died, a figure second among American wars only to the 13 percent lost to the Union side during the American Civil War.

The Revolution also was second only to the Civil War in the ratio of deaths to general population. The future nation's population in the 1770s was 2,640,000 whites and blacks. As Fleming reported, "The Revolutionary dead represented 0.9 percent of the American population." By contrast, the cost in the Civil War was 1.6 percent of the country's population. By contrast again, the ratio of deaths to population during World War II was 0.28.

Incidentally, New Jersey led all future states in the number of engagements fought, with 238 battles and skirmishes of various size fought on its soil. New York came next, with 228.

Hero of Another Revolution

TADUESZ (AMERICANIZED TO THADDEUS) KOSCIUSZKO, the Polish-Lithuanian engineer who designed the defenses of West Point and the American positions at Saratoga, later served with Nathanael Greene during his Southern campaign. One highlight of the Pole's work with Greene was his design of amphibious wagons—with their wheels and axles fully detachable, they became flat-bottomed boats that enabled Greene to cross the rivers in his path as he retreated before Cornwallis in the "Race to the Dan (River)" of early 1781. After the war, Kosciuszko was a founder of the Society of the Cincinnati.

The most dramatic days of Kosciuszko's life still lay ahead when he returned to Poland in 1784—the minor nobleman soon was a military and revolutionary leader as Poland tried to throw off the yoke of Russian rule. Granting freedom to the Polish serfs and gathering the support of virtually all social classes, he briefly served as a "benevolent dictator," noted David Zabecki in *The American Revolution, 1775-1783.*

After achieving significant victories over the Russians in two campaigns for Polish independence, however, Kosciuszko was severely wounded and taken prisoner. "The Third Partition of Poland followed in 1795," wrote Zabecki, "and Poland disappeared from the map for the next 123 years."

Released by the Russians after two years of captivity, the now-crippled Kosciuszko revisited the young United States, where the enthralled and still-thankful citizens of Philadelphia "unhooked the horses from his carriage and drew it through the streets by hand—a gesture they were to repeat for Lafayette a few years later."

After more years of lobbying—and fruitlessly pining—for the Polish cause, the hero moved to Switzerland, where he died in 1817. But he would not be forgotten—as one monument to his memory, the citizens of Krakow built a 150-foot hill from soil taken from "all of his Polish and American battlefields." At West Point, Cadet Robert E. Lee was one of the organizers in the cadet-funded effort establishing a Kosciuszko monument—the first monument erected at the new American Military Academy.

Settling Down

STILL RELATIVELY YOUNG, THIS HARD-FIGHTING Briton went home after Yorktown to a hero's welcome, a continued military career, election to Parliament, partnership in a gambling club, a life of womanizing and drinking—with future King George IV of England among his drinking pals—and a tempestuous, fifteen-year love affair with a woman writer who would make him a thinly disguised figure in a popular novel. But "Bloody Ban," the widely hated Banastre Tarleton, finally settled down in his middle age with a younger wife, became a full general and knight, contracted the gout, and lived out his life in quiet retirement in Shropshire.

Blanket from Bunker Hill

ONLY NINETEEN WHEN THE CONTINENTAL Congress appointed him a major general (unpaid) in 1777, the Marquis de Lafayette still had a lifetime—and a new career or two—ahead of him when he returned to France after the successful conclusion of the American Revolution.

Still pending were: the French Revolution; a mix of political and military roles; five years to be spent as a captive of his country's enemies; an up-and-down relationship with Napoleon, emperor of the French; and a triumphant return to the newly formed United States in his later years.

Back in France, the "hero of two worlds" had inherited a large estate in Brittany, but he and young wife Adrienne chose to live in a mansion on today's Rue de Lille in Paris. Despite his great wealth and prestigious social position, close to King Louis XVI, Lafayette soon showed himself to be an apostle for liberal reforms in the very foundations of French society and government.

The country's finances had been so sapped by the recent military adventure in America that the king turned to the traditional Assembly of Notables for solutions. At that point, Notables-member Lafayette shocked his peers by calling for establishment of a truly democratic parliament, or "National Assembly," diluting the age-old dominance of the nobility and clergy. He would allow Protestants new religious liberties, tax the rich, and help the poor.

None of this was talk expected of a court favorite, and much of it was reaction to his experiences in America . . . in the recent Revolution.

As events turned out, with a push or two from Lafayette, France was teetering on the edge of her own revolution. And in the volcanic tumult that erupted in 1789, Lafayette, commander of the newly created National Guard, briefly emerged as one of the country's most powerful figures. In 1790, on the first anniversary of Bastille Day, the still-young Frenchman led a huge crowd of 300,000 on the Champ de Mars in Paris in taking an oath of allegiance to "the nation, the law and the king."

That, however, was a high point in Lafayette's turbulent political career at home in France. Unwilling, or unable, to seize power himself, the idealistic and liberal Lafayette by 1791 had become an anathema both to the radicals and the conservatives tilting for control of France. Queen Marie Antoinette once was heard to say, "It would be better to perish than be saved by M. de Lafayette."

He found brief respite when war with England broke out in 1792—he commanded a field army in the Netherlands. But this military affair didn't go well and, worse, with a fresh uprising overthrowing the monarchy in mid-1792, Lafayette's troops refused his orders to quell the mob in Paris. Lafayette then fled the country . . . and promptly became a prisoner of the Austrians.

He would not be released until five years later—a release that finally came about as a result of pressure from American diplomats and Napoleon, the new military hero of France who had defeated the Austrians in his northern Italy campaigns. Even then, Lafayette didn't dare return to France until Napoleon took over the country's reins of power in late 1799.

Home once again in 1800, but now largely stripped of his former wealth, Lafayette refused to become an apostle of the new dictator of France; he turned down a diplomatic post in America and a senate seat in France. On the other hand, Lafayette did support Napoleon in the sale of Louisiana to the United States in 1803.

Once Napoleon passed from the scene after Waterloo in 1815, Lafayette, now elected to the Chamber of Deputies, became a leader in political opposition to the more repressive policies of the restored Bourbon monarchy.

After a sentimental, heart-tugging, and year-long tour of his beloved America in 1824 and 1825, Lafayette remained a political force in his own country—as a leader of the revolution of 1830 that dethroned the Bourbon king, Charles V. Still clinging to his longheld ideal of a constitutional monarchy for France, Lafayette supported the installation of Louis-Philippe as the new king . . . turning aside demands that he, himself, become president of a republican France.

Publicly regretting the latest king's lack of zeal for liberal reforms, Lafayette went to his grave in May of 1834 at age seventy-seven. He was active up to his death in the political life of his native country as a leader of the liberal opposition—and, finally, as an advocate of a full-scale republic.

He is buried in Picpus Cemetery in Paris under a blanket of dirt taken, fittingly enough, from America's own hallowed battleground, Bunker Hill.

Contributions Finally Recognized

AFTER THE REVOLUTION, AMERICAN NAVAL hero John Paul Jones bounced around Europe looking for work as an admiral-for-hire, and not always successfully. He was fired from the Russian navy by Catherine the Great, despite his defeat of the Turks in the Liman estuary on the Black Sea, a victory claimed by Russian Prince

Potemkin and French Prince Nassau-Siegen. Jones, forty-five years of age, finished out his life in 1792 as a near-pauper, living in a rented apartment in Paris. He was buried in a French cemetery with little notice or fanfare. Legend holds that the American minister to France, Gouverneur Morris, was too busy hosting a dinner party to attend the funeral ceremony, arranged by the French. The naval hero's remains would stay in France until disinterred in 1905 and placed in a crypt at the U.S. Naval Academy in Annapolis. This time, there was a fitting ceremony, with President Theodore Roosevelt presiding and hailing the determination and heroism of John Paul Jones. Incidentally, the Scots-born navyman has been the subject of more than thirty biographies.

Two Who Rode

PAUL REVERE, LATER MADE IMMORTAL in Longfellow's famous poem *The Midnight Ride of Paul Revere,* had his ups and downs during the Revolution itself. Not long after alerting the Minutemen at Lexington, Massachusetts, the Boston silversmith engraved the official seal still used by the commonwealth of Massachusetts. He operated a gunpowder mill that helped supply his fellow Patriots, and he was given command of the harbor fort called Castle William.

He marched off to war with the John Sullivan forces futilely challenging the British at Newport, Rhode Island, in 1778, and again in 1779, with the Massachusetts contingent dispatched to Penobscot Bay in future Maine in an effort to dislodge British forces establishing a new base on the bay.

The expedition was a disaster, and the Americans were scattered and forced to find their way back home through the wilderness of Maine. In the immediate aftermath, artillery officer Revere was relieved of command, under fire for alleged disobedience of orders, unmilitary behavior, and even cowardice. He returned to Boston under house arrest.

It would be nearly two years before a court-martial convened, but once exonerated on all counts, Revere put that unhappy episode behind him and continued to prove himself a man of many parts. Before the Revolution, he had served in the French and Indian War, taking part in the capture of Crown Point. An early Patriot, he had been a member of the Sons of Liberty, and he had taken part in the Boston Tea Party. Once the Revolutionary War began, he not only gave Massachusetts her seal, he also designed and printed the first Continental money.

In time, he invented a process for rolling sheet copper and operated a copper-rolling and brass-casting foundry near his powder mill in Canton, Massachusetts. His postwar activities included covering the dome of the new Massachusetts State House with copper leaf—and joining Governor Samuel Adams in laying the cornerstone for the same historic structure. Revere also provided the copper sheathing for the hull of the U.S. frigate *Constitution.*

His silverware still widely known and respected today, Revere more obscurely served as Boston's coroner and chief health officer for a time. He also founded an insurance company, Massachusetts Mutual Fire Insurance. No pun intended, he died in 1818 at age eighty-three, a *revered* Bostonian and hero of the Revolution.

An entirely different life awaited Jack Jouett of Virginia, sometimes called the "Paul Revere of the South" for his forty-mile nighttime ride in June 1781 to warn Thomas Jefferson that a British raiding party under Banastre Tarleton was on its way to Charlottesville in an effort to capture Jefferson, the outgoing governor of Virginia, and members of the rebel Virginia legislature, after all had been driven out of Richmond.

The husky young Jouett—six feet four if he was an inch—eluded Tarleton's dragoons the day of the raid (although Virginia legislator Daniel Boone did not and was held overnight in a coal cellar and paroled the following day). Jefferson, lingering at his mountaintop Monticello mansion until the last possible moment, also escaped Tarleton's clutches.

Tarleton's men, it must be said, were kind to Monticello—and they didn't know a Jefferson slave named Caesar was trapped for eighteen hours under the wooden floor of the portico with the family silver and other valuables he had been hiding moments before the British horsemen appeared on the mountaintop in search of Thomas Jefferson.

Other British units visiting Jefferson's Elk Hill plantation at Point of Fork (today's Columbia, Virginia), were far less reverential. They "trashed" this Jefferson property, burning crops and barns, carrying off some of the livestock, cutting the throats of young colts, even forcing helpless slaves into confinement with other slaves suffering from deadly smallpox—causing many additional deaths among the Jefferson slaves at Elk Hill.

But what about Jack Jouett? Westward-minded like fellow Albemarle County natives George Rogers Clark, William Clark, and Meriwether Lewis, Jouett soon headed for the frontier (in 1782) . . . the Kentucky Territory. Following Daniel Boone's Wilderness Road past Cumberland Gap and the Alleghenies, Jouett first settled in Mercer County in central Kentucky, then moved on to adjoining Woodford County in the Kentucky blue grass country.

On the trek west through the untrammeled wilderness of the day, it is said, Jouett was startled one day to hear a woman screaming in distress. Hurrying forward to a lone cabin in the woods, he found she was being beaten by her husband.

Leaping into the fray, he knocked down her consort-assailant, only to have the wife turn on him with a long-handled iron frying pan, which she brought down on his head with considerable force. So much force, in fact, that his head punched out the bottom of the pan leaving Jouett with an iron ring around his neck. He had to travel another thirty-five miles to find a blacksmith who could free him of his frying-pan necklace.

Later, Jouett served in the Virginia Assembly as a Kentucky settler and in Kentucky's own legislature when Kentucky became a state. Among his friends and associates was future President Andrew Jackson, even though Jouett was married to Sallie Robards, sister of Rachel Jackson's first husband, Lewis Robards.

Oddly, Jouett "was mainly responsible for the passage of an act [in the Virginia Assembly] authorizing the courts to determine whether grounds for divorce [of the Robards couple] existed," recalled Virginia newspaper editor and historian Virginius Dabney in an article for the *Ironworker* magazine of Lynchburg, Virginia (summer, 1966).

Apparently misinformed as to what the legislators had done, Jackson and Mrs. Robards then married—but she wasn't really divorced after all. Unhappily, the mixup and their seemingly hasty marriage led to wide criticism, insults, and duels.

Washington's Generals

THE CONTINENTAL CONGRESS GAVE GEORGE Washington a total of twenty-nine major generals and forty-four brigadiers during the Revolutionary War. Of the majors, six were dead by the end of the war in 1783, seven had resigned, and one, Benedict Arnold, had gone over to the enemy as a traitor. What fates awaited Washington's best-known officers?

- Only a short time was left for the man who probably was Washington's best—and favorite—general, Nathanael Greene, commander of the Southern campaign that brought Lord Cornwallis into Virginia and disaster at Yorktown, that subsequently reduced the remaining British outposts throughout the South, one by one.

  Greene briefly returned to his native Rhode Island after the war but soon ran into financial difficulties. His family foundry business had not done well in his absence, and he was stuck with the debts of a cheating army supplier in the South who died bankrupt. Selling out in Rhode Island, he moved south, to a departed Loyalist's estate, Mulberry Grove, a gift from the state of Georgia for his wartime services.

  Still struggling financially, he took ill one day in June 1786 after walking about a friend's rice plantation in the heat. Whether it was sunstroke, a heart attack, or a more commonplace stroke is unknown today, but Greene, only forty-four, died shortly afterward, leaving his wife, Kitty, a widow with five children to raise.

  A few years later, incidentally, their Mulberry Grove plantation would be the site at which Eli Whitney invented his revolutionizing cotton gin.

- William Alexander, otherwise known as the colorful, brave, and loyal "Lord Stirling"—and as a heavy drinker—wasn't well enough to join Washington in the march to Yorktown. He stayed behind as commander of the Northern Department of the Continental Army, was bedridden by Christmastime of

1782 and died on January 15, 1783, in Albany, New York, at age fifty-seven.

- New Hampshire's ramrod-straight General John Stark, a hero at Breed's Hill, victor in the Battle of Bennington, Vermont, and a key player at Saratoga as well, returned home to his farm and lived until 1822. When he died that year at age ninety-three, he may have been the last surviving general of the entire war.

- Controversial John Sullivan, also from New Hampshire, a combative lawyer, early member of the Continental Congress, and one of George Washington's earliest generals, resigned from military service in late 1779 and by 1780 was back in his congressional seat. Also active in politics back home, he would serve as president of post-revolutionary New Hampshire, and then as a federal judge appointed by his old commander in chief, President George Washington. Not always successful in battle, Sullivan by then was drinking to excess. In 1795, he would die young, at age fifty-five.

- Daniel Morgan, considered a brilliant, if untutored, battlefield tactician, French and Indian War veteran, a hero both at Saratoga and Cowpens, was forced into retirement before Yorktown by ill health, but bounced back to lead a light infantry corps from Virginia in Pennsylvania's Whiskey Rebellion of 1794. The "Old Wagoneer," as he liked to call himself, held a seat in the U.S. House in 1797, but retired two years later, again because of ill health. He died in 1802 at the age of sixty-six.

- British-born Charles Lee, once the second in command of American forces in the Revolutionary War, retired to his estate in future West Virginia after a court-martial stemming from his dismissal by Washington in the Battle of Monmouth, New Jersey. Never to command troops again, Lee died at age fifty-one in a visit to Philadelphia in 1782. Buried in that city's Christ Church cemetery, his remains possibly were obliterated or scattered during a later street-widening project.

- John Glover, of the Marblehead Mariners, a fisherman and community leader before the war, returned home after the hostilities and picked up where he left off, both in business and as a local judge and politician.

- Born in England, long an officer in the British army, and a survivor of General Edward Braddock's defeat at the hands of the French and their Indian allies in 1755, Horatio Gates, the victor at Saratoga, did not take up permanent residence in America until purchasing his six-hundred-acre "Travellers Rest" estate in future West Virginia in 1772, on the very eve of the Revolution.

    After Congress forgave his defeat at Camden, Gates returned home in March of 1783 to be by his dying wife Elizabeth Phillips Gates's bedside. Three years after she passed away, no longer in military service, he remarried, to wealthy heiress Mary Vallance. He briefly served as president of the Virginia branch of the Society of the Cincinnati, then with his second wife moved to Manhattan Island, where he died in 1806 after a lingering illness, at age seventy-eight. Like Declaration signer Francis Lewis of New York, Gates was buried in the graveyard at Trinity Church at the top of Wall Street. Like that of signer Lewis, too, the American general's actual gravesite no longer is known today.

- A particularly sad end awaited Henry "Light-Horse Harry" Lee in the postwar years, despite his service as governor of Virginia and a U.S. House member. In charge of the army sent to suppress the Whiskey Rebellion, the onetime commander of Lee's Legion of cavalrymen suffered the humiliation of a year spent in debtors prison, was beaten and disfigured by an angry mob in Baltimore, then felt constrained to rebuild his health in Barbados, leaving his family behind in Virginia. After five years, he was on his way back home when he fell ill aboard ship, was taken ashore on Cumberland Island, Georgia, and died there at age sixty-two. His son, only eleven at the time, was Robert E. Lee, of Civil War fame.

    It was Light-Horse Harry Lee, incidentally, who promulgated that famous epitaph to George Washington, "First in war, first in peace, and first in the hearts of his countrymen."

- Perhaps the most bizarre fate awaiting any of the American military leaders was that of Henry Knox who, after serving as secretary of war under the "Confederation" government, continued in that post in the Washington administration under the newly adopted United States Constitution. He ended his twenty years of public service—both military and govern-mental—in 1794 and retired to his "Montpelier" estate in Maine. Like many of his wartime contemporaries, he then struggled to keep various creditors at bay, in part because of his own speculative risk-taking. He and wife Lucy produced twelve children, but only three lived beyond childhood. Still tall and portly, Knox, fifty-six, died suddenly in 1806—per-haps due to a burst appendix or from swallowing a chicken bone.

• Another to meet a sad and inappropriate end was George Rogers Clark, the hero of Vincennes—an alcoholic in his final years, stroke victim, and amputee (a leg). He was dead in 1818 at age sixty-five. "The mighty oak of the forest has fallen," said eulogizer Judge John Rowan, "and now the scrub oaks sprout all around."

Financing a Banquet

ANOTHER HERO OF THE REVOLUTION to be stalked by poverty and ill-for-tune was Friedrich von Steuben, the Prussian drillmaster who had brought order and real military training into the restless ranks of Continentals wintering at Valley Forge in early 1778. His lack of funds became evident as early as Yorktown, but first he had to settle an affair or two of "honor."

At Yorktown, where he and Lafayette each commanded an American division, the two foreign-born leaders fell into dispute over whose division should be in charge of the trenches at the time of the British surrender. Shouldn't the honor go to Lafayette, whose men were in the trenches when the British sent forth a flag of truce the morning of October 17, 1781? Or should the honor go to Steuben, whose men relieved Lafayette's in the trenches at noon on October 17, then refused to make way for Lafayette's division when normal rotation would have placed the Frenchman's troops back in the trenches? It was Washington who decided the fierce little baron's division could have the honor of occupying the trenches the afternoon of October 19, when the British marched out of Yorktown to surrender.

In another contretemps involving the feisty baron, the Pennsylvania troops of Colonel Richard Butler filed into the vacated British trenches on the day of the surrender to take charge of the entrenchments. This meant planting the regimental colors in a conspicuous spot as symbol of the changeover. The flag was carried by a young ensign at the head of the column—he was supposed to place it on top of the British earthworks, but Steuben seized the staff from him and planted it himself. Butler was so furious they almost settled the matter with a duel.

After the surrender ceremony came a series of dinners hosted by the victors at Yorktown, with the ranking British officers often appearing as guests. Steuben, though, was so short of funds he sold his best horse to raise money and still had to borrow from a friend to put on a banquet of his own. "We are constantly feasted by the French without giving them a bit of bratwurst," he complained at one point. "I will give one grand dinner for my allies, should I eat my soup with a wooden spoon forever after."

Before he could leave Yorktown on November 1, the apparently penniless Steuben asked Washington himself for a loan. "Strongly moved," said Burke Davis in his book *The Campaign That Won America,* the commander in chief gave his old drillmaster twenty guineas and warned that Congress might not ever pay all that it owed for his services.

Steuben insisted on giving a sick aide his carriage and half the Washington loan before leaving Yorktown. The Prussian then hit the road for Philadelphia "with a single gold coin in his pocket." While he would seek—and eventually win—government compensation for his services to the Revolution, it wasn't, as Washington had warned, the full amount due. He should have been awarded $8,500 in cash, reported historian Davis, but instead Steuben received only $1,700.

The balance was paid, added Davis, "in the form of a Treasury Certificate at 6 percent interest—which the Baron later tried in vain to sell at ten cents on the dollar."

Even then, he lost his money to unwise land speculations. In receivership at one point, he had to mortgage 16,000 acres of land presented to him by the state of New York. He won an annual pension of $2,500 from the first Constitutional Congress, but that sum failed to end his indebtedness.

The former inspector general of the Continental Army was living in a two-room log cabin when he died of a stroke in late 1794 at age sixty-four. His "blue book," or training manual for American soldiers, remained in use for many years. He was a cofounder of the Society of the Cincinnati and an early proponent of the U.S. Military Academy, which came into being at West Point in 1802.

A Legend Grows

PILING LEGEND UPON LEGEND FOR the rest of his long life was Daniel Boone, frontiersman, scout, and Virginia legislator captured by Banastre Tarleton in his raid on Charlottesville, Virginia, in 1781. Even earlier, in 1778, Boone had been captured by Shawnee Indians on the Lower Blue Licks off the Licking River in Kentucky, but, typical of this larger-than-life figure, had escaped four months afterward. He would survive additional encounters with the British and Indians on the distant frontier as he fought in the last battles of the Revolution. Long after the war, he would remain a hunter, explorer, and frontiersman extraordinaire.

He lost two sons to Indian conflicts, but he was no Indian-hater; he, in fact, was "adopted" by the Shawnee.

After the war, the great pathfinder continued his treks into the western lands beyond the Alleghenies. He briefly served as a Virginia legislator for a second time; would lose his claims to as much as a million acres in the onetime wilderness lands for lack of the proper paperwork under newly enacted laws; would be robbed of $50,000 in cash he was carrying on behalf of fellow frontier homesteaders, then sell most of his remaining land to pay them back.

Throughout his adult life, Boone was in and out of financial difficulties, but he persevered as a wandering explorer, trapper, and woodsman until old age forced him to stay close to home. Before that, at age seventy-two, he encountered a grizzly bear, but managed to escape into his dugout.

He moved his family to Missouri in 1799, saying that the still sparsely populated Kentucky territory had become "too crowded." Late in life, he lost his wife, Rebecca, who had borne their ten children. Seven years later, just short of his eighty-sixth birthday, Daniel Boone also died, his coffin resting next to his deathbed. His remains (and Rebecca's) were disinterred from their Missouri resting place in 1845 and carried back to Frankfort, Kentucky, for burial there . . . but rumor later arose to suggest that the remains in Daniel's grave were not really his.

Back to England

AMONG THE BRITISH, MEANWHILE, LORD Cornwallis returned home to greetings as a hero . . . after blaming Sir Henry Clinton and the Royal Navy for the surrender at Yorktown. Cornwallis, only forty-two at the time of his defeat, later distinguished himself in dealing with rebellion in Ireland, in British campaigns in India, and as governor-general of the sub-Continent, where he died in 1805 at the age of sixty-six.

The British general who did take much of the blame, fairly or unfairly, was Sir Henry Clinton, who had ordered Cornwallis into Tidewater, Virginia, in June of 1781 to build a naval base. It was Cornwallis, though, who chose the Yorktown site.

After the surrender in October, Clinton, true to his petulant and complaining nature, visibly found fault with the government in England. It wasn't long—May 1782—before Clinton was replaced as the head of the British forces in America by Sir Guy Carleton. Clinton returned home to find he was considered a chief villain among those blamed for the debacle in the former colonies. Out of favor for some years, he recouped much of his lost ground by the 1790s, winning reelection to Parliament, rising to full general and, in 1794, becoming governor of Gibraltar. He died the next year at the age of sixty-five.

British Admiral Sir Thomas Graves, who failed to relieve Cornwallis by sea, also lost favor as a result, served for a time in the Caribbean, and wasn't recalled to England for nearly a year. When finally ordered home, he sailed on a ship that sank from damage suffered in a storm off Nova Scotia. Rescued after several hours spent in a small boat, he spent the next six years in a naval limbo—promotions, but no commands at sea. He finally redeemed his reputation by his actions against the French in 1794 as second in command of the British Channel Fleet—wounded in the same battle, known as the "Glorious First of June," he saw no further active service.

After losing the Battle of Saratoga in 1777, "Gentleman Johnny" Burgoyne returned to England in 1778 as a prisoner of war on parole. He never did return to America, but instead pursued a career in Parliament and as a playwright. Indeed, he attended a theatrical performance the night before he died after a bad attack of the gout in 1792 at the age of seventy.

Returning to bristling criticism in London in 1778 from the still-powerful Lord Germaine and his followers was General Sir William Howe. Victorious in most of his battles against the Americans, Howe was faulted on two counts.

First, he too often failed to follow up his victories with a final, crushing blow. Allowing Washington to evacuate his entire army after the Battle of Long Island was the prime example. Second, Howe was supposed to have moved up the Hudson River early enough in the summer of 1777 to support General Burgoyne's Canadian-launched expedition into upper New York, but Howe was more interested in pursuing Washington's small army in New Jersey and Pennsylvania. Howe finally settled for taking Philadelphia, the rebel capital, and wintering there . . . and never did go to Burgoyne's help.

Scolded in dispatches from Germaine for the failure to help Burgoyne, among other faults, Howe resigned and returned to England in the summer of 1778. He spent some time defending himself in a Parliamentary inquiry and publishing an account of his activities in America. In 1782, as a signal that he still enjoyed the king's favor, he was named lieutenant general of the Ordnance—later becoming a full general. He retired from the military in 1803, and died in 1814 at the age of eighty-five.

Finally, there was Thomas Gage, the first of the Revolutionary

War's British generals to be ordered home in disfavor for lack of success in suppressing the Colonials. Historically, too, Gage often is the scapegoat accused of triggering the war by sending his men to Lexington and Concord. To the contrary, Gage was only following orders from his superiors in England to take forceful steps against the rebels, in the expectation that the restless colonies would then fall into line.

Married to an American woman, Gage was understanding of, if not totally sympathetic with, the colonial grievances. Convinced the Amerians would fight, he was caught between the rioting radicals on the one hand and a distant government calling for tougher measures on the other. He walked the proverbial tightrope trying to keep the two factions at peace with each other, but in the end felt constrained to obey orders from home. He acted as instructed, fully aware that he and his 3,500 troops in Boston faced a more and more rebellious populace of 400,000 in Massachusetts alone.

Known more for his administrative and political abilities than for aggressive command in battle, Gage was called home later in 1775, not long after Major Generals William Howe, Henry Clinton, and John Burgoyne arrived in Boston to prosecute the war against the Americans in the field. Thomas Gage and wife Margaret Kemble of New Jersey spent the rest of their years rather quietly in England, with Gage reaching the rank of full general before he died in 1787 at age sixty-six or so. His widow, the mother of their eleven children (ten of them born in America), lived to age ninety before she died in 1824.

"Old Hickory"

AS IS WELL KNOWN, THE teenage Andrew Jackson, who barely survived smallpox and capture by the British, grew up to become hero of the Battle of New Orleans in the War of 1812 and seventh president of the United States. Always hotheaded, Jackson worked his way up to the pinnacles of his adult career on what is a now-traditional political ladder . . . but with notable and strictly nontraditional personal scrapes along the way.

Early in his career as an attorney in Tennessee, he challenged a rival lawyer to a duel for the latter's remarks in court one day. They only fired their pistols into the air, which was fortunate for the rival, considering that Jackson in later duels (usually over his wife Rachel's honor) would shoot to kill—in one case kill—and in two other duels would suffer gunshot wounds.

He once exchanged gunshots with John Sevier, a leader of the over-the-mountain men who had fought the Battle of King's Mountain during the Revolution. The popular Sevier would be Tennessee's first governor, a post he would hold for six terms. Jackson another time challenged Sevier to a duel and threatened to "cane" him.

After that, their rivalry quieted down. In the meantime, Jackson's pathway to the White House took him to the U.S. House of Representatives, the U.S. Senate, the Tennessee Supreme Court, a major generalship for the Creek War and the War of 1812, and the governorship of Florida. "Old Hickory" was twice elected president, in 1828 and 1832. He then retired to his beloved estate, "The Hermitage," outside Nashville, Tennessee. His and Rachel's onetime home remains open to the public today as one of the nation's most frequently visited historic mansions.

George Washington *"in Extremis"*

JEFFERSON, MADISON, AND WASHINGTON WERE all sick at one time, but it was President Washington himself who was in the worst shape of all . . . who would soon be at death's door.

Abigail Adams was also ill, as was her son Charles.

It was May of 1790, and the flu was on the rampage throughout Manhattan Island, temporary federal capital of the United States.

Thomas Jefferson was only suffering from a migraine, but Congressman James Madison was in bed at a boarding house on

Maiden Lane with the flu. That seems to have been Abigail's problem, and perhaps her alcoholic son's, as well.

At 39 Broadway, the Macomb House, on Sunday May 9, Washington stayed indoors writing letters while battling a "cold." But it turned quickly into "a potentially fatal combination of influenza and pneumonia," reported historian Richard Norton Smith in his book *Patriarch: George Washington and the New American Nation.* By Monday the tenth, " The fifty-eight-year-old President was fighting for his life, and straw was laid on the Broadway pavement to dull the sound of passing carriages."

Blessed with an iron constitution, Washington earlier in life had withstood bouts with smallpox and dysentery, both of them killer diseases, plus a childhood episode of pulmonary disease that left him with a "sunken" chest. At six foot three and roughly two hundred pounds, he otherwise was a magnificent specimen of manhood, his well-being enhanced by an active, energetic, and physically challenging life. Even so, as he advanced in years and commanded his men in time of severe stress, accentuated by the physical hardships of military campaigning, he suffered violent headaches; he contended with the ague, various fevers, the aching of rheumatism, the constant pain of ill-fitting dentures, and "excruciating surgery for a large tumor on his thigh." In that instance, just a year before he fell ill at the Macomb House, the freshly inaugurated—and surprisingly fatalistic—president had told his civilian aide David Humphries, "I know it is very doubtful whether I shall ever rise from this bed, and God knows it is perfectly indifferent to me whether I do or not."

Now, for the crisis of May 1790, First Lady Martha took up her vigil at her husband's bedside on the second floor of their four-story residence, built only three years earlier for New York merchant Alexander Macomb and now considered New York's "grandest address." Located on Broadway below Trinity Church and fairly close to Federal Hall, it suited the presidential couple quite well for its rental fee of $1,000 per annum.

The government had spent $10,000 refurbishing the house after the previous tenant, French Ambassador Comte de Moustier, returned to France. Washington himself financed a new washhouse and "stables to accomodate six Virginia grays and as many milk-white horses to pull the presidential chariot on occasions of state," reported historian Smith in *Patriarch.* A luxury accommodation for its era, the Macomb House boasted "glass doors at the rear leading to a balcony overlooking the swift Hudson River and Jersey shore beyond."

For all that, it wasn't an entirely restful setting for the terribly ill man upstairs, where a watchful Martha Washington sat by the hour knitting and turning away all visitors.

Not entirely restful? "From outside his window," explained Smith, "urban sounds hammered on Washington's brain. Maddening cowbells announced the daily trek north by herds penned on Wall Street. Mingled with the shuffling sounds of the cattle were the sharp cries of vendors peddling straw, hickory wood, and steaming yellow corn. Chimney sweeps out at daybreak left their verbal calling card: 'Sweep ho! from the bottom to the top, with a ladder or a rope, sweep, ho!' Congressmen complained of being unable to hear their own oratory for the street traffic outside Federal Hall, at the intersection of Wall and Broad streets, while the bleating of animals interrupted sessions of the Supreme Court, meeting over a farmers' market in the Royal Exchange building."

As the week progressed, with the patient only sinking further into his fever and labored breathing, the dismaying word went out. *The president! The president is dying!*

His aides sent for an additional doctor, the famous surgeon John Jones of Philadelphia . . . not long from a dutiful stand at Benjamin Franklin's deathbed. For the moment, his treatment steps unknown today, Jones could only apply his ministrations, then watch and wait with all the Washington household members and fellow physicians attending the president.

Four more days passed, and by May 15, "less than a week after his first symptons were reported, Washington was *in extremis.*"

A visiting farmers' lobbyist from Pennsylvania innocently dropped by and found "a household in tears." That was nearly a week after Washington stayed home to pamper his cold. One of the doctors on hand told the visitor that Washington's death was near.

Fearing the worst, Secretary of State Thomas Jefferson soon appeared. As he later reported, however, about four o'clock in the afternoon, "a copious sweat came on." Washington's fever was finally breaking! ". . . [A]nd in the course of two hours it was evident he had gone thro' a favorable crisis."

By the next day, Jefferson was able to record also, Washington was recovering after all—"Indeed, he is thought quite safe." Weak at first, Washington indeed did recover fully. He served out his initial term as president; he then served a second term before finally retiring to Mount Vernon one last time.

For Washington and his newborn nation, it had been a close brush with disaster. As Jefferson said later, "You cannot conceive the public alarm on this occasion. It proves how much depends on his life."

By the time Washington did die, nearly ten years later, the nation he did so much to create was beyond its infancy. Under the stewardship of a second president, John Adams, young America was preparing to move its seat of government—from Philadelphia by now—to its final and permanent home in Washington, D.C. George Washington's death at that time certainly did matter, but it probably would have had a much greater and perhaps even dangerous impact upon the stability of the new nation had it come about during his first term as the nation's first president.

When George Washington did die at the end of 1799, his death was blamed upon a respiratory illness that again began as a cold, apparently contracted while riding about his beloved Mount Vernon plantation on a wet and chilly December day.

What's in a Name?

ONE HUNDRED AND TWENTY-ONE POST offices strewn across the land; nine colleges; seven mountains; ten lakes; eight streams; thirty-three counties; one state; the nation's capital city, and who knows how many streets, avenues, boulevards, byways, and highways in America today all share the same common denominator—all are named Washington, for George, Father of His Country.

Last Gasp

SHE WAITED AND WAITED FOR the return of her war-hero husband for many years ... unsure that he could come back. Eventually, with the passage of so much time, it became obvious he would be one of the last to come home.

She waited and she tried to go on with a normal life. A member of New York's prominent and wealthy Livingston family, she counted one brother as a delegate to the Continental Congress and secretary of foreign affairs and another as a colonel in the Continental Army. Still another, far younger, would be secretary of state under Andrew Jackson. And all were fathered by Judge Robert R. Livingston.

Into this brood in the early 1770s came Richard, raised in Ireland as the son of a member of Parliament. He grew to become a British officer of proven valor and veteran of the Seven Years' War. He later immigrated to the colonies and soon became a zealous convert to the American cause. Arriving in New York in late 1772 and establishing himself as a gentleman farmer at King's Bridge just north of the city, Richard renewed an acquaintance begun when he was stationed in New York for two years during the previous decade.

She was Janet Livingston, and less than a year later, in July of 1773, they became man and wife. For her, she once wrote with surprising frankness for their era, he became "husband, friend and lover." With him, she found "my every hope of happiness."

In the two years before the Revolutionary storm broke over the American colonies, she said further, she came to know "the feast of reason and the flow of soul." As rebellion built around them, however, she had bad dreams. She dreamt he was killed in a sword fight with his brother, and Richard's last words to her were, "No other way, no other way."

She told him about the dream, and he said he knew his happiness could not last. "Let us enjoy it as long as we may," he said, "and leave the rest to God." He brushed aside her expressed wish to have a son. Perhaps in jest, perhaps not, he said: "Be contented, Janet. Suppose we had a son, and he was a fool. Think of that!"

With the storm clouds now darkening, he became a member of the New York Provincial Congress. Then, in June of 1775, the Continental Congress appointed him a brigadier general—one of the first eight American brigadiers. Were the bad dreams coming to fruition? When he told her and gave her a black ribbon to attach to his hat as a cockade, she later said, "I felt a stroke at my heart as if struck by lightning."

He said honor and duty to the cause called him, but she still could hold him from going if she insisted. "Say you will prefer to see your husband disgraced and I submit to go home to retirement," he offered.

Naturally, it was an offer she could not take.

And so he went north in 1775. Plans were made and remade. Suddenly it was he, General Richard Montgomery, who would lead the American invasion of Canada.

They had a last meeting in Saratoga, New York, before he marched off with his troops. His last words to her were, "You shall never blush for your Montgomery."

He and his men soon stormed Fort Chambly, Fort St. Johns, and Montreal, but Quebec still loomed as the most difficult conquest of all. By now, toward the end of 1775, Benedict Arnold and his surviving men had emerged from their starvation march northward through the Maine wilderness.

Even so, the Americans didn't have the numbers to make an assault easy. Indeed, when reminded that Quebec still lay ahead as the real key to conquering the British in Canada, General Richard Montgomery told his brother-in-law and fellow Continental officer Henry Beekman Livingston, "Oh, Harry, that is impossible."

Impossible or not, the attempt had to be made quickly, before the enlistment period for most of his troops expired at the end of the year. And so it was made early on the morning of New Year's Eve, December 31, 1775, with the hope that a bold and direct assault would take the British by surprise.

Of the two generals who led the Americans and fell in the futile assault, the one who survived, as fate would have it, was Benedict Arnold. Richard Montgomery, promoted to major general as he approached Quebec, was the first American general officer killed in the war.

His death had impact on both warring sides. In Quebec, British officers who knew him, who had soldiered with him in the past, were among those according their former comrade a proper and decent burial. In London, Edmund Burke offered a stirring eulogy to Montgomery in Parliament, to which Prime Minister North replied that he could not join in the laments proclaiming Montgomery's death "a public loss."

Reacting prophetically, Lord North also said: "A curse on his virtues! They've undone this country. He was brave, he was noble, he was humane, he was generous, but still he was only a brave, able, humane and generous rebel."

This stirred fresh reactions in the House of Commons, with one-time Montgomery friend Charles James Fox declaring: "The term of rebel is no certain mark of disgrace. The great asserters of liberty, the saviors of their country, the benefactors of mankind of all ages, have all been called rebels."

While the British may have been of two minds over Montgomery's death, a symbolic tragedy at the early stages of the Revolution, there was no such division among his fellow Patriots in America. There, "commemorations, eulogies, and verse celebrated his union with the heroes of antiquity and called Americans to equal his ardor," wrote Charles Royster in his book *Revolutionary People at War.* Thomas Paine, for one, published a supposed dialogue between Montgomery's ghost and a faltering delegate to the Continental Congress in which the deceased hero's spirit argued for independence. Further, "When public spirit faltered later in the war, a call to arms in the newspapers was signed. 'THE GHOST OF MONTGOMERY'," noted Royster.

The widow Janet also figured in the song, rhetoric, poetry, and drama that picked up on the Montgomery story, Royster pointed out. Her friend and longtime correspondent Mercy Otis Warren, a well-known woman of letters in their era, used Montgomery's part-ing words to wife Janet in a history of the Revolution (Mercy Warren's *History of the Rise, Progress and Termination of the American Revolution*).

After the death of her husband ("my General, my soldier"), Janet Livingston Montgomery's life never would be the same. As her out-ward vestments, wrote Royster, she wore mourning to the end of her life. Inwardly, she also wore mourning without cease. Her loss, she once wrote, "always obtrudes itself let me begin with what I will and unfits me for every other Duty."

Always a strong supporter of the revolutionary cause (but a

caustic critic of certain surviving generals), she kept busy both during and after the Revolution. A frequent visitor to President and Mrs. George Washington during the New York residency, she also visited Montgomery's sister in Ireland, Lady Ranelagh.

After buying real estate in lower Manhattan, she began to build a mansion on the Hudson River above New York. "Chateau de Montgomery" was a showplace with a commanding view of the river below. "Her house had high ceilings, great windows, and stone walls two feet thick," wrote Royster.

It boasted a high peak in front of the house with a summit shaped like a bowl, he also noted. "Formerly called Liberty Cap, it became known to local people as 'Mrs. Montgomery's Cap,' in honor of the widow's cap she always wore."

She built her Hudson River mansion in 1802 and 1803, just as she was entering her sixties in age. Congress, in the meantime, back in 1776, had ordered a monument to her General, still buried in Canada. Benjamin Franklin arranged for it to be created by artisans in Paris, but the war naturally caused delays.

Finally, in 1787, it was erected at St. Paul's Church in New York City as the federal government's first such tribute to a hero of the Revolution. But the hero, himself, still had not come home.

Another three decades would pass before that day would come. In 1818, the General's remains were disinterred from their resting place in Quebec and started homeward, an event stirring parades, salutes, and in general "the most impressive public display" since Washington's death in 1799, said Royster.

As the steamboat *Richmond* made its way down the Hudson toward New York for the ceremonial reburial planned at the site of the St. Paul's monument, Janet Montgomery prepared for the culminating moment of her life as a widow. Told exactly what time on July 6 the steamboat would pass on the river below, she asked her guests to leave her while she watched with a spyglass from the riverside porch of Chateau de Montgomery.

The steamer, carrying her husband's remains in a "plumed coffin canopied with crepe" under star-spangled banners, came to a stop below while its band played Handel's Dead March from his *Saul* oratorio. Troops fired a salute, and after a long pause, the steamboat moved on—General Montgomery was close to his final home.

His widow later said she looked on the vessel below and

thought of how he had left her "in the bloom of manhood, a perfect being." And now, "Alas! how did he return!"

She would live on, into her eighties, long enough to dance with Lafayette in his tour of the United States in 1824. But did she ever know another moment like that of July 6, 1818, when her late husband at last was returning home . . . when her guests, going out on the porch after the steamboat had departed, found their hostess, his widow, had fainted?

What's in Another Name?

DURING AND IMMEDIATELY AFTER THE Revolution, many a newborn child was named for the hero Richard Montgomery. Later, at least sixteen counties throughout America were named for him, as were a number of cities—most conspicuously, one state's capital city, Montgomery, Alabama.

X. Select Founding Mothers

by Ingrid Smyer-Kelly

Preamble: "Who Can Be a Silent Spectator?"

LONG BEFORE THE REVOLUTION, MEN *and women* of the American colonies were forming ideas about political liberty. A proliferation of pamphlets, newspapers, even sermons, were exploring the history of political rights. Political writers were passionately concerned that cherished and long-standing political rights were being chipped away by the imperial Mother Country. That great rhetorical cry went out, later to be penned by Jefferson's Declaration, the notion that all men are created equal. But . . . what about the women?

"Are not women born as free as men?" The question was posed by colonial Massachusetts thinker James Otis, brother of Mercy Otis Warren and a leading Patriot, in the opening pages of his 1764 pamphlet, *The Rights of the British Colonies Asserted and Proved.* Many others privately conceded the woman's role extended far beyond the home, although that premise was not to become universally acceptable in America for another two centuries.

During the Revolutionary period, however, there were women who found ways to exert their influence on the great events unfolding before all, even if the same women did not always presume to reach very far beyond the domestic sphere. In their era, after all, neither the pulpit nor the policy-making stage was open to women.

Two thinking women whose power of the pen did reach farther than home and hearth were Mercy Warren and Abigail Adams, both extremely well read for their times, and both admirers of Catharine Macauley, the English historian who had dared to publish her own critiques of political philosophers Hobbes, Burke, and Rousseau.

Abigail's political thought found expression in letters to her husband and friends, many of them politically active male friends, although her letters were not published in her lifetime. In one letter, to husband John Adams in May of 1776, Abigail wrote in a plaintive vein concerning female citizenship: "To be adept in the art of Government is a perogative to which your Sex lay almost exclusive claim." And truly the all-male rebel legislators were not inclined to address the position of women in the proposed new order. Instead, women began to invent their own political character. As Linda K. Kerber points out in her book, *Women of the Republic: Intellect and Ideology in Revolutionary America,* it was a new political role that "merged the domestic domain of the preindustrial woman with the new public ideology of individual responsibility and civic virtue."

While Abigail Adams penned her political ideas in private correspondence, Mercy Otis Warren felt less constrained and used poetry and plays as means of expressing her ideas. Perhaps Mercy, as a writer as well as a wife and mother of four sons, felt that she could advise women as to both private and public responsibilities. In answering a friend who asked for advice on whether it was proper to discuss politics openly in her husband's presence, Mercy wrote, "I know not why any gentleman of your acquaintance should caution you not to enter any particular subject when we meet."

More safely, Mercy added that politics was a subject "much out of the road of female attention." But she was clear in her suggestion that even while maintaining their domestic responsibilities, sometimes women must attend to political matters. Political actions taken by the men, after all, could affect everyone . . . not just the men alone. "[A]s every domestic enjoyment depends on the decision of the mighty Revolutionary contest," she added, "who can be an unconcerned and silent spectator? Not surely the fond mother, or the affectionate wife who trembles lest her dearest connections should fall victims of lawless power, or at least pour out the warm blood as a libation at the shrine of liberty."

The fact is, a good many eighteenth-century women were well aware of the momentous events unfolding around them. They may not have been as visible and outspoken as Mercy Otis Warren, had the political "connections" of an Abigail Adams or, for that matter, had the nearly automatic influence of a Martha Washington, but they often were well informed about the headlong course of events, about the warring councils of government, even about the new political philosophies emerging from the pens or tongues of husbands, brothers, or fathers. All men, of course.

The fact is, too, a good many eighteenth-century women did enter the political arena—but through a variety of back doors, quite aside from whatever pleas or advice they poured into the ears of attentive (or, to be sure, sometimes inattentive) spouses. When the need arose, there was a virtual corps of these additional Founding Mothers who found ways to exert their will that ranged from overt petition and boycott, to covert trickery and spying, even appearance on the field of battle.

"I desire you would Remember the Ladies."
—*Abigail Adams to husband John, delegate to the*
Continental Congress, March 31, 1776

If the men we call Founding Fathers were busy fighting off the British and then reinventing government for the new nation they had secured, who were the Founding Mothers, and what did they do, actually?

To begin with, there were the obvious leaders: Martha Washington, Mercy Otis Warren, Abigail Adams. These and others of their ilk constituted a frankly elite circle of women who gave, gave, and gave yet again, just like their menfolk. Look carefully in the history books and you can find where there is occasional notation of their gallantry, their wisdom, their perseverance and, often, their plain old grittiness in time of peril.

Few trumpets sound for them these days, but there they are, real Founders of a nation also.

Nor were these elites alone. Many others, more on a sewing circle level, also could be considered Founding Mothers. That is to say, women like the "tea party" group in Edenton, North Carolina, who in October of 1774 openly signed their names to a resolution declaring they would boycott English tea and clothing. Instead of real tea, they drank a hot concoction derived from dried raspberry leaves. On a more individual basis, there were women like the famous Deborah Samson, who enlisted in the Continental Army disguised as a man.

Nor should we forget those forced to improvise with quick decisions, women like Hannah Israel, who saved the family's cattle herd from the British raiders one fateful day. The Israel farm on the banks of the Delaware River lay in full view of the moored British frigate *Roebuck*, where her husband and brother were being held captive. The British commander ordered his men to go ashore and drive the cattle from the family's meadow to the edge of the river and there to slaughter them before the eyes of their prisoners. Learning of the British intentions, the brave Hannah, with the help of a young boy, drove the herd into her barnyard amid the whistling balls fired by the British. Since the redcoats were loathe to invade private property in full view of various witnesses, her barnyard became a sanctuary. Not a single cow was lost!

There also were women, individuals, torn between love of their land and loyalty to the Mother Country—even between patriotism and fidelity to husbands who took a Loyalist stance quite different from their own. Elizabeth Graeme, daughter of prominent Dr. Thomas Graeme of Philadelphia, and granddaughter of a governor of Pennsylvania, was known in her own right for her literary accomplishments, among them a translation of the classic *Telemachus* into English verse. Soirees held at her home attracted literary and cultivated folk, and here on one of those evenings she met her future husband, Hugh Henry Fergerson, newly arrived from Scotland.

No sooner had they married than the Revolutionary War erupted. Choices had to be made—recent immigrant Fergerson chose to remain loyal to Great Britain, but his wife would be loyal to the land of her birth. They soon were separated. To complicate matters further, she tried to act as a go-between for the warring parties when the British occupied Philadelphia. But that effort at conciliation only won her rebuffs from the Patriot side as well as a cold reception from many of those who had once gladly partaken of her hospitality at her intellectual gatherings.

Still others had to face up to the enemy himself.

In April of 1781, British Colonel Banastre Tarleton was on the march from Wilmington, North Carolina, with his heart set on conquering Virginia. For several days he and his men were encamped on the grounds of a plantation in such a beautiful setting that Lord Cornwallis earlier had called it "Pleasant Green," the name by which it would be known. The master of the plantation, a Lieutenant Slocumb, commanded a troop of light horse raised in his own neighborhood to act as rangers, leaving Mrs. Slocumb in charge of the affairs of the plantation.

While she was enjoying a beautiful spring day sitting on the veranda of her magnificent home, a horseman rode up, tipped his hat, and greeted her with the question: "Is your husband at home?"

The spunky Mrs. Slocumb answered that he was not. The next question raised her dander. "Is he a rebel?"

Her answer rings down through the ages and exemplifies the courage of women who sustained the homefront: "No sir. He is in the army of his country, and fighting against our invaders; therefore not a rebel."

Despite her tart response, 1,100 of the choicest cavalry of the British pitched their tents on the grounds while Colonel Tarleton set up his headquarters in the grand mansion. Known for her hospitality, Mrs. Slocumb at the dinner hour set a feast before the royal officers, complete with dessert and peach brandy prepared earlier by the absent lieutenant. Amazed at the largess and beauty all around the grand plantation, one officer made the remark, "When we conquer this country, is it not to be divided out among us?"

To this affront the saucy Mrs. Slocumb answered, "The only land in these United States which will ever remain in possession of a British officer, will measure but six feet by two."

While we don't hear much of the Israel or Slocumb wives in most historical accounts of the Revolutionary period—and there were many women like them—most of us are at least dimly aware of the era's best-known women. They would be Martha, Mercy, Abigail, and, for the most part, their respective circles of close friends and associates. While almost every one of these women was the spouse of a famous man, they nonetheless acquired a mantle, an aura, of leadership by their own example and accomplishments.

Martha Dandridge Custis Washington

"GOD BLESS LADY WASHINGTON," SHOUTED the onlookers at Peck's Slip in New York City as she stepped off the gaily bedecked "President's Barge" together with a tall, stately man—the recently inaugurated president of the United States of America.

"Long live President Washington," the crowd also shouted.

Just minutes before, crossing over from Elizabethtown Point on the New Jersey shore, their forty-foot barge had been rowed by a symbolic thirteen oarsmen. While passing the Battery at the tip of Manhattan Island, the couple was treated to a thirteen-gun salute.

And all for Martha, since George had been inaugurated some weeks before this day in May of 1789.

Her long and arduous journey by coach and ferryboat from Virginia had been relieved by stopovers with friends and punctuated by greetings from well-wishers all along the way. Reporters in the crowd had followed Mrs. Washington's coach hoping for a glimpse of the grand lady, and one such eyewitness, impressed with her outfit, wrote in the *Daily Advertizer and Gazette* of Philadelphia, "She was clothed in the manufacture of our Country, in which her native goodness and patriotism appeared to the greatest advantage."

Fancy silks and frills and fashions from the Continent had been taboo during the war for the lady from Virginia. So much so that Martha's homey ways didn't always quite suit her public. On one such occasion, Mrs. Washington was with the General at his winter headquarters in Morristown, New Jersey, when several town ladies decided to pay a social call. A Mrs. Troupe later told the story: "So we dressed ourselves in our most elegant ruffles and silks, and were introduced to her ladyship. And don't you think we found her knitting and with a specked apron on!"

As if that were not enough, Mrs. Troupe also told a local minister, "She received us very graciously, and easily, but after the compliments were over, she resumed her knitting."

Obviously not one to put on airs, the lady from Virginia nonetheless always was quite comfortable in her role as supportive wife of her "General" (as she publicly called him), as a mother and grandmother, and as mistress of their plantation on the Potomac.

As the new nation's first First Lady in 1789, however, she would be negotiating uncharted waters—not even the newly approved Constitution gave any guidelines for the wife of the president. Even so, by education, background, and long exposure to the Revolutionary leadership, she well understood the historical significance of her new role and the precedents she would be setting.

Martha was born on June 21, 1731, to Colonel John Dandridge and Frances Jones on their plantation near Williamsburg. Her father was a wealthy tobacco planter who also served New Kent County as county clerk. Martha's mother came from a long line of clergymen and scholars. Washington biographer Douglas Southhall Freeman considered them "second tier" in the hierarchical society of colonial Virginia.

"Tier-ranking" aside, a teenage Martha made her debut into the blue-ribbon society of Williamsburg. And here she met Daniel Parke Custis, descended from two of the wealthiest families of Virginia. Colonel John Custis objected to his son's courtship of the young Martha, because he had hoped to see his son marry a wealthy cousin. But Martha quickly won the colonel over with her "amiable nature"—or, as some suggest, through her determination.

At the age of eighteen, Martha married Daniel and settled into his "White House" estate on the Pamunkey River. Four children were born to the couple, but two died in infancy. The surviving children, John Parke Custis and Martha Parke Custis, were always called by their pet names, "Jacky" and "Patsy."

Martha's husband died suddenly at the age of forty-five, leaving Martha, at age twenty-six, the wealthiest widow in the Old Dominion.

Less than a year later, legend has it, a handsome military hero on his way to Williamsburg made a hurried stop at a nearby ferry crossing to visit an old friend, a Major Chamberlayne. And here, as fate would have it, a certain young widow was also a guest. The military man and the fair lady met, and he who had been in such a rush to get to Williamsburg delayed his trip until the next day.

Whatever the true story of their first meeting, Martha and George did meet and the rest is history.

To begin their dramatic life together, Martha Custis and George Washington were married on the Twelfth Night after Christmas, January 6, 1759, at White House, her home on the Pamunkey, but it would not be until springtime that the bride would see her new home on another river, Mount Vernon on the Potomac. Little did she know even then, of course, that just upriver one day would appear a vast, almost magical city and national capital named for her new husband.

Thus began what have been called the golden years at Mount Vernon, years during which Martha was content with her domestic duties—priding herself on her ability to cure meat. "Virginia women value themselves on the goodness of their bacon," Washington once explained to a visiting Marquis de Lafayette, according to Joseph E. Fields, editor of the book, *"Worthy Partner": The Papers of Martha Washington*. And nephew Lund Washington, who managed the plantation during the Washingtons' absence, once said that Mrs. Washington's charitable gifts grew in direct ratio to her meat-house successes.

Martha and George had no children of their own but he was very fond of his two stepchildren, Jacky and Patsy, and by all accounts treated them as his own. More generally, Washington the gentleman farmer was the very picture of a happily married man. He, himself, wrote to a friend soon after his marriage, "I am now I believe fixd at this Seat with an agreeable Consort for life and hope to find more happiness in retirement than I ever experienced amid a wide and bustling World."

Their Mount Vernon home, as often was the custom for any fine house in those days, was a favorite stopping place for friends and family, a haven quite often for nieces and nephews in their youth. Both relatives and friends came and went, on occasion spending days or weeks with the happy couple—even in some cases becoming permanent members of the household.

George once offered his aging mother a home at the plantation, but with the warning that the activities there made it seem more like a "busy resort" than a place for privacy and quiet. She apparently took the warning seriously.

Swirling about this idyllic setting, however, were clouds of war. Talk of it was everywhere, and in the busy halls of Mount Vernon notable Patriots came and went.

The women, too, realized that their way of life was about to change—if nothing else, Martha and her friends soon were boycotting goods from England in silent protest to the policies of Parliament and King George III. Since the women of Martha's day couldn't fight or take the reins of political leadership, the boycott simply was the patriotic and effective approach to take. Martha's spinning wheels took on double duty. Sewing, knitting, whatever, her hands were never idle, as her Morristown visitors later would notice. Years later she would report to a friend that at Mount Vernon she often had sixteen spinning and carding machines going at once.

Before the hostilities openly broke out, the year 1773 brought the Washingtons both tragedy and joy. Patsy, never a hardy child, died suddenly in June during a seizure (probably due to epilepsy). That fall, son Jacky, a student at King's College in New York, expressed his desire to come home and to marry his sweetheart, Eleanor Calvert of Mount Airy, Maryland, a direct descendant of the first Lord Baltimore.

Both Jacky and "Nelly," as Eleanor was called, were still in their teens, and Jacky had only completed three months of his two-year course. Still, Martha, always indulgent with her son, acquiesced. The young couple was married the following February at the bride's home in Mount Airy. Martha, still in mourning for her daughter, declined to attend but penned a letter to her new daughter-in-law that revealed the depth of her feelings:

> Dear Nelly—God took from Me a Daughter when June Roses were blooming—He has now given me another daughter, about her Age when Winter winds are blowing, to warm my Heart again. I am as Happy as One so Afflicted and so Blest can be. Pray receive my Benediction and a wish that you may long live the Loving Wife of my happy Son, and a Loving Daughter of
>
> Your Affectionate Mother

Two years later, the Revolutionary storm in full sway, Martha would be saying the first of many farewells to her Virginia gentleman as he left their beloved Mount Vernon for the 1775 session of the Continental Congress in far-off Philadelphia. While she considered the outcome of his trip to be uncertain at best, it might have been a more fearful farewell on her part if she had known he was about to take command of the Continental Army for the duration of a prolonged, eight-year war.

Either way, having her man march off, either to Congress or war, was hardly the best wish of even the patriotic mistress of Mount Vernon, but she knew her duty to home and hearth—clearly she would abide by it. When there were rumors in 1775 that Virginia's royal governor, Lord Dunmore, might want to seize her as a prize hostage, she refused to be frightened away from Mount Vernon, although the mansion on the Potomac clearly would be vulnerable to raiders traveling by boat. Husband George wanted her to seek safety with family elsewhere. But Martha stayed home.

She did join him in Cambridge, Massachusetts, later in 1775, during the siege of Boston and again for a short time in New York the following spring and early summer. For the rest of the war period, it usually was when her General went into winter quarters that she packed her things and left Mount Vernon to the care of Lund Washington and his staff.

The first winter camp actually was at Cambridge on the outskirts of Boston. Here, Martha brightened the dreary camp life for all who knew her. She made many long-lasting friendships with other visiting officers' wives, too. She was especially fond of Lucia (Lucy) Knox, wife of General Henry Knox, and Mercy Otis Warren, wife of the local farmer-politician of note, James Warren—and a poetess and playwright who had gained notice in her own right.

Mercy Warren provided a vivid picture of the General's wife in a letter to her friend Abigail Adams that winter: "I will tell you I think the Complacency of her manners speaks at once the benevolence of her heart, and her affability, Candor and gentleness, qualify her to soften the hours of private life, or to sweeten the cares of the Hero, and smooth the rugged paths of War. . . ."

Others have suggested that Martha saved the Revolution by joining her General and his beleaguered men at Valley Forge the winter of 1777–1778. Her warm presence certainly did inspire the discouraged George, while the cheerful caregiving she offered his men in many cases provided the strength to persevere. As one small example of her willingness to help, she was evermore knitting socks for all—herself included.

Martha returned to Mount Vernon every spring to resume managing its affairs, but when the Continental Army again went into winter quarters, she once more would make the arduous journey to join her General and his men. Once again, she would oversee the care of the soldiers and set a social pace to brighten the long winter days. To think, however, that Martha Washington simply was a passive, nurturing, supportive wife to her husband and den mother to his men is to miss other elements of the picture. She also was privy to confidential military plans by virtue of her occasional secretarial services, and she was often by her husband's side when his officers and military advisers came for discussions.

His staff aides Pierre Etienne du Ponceau and Baron Von Steuben were among her many admirers, with Ponceau once comparing her to the matrons of ancient Rome. With every passing year "Lady Washington's" reputation grew. She soon became quite used to seeing her name in the newspapers, or hearing the fond nickname, "Lady Washington."

These were dramatic and emotional times, but not all the emotion was generated by the war itself. Most Americans have probably forgotten the unhappy shadow that dogged George Washington and his wife at the very moment of the General's triumph at Yorktown.

Behind the siege lines, the General's aide and adopted stepson "Jacky" fell ill with a camp fever that would prove mortal a few days later. A grieving George Washington later wrote that he arrived at the young officer's deathbed just "in time to see poor Custis breathe his last." Jacky's widow and four small children now became part of the Washington household—the younger two children in fact were adopted and raised by Martha and George.

With the surrender of Cornwallis at Yorktown in October of 1781, the war was essentialy over. But for the General and his "Lady" there was much yet to come.

He at last, in late 1783, could rejoin her at their beloved Mount Vernon, thus returning to the "bosom of the land of that country, which gave me birth," as Washington once phrased his greatest wartime wish. But the new bliss for the master and mistress of Mount Vernon would only last a few years before the Father of His Country would answer its call once more.

"I little thought when the war was finished," wrote Martha later, "that any Circumstances could possibly happen which would call the General into public life again. I had anticipated that, from that Moment, we should be suffered to grow old together, in solitude and tranquility."

How wrong she was! Just six years later, a new U.S. Constitution now in place, her General was the natural choice of his countrymen to serve as their first president. So it was that in April 1789 he stood before a crowd of ten thousand in New York City, the temporary federal capital, to take his oath of office. So it was, too, that Martha a few weeks later would journey northward herself and cross that same Hudson River from the Jersey shore to join her Founding Father-husband in another pioneering chapter of their lifetime together.

Abigail Smith Adams

THE WIFE OF FOUNDING FATHER and future President John Adams, mother of four children—one son, John Quincy Adams, also destined to become president—manager of family finances and farm, and life-long adviser to her husband, truly can take her place as a Founding Mother.

Abigail, the definitive letter-writer of the Revolutionary period, probably never dreamed that her letters to her husband, written from the start of a political career that carried him to such heights, would some day be read by others. And it is doubtful that she had any idea of the impact her volumes of personal letters would have on biographers and social historians. Yet it was her ability to take her thoughts to pen so succinctly and to pour out her emotions so endearingly that captures the imagination of her readers.

As wife of the second president and mother of the sixth president of the United States, she had the credentials to be included in the history books, but she is worth knowing in her own right. Her witty, intelligent, and sometimes lecturing letters open a window into her times, into her life at the center of the Revolution and the political events that followed. When a friend suggested in 1818 that her letters be published, her strong reply was, "No. No . . . Heedless and inaccurate as I am, I have too much vanity to risk my reputation before the public."

She was neither heedless nor inaccurate, though she bewailed her lack of formal education. Her love of books was instilled early in her life by her father acting as tutor for his children—she and sisters Mary and Elizabeth were schooled in his library.

Abigail Smith was born in Weymouth, Massachusetts, November 11, 1774, into a prominent New England family. Her mother was descended from Quincys, Nortons, and a long line of respected families of the Bay Colony, while her father, the Reverend William Smith, could boast some degree of wealth and a heritage of merchants and ship captains.

Here in the Boston countryside, Abigail spent her childhood and most of her adult life. It was an idyllic world of an extended family with cousins sometimes visiting for weeks, months, or even years at a time. Abigail often went to Mount Wollaston, home of her maternal grandparents, where she was always warmly welcomed. She was especially close to her grandmother, who seemed to understand and accept her shy but determined ways. Abigail's mother was concerned about what she called her stubborn streak . . . and spending too much time reading books that ladies should not be interested in. But, according to Lynne Withey in her book *Dearest Friend: A Life of Abigail Adams,* the grandmother would answer with pithy adages such as, "Wild colts make the best horses."

While still a colt, but hardly wild, Abigail often visited her uncle and aunt, Isaac and Elizabeth Smith, in Boston, a bustling sophisticated seaport city that captured the young filly's imagination. She formed a strong friendship with her cousin Isaac Jr., and some of his friends, with whom she exchanged letters in hopes of improving her writing skills.

She was still in her early teens when she met the young attorney John Adams, who had recently moved to Weymouth to establish his law practice. He and his friend Richard Cranch, who was courting Abigail's sister Mary, often came calling. John was impressed with the shy Abigail's quick mind—in his eyes, in fact, she was a "constant feast . . . Prudent, modest, delicate, soft, obliging, active." He was especially impressed by her interest in learning and began bringing her books. She, for her part, soon began to take an interest in the young lawyer despite the fact that he was less than handsome, that he was short and had a quick temper. He had endearing qualities as well, she decided—he was sensitive and understanding. And perhaps she saw in him a mirror of her own quiet ambition.

Their courting days were rather erratic, since John was often away in Boston and environs establishing his law practice, but soon the two were passionately in love . . . thus beginning one of America's great love stories.

Struggling to keep their passion in tow, they poured out their hearts on paper. When a snowstorm once kept John away, he wrote to Abigail: "Cruel, Yet perhaps blessed storm!—Cruel for detaining me from so much friendly, social Company, and perhaps blessed to you, or me or both, for keeping me at my Distance . . ."

Once they began talking of marriage, John wrote her a teasing note saying he would never refuse marriage, and, "... on the Contrary am ready to have you at any Time."

The wedding date at last set, Abigail spent a few days shopping in Boston for her trousseau. John was to meet her with a rented cart, gather up all the goods she had bought and take her home. In the interim, she finally answered his teasing note from before with the words, "And—then Sir, if you please you may take me."

Abigail and John were married in the Weymouth parsonage on Octobor 25, 1764, a month before her twentieth birthday.

John took his bride to Braintree, to the little cottage he had inherited from his father. Thus they began a shared life expected to be one of quiet domestic delight near family and friends.

But it would be that way only for the moment. Who could have foreseen the incredible whirlwind that instead swept them up? Who could have dreamed that young Abigail Smith's new husband would become a political leader in the Revolution that separated the American colonies from their mother country of Great Britain, that he in a few short years would take his place as the second ranking governmental officer of the new United States of America?

Or that he also was destined to serve the new nation and its government as the second president?

True to the role she was expected to play, the feminine role usually expected of an eighteenth-century woman, Abigail did become the supportive wife and, later, the nurturing mother. She bore five children over the next ten years, but one died in infancy. Abigail's married life in those early days otherwise seemed perfect . . . if at first rather routine. She could visit her family, who lived nearby, or her favorite sister, Mary, who had married John's good friend Richard Cranch and also lived in the area. But Abigail soon took steps beyond the usual role of dutiful daughter and loving wife—she became an astute businesswoman; managed the couple's farmland; made investment decisions; and, as a surprise to John in later years, designed and planned a major addition to their house in Braintree.

When John was elected to serve in the first Continental Congress in 1774, she became both his pen pal and political advisor. According to Carl Sferrazza Anthony's book, *First Ladies: The Saga of the Presidents' Wives and Their Power 1789-1961,* "She wrote to John on the intricate details of government structure and world economics with more savvy than most congressmen."

She always was interested in events happening around her—in

the early days of the Revolution, she climbed Penn Hill to watch the Battle of Bunker Hill unfolding nearby. Her intelligence and powers of observation were put to excellent use as she became John's eyes and ears in his absence.

Nor was her own husband the only Revolutionary leader who valued her political acumen—his fellow Congress members began asking for her opinions and advice, too.

John spent a great deal of the time away from home in his capacity as a stalwart of the newly forming government, while Abigail was left to run the farm and tend to the children. Her pen became her salvation and was never still. While John received the bulk of her letters, she also carried on a steady correspondence with family members, women friends such as Mercy Otis Warren and Catharine Macauley and even such male notables as Thomas Jefferson and George Washington.

Once the Revolution had run its course, Abigail, by now a married woman of twenty years' standing, at last, in 1784, could join her husband in a heady new life in the capitals of Europe. He first held a diplomatic post in Paris, but the next year, Abigail Smith Adams was privileged to move to London as wife of the first United States Minister to Great Britain. And that was only the beginning for the couple from Braintree.

Still to come for this Founding Mother would be her roles as the wife of the first vice president of the United States, and then as the first First Lady to live in the White House, then called the President's House, in the new capital of Washington.

She found the home unfinished, dank and dreary, and she hung her wash in the future East Room of the drafty structure.

The president's lady, or "Mrs. President," as one of her detractors would call Abigail for her apparent power over the president, regularly sent letters to friendly newspaper editors, unabashedly asking for them to be published with her role as the author disguised. Her more private letters to husband John wouldn't be made public until grandson Charles Francis Adams—son of President John Quincy Adams—published them in the middle of the nineteenth century as a two-volume set.

Speaking of John Adams, he was defeated in his bid for re-election to the brand-new President's House in brand-new Washington, D.C., in 1800 by old Revolutionary-era ally Thomas Jefferson. It was a bitter moment, a bitter parting for the two old friends, with Adams telling Jefferson, "You have put me out! You have put me out!"

They remained on an unfriendly basis for many years, until finally Abigail, by dint of her unceasing correspondence, opened the door to a renewed relationship. When Jefferson's daughter "Polly" died in 1804, Abigail wrote her heartfelt condolences—heartfelt because she knew Polly and once had taken care of her during a two-week visit with the Adamses in London. In time, additional correspondence with Jefferson on various matters succeeded in rekindling the old friendship between these two giants of the Revolutionary era, a bond ultimately marked so symbolically by both men dying on the same day in 1826—on the Fourth of July.

Mercy Otis Warren

HERE, IN THE EYES OF many, was a chronicler of the Revolution with no equal. At a time when women's education consisted mainly of the domestic arts, Mercy Otis haunted the library of her pastor, the Reverend Jonathan Russell, and on his advice she read Raleigh's *History of the World,* which led not only to a love of history but to extensive reading in the classics and English literature.

After her marriage in 1754 to James Warren of Plymouth, Massachusetts, a farmer and political leader at the center of Revolutionary events, she was eager to express her own opinion of those events. Recognized for her sound judgment in political matters, she maintained a rich correspondence with such Patriot leaders as Samuel and John Adams, Thomas Jefferson, General Henry Knox, John Dickinson, and many others.

The Warrens' home became a gathering place for activists both before and after the outbreak of hostilities with the British. As Mercy herself once wrote, "By Plymouth fireside were many political plans originated, discussed and digested." From this vantage she put her pen to work recording the events of the day while also writing poetry and plays. One play in particular, the satirical *Adulateur* (1772) depicting the hapless Governor Thomas Hutchinson of Massachusetts, was prescient in predicting the war to come. Another satire, *The Defeat*, again featured Governor Hutchinson. In 1775 she published *The Group*, a play depicting what would happen to the British king if he rescinded the Massachusetts charter of rights.

In her leisure time she entertained herself with poetry. Often using a classical theme, her verses still reflected her own turbulent times. Most of her poetry was written while spending time at the couple's nearby farm, called Clifford, according to Elizabeth F. Ellet in her three-volume work *The Women of the Revolution.*

Mercy wrote tragedies alluding to suffering—*The Sack of Rome* and *The Ladies of Castille* were two of them. Ellet suggests that they have more "patriotic sentiment than dramatic merit," but says both were read with interest and much praised in after years. As one indication of the seriousness with which Mercy's contemporaries greeted her written work, Alexander Hamilton wrote to the author on July 1, 1791: "It is certain that in the *Ladies of Castille,* the sex will find a new occasion of triumph. Not being a poet myself, I am in the less danger of feeling mortification at the idea that in the career of dramatic composition at least, female genius in the United States has out-stripped the male."

In addition, fellow Massachusetts Patriot John Adams once paid her work the ultimate accolade with his comment that it had "no equal that I know of in this country."

Mercy Otis Warren, sister of early Revolutionary theorist James Otis, is perhaps best remembered for her monumental work *A History of the Rise, Progress, and Termination of the American Revolution,* which not only gives a clear political and philosophical record of the dark days of her country's trials, but invaluable sketches of the leading characters of the times.

Lucy Flucker Knox

IN THE GATHERING STORM OF the Revolution, Thomas Flucker was distressed by one threat in particular to the familiy's political and social position in the colonies. Thomas Flucker, it should be explained here, long had served the British king as secretary of the province of Massachusetts. And it was this position that allowed the Fluckers to enjoy wealth and prestige.

But now, the brewing rebellion threatened their comfortable way of life. Worse, his tall and stately daughter Lucia was romantically attracted to militia Major Henry Knox, not only much "beneath" her in social station but one of those wretched "rebels."

The provincial secretary had great hopes for all his daughters, but he especially desired that "Lucy" would turn her attention to a young British officer whom he regarded as a suitable prospect. To Thomas Flucker's distress, however, Lucy instead frequented the large bookstore in Boston where Knox served as storekeeper. Obviously, the two had a meeting of minds as well as hearts as they met among the bookstands—the lovely Lucy paid no heed to her family's entreaties and soon announced that she would marry her young rebel.

Her Loyalist father, gathering up the remainder of his family and removing to England at the beginning of the hostilities, called her decision "apostacy." He predicted she would miss the life of luxury and social status her sisters would enjoy, in contrast to the dreadful scenes of deprivation Lucy could expect as wife of a soldier committed to a hopeless—and indeed, treasonable—cause.

So much for Thomas Flucker's crystal ball, although he absolutely was correct in one respect: Life on the road with an officer-husband engaged in an uncertain revolution under often-primitive conditions would be no laughing matter.

Lucy Flucker Knox took on her duties as wife of one of Washington's most trusted generals very seriously. Her portly husband won the hearts of his fellow Bostonians early in the Revolution for having brought the heavy guns from Fort Ticonderoga that finally, in the spring of 1776, gave the Americans the advantage in their months-long siege of the port city. Once the big cannon were being dragged into place to bombard the city, the British realized they must evacuate.

Even earlier, right after the Battles of Lexington and Concord in April of 1775, Lucy had joined her husband in fleeing Boston for the American headquarters at Cambridge on the outskirts of the city. Here, she shared the deprivations of her husband and his men. As they fled Boston, say some historians, she managed to carry a concealed sword that he would wear throughout the war by having it quilted into the lining of her cloak.

In the months, and then the years, ahead, whenever the army was in winter quarters, Lucy rejoined her husband no matter how harsh the conditions of camp life. Her cheerful presence during such trying times was a boon to Knox's fellow generals and their men. On these occasions, too, Lucy won the esteem and loyal friendship of Martha Washington, who obviously was buoyed by the younger woman's vitality and cheerful nature—especially by Lucy's delightful, infectious laughter. Their friendship grew as the war wore on—indeed, Lucy stayed at Mount Vernon and reportedly kept up Martha's spirits as they awaited the news to come out of the all-important Siege of Yorktown, where both husbands were engaged against the British.

No great intellectual, philosopher, orator, writer, or politician, Lucy Flucker Knox comes down to us today as one of that small and tight circle of generals' wives, led by Martha, whose steady support of husbands, their soldiers, and the Revolutionary cause itself was a vital, if intangible, factor in bringing about the final triumph.

Catherine Greene

SOME WOMEN BY THEIR CAPTIVATING personality alone are worthy of a place in history—and if they happen to be in a circle of leaders, all the more so. Just such a person was Catherine Greene, wife of Nathanael Greene, perhaps George Washington's best general.

She was born to Phebe Ray and John Littlefield in 1753 in New Shoreham on Block Island. When she was a mere girl, Catherine and a younger sister were sent to live with an aunt married to Governor Greene of Rhode Island, a distant relative of the future general and Revolutionary War hero. Their house was set high on a hill overlooking Narragansett Bay, and it was here that young Nathanael subsequently came calling and met the vivacious "Kate," as she was affectionately called.

Young Kate and Nathanael spent many happy days in Warwick with the Greenes and on Block Island with the Littlefields. They went horseback riding by day and dancing by evening, an activity the future general pursued with vigor despite his Quaker upbringing and his father's stern warnings. Kate had no such parameters— she was described by her friends as the most joyous, frolicsome creature that ever lived.

She was neither tall nor short, but light on her feet. Her fair complexion was highlighted by bright grey eyes that sparkled when she talked. A perceptive conversationalist, she had that added charm of being a good listener. Her limited formal education suited her just fine since she had no love of studies, but when she did open her books she was quick to learn and retain the information. She once amazed a visiting Swedish botanist by having a knowledgeable conversation with him after merely looking over several of his books.

Meanwhile, Nathanael had accumulated a degree of prosperity by working hard in the Greene family gristmills, sawmills, and forges known throughout New England for making anchors. In his business trips to Boston, he came to know Henry Knox, the young bookstore keeper in Boston, and the two spent many congenial hours studying military science, essentially becoming self-taught military experts.

With the blessings of both families, Nathanael and Catherine married on July 20, 1774. The future general took his bride to live in Coventry, Rhode Island, in a newly built home near his new forge. With life looking bright for the young couple despite the political unrest around them, the new bride never dreamed of the adventures and hardships that loomed ahead—that were very soon to come.

After the war's first shots were fired at Lexington and Concord, Nathanael helped to organize the Rhode Island militia. Soon after and before joining in the siege of Boston, his troops were to be inoculated against smallpox. Catherine turned their home into a temporary hospital—and stayed to help the sick men. She would be there, too, when the roar of nearby British shipboard cannon shook the ground.

As the war progressed and her reliable husband became a favorite of George Washington, she did leave home whenever the Continental Army went into winter quarters. During the summer months of active campaigning for the army, she at first, like her friends Martha Washington and Lucy Knox, stayed at home. When her husband resumed his campaign in the South for the two years after Yorktown, however, Catherine Greene went right along, often staying at or near his headquarters or, during the hottest weather, repairing to a coastal island.

Catherine, Mrs. Greene by now, had acquired the gentle sobriquet of "Kitty," most fitting for one so patient and helpful to the soldiers and yet always chipper at difficult moments.

Actually, "Kitty" Greene had become rather famous in Continental Army circles for an incident that took place early in the war, when the hard-pressed Americans received word in the tough winter of 1778 that the French were joining them in an alliance against the British, This obviously called for real celebration. General Henry Knox and his officers put on a grand entertainment at a nearby artillery park. "We danced all night," he wrote to his brother later. But his letter made no reference to the dashing couple who danced for three hours without sitting down once, a tireless couple repeatedly whirling around the dance floor—none other than Kitty and His Excellency, George Washington.

Later, when General Greene was assigned to take over the disastrous Southern campaign late in 1780, he left Washington's northern headquarters so quickly, he and Kitty couldn't meet to say their farewells. He at that point didn't want his wife to make the arduous trip from New England to the South, even though she was willing—and, indeed, desperately wanted to be near him.

Martha Washington later wrote to Kitty that General Greene had spent an evening at Mount Vernon on his way to Richmond and then Charlotte, North Carolina, and that he was doing well.

Still later that year, on December 15, the commander in chief himself wrote to Kitty from his headquarters in New Windsor, New York, enclosed a letter from General Greene, and offered to forward her own letters to her distant husband. Apparently Kitty's absence from the army's headquarters circle already was being felt. "Mrs. Washington, who is just arrived at these my quarters, joins me in most cordial wishes for your every felicity, and regrets the want of your company," General Washington also said.

On a fatherly note, he added, "Remember me to my namesake."

The "namesake" alluded to, the eldest Greene son, some years later was accidentally drowned in the Savannah River. His mother, they say, never quite recovered her joyful spirits after that shock.

Despite the war and the separation it forced upon them, she and Nathanael managed to produce a small brood of three daughters and two sons before all was said and done.

After the war's end, Catherine Greene and her husband returned to Rhode Island to settle their affairs before moving permanently to the South. The foundry business had failed during their absence, and they sold everything but their books. They moved to Mulberry Grove, the plantation the state of Georgia had given the general for his services in liberating the state from the British.

General Greene's early death in 1786 left his younger wife a widow at age thirty, with five children to continue raising, the eldest of them only twelve. She continued to manage the plantation, and ten years later she married Phineas Miller, who had been the children's tutor.

Fate would tap our Kitty yet again, this time giving her a footnote in the history books. A young man who was living with the widow Greene and her children while studying law soon turned his energies to another enterprise, with her encouragement. Given a basement room at Mulberry Grove to work on his ideas, young Eli Whitney invented a better cotton gin, even using Kitty's hairbrush as part of his newfangled machine!

She spent her last years on Cumberland Island off the Georgia coast and died there in 1814. As fate would have it, just four years later, another of George Washington's best-known generals, Henry "Light-Horse Harry" Lee, who in 1781 covered Nathanael Greene's "race to the Dan" across North Carolina to Virginia, would join her in burial on this remote barrier island.

Appendix: Declaration of Independence

(Adopted in Congress 4 July 1776)

The Unanimous Declaration of the Thirteen United States of America

When, in the course of human events, it becomes necessary for one people to dissolve the political bonds which have connected them with another, and to assume among the powers of the earth, the separate and equal station to which the laws of nature and of nature's God entitle them, a decent respect to the opinions of mankind requires that they should declare the causes which impel them to the separation.

We hold these truths to be self-evident, that all men are created equal, that they are endowed by their Creator with certain unalienable rights, that among these are life, liberty and the pursuit of happiness. That to secure these rights, governments are instituted among men, deriving their just powers from the consent of the governed. That whenever any form of government becomes destructive to these ends, it is the right of the people to alter or to abolish it, and to institute new government, laying its foundation on such principles and organizing its powers in such form, as to them shall seem most likely to effect their safety and happiness. Prudence, indeed, will dictate that governments long established should not be changed for light and transient causes; and accordingly all experience hath shown that mankind are more disposed to suffer, while evils are sufferable, than to right themselves by abolishing the forms to which they are accustomed. But when a long train of abuses and usurpations, pursuing invariably the same object evinces a design to reduce them under absolute despotism, it is their right, it is their duty, to throw off such government, and to provide new guards for their future security. —Such has been the patient sufferance of these colonies; and such is now the necessity which constrains them to alter their former systems of government. The history of the present King of Great Britain is a history of repeated injuries and usurpations, all having in direct object the establishment of an absolute tyranny over these states. To prove this, let facts be submitted to a candid world.

He has refused his assent to laws, the most wholesome and necessary for the public good.

He has forbidden his governors to pass laws of immediate and pressing importance, unless suspended in their operation till his assent should be obtained; and when so suspended, he has utterly neglected to attend to them.

He has refused to pass other laws for the accommodation of large districts of people, unless those people would relinquish the right of representation in the legislature, a right inestimable to them and formidable to tyrants only.

He has called together legislative bodies at places unusual, uncomfortable, and distant from the depository of their public records, for the sole purpose of fatiguing them into compliance with his measures.

He has dissolved representative houses repeatedly, for opposing with manly firmness his invasions on the rights of the people.

He has refused for a long time, after such dissolutions, to cause others to be elected; whereby the legislative powers, incapable of annihilation, have returned to the people at large for their exercise; the state remaining in the meantime exposed to all the dangers of invasion from without, and convulsions within.

He has endeavored to prevent the population of these states; for that purpose obstructing the laws for naturalization of foreigners; refusing to pass others to encourage their migration hither, and raising the conditions of new appropriations of lands.

He has obstructed the administration of justice, by refusing his assent to laws for establishing judiciary powers.

He has made judges dependent on his will alone, for the tenure of their offices, and the amount and payment of their salaries.

He has erected a multitude of new offices, and sent hither swarms of officers to harass our people, and eat out their substance.

He has kept among us, in times of peace, standing armies without the consent of our legislature.

He has affected to render the military independent of and superior to civil power.

He has combined with others to subject us to a jurisdiction foreign to our constitution, and unacknowledged by our laws; giving his assent to their acts of pretended legislation:

For quartering large bodies of armed troops among us:

For protecting them, by mock trial, from punishment for any murders which they should commit on the inhabitants of these states:

For cutting off our trade with all parts of the world:

For imposing taxes on us without our consent:

For depriving us in many cases, of the benefits of trial by jury:

For transporting us beyond seas to be tried for pretended offenses:

For abolishing the free system of English laws in a neighboring province, establishing therein an arbitrary government, and enlarging its boundaries so as to render it at once an example and fit instrument for introducing the same absolute rule in these colonies:

For taking away our charters, abolishing our most valuable laws, and altering fundamentally the forms of our governments:

For suspending our own legislatures, and declaring themselves invested with power to legislate for us in all cases whatsoever.

He has abdicated government here, by declaring us out of his protection and waging war against us.

He has plundered our seas, ravaged our coasts, burned our towns, and destroyed the lives of our people.

He is at this time transporting large armies of foreign mercenaries to complete the works of death, desolation and tyranny, already begun with circumstances of cruelty and perfidy scarcely paralleled in the most barbarous ages, and totally unworthy the head of a civilized nation.

He has constrained our fellow citizens taken captive on the high seas to bear arms against their country, to become the executioners of their friends and brethren, or to fall themselves by their hands.

He has excited domestic insurrections amongst us, and has endeavored to bring on the inhabitants of our frontiers, the merciless Indian savages, whose known rule of warfare, is undistinguished destruction of all ages, sexes and conditions.

In every stage of these oppressions we have petitioned for redress in the most humble terms: our repeated petitions have been answered only by repeated injury. A prince, whose character is thus marked by every act which may define a tyrant, is unfit to be the ruler of a free people.

Nor have we been wanting in attention to our British brethren. We have warned them from time to time of attempts by their legislature to extend an unwarrantable jurisdiction over us. We have reminded them of the circumstances of our emigration and settlement here. We have appealed to their native justice and magnanimity, and we have conjured them by the ties of our common kindred to disavow these usurpations, which, would inevitably interrupt our connections and correspondence. We must, therefore, acquiesce in the necessity, which denounces our separation, and hold them, as we hold the rest of mankind, enemies in war, in peace friends.

We, therefore, the representatives of the United States of America, in General Congress, assembled, appealing to the Supreme Judge of the world for the rectitude of our intentions, do, in the name, and by the authority of the good people of these colonies, solemnly publish and declare, that these united colonies are, and of right ought to be free and independent states; that they are absolved from all allegiance to the British Crown, and that all political connection between them and the state of Great Britain, is and ought to be totally dissolved; and that as free and independent states, they have full power to levy war, conclude peace, contract alliances, establish commerce, and to do all other acts and things which independent states may of right do. And for the support of this declaration, with a firm reliance on the protection of Divine Providence, we mutually pledge to each other our lives, our fortunes and our sacred honor.

New Hampshire: Josiah Bartlett, William Whipple, Matthew Thornton

Massachusetts: John Hancock, Samuel Adams, John Adams, Robert Treat Paine, Elbridge Gerry

Rhode Island: Stephen Hopkins, William Ellery

Connecticut: Roger Sherman, Samuel Huntington, William Williams, Oliver Wolcott

New York: William Floyd, Philip Livingston, Francis Lewis, Lewis Morris

New Jersey: Richard Stockton, John Witherspoon, Francis Hopkinson, John Hart, Abraham Clark

Pennsylvania: Robert Morris, Benjamin Rush, Benjamin Franklin, John Morton, George Clymer, James Smith, George Taylor, James Wilson, George Ross

Delaware: Caesar Rodney, George Read, Thomas McKean

Maryland: Samuel Chase, William Paca, Thomas Stone, Charles Carroll of Carrollton

Virginia: George Wythe, Richard Henry Lee, Thomas Jefferson, Benjamin Harrison, Thomas Nelson, Jr., Francis Lightfoot Lee, Carter Braxton

North Carolina: William Hooper, Joseph Hewes, John Penn

South Carolina: Edward Rutledge, Thomas Heyward, Jr., Thomas Lynch, Jr., Arthur Middleton

Georgia: Button Gwinnett, Lyman Hall, George Walton

Chronology of Events

Colonial Grievances Pile Up: *February 10, 1763,* Treaty of Paris ending the French and Indian War, also known as the Seven Years' War. Colonials resent king's proclamation of *October 7* the same year forbidding settlement of the trans-Allegheny west. *1764,* Stamp Act proposed in Parliament, with colonial agitation resulting.

February 27, 1765, Parliament decrees Stamp Act will go into effect November 1—twenty-five pages of taxation rules to contend with. *May 30,* first of Patrick Henry's defiant Stamp Act Resolves adopted by Virginia House of Burgesses after hot debate marked by his dramatic utterance, "If this be Treason, Make the Most of it!" *September 1765,* Stamp Act Congress held in New York—twenty-seven delegates from nine colonies represent first united American protest against British actions.

March 18, 1766, Stamp Act repealed by Parliament, only to be replaced, in *1767,* by Townshend Acts imposing new duties upon items such as paper, glass and tea, with even greater colonial agitation and protest resulting. *May 1769,* Virginia House of Burgesses dissolved by Royal Governor Botetourt after passing defiant resolutions, whereupon the legislators meet in a private home under their own authority and adopt a proposal to boycott British goods and invite sister colonies to join in.

1770, further colonial restiveness when duty on tea remains in force despite repeal of Townshend Acts. *June 9, 1772,* burning of British revenue vessel *Gaspee* in Rhode Island waters stirs new round of intra-colonial communications through committees of correspondence. *December 16, 1773,* inflammatory Boston Tea Party destroying imported British tea, followed by Parliament's punitive Intolerable Acts of *1774* closing the port of Boston, moving the customs house to Salem, Massachusetts, and placing British ships in Boston Harbor to enforce British edicts.

September 1774, first meeting in Philadelphia of the Continental Congress, soon to represent all thirteen colonies; the Second Continental Congress will meet *May 10, 1775,* after Lexington-Concord and act as the Revolutionary Government until a new government is formed under the Articles of Confederation, to be adopted in *1781.*

Events of the Revolutionary War: Year *1775—April 19,* Battles of

Lexington, Concord, and Menotomy, Massachusetts; Americans begin siege of Boston. *May 10,* Fort Ticonderoga falls to the Americans. *June 17,* Battles of Bunker/Breed's Hill. *July 3,* George Washington takes command. *September-December,* campaign against British in Canada, led by Benedict Arnold and Richard Montgomery. *December 31,* Americans fail to take Quebec, Montgomery killed, Arnold wounded.

Year *1776—February 27,* Patriot victory at Moore's Creek Bridge, North Carolina. *March 17,* British abandon Boston. *June 28,* beginning of Sir Henry Clinton's futile assault on Charleston Harbor and Sullivan's Island. *July 4,* Declaration of Independence adopted by the Second Continental Congress, assembled in Philadelphia. *August 27,* American defeat in Battle of Long Island, followed by American withdrawal from Brooklyn to Manhattan Island. *September 15,* British land at Kip's Bay, Manhattan Island. *October 11,* Benedict Arnold's heroics in losing Battle of Valcour Island, Lake Champlain. November, Americans lose Forts Lee and Washington on New Jersey and New York shores of the Hudson River. *December 13,* General Charles Lee captured by British. *December 26,* stunning American victory at Trenton, New Jersey.

Year *1777—*For Patriots, good news also at Princeton, *January 3. Summer,* British invade upper New York from Canada, capture Ticonderoga, battle Americans at Bennington, Vermont, and Oriskany and Fort Stanwix, New York. *July 9-10,* British General Richard Prescott captured in his bed in Rhode Island, with expectations of an exchange for Charles Lee. *August 25,* Sir William Howe's army, formerly based in New York, poised to strike at Philadelphia after landing at Head of Elk, Maryland. *September 11,* Washington outflanked at Brandywine Creek. *September 17* and *October 7,* British General "Gentleman Johnny" Burgoyne loses two-step Battle of Saratoga, New York, and surrenders his invading army. At Saratoga, too, more heroics by Benedict Arnold and another wound to his bad leg. *September 16,* Howe takes over American capital of Philadelphia. *October 4,* Americans stymied at Germantown, Pennsylvania. *December 17,* Americans retire to Valley Forge for the winter.

Year *1778—February 6,* French decide to support the American cause, and on *May 6,* shortly after the news finally reaches America, the Continental Army celebrates at Valley Forge with great excitement. *June 16-18,* British abandon Philadelphia to the Americans again. *June 16,* much restored and better trained, Continental Army marches out of Valley Forge for renewed campaigning, soon pursuing the British as they march toward New York. *June 19,* Benedict Arnold, permanently lamed by his most recent leg wound, in effect becomes military governor of

Philadelphia. *June 28,* Battle of Monmouth, New Jersey, marked by dismissal of General Charles Lee from field of battle. *August,* American land forces and French fleet frustrated in effort to dislodge British from Newport, Rhode Island, due in part to lack of coordination. *December 19,* British take Savannah, Georgia.

Year *1779—February 24,* in the "Northwest Country" George Rogers Clark crosses impossible terrain to seize Vincennes. *July–August,* Americans experience small disaster at Penobscot Bay, Maine, but achieve morale-boosting victories at Stony Point, New York, and Paulus Hook, New Jersey. *September 23,* John Paul Jones makes his mark with the triumph of his *Bonhomme Richard* over the British frigate *Serapis* off the English coast. *October 9,* French and Americans driven off in attempt to recapture Savannah. Heroic Polish Count Kasimir Pulaski fatally wounded. *December 1,* George Washington and the vanguard of his Continental Army arrive at winter quarters at Morristown, New Jersey, for what will become known as the worst winter of the eighteenth century.

Year *1780—January 14,* American "Lord Stirling's" abortive raid by sled against British at Staten Island. *January 26,* Benedict Arnold court-martial finds him guilty on two minor charges of abusing command position at Philadelphia, recommends mild penalty—Arnold, already spying for the British, is outraged. *April 28,* Landing in Boston, Lafayette returns from France with news the French will be sending an army to help the Americans. Turncoat Benedict Arnold secretly passes on this intelligence to the British. *March 14,* Spanish seize Mobile in West Florida. *May 12,* Charleston finally falls to the British, followed by Battle of the Waxhaws, also in South Carolina, on *May 29,* an American rout. *July 11,* the French army under Count Rochambeau debarks at Newport, Rhode Island, recently evacuated by the British. *August 16,* American disaster at Camden, South Carolina, Lord Cornwallis over Horatio Gates. Nathanael Greene now will take over the war in the South for George Washington. *September 25,* Benedict Arnold goes over to the British after the capture of his contact, Major John André. *October 5,* André executed as spy. *October 7,* Battle of King's Mountain, South Carolina, victory for the American "over-the-mountain" men. *December 30,* Benedict Arnold leads British forces into Virginia.

Year *1781—January 1,* mutiny among Pennsylvania Continentals. *January 4,* Benedict Arnold captures Richmond, Virginia's capital. *January 17,* decisive American victory at Cowpens, South Carolina, Daniel Morgan over Banastre Tarleton. *February 3,* Nathanael Greene lures Lord Cornwallis into weeks-long "race to the Dan" (the Dan River on the Virginia-Carolina border) as part of Greene's overall campaign strategy of harassing and weakening the main British force in the South without risking all in a single, face-to-face battle. Plunging back into North Carolina, however, Greene does directly take on Cornwallis at Guilford Courthouse (today's Greensboro, North Carolina) on *March 15,* technically a victory for the British—but they are weakened further by their losses. *March 18,* his supplies and even foodstuffs exhausted, Cornwallis sets off for British riverside base at Wilmington, North Carolina, leaving his wounded behind.

Nathanael Greene ignores Cornwallis now and returns to lower South to begin systematic reduction of British outposts —and eventual recapture of Charleston—over the next two years. Meanwhile, on *April 6,* Lafayette is ordered into Virginia with instructions to recapture Richmond. *April 24,* Lord Cornwallis leaves Wilmington for campaigning in Virginia as well. *April 29,* with Arnold and British allies still on the loose nearby, Lafayette retakes Richmond. *May 9,* British garrison at Pensacola falls to Bernado de Galvez— Spain controls both East and West Florida. *May 20,* Cornwallis appears in Petersburg, Virginia, with his reduced army of 1,500—reinforcements soon will swell his ranks to 7,200. *June 4,* British dragoons under Banastre Tarleton just miss capturing outgoing Virginia Governor Thomas Jefferson and his legislature in lightning raid on Charlottesville, Virginia. *June 10,* Anthony Wayne and his troops join Lafayette in Virginia; Cornwallis by *June 20* begins to move down the Virginia peninsula. He soon will pass through Williamsburg, cross the James River for brief respite at Portsmouth, Virginia, then recross the James and settle into Yorktown on the York River, also holding Gloucester Point on the far shore to protect his flank. Cornwallis is fully confident that he can be safely supplied by sea.

August 14, in the North, French Count Rochambeau receives word from French Admiral de Grasse that he and his fleet are prepared to sail into the Chesapeake Bay as a screen between Cornwallis and his Royal Navy. *August 21,* George Washington and Rochambeau begin hasty march south to Virginia, hoping to find Cornwallis bottled up at Yorktown. *August 26,* de Grasse arrives off Virginia and can now plug the approaches to Yorktown well ahead of any British naval force trying to rescue or resupply Cornwallis. *September 2,* the French and Americans marching southward reach Philadelphia. *September 5,* French and British fleets engage off Virginia's Cape Henry—victory goes to the French. With their naval relief force denied access and a large Franco-American land force approaching, the fate of the British at Yorktown is sealed. *September 28,* French and Americans take siege positions around Yorktown. *October 19,* formal surrender of the British forces at Yorktown, a French-American victory widely considered ever since the symbolic end of the Revolutionary War . . . but not quite so in practical fact. Many minor battles and skirmishes remain to be fought over the next two years as negotiators in Paris tackle their assignment of producing a final peace treaty recognizing American independence and an end to her war with Great Britain.

Year *1782—July 11,* British leave Savannah. *August 15-19,* frontier battles of Bryan's Station and Blue Licks, both in Kentucky. *November 30,* preliminary peace terms signed in Paris. *December 11,* British disengagement continues with evacuation of Charleston.

Year *1783—September 3,* Treaties of Paris and Versailles officially end the war and all hostilities among the warring parties. *November 25,* last British garrison still in the future United States departs the long-held city of New York, along with about 7,000 Loyalists, or 7 percent of the 100,000 Loyalists who have fled the former colonies as a result of the Revolution. *December 4,* George Washington's tearful farewell to his officers gathered at Fraunces' Tavern in New York, followed by his own departure from the city. *December 23,* more emotion as George Washington bids farewell to Congress, assembled now at Annapolis, Maryland, and turns in his commission as commander in chief of the Continental Army. He is wrong when he says, "I . . . take my leave of all the employments of public life." He will soon reappear in public life as the new republic's first president. In the meantime, however, this chapter of American history is over.

Select Bibliography

Akers, Charles W. *Abigail Adams: An American Woman.* Boston: Little, Brown, 1980.

Alotta, Robert I. *Another Part of the Field: America's Revolution, 1777-78.* Shippensburg, Penn.: White Mane, 1991.

Anthony, Carl Sferrazza. *First Ladies: The Saga of the Presidents' Wives and their Power, 1789-1961.* New York: William Morrow, 1990.

Bahne, Charles. *The Complete Guide to Boston's Freedom Trail,* 2nd ed. Cambridge, Mass.: Newtowne Publishing, 1993.

Bailyn, Bernard. *Faces of the Revolution: Personalities and Themes in the Struggle for American Independence.* New York: Vintage Books, 1992.

Bakeless, John. *Background to Glory: The Life of George Rogers Clark.* Lincoln, Neb.: University of Nebraska Press, 1992.

Best, Nicholas. *The Kings and Queens of England.* London: Weidenfeld & Nicolson, 1995.

Billias, George Athan. *General John Glover and his Marblehead Mariners.* New York: Holt, Rinehart and Winston, 1960.

———, ed. *George Washington's Generals and Their Opponents: Their Exploits and Leadership.* New York: Da Capo Press, 1994.

Blanco, Richard L., ed. *The American Revolution, 1775-1783,* two-volume encyclopedia, New York and London: Garland Publishing, 1993.

Bridges, Edwin, Harvey H. Jackson, Kenneth H. Thomas Jr., and James Harvey Young. *Georgia's Signers and the Declaration of Independence.* Atlanta: Cherokee, 1981.

Clark, Harrison. *All Cloudless Glory: The Life of George Washington from Youth to Yorktown.* Washington, D.C.: Regnery, 1995.

Cohen, Sheldon S. *Yankee Sailors in British Gaols: Prisoners of War at Forton and Mill, 1777-1783.* Newark, Del.: University of Delaware Press, 1995.

Collins, James. *Autobiography of a Revolutionary Soldier.* "Revised and Prepared" by John M. Roberts. New York: Arno Press, 1979.

Concord Chamber of Commerce. *The Lexington-Concord Battle Road: Hour-by-Hour Account of Events Preceding and on the History-making Day April 19, 1775.* Concord, Mass.

Dabney, Virginius. *Virginia: The New Dominion, a history from 1607 to the present.* Charlottesville, Va.: University Press of Virginia, 1983.

————, From Cuckoo Tavern to Monticello. *The Iron Worker* magazine, Lynchburg, Va., summer, 1966.

Dann, John C., ed. *The Revolution Remembered: Eyewitness Accounts of the War for Independence.* Chicago: University of Chicago Press, 1980.

Davis, Burke. *The Campaign That Won America: The Story of Yorktown.* Conshohocken, Penn.: Eastern Acorn Press, 1996.

Dictionary of American Biography. New York: Charles Scribner's Sons.

Ellet, Elizabeth. *The Women of the American Revolution,* three volumes. Williamstown, Mass.: Corner House, 1980 (first published in 1848 by Baker and Scribner, New York).

Evans, Sara M. *Born for Liberty: A History of Women in America.* New York: Free Press, 1989.

Fast, Howard. *The Crossing.* New Jersey Historical Society, Newark, N.J., 1984, (reprinted from William Morrow, New York, 1971).

Ferling, John, ed. *The World Turned Upside Down: The American Victory in the War of Independence.* Westport, Conn.: Greenwood Press, 1988.

Fields, Joseph E., ed. *"Worthy Partner": The Papers of Martha Washington.* Westport, Conn.: Greenwood Press, 1994.

Fleming, Thomas. *Liberty! The American Revolution.* New York: Viking, 1997.

Franklin, Benjamin. *The Autobiography of Benjamin Franklin.* New Haven: Yale University Press, 1964.

Fraser, Walter J. Jr. *Patriots, Pistols and Petticoats: "Poor Sinful Charles Town" during the American Revolution.* Columbia, S.C.: University of South Carolina Press (reprinted from Charleston County Bicentennial Committee, 1945).

Freeman, Douglas Southall. *George Washington: A Biography,* seven volumes. New York: Charles Scribner's Sons, 1948.

Fuller, J. F. C. *Military History of the Western World,* three volumes, New York: Da Capo Press (reprinted from Funk and Wagnalls, New York, 1954-57).

Gallagher, John J. *The Battle of Brooklyn 1776.* New York: Sarpedon, 1995.

Gelles, Edith B. *Portia: The World of Abigail Adams.* Bloomington, Ind.: Indiana University Press, 1992.

Gragg, Rod. *Planters, Pirates and Patriots: Historical Tales from the South Carolina Grand Strand.* Nashville, Tenn.: Rutledge Hill Press, 1994.

Hilborn, Nat and Sam. *Battleground of Freedom: South Carolina in the Revolution.* Columbia, S.C.: Sandpiper Press, 1970.

Historic Black Women: A Gift of Heritage. Chicago: Emback Publishing Company, 1990.

Hoffecker, Carol E. *Delaware, The First State.* Wilmington, Del.: Middle Atlantic Press, 1988.

Humes, James C. *The Wit & Wisdom of Benjamin Franklin: A Treasury of more than 900 Quotations and Anecdotes.* New York: HarperCollins, 1995.

Irving, Washington. *Life of George Washington.* Edited and abridged from 1855-59 edition by Jess Stein. Tarrytown, N.Y.: Sleepy Hollow Restorations, 1975.

Johnson, Gerald W. *Andrew Jackson, An Epic in Homespun.* New York: Minton Balch, 1927.

Johnson, James M. *Militiamen, Rangers, and Redcoats: The Military in Georgia, 1754-1776.* Macon, Ga.: Mercer University Press, 1992.

Kelly, C. Brian. Various articles, *Military History* magazine, Leesburg, Virginia, 1984-98. *Country's Best Log Homes* magazine, Reston, Virginia, January 1998 and July 1998. *The Washington Star* newspaper, Washington, D.C., 1975-76.

Kerber, Linda K. *Women of the Republic: Intellect & Ideology in Revolutionary America.* New York: W. W. Norton, 1986.

Lancaster, Bruce, and J. H. Plumb. *The American Revolution.* New York: American Heritage, 1971.

Leach, Douglas Edward. *Roots of Conflict: British Armed Forces and Colonial Americans, 1677-1763.* Chapel Hill, N.C.: University of North Carolina Press, 1986.

Leamon, James S. *Revolution Downeast: The War for American Independence in Maine.* Amherst, Mass.: University of Massachusetts Press, in cooperation with the Maine Historical Society, 1993.

Lexington Historical Society, *Lexington: Birthplace of American Liberty.* Lexington, Mass., 1995.

Longford, Elizabeth, ed. *The Oxford Book of Royal Anecdotes.* New York: Oxford University Press, 1991.

Malone, Dumas. *The Story of the Declaration of Independence.* New York: Oxford, 1976.

Martin, David G. *The Philadelphia Campaign: June 1777-July 1778.* New York: Combined Books, 1993.

Martin, Michael and Leon Gelber. *Dictionary of American History,* revised by A. W. Littlefield. New Jersey: Littlefield, Adams, Totowa, 1968.

Moore, John Hammond. *Albemarle: Jefferson's County: 1727-1976.* Charlottesville, Va.: University Press of Virginia, 1976. (Albemarle Historical Society, reprint, 1986.)

Morrill, Dan L. *Southern Campaigns of the American Revolution.* Baltimore, Md.: Nautical & Aviation Publishing, 1996.

Rankin, Hugh and George F. Scheer., eds. *Rebels & Redcoats: The American Revolution Through the Eyes of Those Who Fought and Lived It.* New York: Da Capo Press, 1957.

Ravages of the King's Troops on the 19th of April 1775. New England & Virginia Co., Salem, Mass., facsimile of printed depositions by witnesses to the events of April 19, 1775.

Reed, John F. *Campaign to Valley Forge, July 1, 1777–December 19, 1777.* Pioneer Press, Copyright 1965, trustees of University of Pennsylvania, also published by Oxford University Press.

Remini, Robert V. *The Life of Andrew Jackson,* condensation. New York: Harper & Row, 1988. New York: Penguin Books, 1990.

Robbins, Peggy. *Military History* magazine, Leesburg, Va., October 1989.

Robinson, Blackwell. *Moore County, North Carolina, 1747-1847.* Southern Pines, N.C.: Moore County Historical Association, 1956.

Royster, Charles. *A Revolutionary People at War: The Continental Army and American Character, 1775-1783.* New York: W. W. Norton, 1981, (reprint from University of North Carolina Press, Chapel Hill, N.C., 1979).

Sawtell, Clement C. *The Nineteenth of April, 1775: A Collection of First Hand Accounts.* Sawtells of Somerset, Mass., 1968. Reissued by Eastern National Park & Monument Association, Conshohocken, Penn., 1991.

Shreve, L. G. *Tench Tilghman: The Life and Times of Washington's Aide-de-Camp.* Centreville, Md.: Tidewater, 1982.

Smith, Richard Norton. *Patriarch: George Washington and the New American Nation.* New York and Boston: Houghton Mifflin, 1993.

Smith, Rev. Samuel Abbot. *West Cambridge, 1775.* Presented as a lecture in 1864, reprinted by the Arlington (Mass.) Historical Society, 1974.

Smyer, Ingrid. *First Ladies in Review,* from *Best Little Stories from the White House,* by C. Brian Kelly and Ingrid Smyer. Charlottesville, Va.: Montpelier, 1992.

Stokesbury, James L. *A Short History of the American Revolution.* New York: Quill/William Morrow, 1991.

Tebbel, John. *George Washington's America.* New York: E. P. Dutton, 1954.

The World Book Encyclopedia, Volume 11. Field Enterprise, Chicago, 1962.

Valiant, Joseph N. Jr. *Military History* magazine, Leesburg, Virginia, October 1995.

Van Tyne, Claude Halstead. *The Loyalists in the American Revolution.* New York: Macmillan, 1902 (fascimile reprint, HeritageBooks, Bowie, Md., 1989).

Virginia State Department of Education, *The Road to Independence: Virginia, 1763–1783.* Guidebook for teachers, Commonwealth of Virginia, Richmond.

Wallace, Willard M. *Appeal to Arms: A Military History of the American Revolution.* Chicago: Quadrangle Books, 1964.

Watterson, John S. III. *The North Carolina Historical Review.* Raleigh, N.C., April 1971.

Wharton, Anne Hollingsworth. *Martha Washington.* New York: Charles Scribner's Sons, 1897.

Wilson, Vincent, Jr. *The Book of the Founding Fathers.* Brookeville, Md.: American History Research Associates, 1974.

Withey, Lynne. *Dearest friend: A life of Abigail Adams.* New York: Free Press, 1981.

Women in American History, Britannica Online. *Encyclopedia Britannica,* women.eb.com, 1998.

Index